Aircraft Operating Leasing

Aerospace Law and Policy Series

VOLUME 9

Editors

Introduction

The *Aerospace Law and Policy Series* critically examines the fundamental changes that international aviation and space activities have undergone since the last century, growing up as mature industries while freeing themselves from traditional regulatory constraints and displaying a variety of innovative applications that call for creative legal solutions.

Objective

The objective of the Series is to make a contribution to legal thinking on public international air and space law and policy, and their implementation at the regional and national levels, responsibility and liability of public bodies and service providers, competition law, insurance law, company law, and the complex relationship between EU law and public international law.

Readership

Aviation and space lawyers, academics, representatives of governments, international organizations, and companies involved in aviation and space activities.

The titles published in this series are listed at the end of this volume.

Aircraft Operating Leasing

A Legal and Practical Analysis in the Context of Public and Private International Air Law

Third Edition

Donal Patrick Hanley

Wolters Kluwer

Published by:
Kluwer Law International B.V.
PO Box 316
2400 AH Alphen aan den Rijn
The Netherlands
E-mail: international-sales@wolterskluwer.com
Website: www.wolterskluwer.com/en/solutions/kluwerlawinternational

Sold and distributed by:
Wolters Kluwer Legal & Regulatory U.S.
7201 McKinney Circle
Frederick, MD 21704
United States of America
E-mail: customer.service@wolterskluwer.com

ISBN 978-94-035-4030-6

e-Book: ISBN 978-94-035-4031-3
web-PDF: ISBN 978-94-035-4032-0

A.M.D.G.

To my beloved wife Helen

About the Author

Donal Patrick Hanley is an Adjunct Professor at the Institute of Air and Space Law of McGill University, a Visiting Lecturer at the International Institute of Air and Space Law of Leiden University, an Instructor at the Training and Development Institute of the International Air Transport Association (IATA), and a Fellow of the Royal Aeronautical Society.

Born in 1964 in Ireland, he was educated first in Dublin at Belvedere College, SJ and the Law Schools of Trinity College, Dublin and the Law Society of Ireland. He then received a European Commission scholarship to study Japanese language and business at the Tokyo School of Japanese Language and Sophia University, SJ, as part of its Executive Training Programme in Japan. He has an MA degree in Linguistics from Monash University, which he studied by distance learning, as well as an MBA degree in International Aviation from Concordia University, Montréal and a Diploma in Air Law from IATA. He graduated *cum laude* with an LLM (Adv) in Air and Space Law from Leiden University and obtained his doctorate there in 2011.

A non-executive board director of a number of aviation-related companies, he was previously the founding Managing Director of ACG Aircraft Leasing Ireland Limited, a Dublin-based wholly owned subsidiary of Aviation Capital Group LLC (ACG), a large California-based aircraft leasing company, and served as a board director of its Irish, French and Swedish subsidiaries. With the late Dr Donald H. Bunker and others, he co-founded and served as a board director of CIAF Leasing, an Egyptian aircraft leasing company.

For many years, he represented ACG on the Aviation Working Group (AWG), an industry association of major aircraft and aircraft engine manufacturers, lessors and financiers, and was a member of the AWG team negotiating legal documentation standardization with IATA.

Before joining ACG, he was an aircraft leasing and finance lawyer with extensive experience, both in private practice and in-house, in Ireland and England for McCann FitzGerald, in Japan for Linklaters and in the United States of America and The Netherlands for Tombo Aviation Inc. and other group companies of Mitsui & Co., Ltd.

He is a non-practising solicitor admitted in Ireland, England and Wales and is an active member of the State Bar of California, serving as Chair of its International Law Section from 2006 to 2007.

He is a Knight of the Holy Sepulchre, a Knight of Malta and a member of the Stephen's Green Club in Dublin and of the Royal Air Force Club in London.

Table of Contents

About the Author vii

List of Abbreviations xv

Preface to the Third Edition xvii

Preface to the Second Edition xix

Preface to the First Edition xxi

Acknowledgements xxiii

Chapter 1
Introduction 1
§1.01 Context 1
§1.02 'Practical' Versus 'Legal' 3
[A] 'Practical' 4
[B] 'Legal' 6
§1.03 Aim and Methodology 7

Chapter 2
Overview 13
§2.01 Aircraft Operating Leasing and Other Forms of Leasing and Financing 13
§2.02 Structuring the Lease 18
§2.03 The Letter of Intent 20
§2.04 The Jurisdictional Questionnaire 23
§2.05 The Legal Opinion 24
§2.06 The Layout of the Lease 25
[A] Pre-delivery 25
[B] Post-delivery 26
[C] Post-lease Term 27

CHAPTER 3
The Aircraft Operating Lease 31
§3.01 Parties 31
§3.02 Recitals 32
§3.03 Definitions 32
§3.04 Representations and Warranties 34
[A] Representations as to Present and Past Facts 34
[B] Repetition of Representations 34
[C] Representations of Law 35
[D] Warranties 35
[E] Conclusions 36
§3.05 Conditions Precedent 36
[A] General Conditions Precedent 37
[1] Payments 37
[2] Constitutional Documents 38
[3] Corporate Approvals 38
[4] Filings and Consents 38
[5] Legal Opinions 39
[6] Process Agent Letter 39
[B] Airline-Specific Conditions Precedent 40
[1] Certificate of Insurance and Broker's Letter of Undertaking 40
[2] Certificate of Registration 41
[3] Certificate of Airworthiness 42
[4] Radio Station Licence 42
[5] Air Transport Licence 42
[6] Air Operator's Certificate 44
[7] Eurocontrol Letter 44
[C] Waivers and Conditions Subsequent 44
[D] Conclusions 45
§3.06 Term and Delivery 46
[A] Term 46
[B] Delivery 46
[1] Delay in or Failure of Delivery 47
[2] Failure to Meet Delivery Condition Prior to Delivery 47
[3] Effect of Acceptance of Delivery 48
[C] Conclusions 52
§3.07 Payments 52
[A] Rent 52
[B] Security Deposit 55
[1] Security Deposit Rationale 55
[2] Charge over the Security Deposit 56
[3] Commitment Fee 57
[4] Market Reality 57

[C] Maintenance Reserves 57
[1] Maintenance Reserves Rationale 57
[2] Charge over Maintenance Reserves 59
[3] Supplemental Rent 59
[4] Limited Reimbursement Obligation 59
[D] Standby Letters of Credit and Guarantees 60
[1] Standby Letters of Credit 60
[2] Guarantees 62
[E] Late Payment 62
[F] Conclusions 63
§3.08 Taxes 63
§3.09 Manufacturer's Warranties 64
§3.10 Covenants 66
[A] Lessor's Covenants 66
[1] Quiet Enjoyment 66
[2] Reimbursement from Reserves and Other Payments 67
[B] Lessee's Covenants 68
[1] Maintenance 68
[2] Liens 70
[a] Mechanics' Liens 70
[b] Eurocontrol and Similar Liens 73
[c] Emissions Lien 78
[d] Tax Liens 81
[3] Chicago Convention and Registration 84
[a] Owner-Only Registration 87
[b] Owner or Operator Registration 89
[c] Owner and Operator Registration 89
[d] Operator-Only Registration 91
[4] Possession and Replacement of Parts and Engines 91
[a] Possession 91
[b] Replacement of Parts 92
[c] Replacement of Engines 93
[C] Conclusions 100
§3.11 Indemnities 101
[A] Damage to Aircraft or Other Loss to Lessor 101
[B] Liability for Damage to Third Parties 101
[1] Liability to Non-passengers 101
[2] Liability to Passengers 104
[3] Product Liability 115
[4] A Note on Public International Air Law Instruments 116
[a] Tokyo Convention (1963) 117
[b] Hague Convention (1970) 118
[c] Montreal Convention (1971) 119
[C] Negligent Entrustment 120

[1] Extension to Aircraft Operating Leases 120
[2] US Federal Law 122
[3] AAR Cases 123
[4] Liability Insurance and Indemnities 125
[D] Conclusions 126
§3.12 Insurances 127
[A] Liability Insurances 128
[B] Hull Insurances 131
[1] Agreed Value 131
[2] Determination of Total Loss 132
[C] Deductibles 132
[D] Reinsurance and Cut-Through Clause 132
[E] Termination of Insurances 133
[F] Conclusions 134
§3.13 Redelivery 134
[A] Redelivery in Redelivery Condition 134
[B] Timely Redelivery 135
[C] Non-compliance with Redelivery Condition 136
[D] Residual Value Guarantee 137
[E] Records 138
[F] Conclusions 138
§3.14 Events of Default 139
[A] Payment 140
[B] Breach of Other Obligations 140
[C] Insurance 140
[D] Bankruptcy 140
[1] US Bankruptcy Code 141
[2] Cape Town Convention (2001) 142
[a] Alternative A 142
[b] Alternative B 142
[3] Non-insolvency Restructuring and the Cape Town Convention (2001) 144
[4] Conclusions 145
§3.15 Remedies 145
[A] Repossession 146
[B] Rome Convention (1933) 149
[C] Cape Town Convention (2001) 151
[D] Geneva Convention (1948) 151
[E] Subleasing 152
[F] Deregistration 152
[G] Deregistration Power of Attorney 153
[H] Article 83*bis* Transfer 153
[I] Irrevocable Deregistration and Export Request Authorization 157
[J] Indemnity Claim 159

[K] Voluntary Restructuring 160
[L] Conclusions 161
§3.16 Assignment 162
[A] Absolute Assignment 163
[B] Assignment by Way of Security 163
[C] Conclusions 165
§3.17 Governing Law 165
§3.18 Dispute Resolution 167
[A] Contractual Agreement 167
[B] Third Parties and Forum Non Conveniens 169
[C] Conclusions 170
§3.19 Miscellaneous 171
[A] Time of the Essence 171
[B] No Waiver 172
[C] Entire Agreement 172
[D] Waiver of Sovereign Immunity 173
[E] Conclusions 175
§3.20 Execution 175

CHAPTER 4
Conclusion 177
§4.01 Overall Conclusions 177
[A] Pre-delivery 178
[B] Post-delivery 178
[C] Post-lease Term 179
§4.02 Recommendations 180
[A] Article 83*bis* of the Chicago Convention (1944) 181
[B] Cape Town Convention (2001) and IDERA 182
[C] Eurocontrol Liens, Emissions Liens, and Similar Liens 183
[D] Standardization of Documentation 185
[E] Lessor's Civil Liability for Acts of the Airline 186
[F] Lessor's Criminal Liability for Acts of the Aircraft Commander and Crew (Tokyo Convention (1963)) 188
[G] Hell or High Water 188
[H] Conclusivity of Acceptance 189
[I] Jurisdictional Rankings 189
§4.03 Closing Words 190

Annexes 193

Annex 1 195

Annex 2 197

Annex 3 199

Annex 4 201

Annex 5 203

Annex 6 205

Annex 7 207

Annex 8 209

Annex 9 211

Annex 10 213

Annex 11 215

Annex 12 217

Supplement: Sample Aircraft Lease Agreement 223

Bibliography 347

Table of Cases 355

Table of International Conventions and Other Agreements 359

Table of Legislation and Regulations 363

Index 367

List of Abbreviations

ABCA	Alberta Court of Appeal
AC	Appeal Cases
ACG	Aviation Capital Group
All ER	All England Reports
AOC	Air Operator's Certificate
AWG	Aviation Working Group
BGB	German Civil Code (Bürgerliches Gesetzbuch)
Ch	Chancery
Civ	Civil
Comm	Commercial
CORSIA	Carbon Offsetting and Reduction Scheme for International Aviation
CRCO	Central Route Charges Office
CSA	Conditional Sale Agreement
CSOH	Court of Session Outer House
EASA	European Aviation Safety Agency
ECHR	European Convention on Human Rights
EEA	European Economic Area
EHRR	European Human Rights Reports
EU	European Union
EWCA	England and Wales Court of Appeal
EWHC	England and Wales High Court
FAA	Federal Aviation Administration of the United States of America
FASB	Financial Accounting Standards Board

HLR	House of Lords Reports
IASB	International Accounting Standards Board
IATA	International Air Transport Association
ICAO	International Civil Aviation Organization
ICLQ	International and Comparative Law Quarterly
IDERA	Irrevocable Deregistration and Export Request Authorization
IEHC	Ireland High Court
MRO	Maintenance, Repair and Overhaul
OECD	Organisation for Economic Co-operation and Development
RORA	Recognition of Rights Agreement
SARP	Standards and Recommended Practice
SCC	Supreme Court of Canada
SDNY	Southern District of New York
SPV	Special Purpose Vehicle
UCTA	United Kingdom Unfair Contract Terms Act 1977
UKHL	United Kingdom House of Lords
UKPC	United Kingdom Privy Council
US	United States
WLR	Weekly Law Reports

Preface to the Third Edition

Feast of Blessed Fra' Gerard, 2021

In the few years since the second edition of this work, the universally shared experience of the COVID-19 pandemic and the restrictions imposed in its wake have changed much in the practical operation of the aircraft operating leasing, if not directly, yet, in the law itself.

One thing which this experience has awakened in me is not just the natural wish for freedom, health and safety for all those close to me, but the ability for us all to travel to see one another safely and affordably. To the extent that the advent of aircraft operating leasing helps us to achieve such goals, it has an important public benefit. Air travel is a powerful antidote to xenophobia. Environmental initiatives will help to ensure that this particular form of public transport continues in a sustainable manner for the benefit of all. None of us, I hope, wishes to see a return to the days of air travel as the reserve of an *élite*.

Nobody can know exactly what the future holds for aviation in general, and aircraft operating leasing in particular, but, thankful for the life which aviation has afforded me to live thus far, it is my strong wish and hope that this small work may in some small way help to ensure the availability of air transport to all.

At the risk of repeating myself from my preface to the second edition, I would remind my dear readers that, not only are any errors in this book entirely my own responsibility, but all opinions stated herein are purely my own personal ones and do not represent those of any current or previous employer or any other party. I welcome any corrections, comments and criticisms.

The law is stated as of 31 August 2021.

Donal Patrick Hanley
Montréal, Québec, Canada

Preface to the Second Edition

The Feast of Our Lady of Victory, 2016

Four years have passed since the first edition of this work. This second edition takes account of developments in law and practice since the first edition and builds on the feedback received on the first edition. I am grateful for all feedback received, including suggestions for improvement.

One important development since the first edition has been the development of the Cape Town Convention Academic Project[1] and, in particular, its repository of legal materials, making available not only reports of judicial activity involving the Cape Town Convention but also reports of administrative and non-judicial activity. All those involved, as well as the members of the Aviation Working Group[2] and its Legal Advisory Panel are to be commended for this important work.

It is perhaps best not to let it go without saying that, not only are any errors in this book entirely my own responsibility, but that all opinions stated herein are purely my own personal ones and do not represent those of my employer or any other party.

The law is stated as of 30 September 2016.

Donal Patrick Hanley
Montréal, Québec, Canada

1. http://www.ctcap.org.
2. http://www.awg.aero.

Preface to the First Edition

The Feast of St Joseph the Worker, 2012

Men have always sought to reach the heavens. We see, for example, in The Holy Bible how men sought to build a city and a tower 'the top whereof may reach to heaven'[1] and we see how the Lord decided, as a result, to confound their tongue and they ceased to build the city,[2] thence called 'Babel … That is, confusion.'[3] Notwithstanding the failure of the Tower of Babel project, ever since, men have continued with their efforts to reach the heavens until, finally, in our day, air travel and even space travel have become commonplace. The concept of leasing also goes far back through history – at least to Babylonian times[4] – and has also developed since then until it is commonplace nowadays for aircraft.

Bringing together both air travel and leasing is a somewhat more recent endeavour and the laws and practices surrounding both need to take account of one another. Perhaps, in this regard, a certain aspect of the confusion of Babel is seen to this day, given the many legal systems and legal provisions that can be very hard, if not sometimes seemingly impossible, to reconcile, written, as they are, in many languages and not always taking into account one another.

It is the intent of this author that this work may serve to reduce that confusion and increase the common understanding of the legal and practical aspects of the aircraft operating lease and to clarify, at least to some extent, its place in the firmament of public and private international air law.[5]

This author's motivation in tackling this subject lies in his surprise at how comparatively little has been written on it academically given its ever increasing importance and in his opinion, after more than twenty years of legal practice in the

1. Genesis 11:4, Old Testament, Holy Bible, Douay-Rheims, 1610, revised by Bishop Richard Challoner, 1752.
2. Interestingly, we are not told that the tower itself was destroyed.
3. *Ibid.*, 11:9.
4. *See* Chapter 1 section §1.01 *infra*.
5. The reader's attention is drawn in particular to Chapter 1 section §1.03 *infra*, which sets out a detailed road map as to what lies ahead.

field, that there is an as yet undefined gap between law and practice in aircraft operating leasing.

Parties to a lease should be aware of the law so as not to include unenforceable provisions in their leases. Drafters of laws should at least be aware of practice when drafting laws that will affect such practice. Assuming that, having bridged any identified gaps between law and practice, leases contain only enforceable provisions, courts should swiftly and unambiguously enforce such provisions as drafted.

The law is stated as of 30 April 2012.

Donal Patrick Hanley
Montréal, Québec, Canada

Acknowledgements

First, I wish to thank my parents, Donal and Norma, for having suggested a career in law to me, as well as my classmates, teachers, professors, colleagues and superiors, past and present, for having inspired me to want to learn more and for invaluable advice throughout my career.

In particular, I thank my doctoral dissertation supervisors, Professor Pablo Mendes de Leon of Leiden University and the late Professor Donald H. Bunker of McGill University, the members of my doctoral and opposition committees and the late Ms Paula van der Wulp of the International Institute of Air and Space Law at Leiden University.

Next, I thank my sister, Ciara, and my brother, Cormac, for acting as my *paranymfs* during the defence of my doctoral dissertation on which this work is based. *Deo gratias*, the defence was successful.

I also thank Loren M Dollet, Esq, formerly Executive Vice President of Aviation Capital Group Corp, Newport Beach, California, for his kind consent to include the Supplement to this work.

Further, I wish to thank the libraries of Leiden University, McGill University and the International Civil Aviation Organization (ICAO) for the use of their facilities during my research. I also thank the Organisation for Economic Co-operation and Development and ICAO for their kind permission to reproduce Annexes 11 and 12, respectively.

Finally, but most of all, I wish to thank in a special way my wife, Helen, to whom this work is dedicated, for her loving support and patience with me during the long process involved in this study from start to finish.

In undertaking a study such as this, I am very much aware of how interdependent we all are. Nevertheless, writing is essentially an individual task: any errors that may be found herein are entirely my responsibility.

Go raibh maith agaibh go léir.

CHAPTER 1
Introduction

§1.01 CONTEXT

The aim of this work is to examine the aircraft operating lease from both a legal and practical point of view and, in particular, to contextualize it in light of both public and private international air law.

Personal property leasing can be traced back to ancient times: Lawrence and Minan[1] note that chartering of ships originated in the times of the Phoenicians and that the code of the Babylonian king Hammurabi[2] referred to the leasing of personal property.[3]

Although aircraft, not constituting or being attached to land, or real estate, do indeed constitute personalty, or personal property,[4] commercial aviation is very much a product of the twentieth century.

As a discrete field of jurisprudence, aircraft leasing is, therefore, comparatively young, having taken off, as it were, only on a major scale since the 1980s[5] – and yet already by 2007 over a quarter of the world's commercial aircraft fleet was leased,[6] rising to about half already by 2020.[7] The legal implications of fully half of the world's commercial aircraft being operated by an airline which is not the owner of the aircraft,

1. Lawrence W.H. and Minan J.H., *The Law of Personal Property Leasing*, Thomson West, 2003, 1.01.
2. *Floruit circa* 1750 BC.
3. Code of Hammurabi: '236. If a man rent his boat to a sailor, and the sailor is careless, and the boat is wrecked or goes aground, the sailor shall give the owner of the boat another boat as compensation', as set out in http://avalon.law.yale.edu/ancient/hamframe.asp on 9 Sep. 2021.
4. Nolan J.R. and Nolan-Haley J.M., *Black's Law Dictionary*, 6th Edition, West Publishing Co., 1990.
5. Abeyratne R.I.R., *Aviation Trends in the New Millenium*, Ashgate, 2001, 1.
6. Morrell P.S., *Airline Finance*, 3rd Edition, Ashgate, 2007, 196.
7. CAPA Centre for Aviation, *Aircraft lessor fleet falls disproportionately; lease rates plummet*, Analysis, 15 Jul. 2020 as set out in https://centreforaviation.com/analysis/reports/aircraft-lessor-fleet-falls-disproportionately-lease-rates-plummet-530864 on 9 Sep. 2021.

with much of the remainder of the commercial aircraft fleet being subject to a mortgage or other security in favour of secured lenders, are great both in the fields of public and private international air law.

The duty of lawyers specializing in aircraft operating leasing is to record with certainty the commercial terms agreed between the leasing company (the lessor) and the airline (the lessee) in the hope that good drafting will enable the parties to be clear about their respective rights and obligations under the contract and about their rights in the event of a breach of the terms thereof by the other party.

This desire was well summarized by Hamblen J of the English High Court in *Celestial Aviation Trading 71 Limited v. Paramount Airways Private Ltd.*[8] where he stated:

> The lessor, having a reversionary right to the asset, needs to know and agree with precision with the lessee: (a) the obligations of each party, (b) the events that will entitle the lessor to terminate the contract and recover its asset and (c) provisions which will show how, as a matter of business practicality, the contract will be terminated, the asset recovered and possession returned by the lessee to the lessor.

Typically, aircraft operating leases may run from 100 to 200 pages or so. As Wilson has noted, in the context of short-term aircraft engine operating leases:

> As much as a lessee may complain about the complexity of a lease, lessors have a point in justifying complex documentary requirements. Thorny legal issues exist, and lessors are entitled to ensure that sufficient legal protections are in place before transferring possession of their expensive assets.[9]

Nevertheless, the two parties do not enjoy complete freedom to contract on whatever terms they wish. For example, the lessor, in particular, may be subject to constraints imposed by its financier. Likewise, the lessee may be subject to regulatory constraints concerning aircraft registration or foreign remittances or other matters depending on its jurisdiction.

The European Civil Aviation Conference,[10] for example, has, while recognizing that leasing is a common practice in the airline industry and that a flexible approach to it can bring economic benefits to air carriers and consumers alike and help air carriers to meet market needs better, also recognized that:

> leases should not be used as a means to circumvent applicable laws, regulations or international agreements.[11]

8. [2010] EWHC 185 (Comm) at para. 72.
9. Wilson F.S., *Mastering Engine Leasing: The Master Short-Term Engine Lease Agreement Will Serve as Models for Future Standardization in the Aviation Industry*, Airfinance Journal, Sep. 2007.
10. ECAC Recommendation on Leasing of Aircraft, Recommendation ECAC/21-1, 2–3 Jul. 1997 in *Study on Aircraft Leasing*, Air Transport Committee, 156th Session of the Council, ICAO, 1999, at Appendix B.
11. *Ibid.*

and, accordingly, it went on to recommend, *inter alia*, that:

> [f]or the purpose of ensuring safety and liability standards and compliance with any applicable economic conditions, all leasing arrangements entered into by air carriers[12] should receive prior approval from the appropriate authorities.[13]

While concerned that a rigid approach to leasing would be counter-productive, Abeyratne[14] cautions against allowing overly flexible arrangements to the point where safety might be threatened, and calls for the two aspects of freedom of contract in leasing and safety to be addressed harmoniously so that 'a cautious balance of the elements of freedom and compulsion is maintained'.

With due respect to Abeyratne, this is somewhat confusing: it is hard to imagine (and indeed he does not explain) how safety could be compromised by virtue only of an airline operating an aircraft pursuant to a dry operating lease[15] rather than pursuant to a finance lease or pursuant to a secured loan or, for that matter, pursuant to outright ownership and it is submitted that safety is not really a valid concern in this context. It should be borne in mind that he was writing some sixteen years ago when aircraft leasing was not as widespread or as familiar as it is now and his caution was not unusual among those rightly concerned with aircraft safety at that time. Maintenance and safety in the context of aircraft operating leases will be discussed in Chapter 3 sections §3.10 (Covenants) and §3.11 (Indemnities), *infra*.

The seasoned legal practitioner may be familiar with how various issues are typically resolved in the aircraft operating lease but may not always be familiar with the theoretical reasoning underlying such resolution. This is particularly so because many aircraft finance lawyers come to their field through more general financing law rather than through more general air law and thus may not be immediately familiar with applicable principles of public and private international air law. Likewise, when negotiating a lease, practitioners should bear in mind that ultimately if it comes to litigation, it will be adjudicated by a judge who may be unfamiliar with the commercial background: it is crucial, therefore, that the lease be properly drafted to reflect the intent of the parties and with an awareness of the regulatory and legal framework within which the judge must analyse the lease.

§1.02 'PRACTICAL' VERSUS 'LEGAL'

At this stage, it is appropriate to explain what is meant by 'practical' and 'legal' in the title of this work and why such contextualization is necessary or at least desirable. It is

12. This is somewhat ambiguous – it is unclear whether the reference is to all leasing arrangements entered into by air carriers as lessees or only those leasing arrangements entered into by air carriers as lessors, as contrasted with non-airline lessor. *See* Chapter 3 section §3.05[A][4] *infra*.
13. *Ibid.*
14. Abeyratne R.I.R., *Aviation Trends in the New Millenium*, Ashgate, 2001, 459.
15. *See* Chapter 3 section §3.05[A][4] *infra*.

conceded that perhaps other terms could be used, but they seem as good as any others with some explanation.[16]

This work, limited as it is to the aircraft operating lease, has been influenced by the works of those who have gone before. In particular, this author draws attention to the work of, while in no way comparing himself to, Sir Roy Goode whose book, Commercial Law, is 'a synthesis of the theory underlying commercial relationships and the practice which governs their operation'.[17] As Goode points out, for such a synthesis:

> [t]he greatest difficulty ... lies not in the sophisticated rule but in the fundamental concept. Rules may change, concepts are more permanent. Hence it is the theoretical framework of a subject which commands the closest attention, for it is that which endures when the detailed rule has passed into oblivion.[18]

[A] 'Practical'

By 'practical' is meant the approach of the legal practitioner in the field of aircraft operating leasing.[19] Such a practitioner may work in a commercial aircraft leasing company, as lessor, an airline, as lessee, or a private practice law firm representing either lessor or lessee. Practitioners in this field are, for the most part, highly qualified and experienced lawyers dealing in assets worth in the many millions of US dollars (USD). Certain practices are common among them, and the format of this work will broadly follow that of a typical aircraft operating lease deal for such practitioners, with such practices being discussed where they arise in Chapter 3.

Given the large sums of money involved, industry practice is highly developed, and all practitioners wish to ensure that such practice is, save where specifically negotiated otherwise, followed should matters end in litigation - the last thing they want is to find that a court has refused or is unable to enforce a provision of an aircraft operating lease on which they seek to rely due to a contrary judicial precedent, persuasive academic article, regulation, statute, or international treaty or other agreement or instrument.

In terms of the aircraft operating lease, each deal involves a high-value asset and tends to be something of a tailor-made or bespoke agreement, based on a model lease produced by the lessor (occasionally, in the case of a powerful airline, by the lessee), with each lessor having its own preferred form. Thus, forms of lease vary even if overall their content is similar in effect to reflect then-prevailing market practice.

---

16. Originally, this author had considered using 'theoretical' instead of 'legal' but was swayed in his final choice by the title of the DCL Thesis of Margo R.D., *Aviation Insurance in the United Kingdom: Law and Practice*, McGill University, 1979.
17. Street H., Foreword to First Edition, in Goode CBE QC Sir Roy, *Commercial Law*, 2nd Edition, Penguin Books, 1995, at xxiv.
18. Goode CBE QC Sir Roy, *Commercial Law*, 2nd Edition, Penguin Books, 1995, at xxvi.
19. Other forms of aircraft leasing and financing, such as finance lease, are discussed in Chapter 2 section §2.01, *infra*.

To that extent, such leases, being fully negotiated by the parties, differ both from wet leases[20] and from short-term engine leases, where lessees typically have less bargaining power and the leases are correspondingly more one-sided, leading to difficulty in enforcement in case of breach by the lessor.[21] This is because these are more typically entered into at short notice on an emergency basis where an airline finds itself needing an aircraft or engine at short notice due to a problem with another of its aircraft, or one of the engines on such aircraft.

Bunker[22] sets out in detail some of the problems which can be encountered with wet leasing, especially given the fact that generally, the immediate need is so intense that there is less than ideal negotiation of the terms of the wet lease[23] or adequate due diligence: one of his primary cautions is to identify the wet lessor and to establish its bona fides.[24]

With short-term engine leasing, the International Air Transport Association (IATA),[25] in conjunction with the Aviation Working Group (AWG),[26] has prepared an agreed form Master Short-Term Engine Lease Agreement[27] which is freely available for use and adaptation by parties. It is only suitable for short-term leases of engines, but there has been some discussion of extending such standardization process further. Wilson[28] has commented:

> While some might say that it remains to be seen if document standardization comes to other aspects of aircraft finance, others think it inevitable and that the only question is, 'When'?

It is the intent of this author that this work should flag the principal legal issues to be considered in developing a standard form aircraft operating lease and he will make certain recommendations in that regard.

20. 'Wet leasing of an aircraft entails the transfer for use of an aircraft along with the cockpit crew, cabin crew, maintenance and hull insurance … . A wet lease is generally concluded for a very short term … . A wet lease is similar to an aircraft charter, except that the wet lessee must be an airline holding its own operating licenses and permits, and the aircraft must be operated under the lessee's flight designator codes and route authorities': Bunker D.H., *Aircraft Wet Leasing: The Perils and the Benefits*, Annals of Air and Space Law, Volume XXV, 2000, 67–82, at 67–68.
21. '… a judge's hands may be tied where, for example, a one-sided lease agreement fails to include any lessor default or adequate termination provisions in favour of the lessee', Bunker, *supra*, at 81.
22. Bunker D.H., *International Aircraft Financing, Volume 1: General Principles*, 2nd Edition, IATA, 2015, at 180–191.
23. *Ibid.*, at 241.
24. *Ibid.*, at 243.
25. *See* http://www.iata.org on 9 Sep. 2021.
26. *See* http://www.awg.aero on 9 Sep. 2021.
27. IATA Document No. 5016-00, *Master Short-Term Engine Lease Agreement*, 2002.
28. Wilson F.S., *Mastering Engine Leasing: The Master Short-Term Engine Lease Agreement Will Serve as Models for Future Standardization in the Aviation Industry*, Airfinance Journal, Sep. 2007.

[B] 'Legal'

By 'legal', on the other hand, is meant *not* a body of law that somehow exists only in theory and is not applied, as contrasted with practice, but rather that body of law, involving public and private international air law, statutes, regulations, and judicial precedent which indeed applies to any legal issues which may arise under an aircraft operating lease.[29] These will be examined as they arise in the context of an operating leasing transaction in the following pages. Such body of law may differ from the industry practice but, ultimately, while courts may take note of industry practice, in the case of disputes as to the interpretation or enforcement of provisions of aircraft operating leases, the courts will, or should, apply the *lex lata*, the law as it is, and cannot easily ignore it simply because the outcome is inconvenient from the point of view of the aircraft operating lease industry.

It is certainly desirable, therefore, that such courts, and those practising before it in the context of contentious litigation, should at least be familiar with the industry practice in respect of which they are asked to adjudicate. Likewise, it is incumbent on legal practitioners specializing in putting the transactions together to be aware of the legal framework within which those courts, who will adjudicate in case of dispute, operate.

To put it another way, the practical approach, guided by a desired certain commercial outcome, is deployed in putting the lease together, but the legal, or more theoretical, approach, applying the law to disputes arising thereunder, takes the lease apart in order to analyse it and to apply the law to it.

If it may be said that many aircraft finance lawyers are not as familiar with public and private international air law, it may fairly be said also that public and private international air law did not always, until relatively recently, take full account of the fact that ownership and operation of a given aircraft may be in different hands. This is not surprising, since the aircraft operating lease only really took off after the 1970s,[30] growing rapidly in the 1980s and 1990s.[31]

By contrast, most public and private international air law treaties have been in place before the mid-1970s, the Montreal Convention (1999)[32] and the Cape Town Convention (2001)[33] being the more recent developments in the field of private air law treaties and the amendment to the Chicago Convention (1944)[34] by the addition of

29. For more on the source of public and private international air law, *see* Mendes de Leon P.M.J., *An Introduction to Air Law*, 10th Edition, Kluwer Law International, 2017; Bunker D.H., *International Aircraft Financing, Volume 1: General Principles*, 2nd Edition, IATA, 2015, at 457 et seq., and Dempsey P.S., *Public International Air Law*, McGill University, 2008, at 5-6.
30. Bunker D.H., *The Law of Aerospace Finance in Canada*, McGill, 1988.
31. *Study on Aircraft Leasing*, Air Transport Committee, 156th Session of the Council, ICAO, 1999.
32. Convention for the Unification of Certain Rules for International Carriage by Air, signed at Montreal on 28 May 1999.
33. Convention on International Interests in Mobile Equipment signed at Cape Town on 16 Nov. 2001.
34. The Convention on International Civil Aviation, signed at Chicago on 7 Dec. 1944.

Article 83*bis*[35] being a more notable relatively recent development in the field of public air law treaties.

It is desirable, it is submitted, for those putting a lease together to know how it may be taken apart later, and it is equally desirable for those taking a lease apart later to know how and why it was put together the way it was.

Goode has written that:

> [t]he commercial lawyer of today needs to know not only his or her own law but of developments in what has come to be known as transnational commercial law, the corpus of law that grows from international conventions and other instruments of harmonization and from conscious and unconscious parallelism in judicial thinking in different jurisdictions.[36]

This statement, it is submitted, is equally true if 'aircraft finance lawyer' is substituted for 'commercial lawyer' and 'public and private international air law' for 'transnational commercial law'.

§1.03 AIM AND METHODOLOGY

It is the aim of this work to provide an original contribution to legal science by examining, from a legal perspective, a typical lease transaction from the start of the deal through to execution of the documentation, discussing not only the typical issues that arise and their resolution, but the reasons underlying them. It is submitted that a comprehensive examination of the interrelationship between the law, on the one hand, and the practice of the typical provisions aircraft operating leases, on the other hand, has been a somewhat understudied area of aircraft finance law to date.

In terms of layout, this work is divided into four parts in addition to the various Annexes and Tables at the end:

(1) introduction, which as its name implies is introductory;
(2) overview, which is largely descriptive;
(3) the Aircraft Operating Lease, which is largely analytical and based on research, and constitutes by far the greater body of this work; and
(4) conclusion, which is largely prescriptive.

Finally, a Supplement is added after the end of this work which sets out a real example of a form of aircraft operating lease for a used aircraft, in a form as previously used by a leading commercial aircraft leasing company.[37] This form will differ in detail from those used by other leasing companies, but in overall terms of layout and content, it is representative of the current state of the market. This Supplement should be

35. *See* Chapter 3 section §3.15[H] *infra*.
36. Goode CBE QC Sir Roy, *Commercial Law*, 2nd Edition, Penguin Books, 1995, at xx.
37. The company is Aviation Capital Group Corp. of Newport Beach California. Until April 2019, this author was employed as Managing Director of its Irish based subsidiary, ACG Aircraft Leasing Ireland Limited.

valuable in illustrating many of the points made in the body of the text itself and cross-references are made where appropriate.

In terms of methodology, there are two main ways of undertaking the analysis of this subject.

One is a systematic overview of public and private international air law, examining each international agreement in turn, and discussing where the provisions of each have an impact on aircraft operating leasing. Such a methodology may be seen in, for example, Pompongsuk.[38]

The other is a systematic overview of the aircraft operating lease, examining each major section thereof in turn, and researching and discussing where the provisions thereof have been impacted, *inter alia*, by relevant provisions of substantive law. Such a methodology may be seen, for example, in Bunker.[39]

The methodology chosen in this work is the latter rather than the former for several reasons, among them, the following:

- Many provisions of substantive law (the theory, as discussed in section §1.02 *supra*) need to be considered, not only those set out in public and private international air law agreements but also case law, statutes and regulations (which differ by jurisdiction), taking into account both common and civil law systems where appropriate.
- It is arguably more important to avoid problems in the interpretation of leases by addressing these issues at the time when the lease is being put together during the drafting and negotiation stage rather than *ex post facto* when it is being taken apart for analysis during litigation, by which stage it is too late to remedy any problems.
- This author was personally more familiar, at the outset of this research, with the situation of the legal practitioner who needs to understand better the theoretical framework in which he operates rather than vice versa.

This work differs from Bunker,[40] however, in having a more detailed discussion in relation to each section of the typical aircraft operating lease agreement under analysis. The reason for this is that Bunker is not confined to aircraft operating leasing but examines other forms of lease and indeed of aircraft financing. Further, although the major sources of air law are considered,[41] a detailed contextualization of the aircraft operating lease in that setting is outside the scope of that work.

This examination will be carried out in the context of reviewing the current literature in this area and making reference, where appropriate, to the results of extensive research into relevant learned articles and texts, case law, regulations, statutes, and international treaties, particularly those relating to public and private international air law.

38. Pompongsuk P., *International Aircraft Leasing: Impact on International Air Law Treaties*, LLM Thesis, McGill University, 1997.
39. Bunker D.H., *International Aircraft Financing*, Volume 2, 2nd Edition, IATA, 2015.
40. *Ibid.*
41. *Ibid.*, Volume 1, Chapter 6.

In that regard, many different domestic legal systems may come into play: the governing law of the lease itself, the law of the jurisdiction of the lessor, the law of the jurisdiction of the lessee, the law of the state of registration of the aircraft pursuant to Article 17 of the Chicago Convention (1944), and the *lex situs* of the aircraft all come to mind. To that extent, the examples given should be seen as precisely that. The particular combinations of laws that may apply in a given case will often vary from deal to deal as each of the factors just cited changes.

Cross-border aircraft operating leasing is thus characterized by what Simon Hall describes as an 'absence of a uniform body of law',[42] with the rules of private international law governing, for the time being, 'what law applies, and, accordingly, what laws will govern the consequences of the contractual relations involved'.[43]

The governing law of the cross-border aircraft operating lease will, in the majority of cases, be English or New York law, since the English and New York courts have great experience in interpreting and enforcing operating lease provisions, thus reducing uncertainty of interpretation. This author has rarely seen in over twenty years of practice in the field a cross-border aircraft operating lease governed by the laws of any other common law jurisdiction and has never seen one governed by the laws of a civil law jurisdiction.[44]

This work will focus primarily, therefore, on English and, to an extent, New York law as the governing law of the lease, as well as to relevant principles and provisions of European Union (EU) law, but will refer to other systems of law elsewhere in the world where appropriate in addition to relevant principles of public and private international air law.

It is important to examine the structuring of the transaction and the letter of intent which precedes the negotiation of the lease first since these will set the parameters for the lease itself – for example, by determining who will be the parties to the lease and whether the lease will be directly from the lessor to the lessee or will consist of a head lease from the lessor to a special purpose company set up by the lessor for that purpose and a sublease from such special purpose company to the lessee. Even more complicated structures may be required depending on the particular jurisdiction and the requirements of the lessor's financiers.

Turning then to the lease itself, the major issues in aircraft operating leasing will be analysed from both a legal and practical point of view, with subjects divided according to the main typical sections of an aircraft operating lease. One reason for this is that, in practice, this is typically how, in this author's experience, leases are negotiated and legal, as well as commercial, technical and other issues are encountered

42. Clark T. (ed.), *Leasing Finance*, Euromoney, 1985, at 73.
43. *Ibid.*, at 75.
44. That is not to say, of course, that it does not or cannot happen. *See*, e.g., Fortier J.M., *Leasing of Aircraft in the Province of Quebec*, Annals of Air and Space Law, Volume XV, 1990, at 61–73, where the author discusses finance (but not operating) leasing in the Canadian civil law province of Québec, in particular, the exemption of aircraft on finance lease, or *crédit-bail*, as defined in Art. 1603 of the then Civil Code of Lower Canada, from the provisions of Chapter First of the Lease of Things of such Civil Code, from the requirement that it be in good repair and that lessor grant a warranty against latent defects.

– by a page by page-turning through the draft lease, section by section, by counsel for both lessor and lessee together with other representatives of either party.

As will be seen in Chapter 3, the influence of the public and private air law treaties is to be found mainly in respect of safety and maintenance, licensing and certification, liability to third parties, as well as issues pertaining to registration and enforcement of remedies. Less evident, if evident at all in some cases, is a concern with the commercial aspects of the operating lease or the allocation of risk by the parties *inter se.*[45] Accordingly, as the provisions of the lease are gone through, this work shall, depending on the section in question, dwell to a greater or lesser extent on applicable public and private international air law.

Goode,[46] in his Official Commentary[47] to the Cape Town Convention (2001), distinguishes private and public international air law. He echoes Abeyratne[48] in referring to States' balancing of each state's legal philosophy and the need to respect a high degree of autonomy for the parties.

Further, he points out that, although the Cape Town Convention (2001) is framed on a basis consistent with the preamble to the Chicago Convention (1944) that:

> international civil aviation may be developed in a safe and orderly manner and that the international air transport services may be established on the basis of equality of opportunity and operated soundly and economically,

the third preamble to the Aircraft Equipment Protocol to the Cape Town Convention (2001) is carefully worded so as to 'avoid any implication that the Convention has to be construed by reference to the provisions of the Chicago Convention'[49] as follows:

> MINDFUL of the principles and objectives of the Convention on International Civil Aviation, signed at Chicago on 7 December 1944.

According to the Official Commentary,[50] the Cape Town Convention (2001), together with the Aircraft Equipment Protocol thereto, provides 'an international legal regimen for security and related interests in aircraft', thus helping:

> to reduce legal uncertainty caused by differences in national laws and thereby opening up to developing countries access to finance at reasonable cost.

45. As will be discussed in Chapter 3 *infra*, only the Cape Town Convention and Aircraft Equipment Protocol thereto, of the international air law instruments, is directly concerned with contractual rights *inter partes*; for the most part, the others deal with the rights and obligations of third parties, such as passengers, those on the ground, tax authorities, air navigation and other service providers, etc.
46. Goode was chairman of the UNIDROIT Study Group which initiated the Cape Town Convention as an ambitious private international law project.
47. Goode R., *Convention on International Interests in Mobile Equipment and Protocol Thereto on Matters Specific to Aircraft Equipment: Official Commentary*, UNIDROIT, 2002, at 175–180.
48. *See* section §1.01 *supra.*
49. *Ibid.*, at 176.
50. *Supra*, at back cover page.

Goode continues that, although both the Cape Town Convention (2001) and Chicago Convention (1944) have a similar set of principles and objects,[51] nevertheless, they address different subjects: the Chicago Convention (1944) is a public law convention establishing an international system centred on sovereignty to promote safe and secure flight operations whereas the Cape Town Convention (2001) is a private law convention designed to facilitate the financing and leasing of aircraft.[52] In his view, in any event, 'principles of interpretation employed in dealing with one text are unlikely to apply in dealing with the other'.[53]

Even if that is so, in the context of aircraft leasing, the key word is to be found in the above-quoted third preamble to the Aircraft Equipment Protocol to the Cape Town Convention (2001): allowing that Goode is correct that the Cape Town Convention (2001) does not *have to be* construed by reference to the Chicago Convention (1944), it is still necessary to be *mindful* of both applicable principles of public international air law and of private international air law.

Perhaps his distinction is somewhat artificial – by way of comparison, the Warsaw Convention (1929) does not refer to the Paris Convention (1919),[54] the predecessor of the Chicago Convention (1944),[55] at all; and the Montreal Convention (1999), in its fourth recital, simply 'reaffirms' the 'desirability' of an orderly development of international air transport operations 'in accordance with the principles and objectives of' the Chicago Convention (1944). Indeed, the other public and private air law instruments referred to in this work do not refer to the Chicago Convention (1944) in this context at all.

Notwithstanding the great respect due to Goode's role as chairman of the UNIDROIT Study Group which initiated the Cape Town Convention (2001), it is not clear to this author that the word 'mindful' in the context of the Cape Town Convention (2001) connotes as great a sense of separation from the Chicago Convention (2001) as Goode implies it does.

Given that one of its aims is to 'ensure greater degree of certainty and enforceability of a lessor's contractual rights and obligations',[56] the Cape Town Convention (2001) will be discussed at length throughout this work.

The main premise of this author is that, under the operating lease, the lessor wishes to pass all operational risk to the airline lessee, retaining only the credit risk of the lessee and the risk of the residual value of the aircraft at the end of the lease term

51. The preamble to the Chicago Convention states that it was concluded 'in order that international civil aviation may be developed in a safe and orderly manner and that international air transport services may be established on the basis of equality of opportunity and operated soundly and economically'. The preambles to the Cape Town Convention and Aircraft Equipment Protocol refer to the need for clear rules to facilitate the financing of the acquisition and use of aircraft equipment.
52. *Ibid.*, at 180.
53. *Ibid.*
54. The Convention relating to the Regulation of Aerial Navigation signed at Paris on 13 Oct. 1919, henceforth also referred to as the Paris Convention (1919).
55. *See* Art. 80 of the Chicago Convention.
56. Djojonegoro A., *The Unidroit Proposal for a Uniform Air Law: A New Aircraft Mortgage Convention?*, Annals of Air and Space Law, Volume XXII, Part II, 1997, at 54.

but that, while this may work *inter partes*, this does not bind third parties whose rights are founded not in contract but in law.

Too often, in this author's experience, lawyers in this field believe in absolute freedom of contract to allocate risk and too often find out, when it comes to litigation, that the courts refuse to enforce lease provisions in the way in which such lawyers had originally envisaged or even to enforce them at all. Practitioners should draft clearly, within the applicable legal and regulatory framework, so that courts can simply enforce the leases as drafted. Once that is done, for their part, courts should indeed simply enforce the leases as drafted.

In short, this work, then, aims to bring the lawyer through an aircraft operating lease in such a manner as to give him/her a thorough understanding not only of the practical manner in which leases are typically negotiated, drafted and executed[57] but of the theoretical legal reasons under applicable domestic and international law, whether by way of case law, statute or treaty, which underpin, or which should underpin, such practical manner.

More importantly, based on the research and analysis set out in this work, this author will consider if any patterns emerge in cases of divergence between the practical and the legal and will consider what implications such divergence may have in particular for the fields of public and private international air law.

57. As to which, *see also* Bunker D.H., *International Aircraft Financing, Volume 2: Specific Documents*, 2nd Edition, IATA, 2015, at 38–204.

CHAPTER 2

Overview

§2.01 AIRCRAFT OPERATING LEASING AND OTHER FORMS OF LEASING AND FINANCING

In the context of personal property, such as an aircraft, a lease may be defined as:

> a contract by which one owning such property grants to another the right to possess, use and enjoy it for a specified period of time in exchange for periodic payment of a stipulated price, referred to as rent.[1]

However, this definition, although it may work for most purposes, may not be entirely correct or comprehensive.[2]

There seems no good reason why such grant must be in exchange for a periodic payment (rent could be paid in advance in full, for example) of a stipulated price (the rent may be floating by reference to interest rate fluctuations, rather than fixed, or may otherwise be reviewable during the term) or at all (there could be a power by the hour arrangement whereby the airline is only obliged to store, maintain and use the aircraft, but is only obliged to pay rent, howsoever described, based on actual usage, with or without minimum usage requirements).[3]

The Cape Town Convention (2001) perhaps comes closer to a comprehensive definition by defining a lease agreement as:

> an agreement by which one person (the lessor) grants a right to possession or control of an object (with or without an option to purchase) to another person (the lessee) in return for a rental or other payment.[4]

1. Nolan J.R. and Nolan-Haley J.M., *Black's Law Dictionary*, 6th Edition, West Publishing Co., 1990, at 889.
2. For example, the lessor may not be the owner where it itself holds the leased property pursuant to a head lease.
3. Thus, the various attempts to define a lease in Abeyratne R.I.R., *Aviation Trends in the New Millenium*, Ashgate, 2001, 14 et seq., while good, likewise are not comprehensive.
4. Article 1(q).

The International Civil Aviation Organization (ICAO), the specialized agency of the United Nations dealing with international civil aviation, has, perhaps wisely, declined to define what constitutes a leased aircraft other than as one 'used under a contractual leasing arrangement' according to its Manual on the Regulation of International Air Transport.[5] Given the tailor-made nature of leases negotiated for specific situations, its Air Transport Committee has stated that a more precise definition has not proven possible.[6]

Aircraft leases are classified as being either operating or true leases on the one hand or finance or capital leases on the other hand.[7] This work will examine the aircraft operating lease.[8]

For accounting purposes, the International Accounting Standards Board (IASB)[9] adopted Standard 17 (IAS 17) which provides that:

> The classification of leases adopted in this Standard is based on the extent to which risks and rewards incidental to ownership of a leased asset lie with the lessor or the lessee.
>
> A lease is classified as a finance lease if it transfers substantially all the risks and rewards incidental to ownership. A lease is classified as an operating lease if it does not transfer substantially all the risks and rewards incidental to ownership.

In the United States (US), the Financial Accounting Standards Board (FASB)[10] adopted the Statement of Financial Accounting Standards 13 (FAS 13), which is more detailed than IAS 17.

Under paragraph 7 of FASB 13, a capital lease is one in which, *inter alia*:

(1) the lease transfers ownership of the property to the lessee by the end of the lease term;
(2) the lease contains a bargain purchase option;
(3) the lease term is equal to 75% or more of the estimated economic life of the leased property; or
(4) the present value of the lease payments, discounted at an appropriate discount rate, exceeds 90% of the fair market value of the asset.

An operating lease is simply defined as any lease which is not a capital lease.

5. Doc 9626.
6. *Study on Aircraft Leasing*, Air Transport Committee, 156th Session of the Council, ICAO, 1999, at 1.1.
7. *See* discussion in Vasigh B., Fleming K. and Humphreys B., *Foundations of Airline Finance: Methodology and Practice*, Routledge, 2015, at 495–530.
8. Specifically, the dry aircraft operating lease. For the distinction between dry and wet leases (which latter are more akin to charters of aircraft in certain respects and in any event beyond the scope of this work), *see* Chapter 3 sections §3.05[A][4] and §3.05[B][5] *infra*. Also note Hamilton's statement that the United States Federal Aviation Administration has a basic presumption that, where an aircraft and crew are provided from the same source, the arrangement is a charter and not a lease, with wet leases being closely scrutinized: Hamilton J.S., *Practical Aviation Law*, 4th Edition, Blackwell, 2005, at 218.
9. http://www.ifrs.org on 9 Sep. 2021.
10. http://www.fasb.org on 9 Sep. 2021.

The IASB and the FASB harmonized their approach to lease accounting by requiring a lessee to recognize assets and liabilities for the rights and obligations created by leases, of whatever type.[11] Harmonization of IASB 17 and FAS 13 was achieved in January 2016 with the publication of International Financial Reporting Standards (IFRS) 16 Leases,[12] taking effect from 1 January 2019, which provides a new definition of a lease as follows:

> A lease is defined as a contract, or part of a contract, that conveys to the customer the right to use an asset for a period of time in exchange for consideration.

The UNIDROIT Convention on International Financial Leasing (1988),[13] which has not been widely adopted,[14] sets out provisions dealing with 'financial leasing' which it defines as including, *inter alia*, the characteristic that:

> the rentals payable under the leasing agreement are calculated so as to take into account in particular the amortisation of the whole or a substantial part of the cost of the equipment.[15]

From a commercial and accounting point of view, the main difference between an operating and a finance lease is that, with the former, the lessor is expecting to receive the aircraft back while it still has a useful economic life and thus will be more concerned as to the physical condition of the aircraft since it must lease it out afterwards to a subsequent lessee. The aircraft remains accounted for as an asset on the books of the lessor, who is entitled to depreciation of the aircraft since the risks and rewards of ownership lie with it. Further, a benefit for the lessee in entering into an operating lease is the corollary that the operating lease does not appear on its books as a liability[16] since, with it:

> lease structures can be devised to meet accounting objectives of removing liabilities from a balance sheet – thereby, among other things, preserving the lessee's debt-to-equity ratio.[17]

With the finance lease, on the other hand, the aircraft is accounted for as an asset on the books of the lessee, with the depreciation rights which that entails since the risks and rewards of ownership have been assumed by it. Barring a default on the part of the lessee, the lessor does not expect to retake possession of the asset.

11. https://www.fasb.org/leases on 9 Sep. 2021.
12. *Ibid.*
13. Signed at Ottawa on 28 May 1988.
14. It is only in force in eleven states – http://www.unidroit.org/status-leasing-conv-1988 on 9 Sep. 2021.
15. Article 2(c).
16. This is, of course, only one benefit to the lessee of an operating lease. Even without such accounting treatment, the operating lease would still offer flexibility in terms of a finance lease in terms of committing the airline to an aircraft for only a portion of its economic life.
17. Bunker D.H., *Aircraft Financing in the Future*, Annals of Air and Space Law, Volume XXVII, 2002, 139–160, at 149.

In *Lithoprint (Scotland) Ltd. v. Summit Leasing Ltd. & Ors.*,[18] a case before Lord Milligan of the Scottish Court of Sessions, the dispute did not concern whether the lease in question was an operating lease or a finance lease. In it, the pursuers[19] asserted, and the defenders[20] did not dispute that 'a finance lease typically transfers many of the risks and rewards of ownership to the lessee in return for payment of a rental, that most finance lessors fix the rental as if the transaction is a loan'[21] and 'that the rental is fixed with a view to a full return to the lessor of capital and interest'.

To that extent, the finance lessor can be considered as essentially akin to a secured lender, choosing to structure its security by way of ownership where the asset is subject to a finance lease in favour of what is thus essentially akin to a borrower rather than by allowing the borrower legal ownership while taking a mortgage over the aircraft.[22]

This argument was raised before Hamblen J of the English High Court in *Celestial Aviation Trading 71 Limited v. Paramount Airways Private Ltd.*[23] In that case, Hamblen J considered *Shiloh Spinners Ltd. v. Harding (HL)*,[24] which allowed the court to consider whether the insertion of a right of forfeiture essentially to secure the payment of money was a ground on which relief against forfeiture could be granted. In *Celestial*, Hamblen J held that the lease in question was an operating, not a finance lease, that possessory rights for the lease term only were transferred not proprietary rights, and rejected the claimant's argument that relief against such forfeiture should be granted since, *inter alia*, the total of all lease rentals and supplemental reserves (as to which *see* Chapter 3 section §3.07 *infra*) to be paid to the defendant would exceed the cost of the aircraft. His reasoning included the fact that this was an operating lease and that, for leases of this type, the rent was set by reference to prevailing demand and supply for aircraft of the same type. He also rejected the claimant's method of calculation (specifically excluding supplemental rent since that is a fund to be used for major aircraft maintenance).[25]

Both the IASB and FASB considered abolishing the distinction between operating and finance leases for accounting purposes. In the end, the IASB issued a final standard with a single lessee accounting model, whereas the FASB decided to have a dual lessee accounting model.[26]

Even with a change to a single lessee accounting model for accounting purposes, it is submitted that this should not have any effect on the legal distinction between operating and finance leases, at least under English law. In *Celestial*,[27] Hamblen J

18. [1998] ScotCS 36 (23 Oct. 1998).
19. Plaintiffs in Scottish courts.
20. Defendants in Scottish courts.
21. At p. 2.
22. *See* the discussion 'Scope Problem: True Lease or Disguised Security Interest?' in Clark B., *The Law of Secured Transactions under the Uniform Commercial Code*, Volume 1, Thomson Financial, 2000, at 1-45 et seq.
23. [2010] EWHC 185 (Comm.).
24. [1973] AC 691.
25. *Ibid.*, at 47.
26. https://www.iasplus.com/en/news/2016/01/ifrs-16 on 9 Sep. 2021.
27. At 55.

referred to the distinction in accounting treatment[28] between operating leases and finance leases but did not base his judgment on it. He based his judgment on the following:

> In the present case ..., Paramount only has a right to possess the Aircraft for a proportion of its economic life. As such, Celestial retains a very real interest in the Aircraft themselves, including their proper maintenance, the extent of their use, their condition, and their rental and resale value. Possession of the Aircraft will revert to it at a time when the bulk of their economic life is still to run, and there are detailed terms addressing the return of the Aircraft and their required redelivery condition. Celestial therefore retains many of the risks and rewards of ownership. Moreover, rent was not calculated on the basis of recouping the cost of the Aircraft together with interest and profit.[29]

The Cape Town Convention (2001), which will be examined in detail in Chapter 3 later,[30] particularly in the context of remedies, does not distinguish between operating and finance leases and thus a change in accounting treatment of operating leases would have no effect thereunder. This is not surprising since one of the main purposes of the Cape Town Convention (2001) is to establish 'clear rules to govern' asset-based financing and leasing alike: Article 1(i) thereof defines a creditor as being variously 'a charge under a security assignment, a conditional seller under a title reservation agreement and a lessor under a leasing agreement'.

Accordingly, this lack of distinction between operating and finance leases in the Cape Town Convention (2001) makes sense when one considers that it protects both the lessor under a lease (whether operating or finance) and the lender under a secured financing. If the lender chooses to lend under a finance lease, it will be protected as a lessor under the Cape Town Convention (2001). If it chooses to lend instead with the security of a mortgage over the aircraft, it will be protected as the holder of a charge thereover.

Further, Article 83*bis* of the Chicago Convention (1944), also dealt with in detail in Chapter 3[31] and dealing with leasing, likewise does not distinguish between operating and finance leases. Therefore, a change in the accounting treatment of operating leases would not have any effect under the Chicago Convention (1944) either.

The many other forms of aircraft financing available to an airline are beyond the scope of this work. They are discussed in detail in Bunker[32] but there is one thing worth pointing out here - operating leasing, as with finance leasing, secured finance and outright purchase are all tools available to the airline to choose how it wishes to acquire and pay for the aircraft it uses. Although operating leasing may have once been seen as the preserve of carriers with a lower credit quality (who, lacking sufficient financial

28. Referring there to a Statement of the Institute of Chartered Accountants, SSAP 21.
29. At 54.
30. *See* Chapter 3 section §3.15[C] *infra*.
31. *See* Chapter 3 section §3.15[H] *infra*.
32. Bunker D.H., *International Aircraft Financing*, 2nd Edition, IATA, 2015.

resources to place their own orders for new aircraft, were forced to rely on a small number of leasing companies), such has not been the case for a long time now.[33]

With the option of operating leasing, airlines can target certain aircraft for ownership as strategic long-term assets, but using additional aircraft more flexibly on operating lease, which they can allow to expire at the end of the lease term or extend, depending on their needs at that time. Further, whereas, upon a strict comparison, operating leasing may appear expensive compared with other sources of finance, this is not necessarily the case, especially when the cost of pricing in the lessor's assumption of the residual value risk is factored in.[34] In all cases other than operating leases, the airline assumes the residual value risk of the aircraft and this assumption should be priced into a comparison when deciding whether to buy or to lease.

§2.02 STRUCTURING THE LEASE

Having decided to proceed with an aircraft operating lease, the airline must next determine with the lessor how it should best be structured.[35]

In the simplest case, the lessor will own the aircraft and lease it to the lessee. However, many other permutations and combinations are possible and it is desirable for the team putting a lease together to obtain relevant legal advice pursuant to the jurisdictional questionnaire,[36] accounting advice, and technical advice[37] before fixing on the structure, which should be clear before committing to the letter of intent.[38]

For example, the owner and the lessor may not be the same. In such a case, typically, the owner will lease the aircraft to the lessor under a head lease and the lessor will then lease the aircraft to the airline under a sublease.[39] The reasons for this may vary for reasons discussed below.

The lessor's financier (if it has one) may insist on having ownership of the aircraft placed in a special purpose vehicle (SPV) set up by the lessor but over which the financier has a pledge of shares[40] rather than allowing the lessor to retain ownership of the aircraft and accepting a mortgage of the aircraft. Reasons for so doing may be the greater ease of enforcement of a pledge of shares in the jurisdiction of incorporation of the SPV as compared with enforcement of a mortgage in the jurisdiction where the aircraft is registered or was located at the time of the creation of the mortgage or is located at the time of enforcement of the mortgage.[41]

---

33. Lobkowicz P. and Detrich B., *Operating Leasing: Who Wins Economically?* Airfinance Journal: A Guide to Operating Lease, June 1997.
34. *Ibid.*
35. *See* Bunker D.H., *International Aircraft Financing, Volume 2: Specific Documents*, 2nd Edition, IATA, 2015, at 37.
36. *See* section §2.04 *infra*.
37. For example as to the desirability of one aircraft nationality register over another.
38. *See* section §2.03 *infra*.
39. *See* Annex 1 *infra*.
40. *See* Annex 3 *infra*.
41. Likewise, stamp duty in certain jurisdictions on mortgagers must be such as to make a mortgage uneconomical to pursue, in which case the lender will likely look to a solution involving its reliance instead on ownership in an SPV. In some cases, a lender will pursue a 'belt and braces'

Alternatively, there may be a withholding tax which, subject to any relevant tax treaty, the lessee would be obliged to withhold on payments to the owner's jurisdiction under the lease, and in respect of which the owner would oblige the lessee to gross up so as to ensure that, after making the necessary withholding, the lessor receives net the amount specified in the lease.[42] However, such a withholding tax may not apply with respect to another jurisdiction or it may apply at a lower rate. In such an event, the owner will set up an SPV in a tax favourable jurisdiction and lease the aircraft to the SPV under a head lease. The SPV will then lease the aircraft to the airline under a sublease.

In the two examples above, the structure is the same (head lease and sublease) but the substantial party differs: in the first case, it is the lessor (the owner being simply an SPV); in the latter, it is the owner (the lessor being simply an SPV).

Another example of the same structure on paper is a head lease and sublease where the airline is owned by a parent company which does not hold an air operator's certificate (AOC) or air transport licence[43] but which, for whatever reason, wants to be the immediate lessee of the aircraft. That parent will then sublease to its certificated and licensed airline subsidiary.

A different structure may occur where, for example, the owner wants to use an owner trust. This may be required due to restrictions on registration of aircraft on the nationality register of the airline's jurisdiction. For example, a non-US owner may wish to lease to a US airline with the aircraft being registered in the US. It may enter into a trust agreement as beneficiary with a US owner trustee which will then lease the aircraft, not in its individual capacity, but solely in such capacity as owner trustee, to the airline.

In this case, and in the first two cases, the airline may well want a guarantee if the lessor is not leasing in its own capacity or is not the party in the transaction structure with substantial assets, and it should seek a letter of quiet enjoyment whereby any owner, head lessor or trust beneficiary undertakes not to interfere with the airline's quiet enjoyment and use of the aircraft so long as it is performing its obligations under the lease.

Indeed, owner trusts as lessors are not restricted to this instance: a non-US airline wishing to have an aircraft registered in the US may also rely on an owner trust. In May 2010, the Federal Aviation Administration of the United States of America (FAA) expressed concern in a Notice of Proposed Rulemaking[44] over the situation where the beneficiary of the owner trust is the same entity as the entity that has operational

approach, wanting both ownership in an SPV over which it has a pledge of shares and also a mortgage by that SPV in its favour securing the amounts due to it.

42. This is the so-called hell or high water clause (as in, come hell or high water the lessee must ensure that the lessor receives the full amount of rent referred to in the lease). *See* Chapter 3 sections §3.07[A] and §3.08 *infra*.
43. *See* Chapter 3 sections §3.05[B][5] and §3.05[B][6] *infra*.
44. 73 Fed. Reg. 10, 701 (proposed 28 Feb. 2008).

control over the aircraft[45] – it did not express concern about where the parties are different (such as where the beneficiary of the owner trust is a lessor and the party with operational control of the aircraft is a lessee).

Although this issue remains under review, there has been no change so far in regulations or FAA practice and the issue, in any event, did not concern non-US lessors using owner trusts.[46]

The different possibilities involved due to aircraft registration are discussed in further detail in Chapter 3 section §3.10[B][3] *infra*.

The cost of a structure more complicated than that of a simple lease from the owner to the airline should be calculated in advance, and agreement reached as to how those costs are borne or shared, to determine their impact on the economics of the deal before the parties are committed to proceeding with it. In this regard, the reason for the structure (to accommodate the lessor or the lessee) will play a role but, ultimately, the relative bargaining power of the parties will determine.

A useful source of reference in this regard is *Advanced Contract and Opinion Practices under the Cape Town Convention*[47] which assesses the implications of the Cape Town Convention (2001)[48] on a hypothetical but realistic transaction, from term sheet to closing.[49]

Having determined the structure of the lease, the parties are then in a position to enter into a letter of intent (which will be examined next) setting out the principal commercial terms of the desired leasing transaction. Alternatively, they may, if they so wish, reverse the order and agree to the letter of intent first, leaving the precise structuring of the lease to be determined after the letter of intent is signed but before definitive lease documentation is agreed.

§2.03 THE LETTER OF INTENT

The lease is almost always preceded by a letter of intent[50] which sets out in summary form the principal terms. Legal issues here include the binding versus the non-binding letter of credit and the issue of refundability of the deposit which is typically paid upon execution of the letter of intent so that the aircraft will be removed from the market pending negotiation and execution of the definitive lease.

With a non-binding letter of intent or other letter of intent that does not include a deposit which is forfeitable in certain events, the lessor will have little motivation to remove the aircraft from the market.

45 Gerber D.N., *Aircraft Finance Issues: The Blue Sky Ruling; The New ASU and the 'Home Country Rule'; and Recent Developments at the FAA Registry*, a paper presented at the American Bar Association Air and Space Law Forum 2010 Annual Meeting in Seattle, Washington on 26 Oct. 2010.

46 *Ibid.*

47 Legal Advisory Panel of the Aviation Working Group, *Advanced Contract and Opinion Practices under the Cape Town Convention*, Cape Town Paper Series, Volume 2, UNIDROIT, 2008.

48 Considered in Chapter 3 sections §3.01, §3.10, §3.15[C], et seq., *infra*.

49 *Ibid.*, at xix.

50 Also commonly referred to as a term sheet or memorandum of understanding.

The letter of intent is normally signed as soon as a commercial agreement is reached in principle between the lessor and the airline with respect to the leasing of the aircraft. It will normally set out[51] the main commercial provisions, such as the parties, the aircraft, the target delivery date and lease term, the rent and other payment provisions (such as security deposit and maintenance reserves), any pre-approved subleasing by the lessee, key insurance requirements (such as stipulated loss value, minimum liability coverage and maximum deductible), and delivery and redelivery locations and (to a greater or lesser degree) conditions.

It is very desirable for a letter of intent to be reviewed by legal counsel to both parties (without slowing down the process unduly) since other matters, such as the governing law and jurisdiction provisions, the timeline for requisite corporate approvals subject to which the letter is signed, and other legal matters such as those identified above should be set out.

The more detailed the letter of intent, the less negotiation, in theory, there should be when it comes time to negotiate the lease itself and other definitive legal documentation, although this is not always the case. For example, if the lessor has legal, financing or other restrictions on where it can permit the lessee to operate the aircraft, it would be prudent to raise the issue at the letter of intent stage rather than leaving it until the definitive documentation, since such particular requirements could run contrary to the lessee's immediate or potential future plans for the aircraft.

A provision in the letter of intent that the transaction is subject to agreement of definitive legal documentation does not of itself make the letter of intent void for uncertainty or allow a contract party to evade its responsibilities by refusing to agree to the definitive legal documentation following a change of heart about the transaction. Leggatt J, in the English High Court, has held in *Novus Aviation Limited v. Alubaf Arab International Bank BSC*[52] that it is:

> well established that, in the absence of very clear language to the contrary, a contractual discretion must be exercised in good faith for the purpose for which it was conferred, and must not be exercised arbitrarily, capriciously or unreasonably.[53]

Leggat J went on to make clear that this discretion included reviewing the documentation in a reasonable manner but did not include the right to review whether the counterparty still wanted to pursue the transaction at all. It is submitted that it is prudential to include an express provision in the letter that where the transaction is subject to agreement on definitive documentation, the parties will act reasonably and in good faith to agree in a timely manner such documentation on terms typical in the industry for such transactions save as expressly provided in the letter of intent.

Having agreed to the letter of intent, the matter of drafting the lease is then turned to the legal counsel for the parties, with counsel to the lessor normally providing the

51. *See* Bunker D.H., *International Aircraft Financing, Volume 2: Specific Documents*, 2nd Edition, IATA, 2015, at 16–37.
52. [2016] EWHC 1575 (Comm).
53. At 64.

first draft (after technical and commercial review by his or her colleagues) for review by counsel to the lessee. This author has often noted that the lawyer's task at this point is to say in between 100 and 200 pages what the parties had already agreed to in fewer than twenty pages in the letter of intent – the additional pages being accounted for in no small measure by consideration of the legal considerations which are the subject matter of this work.

For cases where the Cape Town Convention (2001) applies,[54] the *Advanced Contract and Opinion Practices under the Cape Town Convention*[55] published by the Legal Advisory Panel of the AWG[56] recommends[57] that the letter of intent should be binding in order:

(1) to constitute an 'agreement for registration' if the intended nationality registration of the aircraft is to be the connecting factor under Article 3(3);[58] or
(2) to create an enforceable obligation to remove prospective registrations[59] if the Transaction does not close or the beneficiary of such registration ceases to have an interest.

That same publication also advises[60] that the letter of intent should make clear which international interests thereunder are to be registered pursuant to the Cape Town Convention (2001) but even if this is not done, it should be clear from the interests provided for in the letter of intent and the provisions of the Cape Town Convention (2001) which interests are registrable thereunder and which are not.

Typically, with a binding letter of intent, the lessee will pay a deposit to the lessor in consideration of the lessor's removal of the aircraft from the market.

In *JSD Corporation PTE Ltd v. Al Waha Capital PJSC and Second Waha Lease Limited,*[61] before Smith J in the English High Court, the plaintiff sought the return of a deposit paid by it under a letter of intent for the purchase by it of an aircraft where the sale did not proceed.

The letter of intent stated that the deposit was non-refundable except in case of total loss of the aircraft or a default by seller, either of which events would result in the deposit being returned to the buyer.

---

54. Considered *infra* in Chapter 3 sections §3.01, §3.10, §3.15[C] and elsewhere.
55. *Advanced Contract and Opinion Practices under the Cape Town Convention*, Cape Town Paper Series 2, Volume 2, The Legal Advisory Panel of the Aviation Working Group, 2008.
56. An industry association of leading aircraft and aircraft engine manufacturers, lessor and financiers: *see* http://www.awg.aero.
57. At 11.
58. This provides for applicability of the Cape Town Convention where the aircraft is registered in the aircraft register of a contracting State or is to be so registered pursuant to an agreement for such registration in addition to Art. 3(1) which provides for applicability of the Cape Town Convention where the lessee is situated in a contracting State.
59. Prospective international interests may be registered under the Cape Town Convention pursuant to Art. 6 but there should be a mechanism to remove them if the transaction does not close.
60. At 12.
61. [2009] EWHC 583 (Ch).

In its defence, the plaintiff argued that the defendant did not negotiate in good faith to finalize the documentation. Smith J was clear that there is no such obligation under English law. He held, however, that the defendant was in breach of the terms of the letter of intent because, however, inadvertently, it continued to advertise the aircraft for sale on Speednews, a trade publication, and thus failed, as agreed, to remove the aircraft from the market.

But for this clause, the plaintiff would not have succeeded – thus, it is imperative that lessors, as well as sellers of aircraft, ensure that, where a deposit is accepted in consideration for their removal of the aircraft from the market, all marketing efforts immediately cease and all advertisements lined up be cancelled.

Consistent with this approach, in *Tandrin Aviation Holdings Ltd v. Aero Toy Store LLC*,[62] the English Commercial Court upheld a seller's right to keep a deposit under a definitive sale agreement for the sale of an aircraft where a buyer failed to complete the purchase of an aircraft in a depressed market, holding on the facts that the amount of the deposit did not amount to a penalty and should be accepted in the circumstances as a true bargain between the parties as to a pre-estimate of seller's loss if buyer wrongly refused to complete the aircraft purchase. Similarly, in *Aercap Partners 1 Limited v. Avia Asset Management AB*,[63] the same court upheld a claim by an aircraft seller against a buyer where the buyer failed to pay the final instalment of a deposit. Gross LJ held that:

> it seems to me to follow that AerCap is entitled to base its loss of bargain claim on the difference between the contract ... price and the market price once there was a market price.

Finally, if the obligation of either party to proceed is subject to its obtaining the approval of its board of directors, or to a satisfactory inspection of the aircraft by the lessee, or to any other condition or contingency, this should be made clear in the letter of intent, together with a clear deadline by which the conditions must be met, failing which the letter of intent should terminate and the deposit be returned to the lessee.

On the other hand, if the conditions are met, typically, the deposit paid under the letter of intent is applied towards the deposit payable under the lease once definitive lease documentation is signed.

§2.04 THE JURISDICTIONAL QUESTIONNAIRE

The jurisdictional questionnaire is a vital tool to help the lawyer assess the risk of leasing to an airline incorporated in a particular jurisdiction and allowing it to register the aircraft on that country's or another country's register.

Issues here include many of the items that will later be covered in the legal opinion to be given by the airline's lawyers to the leasing company but in general terms

62. [2010] EWHC 40.
63. [2010] EWHC 2431, at 113.

to help to identify jurisdictional risk and to determine any tax or legal issues which might affect the structuring of the deal.

For example, if the English courts are chosen as a forum for settlement of disputes under the lease, will the courts of the airline's jurisdiction enforce such judgment? If not, would they more readily enforce an arbitral award?

The lessor will usually obtain such a questionnaire from its local counsel in the jurisdiction in question.

Typical areas covered in a jurisdictional questionnaire given by lessor's counsel include those set out at Annex 5.

§2.05 THE LEGAL OPINION

The legal opinion is typically not obtained until after the lease is signed and is a condition to the lessor's obligation to deliver the aircraft to the lessee. Nevertheless, the likely contents should be discovered beforehand pursuant to a draft opinion so as not to contain any unpleasant surprises. It typically covers many of the matters covered in both the jurisdictional questionnaire (as to which, *see* section §2.04 *supra*) but is more specific, dealing with the lease in hand, rather than leases in general, and also the lessee's representations and warranties in the lease itself (as to which, *see* Chapter 3 section §3.04 *infra*).

The legal opinion should be addressed to the lessor and (if any) its financiers,[64] given by counsel to lessee acceptable to the lessor, and can be expected to contain various assumptions and qualifications which should be checked against typical practice for reasonableness.

The legal opinion should reference whether or not the Cape Town Convention (2001) is applicable. It is applicable where the lease constitutes an international interest under Article 2 thereof which may be registered if the airframe is registered as part of an aircraft in a contracting State, if the engine is registered as part of an aircraft in a contracting State or otherwise the engine is located in a contracting State[65] or if the lessee is situated in a contracting State.[66]

For transactions to which the Cape Town Convention (2001) is applicable, the Legal Advisory Panel of the AWG[67] has made certain recommendations as to provisions dealing with the Cape Town Convention (2001) as well as assumptions and qualifications. Interestingly, a footnote to its recommendation provides that:

> Law firms may give an opinion on the Convention as a matter of international law even though they are not counsel in the jurisdiction of any particular Contracting

64. Lessees may object to extension of the opinion to lessors' financiers with whom they have no direct relationship but lessors may respond that there is no additional cost involved and no additional obligation on the part of the airlines.
65. Article IV(1) of the Aircraft Protocol thereto.
66. Article 3(1) of the Convention.
67. *Advanced Contract and Opinion Practices under the Cape Town Convention*, Cape Town Paper Series 2, Volume 2, The Legal Advisory Panel of the Aviation Working Group, 2008, 25 et seq.

> State. A legal opinion should cover the law of the Contracting State where the aircraft is registered ... and also, if not the same, where the debtor[68] is situated ....

Typical areas covered in a legal opinion on a lease given by lessee's counsel include those set out at Annex 6.

§2.06 THE LAYOUT OF THE LEASE

Before examining the lease itself in detail, the overall typical layout of the lease will be examined first. Aircraft operating leases are typically fairly long documents, as noted, often between 100 and 200 pages in length, but, even if the order may differ somewhat,[69] typically, they may be seen as narratives with a start, pre-delivery (the period before the leasing of the aircraft begins), a middle, post-delivery (the period when the aircraft is on lease) and an end, post-lease term (the period after the leasing of the aircraft ends).

[A] Pre-delivery

Parties: The lease will, of course, need to state who are the parties to the lease so that the contract parties are clear. Often guarantors will be necessary also where the contract party is of insufficient credit, but the guarantee will normally be set out in a standalone document.[70]

Recitals: Although not essential, it is useful to set out recitals showing the background to the lease as an aid to the reader in reading the substantive provisions of the lease itself.

For example, if the lease is part of a sale and lease back deal whereby the lessor purchases the aircraft from the lessee and then immediately leases it back to the lessee, setting forth this fact in the recitals will make apparent to the reader why, later on in the lease, there are no delivery conditions which must be met before the lessee is obliged to accept the aircraft from the lessor.[71]

Definitions: Rather than setting out what is meant by terms each time they are used, or defining them in different places throughout the document, which may make reference difficult, it is also an aid to the reader to set out in one place, either here or in a schedule to the lease, the agreed meaning of certain terms, such as what is meant by an Engine Shop Visit, or a Business Day, where the meaning may not be completely clear simply by reference to industry usage.[72]

Representations and Warranties: The representations and warranties actually fall both into the start and the middle in this view of the lease as narrative.

---

68. Under Art. 1(r) of the Cape Town Convention, the term 'debtor' where used in the Convention includes 'a lessee under a leasing agreement' *inter alia*.
69. *See*, for example, Bunker D.H., *International Aircraft Financing, Volume 2: Specific Documents*, 2nd Edition, IATA, 2015 at 38–204.
70. *See* Chapter 3 section §3.01 *infra*.
71. *See* Chapter 3 section §3.02 *infra*.
72. *See* Chapter 3 section §3.03 and section 1 of the Supplement *infra*.

Although they are set out together, representations are pre-contractual inducements made by each party to the other to enter into the contract in the first place, with remedies for their breach, whereas warranties are part of the contract itself, with legally distinct remedies for their breach.[73]

Conditions Precedent: Conditions precedent are those conditions which must be satisfied by one party before the obligations of the other party take effect. For example, a lessor may not want to be obliged to deliver the aircraft to the lessee until it has been paid the first month's rent and been assured that the aircraft is insured by the lessee. Likewise, a lessee may not want to be obliged to take delivery of the aircraft from the lessor until the lessor has title to that aircraft (a concern particularly for new aircraft orders where the lessor will want to conclude a lease for an aircraft which the manufacturer has not yet delivered to it).[74]

[B] Post-delivery

Having clarified who the parties are, the background to the lease, the meaning of the terms used in it, the inducements each party made to the other to enter into the lease, and the conditions which each party must first satisfy before the aircraft is delivered under the lease, the middle part of the lease in this narrative is next to be examined.

Term and Delivery: This is the core of the lease contract where the lessor and lessee agree that the lessor shall lease the aircraft to the lessee, and the lessee shall lease the aircraft from the lessor, on and subject to the terms set out in the lease agreement. The lease will make clear what the term of the lease is, and any extension options or early termination options to that term. It will also set out the delivery procedures and (although this may also be seen as part of the start) the physical condition required of the aircraft at the time of delivery to the lessee.[75]

Payments: The lease will also make clear what security deposit, if any, must be paid by the lessee to the lessor as security for its obligations, what rent must be paid and when throughout the term of the lease, and what maintenance reserves, if any, must be paid by the lessee to the lessor. The obligation of the lessor to return the security deposit may be set out here or elsewhere, as will the obligation of the lessor to return any maintenance reserves to the lessee (or any third party designated by it) as it performs certain scheduled maintenance work to the aircraft during the term.[76]

Taxes: The lease will set out the respective obligations of the parties for payment of taxes in connection with the leasing of the aircraft and which tax risks are borne by which party.[77]

73. *See* Chapter 3 section §3.04 and section 2 of the Supplement *infra*.
74. *See* Chapter 3 section §3.05 and section 3 of the Supplement *infra*.
75. *See* Chapter 3 section §3.06 and section 4 of the Supplement *infra*.
76. *See* Chapter 3 section §3.07 and section 5 of the Supplement *infra*.
77. *See* Chapter 3 section §3.08 and section 5 of the Supplement *infra*.

Manufacturer's Warranties: If the aircraft is still covered by manufacturer's warranties, the lease will make clear how these may be enforced if a problem covered by such warranties develops during the lease term.[78]

Covenants: The lease will set out covenants from each party to the other. As the lessee will have operational control of the aircraft, most covenants will be made by the lessee in favour of the lessor. Such covenants may be positive covenants, such as to register the aircraft as agreed in the lease, to operate the aircraft lawfully, to maintain the aircraft as required by law and the lease contract, etc., or negative covenants, such as not to abandon the aircraft and not to hold itself out as owner of the aircraft.[79]

Indemnities: The lease will also provide indemnification by the lessee of the lessor and its financiers for any claim brought against the latter as a result of the lessee's possession and operation of the aircraft during the lease term and (although this goes to the end part of the narrative) such indemnities should survive the termination of the leasing of the aircraft under the lease since it is possible that a claim may not be brought against the lessor or its financiers until after the end of the lease period.[80]

Insurances: The indemnities given by the lessee are only as good as its credit and as airlines tend to go into bankruptcy with greater frequency than lessors, and since the amount of claims may exceed that which even an airline in good condition could afford to pay, the prudent lessor will require that the lessee take out insurances satisfactory to the lessor which protect the lessor and its financing parties in the event of a claim.[81]

[C] Post-lease Term

By now, the parties have delivered the aircraft, and know their respective rights and obligations during the term of the lease. However, as the parties are here dealing with an operating rather than a finance lease, both sides must prepare for the end of the contractual relationship and the return of the aircraft by the lessee to the lessor. The termination of the relationship may take any of several forms: natural expiration as envisaged in accordance with the lease, early termination by mutual agreement or by lessor due to a breach of the lease by lessee, or an end to the particular contractual relationship due to a sale of the aircraft by the lessor to another owner during the lease term or (occasionally) due to the transfer (with the lessor's consent) of the lessee's rights and obligations[82] under the lease to another airline.

Redelivery: Assuming agreed redelivery in accordance with the lease, this section should set out the procedures required and the condition which the aircraft should meet at the time of redelivery.[83]

78. *See* Chapter 3 section §3.09 and section 6 of the Supplement *infra*.
79. *See* Chapter 3 section §3.10 and sections 7 and 8 of the Supplement *infra*.
80. *See* Chapter 3 section §3.11 and section 10 of the Supplement *infra*.
81. *See* Chapter 3 section §3.12 and sections 9 and 11 of the Supplement *infra*.
82. Rights may be assignable, but obligations can only be transferred pursuant to a novation or assignment and assumption.
83. *See* Chapter 3 section §3.13 and section 12 of the Supplement *infra*.

Events of Default: Although these may not necessarily result in a termination of the contract, the parties will need to set out the events which, if they occur, give the lessor the right to terminate the lease or to take other remedial action.[84]

Remedies: While a party will have rights at law in the event of a breach, it will want contractual certainty, insofar as applicable laws allow, to set out its remedies and claims against the other party in the event of a breach.[85]

Assignment: This section will set out the agreement between the parties whereby either may assign its rights and the lessor may, in addition, cause its obligations to be assumed under certain conditions by a third party.[86] The lessor needs to keep flexibility to sell the aircraft with the benefit of the lease attached whereas the lessee will want to ensure that it is not materially prejudiced by this, whether by virtue of a transfer to a leasing company with a much lower net worth or otherwise.[87]

Governing law: In the event of a dispute which ends in litigation or other adversarial proceedings, the lease will set out what law has been agreed by the parties to govern the contract.[88]

Dispute resolution: If the parties cannot agree on the correct interpretation of the lease or the facts in hand, the lease should make clear in what jurisdictions any claim may be brought. Enforceability of a judgment against the lessee in particular will always be primarily a concern of the lessor.[89]

Miscellaneous: These final clauses are sometimes called 'boiler plate' since they appear in most leases but their importance should not be overlooked.[90]

Execution: Finally, although this will normally only become an issue in the event of a dispute, the lease will need to be duly executed by both parties observing any formalities required and bearing in mind any stamp duty or other tax implications as to the place of execution.[91]

Thus, the typical aircraft lease can be seen simply as an agreement between two parties for one to deliver to the other possession of a specified aircraft for an ascertainable period in return for an ascertainable consideration, with certain obligations being placed on the parties during such period and in respect of the return of the property at the end, and with consequences for breach, and allocation of risk for damage by and to the aircraft being set out as between the parties.

Having such a rather high-level overview of the layout of the typical aircraft operating lease, the heart of this work follows in Chapter 3 – a detailed examination of each of these parts of the lease with particular reference to the impact on each of them of the results of this author's research into relevant case law, statutes and regulations,

84. *See* Chapter 3 section §3.14 and section 13 of the Supplement *infra*.
85. *See* Chapter 3 section §3.15 and section 13 of the Supplement *infra*.
86. Surely a lessee would never be allowed to rid itself of its obligations!
87. *See* Chapter 3 section §3.16 and section 14 of the Supplement *infra*.
88. *See* Chapter 3 section §3.17 and section 15 of the Supplement *infra*.
89. *See* Chapter 3 section §3.18 and section 15 of the Supplement *infra*.
90. *See* Chapter 3 section §3.19 and section 16 of the Supplement *infra*.
91. *See* Chapter 3 section §3.20 *infra*.

and international treaties, especially in the context of public and private international air law, which in turn is followed by Chapter 4 – conclusions together with recommendations of this author in relation to issues that have come to light as a result of the research examined in Chapter 3.

CHAPTER 3
The Aircraft Operating Lease

§3.01 PARTIES

The preliminary steps identified in Chapter 2 (Overview) *supra* will help to clarify who should be the parties to the lease – that is, whether a head lease/sublease structure, owner trust or other structure which may cause a change in the parties is required.

If so, whether or not there should be a guarantee of the obligations of either or both parties under the lease should be clear by this stage.

If the lessor is, for whatever reason, not the leasing company itself, but an intermediary vehicle of the leasing company or an owner trust under which the leasing company is the beneficiary,[1] the lessee should consider obtaining a guarantee of the lessor's obligations from the leasing company itself. Although the lessee is primarily the debtor under the lease and the lessor is primarily the creditor (and the parties are respectively seen as such under Article 1 of the Cape Town Convention (2001)), the lessee is a creditor in respect of refund of any security deposit and maintenance reserves it pays as well as for other contractual obligations and thus has a legitimate interest in the creditworthiness of the lessor.

If the lessee's credit is such that a guarantee of its obligations is required by the lessor, this should be demanded and reflected where appropriate in the drafting.

In particular, any representations and warranties given by a party in the lease should also be given by that party's guarantor, and any events of default relating to the creditworthiness of the lessee should be extended to such events in the context of the guarantor also since the lessor will in such instance be looking to the credit of the guarantor.

1. Since invariably in such case, the owner trustee will insist on undertaking obligations in the lease 'not in its individual capacity but solely as owner trustee'.

§3.02 RECITALS

Although not legally required, the recitals can be a useful introduction to the lease for the reader. *See also* Chapter 2 section §2.06[B] *supra*. They help put the lease in context but, under English law, are only used as an aid to construction in case of ambiguity.[2]

They can set out the context to the lease, which may be particularly useful, for example, where there is a complicated ownership structure, where the owner, the head lease from the owner as head lessor to the lessor as head lessee, and the intention of the lessor to lease the aircraft as sub-lessor to the airline as sub-lessee can be made clear.

Recitals are typically set out following the word 'Whereas' to indicate that they set out the background to the lease, and are then followed by such words as 'Now therefore, it is agreed between the parties as follows', and the actual agreement of the parties is set out.

Thus, the argument may be raised that the recitals do not form part of the contract itself.

It is typical, therefore, to include a provision whereby not only the recitals, but also any schedules, annexes and appendices to the lease are deemed to form part of the lease – this avoids any argument, for example, as to whether terms defined in the recitals and used elsewhere in the lease form part of the lease and as to whether any representation, warranties, or undertakings set out therein are representations, warranties or undertakings under the lease such that the remedies for breach thereof under the lease are not lost simply because they appeared in the recitals, that is, before the words 'Now therefore, it is agreed between the parties as follows.'

§3.03 DEFINITIONS

The definitions used are vital to the interpretation of the lease. They may be set out for ease of reference either at a particular place in the lease or as a separate schedule attached to the lease but it is desirable that they be set out in one place.[3]

One advantage of setting the definitions in a separate schedule is that technical staff for the lessor and the airline may request that technical provisions, particularly as to delivery and redelivery conditions, also be set out in separate schedules. If the definitions are also set out in a separate schedule, they can simply extract the relevant schedules, including that for definitions, and refer to those alone. This is not a legal consideration but is a practical one where cross-border aircraft dry operating leases typically run up from 100 to 200 pages in length.

One reason to use definitions is consistency, which will help in the correct construction of the contract.

2. Clark T. (ed.), *Leasing Finance*, Euromoney, 1985, at 52.
3. *See* section 1 of the Supplement *infra*.

For example, in the context of insurance, one may refer to agreed value[4] or to stipulated loss value but one should be consistent in one's choice of words to make sure that it is clear that the same concept is being referred to each time.

Likewise, one may refer to either security deposit or commitment fee,[5] and one may refer to either maintenance reserves or supplemental rent[6] but one should be aware of the possible implications of one's choice of terminology (e.g., different treatment in the case of bankruptcy of the lessee)[7] and use the same words consistently when referring to the same concept.

Maintenance reserves may be defined by reference to the number of hours utilized by the aircraft. In this case, the draftsman should be clear whether flight hours or block hours are the relevant unit of reference and the relevant term defined clearly and used consistently to avoid confusion.

For example, a 'Flight Hour' means:

> each hour or part thereof elapsing from the moment at which the wheels of the Aircraft leave the ground on the take-off of the Aircraft until the wheels of the Aircraft touch the ground on the landing of the Aircraft following such take-off.[8]

whereas a 'Block Hour' means:

> [t]he number of hours incurred by an aircraft from the moment it first moves for a flight until it comes to rest at its intended blocks at its next point of landing ... .[9]

If, therefore, only the term 'hours' were used, it would not be clear how to calculate the number of hours desired – hours in the air or hours in motion, whether on the ground or in the air.

Likewise, if 'Block Hours' were used where 'Flight Hours' was intended, or vice versa or they were wrongly defined, the lessee could end up paying either too much or too little by way of maintenance reserves calculated based on hourly usage of the aircraft.

How terms are defined in leases will be looked at under the heading of the relevant part of the lease where they are most relevant. *See also* Chapter 2 section §2.06[A] *supra*.

4. *See* section §3.12[B][1] *infra*.
5. *See* section §3.07[B] *infra*.
6. *See* section §3.07[C] *infra*.
7. *See* sections §3.07[B] & §3.07[C] *infra*.
8. Bunker D.H., *International Aircraft Financing: Volume 2: Specific Documents*, 2nd Edition, IATA, 2015, at 52.
9. *Ibid.*

§3.04 REPRESENTATIONS AND WARRANTIES

Each party will give each other representations and warranties, which may be repeated periodically, breach of which gives rise to remedies[10] for breach of contract.[11] Typical representations and warranties of a lessee include those set out at Annex 7.

[A] Representations as to Present and Past Facts

Representations are made by each party to the other to induce the other to enter into the lease. They should be made with respect to present and past only. Representations as to the future are not possible and should be covered as covenants or events of default, which will be examined in sections §3.10 and §3.14 *infra* respectively.

[B] Repetition of Representations

It is not uncommon for a lessor to request that a lessee repeat its representations and warranties (with respect to facts and circumstances then existing) at delivery of the aircraft under the lease and possibly also periodically throughout the term of the lease - typically, throughout the lease term or at least on each rent payment date.

It is debatable as to whether there is much need to insist on this or much risk in acceding to such a demand since breach of a given repeated warranty will most likely be caught by one or other of the events of default anyway but the drafter should check rather than assume that such is indeed the case.

A stronger objection to automatic repetition of representation and warranties is that it may force a lessee into making a false representation and warranty. For example, the lease may provide that the representation and warranties will automatically be deemed to be repeated (with respect to facts and circumstances then existing) on each rent payment date. The lease may further provide a representation and warranty on the part of the lessee there are no withholding taxes payable on the rental payments and that such statement was correct when the lease was signed but subsequently the law is changed and a withholding tax is introduced. The lessor should be protected by the gross-up clause in the taxation section (as to which *see* section §3.08 *infra*) requiring the lessee to pay a sufficient amount in rent such that, after making the requisite withholding, the lessor still receives the same net payment of rent as if there had been no withholding. With an automatic repetition of representations and warranties, however, on the next rent payment date after the change in law, the lessee will be deemed to have made a representation and warranty that is untrue, thus entitling the lessor to terminate the lease.

One instance where a lessor will have a strong need for repetition of representations and warranties will be if it decides to sell the aircraft to another party with the benefit of the lease attached. The purchaser will invariably want the lessee to repeat in

10. *See* section §3.15 *infra*.
11. *See* section 2 of the Supplement *infra*.

its favour the representations and warranties set out in the lease before entering into a contractual relationship with the lessee. Lessees often refuse this on the basis that they are not so obliged under the lease - one possible compromise would be for the lessor to agree that the only repetition of representations and warranties in the lease by the lessee would be upon an assignment or novation of the lease to a purchaser of the aircraft and that even then if the lessee could not truthfully repeat such representations and warranties with respect to facts and circumstances then existing, it could then qualify such representations and warranties accordingly.

[C] Representations of Law

A representation must be a statement of fact, not of opinion or (with some exceptions) of law.[12]

The fact that representations generally cannot be given as to law is sometimes relied upon by lessees who wish to limit their representations and warranties strictly to factual matters only and who wish to deal with representations as to law only in the legal opinion to be provided to the lessor by their lawyers as one of the conditions precedent to the lessor's obligations under the lease. This argument ignores two points.

The first is that representations as to foreign law, with which the lessor is not expected to be familiar itself, may be binding.[13] Most leases are cross-border leases where the lessor and lessee are based in different jurisdictions.

The other is that if a particular representation as to foreign law is incorrect if it is only in the legal opinion, the lessor's only remedy is for damages against the lawyer giving the incorrect legal opinion whereas if it is in the lease, the lessor will have the full range of remedies as set out in the lease available to it, including the right not only to seek damages but to terminate the leasing of the aircraft and to recover possession of the aircraft.

If a representation misrepresented a relevant fact, under English common law, unless such representation was incorporated into the contract, no remedy for damages lay, although the party to whom such misrepresentation was made could seek to rescind the contract.[14]

[D] Warranties

A warranty does form part of the contract but is contrasted with a condition. Under the English Sale of Goods Act 1893, a condition was defined as a provision of a contract the 'breach of which may give rise to a right to treat the contract as repudiated'[15] whereas a warranty was a provision of a contract the 'breach of which may give rise to a claim

12. Furmston M.P., *Cheshire & Fifoot's Law of Contract*, 10th Edition, Butterworths, 1981, at 235–240.
13. *Ibid.* and Bunker D.H., *International Aircraft Financing, Volume 2: Specific Documents*, 2nd Edition, IATA, 2015, at 60–62.
14. Furmston, *supra*, at 235–240.
15. Section 11(1)(b).

for damages but not to a right to … treat the contract as repudiated'.[16] Such dichotomy between condition and warranty has since become 'a general but not a universal feature' of English contract law.[17]

To avoid the issues of whether a particular representation was made at all, whether it induced the lessor to enter into the contract, whether it forms part of the contract, whether, as part of the contract, it is, even if described as a warranty, a condition or a warranty for the purposes of English contract law, common drafting practice is to set out the relevant facts relied upon in the lease itself as both representations and warranties together and to provide for the lessor's remedies for their breach in the lease itself, such remedies invariably including the right to terminate the leasing of the aircraft and to demand repossession thereof.

It should not be thought, however, that in aircraft operating leases, representations and warranties have thus fallen together for all purposes. In *Sabena Technics SA v. Singapore Airlines Limited,*[18] Colman J of the English High Court held on the facts that an incorrect statement with respect to the condition of the aircraft in question on the part of the lessor constituted a breach of warranty[19] even though it did not constitute a misrepresentation under section 2(1) of the English Misrepresentation Act 1967[20] or negligent misrepresentation.[21]

[E] Conclusions

In the context of representations and warranties, on the basis of which the parties enter into the aircraft operating lease, thus far, no particularities relating to public or private international air law have been disclosed. As seen in section §3.04[D] *supra*, the governing law of the lease contract may have statutory provisions but these are of the sort which may be expected in the context of any contract, regardless of whether or not related to international aviation. The lease contract having been entered into on foot of those representations and warranties, the review turns next to conditions precedent which must be fulfilled before the respective obligations of the parties thereunder take effect.

§3.05 CONDITIONS PRECEDENT

Conditions precedent of a party are those conditions which must be satisfied before the obligations of that party under the lease become effective.[22] The major conditions will be examined in detail. Typical conditions precedent to be satisfied by a lessee in order

16. *Ibid.*
17. Furmston, *supra*, at 132.
18. [2003] EWHC 1318 (Comm).
19. At 94.
20. At 111.
21. At 114.
22. *See* section 3 of the Supplement *infra*.

for the obligations of the lessor under the lease to become effective include those set out at Annex 8.

It is important to define what is meant by conditions precedent, which in Roman law was treated not as part of the contract itself but an external fact on which the existence of the obligation depends.[23] It may be that the whole existence of a contract is suspended until the happening of a stated event, that is, until satisfaction of a condition precedent.[24] On the other hand, it may be that such a condition may operate:

> not to negate the very existence of a contract but, to suspend, until it is satisfied, some right or duty or consequence which would otherwise spring from the contract.[25]

In the case of the aircraft operating lease, the latter is the more likely since it will typically provide that, if the lessor does not satisfy the conditions to be satisfied by it within the time specified, the lessee shall not be bound to accept delivery of the aircraft and, if the lessee does not satisfy the conditions to be satisfied by it within the time specified, the lessor shall not be bound to tender delivery of or to deliver the aircraft to the lessee. However, even in such an event, the parties will want the lease agreement itself to survive since they will want such matters as representation and warranties, waivers of liability, and perhaps certain other matters to survive notwithstanding non-delivery of the aircraft. Commercially, the parties will wish to be clear as to the return or forfeiture of any deposits paid.

Further, the lessee generally will want to ensure that it is a condition precedent to its being obligated to take delivery of the aircraft under the lease that the aircraft meet the agreed delivery conditions.

[A] General Conditions Precedent

Certain conditions precedent (as set out below) should be satisfied by both parties, and generally, the language required of each party will mirror that required of the other.

[1] Payments

For example, it is normally a condition precedent to the lessor's obligations under the lease that the lessor should have received in full payment of the security deposit and the rent in respect of the first rent period, usually one month payable in advance or as otherwise provided for in the lease.[26]

Although the lessor will not normally have payment obligations to the lessee, occasionally these do arise such as where a lessor agrees to make a payment to the lessee in lieu of a certain non-compliance with delivery condition or in order for certain

23. Furmston, *supra*, at 129.
24. *Ibid.*
25. Furmston, *supra*, at 130.
26. *See* Bunker D.H., *International Aircraft Financing, Volume 2: Specific Documents*, 2nd Edition, IATA, 2015, at 63.

work to be undertaken on the aircraft. Such obligations may, however, take the form of a credit against future rent.

[2] Constitutional Documents

Both parties should provide copies of their constitutional documents to the other, showing their legal capacity to enter into the aircraft operating lease. These will normally be outside the ability of the other party to interpret; hence, they should be read in conjunction with the legal opinions referred to in section §3.05[A][5] *infra*.

[3] Corporate Approvals

Likewise, both parties should provide copies of their corporate approvals, whether board resolutions or otherwise, to the other, showing that all necessary internal corporate approvals have been obtained to enter into the aircraft operating lease. These will normally be outside the ability of the other party to interpret, at least in the case of cross-border leases; hence, they also should be read in conjunction with the legal opinions referred to in section §3.05[A][5] *infra*.

[4] Filings and Consents

Proof that any filings or external consents necessary for the lessor or the lessee to meet its obligations under the lease have been made or obtained as appropriate should be required by the other party.

For example, under Commission Regulation (EC) 859/2008, OPS 1.165(c)(1)(i), an EU operator shall not dry lease in[27] an aeroplane from an entity other than another such operator unless approved by its authority. Any conditions which are part of this approval must be included in the lease agreement. *See also* section §3.05[B][5] *infra*.

Bilateral air transport agreements between countries may come into play.[28] According to the Air Transport Committee of ICAO, out of forty-one bilateral air service agreements found to contain provisions on leasing, three had clauses dealing with safety aspects requiring the aviation authority of the operator to be satisfied that airworthiness standards will be maintained.

27. A dry lease is described as 'a lease of an aircraft where the aircraft is operated under the AOC of the lessee. It is normally a lease of an aircraft without crew, operated under the commercial control of the lessee and using the lessee's airline designator code and traffic rights' in ECAC Recommendation on Leasing of Aircraft, Recommendation ECAC/21-1 in *Study on Aircraft Leasing*, Air Transport Committee, 156th Session of the Council, ICAO, 1999, at Appendix B.
28. Article 6 of the Chicago Convention requires permission or authorization of a state for scheduled international service over or into its territory. Accordingly, the majority of international scheduled fights are regulated by bilateral or multilateral air transport agreements. *See* Bunker D.H., *International Aircraft Financing, Volume 1: General Principles*, 2nd Edition, IATA, 2015, at 276.

Greater concern is shown therein for leases from one airline to another airline, with a desire to make clear that no additional traffic rights are granted being evident, and, importantly, in the context of the present work, a distinction being made in certain cases between leases from other airlines, on the one hand, and leases from non-airline lessors, on the other hand. For example, in certain cases, notification only rather than approval is required in the case of leases from non-airline lessors.[29]

Again, these should be read in conjunction with the legal opinions referred to in section §3.05[A][5] *infra*.

[5] Legal Opinions

The lessee should provide a legal opinion, from its qualified legal counsel[30] acceptable to the lessor, confirming the overall legal viability of the structure from a legal point of view. Where the governing law of the lease, the jurisdiction of registration of the aircraft, and the jurisdiction of incorporation and residence of the lessee differ, multiple legal opinions may be necessary, one from each relevant jurisdiction.

As the lessor will also owe certain obligations to the lessee, such as return of the security deposit, return of maintenance reserves and the covenant of quiet enjoyment during the lease term, a legal opinion or opinions from its qualified legal counsel acceptable to the lessee may also be appropriate.

See also Chapter 2 section §2.05 *supra* and Annex 6 *infra*.

[6] Process Agent Letter

Unless the lessee is domiciled in the jurisdiction (or otherwise subject to the jurisdiction of its courts) chosen as a venue for resolution of disputes (such as an English airline where the courts of England are chosen in the lease as having jurisdiction over any disputes that arise under the lease), a letter from an agent for the lessee agreeing to act as its agent for service of process within such jurisdiction should be obtained.

The lessee should likewise require a similar letter from the lessor.

Without such a letter, a party seeking to sue the other may be subject to cumbersome procedures to serve a party outside the relevant court's jurisdiction.

Even with such a letter, without substantial assets in such jurisdiction, the value of any favourable judgment will depend on the ability of the victorious plaintiff to enforce such judgment in a jurisdiction where the other party has indeed substantial assets.

29. *Study on Aircraft Leasing*, Air Transport Committee, 156th Session of the Council, ICAO, 1999, 4.3–4.14.
30. This need not necessarily be from an independent law firm retained by the lessee but may, if the lessor agrees, be from in-house legal counsel in the employment of the lessee.

[B] Airline-Specific Conditions Precedent

Certain documentary conditions precedent must be satisfied by the lessee before the lessor will agree to deliver the aircraft. These are necessary for various reasons: the lessor will want to ensure that the lessee has all necessary approvals and is competent to operate the aircraft. Even if the lessor does not ask for them, the lessee must have them in order to satisfy its legal requirements.

These documents include the certificate of insurance, certificate of registration, certificate of airworthiness, radio station licence, air transport licence, AOC, and Eurocontrol letter. There may be others, which should be determined by the lessor's local counsel, and which should have been identified pursuant to the jurisdictional questionnaire discussed in Chapter 2 section §2.04 *supra*.

Article 19 of the Paris Convention (1919), required that an aircraft covered by it be 'provided with', *inter alia*, certificate of registration, airworthiness, crew licences and a licence for any equipped radio[31] apparatus but did not expressly require that these be carried on board the aircraft – under Article 29 of the Chicago Convention (1944), the aircraft must, *inter alia*, 'carry' such documents. Under Article 80 of the Chicago Convention (1944), this convention superseded the Paris Convention (1919). Within the EU, these documents together with the certificate of insurance, *inter alia*, must be carried on each flight pursuant to OPS 1.125 of Commission Regulation (EC) 859/2008.

Each will be examined in further detail below.

[1] Certificate of Insurance and Broker's Letter of Undertaking

The lessor will want to know that the aircraft is adequately insured[32] and that it, and any of its financiers, are covered adequately as to liability, as required by the lease (*see* section §3.12 *infra*) and will also want to receive a broker's letter of undertaking whereby, if the insurances should be cancelled, for example, due to non-payment of premium by the lessee, the broker will give a certain minimum notice first to the lessor to enable it to ensure continuation of coverage.

The certificate of insurance need not necessarily be kept on board the aircraft.[33]

In an English Court of Appeal case, *First Security Bank National Association (acting as owner trustee for the benefit of Leopard Leasing No 2 Ltd) v. Compagnie*

31. Termed 'wireless' in the Paris Convention (1919).
32. Typically, in accordance with the standard Lloyd's market endorsement for lessors and financiers AVN 67B or its replacement AVN 67C – http://www.awg.aero/project/insurance-and-liability/ on 9 Sep. 2021. As the separation between aircraft owner and operator has developed, aircraft financiers had to become familiar with nuances of insurance in an effort to avoid last minute pressure to approve insurance provisions. AVN 67B was developed to standardize policy endorsements for finance and lease contracts in the London market which insurers elsewhere generally follow: Margo R.D. and Houghton A.T., *The Role of Insurance in Aviation Finance Transactions*, in Butler G.F. and Keller M.R., executive editors, *Handbook of Airline Finance*, 1st Edition, Aviation Week: McGraw-Hill, 1999, at 279 et seq.
33. But *see* section §3.05[B] *supra* on Commission Regulation (EC) 859/2008.

Nationale Air Gabon,[34] May LJ upheld a refusal on discretionary grounds by Timothy Walker J in the English High Court to grant an injunction to lessor preventing lessee from flying the leased aircraft (which in this case had already been delivered) from France to Gabon where the proof of insurance was incomplete and not fully legible and the broker's opinion was missing. The judgment was without prejudice to the issue of damages.

[2] Certificate of Registration

The aircraft is required to carry its certificate of registration issued in compliance with Articles 17 and 18 of the Chicago Convention (1944).[35]

This may not always issue in time for delivery of the aircraft to the lessee and it is customary, where necessary, to allow a copy of such certificate to be forwarded to the lessor within a few days of delivery.

In practice, until now, a certified copy of the certificate of registration was simply collected pursuant to the conditions precedent around the time of delivery and forgotten about unless, pursuant to a sublease or some other development, a change in the state of registration was required during the lease term. This approach may change, certainly for aircraft registered in the US, and for other countries which may follow its approach in introducing new regulations requiring re-registration of aircraft every three years pursuant to particular procedures which, if not followed, will lead to the aircraft being removed from its register.

Prior to such new regulations, registration was indefinite[36] – the purpose of the new regulations[37] is to clean up the register, burdened by thousands of outdated and inaccurate registrations.[38] Henceforth, certificates of registration issued by the US Federal Aviation Administration will contain an expiry date dated three years later. One hundred and eighty days prior to such expiration, a reminder will be sent to owners, as befits an ownership-based system.[39]

The owner should beware that, if it fails to renew the registration of the aircraft, the registration of the aircraft will lapse, and the lessee will be unable to operate the aircraft – this would leave the owner/lessor open to a claim by the airline lessee for breach of its covenant of quiet enjoyment.[40]

Lessors should thus be careful to have systems in place to ensure renewal of such registration.

34. Royal Courts of Justice, 10 May 1999.
35. *See* section §3.10[B][3] *infra.*
36. Gerber D.N., *Aircraft Finance Issues: The Blue Sky Ruling; The New ASU and the 'Home Country Rule'; and Recent Developments at the FAA Registry,* a paper presented at the American Bar Association Air and Space Law Forum 2010 Annual Meeting in Seattle, Washington on 26 Oct. 2010.
37. 14 C.F.R. section 47.40(a)(1).
38. *Ibid.*
39. *See* section §3.10[B][3] *infra.*
40. *See* section §3.10[A] *infra.*

If similar requirements are brought in by jurisdictions with operator-based registries,[41] lessors should build in systems to ensure the lessee is required to show timely proof of such renewal.

[3] Certificate of Airworthiness

The aircraft is required to carry a certificate of airworthiness issued in compliance with under Article 31 of the Chicago Convention (1944).[42] It is the responsibility of the aviation authority where the aircraft will be registered during the term to inspect the aircraft and to issue the certificate of airworthiness (except in the case of an Article 83*bis* delegation, as to which, *see* section §3.15[H] *infra*).

[4] Radio Station Licence

The aircraft is required to carry a licence for any radio apparatus with which it is equipped issued in compliance with under Article 30 of the Chicago Convention (1944).

[5] Air Transport Licence

Council Regulation (EC) 1008/2008,[43] Article 3.1, provides that no undertaking established in the EU shall be permitted to carry by air passengers, mail, and/or cargo for remuneration and/or hire unless it has been granted the appropriate operating licence, commonly known as an air transport licence.

Article 4 sets out the conditions for granting such a licence and it is worth setting them out here in full:

> An undertaking shall be granted an operating licence by the competent licensing authority of a Member State provided that:
>
> (a) its principal place of business is located in that Member State;
> (b) it holds a valid AOC issued by a national authority of the same Member State whose competent licensing authority is responsible for granting, refusing, revoking or suspending the operating licence of the Community air carrier;
> (c) it has one or more aircraft at its disposal through ownership or a dry lease agreement;
> (d) its main occupation is to operate air services in isolation or combined with any other commercial operation of aircraft or the repair and maintenance of aircraft;
> (e) its company structure allows the competent licensing authority to implement the provisions of this Chapter;

41. *See* section §3.10[B][3] *infra*.
42. This supersedes.
43. Regulation (EC) 1008/2008 of the European Parliament and of the Council of 24 Sep. 2008 on common rules for the operation of air services in the Community.

(f) the Member States and/or nationals of Member States own more than 50% of the undertaking and effectively control it, whether directly or indirectly through one or more intermediate undertakings, except as provided for in an agreement with a third country to which the Community is a party;
(g) it meets the financial conditions specified in Article 5;
(h) it complies with the insurance requirements specified in Article 11 and in Council Regulation (EC) No 785/2004; and
(i) it complies with the provisions on good repute as specified in Article 7.

A practical issue here is that the airline must have one or more aircraft at its disposal. For a start-up airline, the lessor can sign up a lease for the first aircraft, and, indeed may have to in order for the lessee to be able to obtain an air transport licence, but it should require confirmation that such licence has been obtained before it delivers the aircraft – the lessee in any event will need such licence in order to put the aircraft into service.

Under Article 13.2, a dry or wet-lease agreement[44] to which a Community air carrier is a party shall be subject to 'prior approval in accordance with applicable Community or national law on aviation safety'.

Under Article 13.3, in the case of an aircraft registered in a third country, a wet-lease agreement to an EU air carrier is, unlike a dry lease, additionally subject to prior approval for the operation from the competent licensing authority which may, *inter alia*, require one of the following conditions to be fulfilled:[45]

(i) the Community air carrier justifies such leasing on the basis of exceptional needs, in which case an approval may be granted for a period of up to seven months that may be renewed once for a further period of up to seven months;
(ii) the Community air carrier demonstrates that the leasing is necessary to satisfy seasonal capacity needs, which cannot reasonably be satisfied through leasing aircraft registered within the Community, in which case the approval may be renewed; or
(iii) the Community air carrier demonstrates that the leasing is necessary to overcome operational difficulties and it is not possible or reasonable to lease aircraft registered within the Community, in which case the approval shall be of limited duration strictly.

The above requirements are not expressly extended to dry leases, but it is not clear whether or not similar requirements for dry leases could be invoked anyway pursuant to the more general language of Article 13.2, particularly where it is proposed

44. A wet lease is described as 'a lease of an aircraft where the aircraft is operated under the AOC of the lessor. It is normally a lease of an aircraft without crew, operated under the commercial control of the lessee and using the lessee's airline designator code and traffic rights' in ECAC Recommendation on Leasing of Aircraft, Recommendation ECAC/21-1 in *Study on Aircraft Leasing*, Air Transport Committee, 156th Session of the Council, ICAO, 1999, at Appendix B.
45. Article 13.3(b).

to keep the aircraft on the register of a third country whether pursuant to Article 83*bis* of the Chicago Convention (1944) or otherwise.[46]

The licence may be suspended or revoked pursuant to Article 9.

[6] Air Operator's Certificate

Commission Regulation (EC) 859/2008, Subpart C, OPS 1.175 et seq., deals with rules for the issuance of an AOC to an EU carrier and certifies that the operator has the professional ability and organization to ensure the safety of operations specified in the certificate.

Whereas the air transport licence is concerned with the overall viability of the proposed enterprise, the AOC is concerned with safety. Indeed, as seen in section §3.05[B][5] *supra*, in the EU it is a requirement[47] that an enterprise seeking an air transport licence demonstrates that it already holds an AOC.

[7] Eurocontrol Letter

For leases of aircraft which are, or are likely to be, operated into the EU or any other territory in respect of which Eurocontrol provides air navigation services, it is, in this author's experience, standard practice for lessors to require that the lessee first supply it with a letter, in a form satisfactory to it and to Eurocontrol, authorizing it to obtain information from time to time concerning the status of the lessee's account with Eurocontrol in respect of air navigation charges.

Without such a letter, Eurocontrol is not free to divulge what are otherwise private matters between it and the lessee airline. Having obtained such a letter,[48] it is then up to the lessor to check such status regularly with Eurocontrol so as to monitor any airlines whose overdue debts may become of concern, especially given the extent of Eurocontrol's in rem lien over the aircraft for unpaid charges.[49]

[C] Waivers and Conditions Subsequent

With the exception of insurances and, usually, payments, sometimes a lessor will agree to deliver an aircraft to a lessee notwithstanding that the lessee has not then satisfied all conditions to be satisfied by it. Such unsatisfied conditions will, in such event, be waived permanently or temporarily by lessor.

In particular, quite often, the certificate of registration may not be available until some short time after delivery, allowing for processing time.

---

46. *See* section §3.15[H] *infra.*
47. Article 4(b) of European Commission Regulation 1008/2008.
48. This assumes, of course, that Eurocontrol abides by its provisions. It is submitted that this letter, which is the lessor's primary means of monitoring a situation which could result in loss of title to its aircraft for reasons outside its control, be put on a legal footing which clearly obliges Eurocontrol to abide by it.
49. *See* section §3.10[B][2][b] *infra.*

In such circumstances, the parties should agree to a short letter setting out which conditions precedent have not yet been satisfied by the lessee, agreeing that delivery may nevertheless proceed, but providing that such unsatisfied conditions, if not permanently waived, are temporarily waived by being converted into conditions subsequent to be satisfied within a mutually agreed period after delivery.

Such a letter will only be of real value to the lessor if it also provides that failure to satisfy any relevant condition subsequent within such agreed time period shall constitute an event of default under the lease, thus allowing the lessor to exercise its remedies for breach under the lease.

This can be seen from Cheshire & Fifoot's definition of a condition subsequent as follows:

> If a contract has come into existence but is to terminate upon the occurrence of some event, it is said to be subject to a condition subsequent.[50]

Such a definition also encompasses events of default the occurrence of which entitle the lessor to terminate the leasing of the aircraft to the lessee under the lease agreement.

[D] Conclusions

The conditions precedent reviewed in section §3.05[A] *supra* are of the type which are to be expected in any commercial cross-border contract and are not, of themselves, specific to international aviation, even if some of the specific examples are.

The conditions precedent set out in section §3.05[B] *supra*, however, disclose for the first time in this work the relevance of public and private international air law to the aircraft operating lease contract.

The conditions examined in section §3.05[B] *supra* may, in turn, be divided into those which the lessor simply requires to see simply as a matter of due diligence and those which it contractually imposes on the lessee before it is willing to part with possession of its aircraft in favour of the lessee.

Examples of the former, which the lessor requires as a matter of due diligence but which the lessee is required as a matter of law to have any way in order to operate the aircraft, whether they are set out contractually as conditions precedent in the lease or not, are that the lessee holds an air transport licence and an AOC.

An example of the latter is the requirement that the lessee provides the lessor with a letter authorizing Eurocontrol to disclose details of its account with Eurocontrol to the lessor. This is a purely contractual requirement of the lessor: the lessee is required to pay Eurocontrol fees for navigation services but disclosing details of its account to a lessor is not a legal requirement of Eurocontrol or any other entity.

A hybrid example is the requirement that the lessee provides the lessor with an insurance certificate – liability coverage is legally required anyway but the lessor may

50. Furmston, *supra*, at 131.

impose higher contractual requirements as to liability insurance and will require hull insurance.[51]

In the case of these latter types of conditions precedent, therefore, the provisions of public and private international air law come into play in the aircraft operating lease, with particular concerns for the lessor in the case of non-compliance therewith by the lessee, and these are examined in detail as they arise throughout Chapter 3 of this work.

Having satisfied the conditions to the obligations of the parties under the lease, the examination turns next to the delivery of the aircraft by the lessor to the lessee thereunder.

§3.06 TERM AND DELIVERY

[A] Term

The term of the lease together with any early termination or extension options should be set out with certainty.[52] Any minimum time-period notice provision to terminate early or to extend should be clear and should be irrevocable once given.

The term must be ascertainable but need not necessarily be a fixed date: for example, it could be stated to end on a given date, or after a given period from the delivery date, or even something not fixed (but ascertainable) such as completion of the first scheduled heavy check (suitably defined) to occur before or after a certain date.

Once all conditions precedent to delivery are satisfied or waived, the aircraft may be tendered for delivery at the agreed delivery location, which should be specified in the lease since this will have cost implications in terms of fuel, crew, and insurance. Also, as the lessee will generally bear the tax risk of any taxes being imposed by virtue of the delivery in the jurisdiction of the delivery location (as to which, *see* Chapter 2 section §2.06[H] *supra*), the lessee should satisfy itself beforehand that it will not face any untoward tax consequences by agreeing to accept delivery in a particular location.

[B] Delivery

The agreement to lease is typically set out here and constitutes the core of the contract between the parties whereby the lessor agrees to lease the aircraft to the lessee and the lessee agrees to lease the aircraft from the lessor on and subject to the terms set out in the lease agreement.

Passing of risk on delivery, the requirement that the aircraft be in delivery condition, and delay in delivery are also issues to deal with here.

51. *See* section §3.12 *infra*.
52. *See* section 4 of the Supplement *infra*.

[1] Delay in or Failure of Delivery

The lease should provide for what happens in the case of delay or failure to deliver the aircraft in the delivery condition set out in the lease within the timeframe set out in the lease as well as the effect of accepting delivery of the aircraft by the lessee.

If the lessee fails to accept delivery when properly tendered, the lease will normally give the lessor the right to keep the security deposit.[53] Normally, some delay in delivery is contemplated but typically a final date for delivery will be set out, failing which, the security deposit will be returnable to the lessee, if failure is not attributable to the lessee, or the security deposit may be retained by the lessor, if failure is attributable to the lessee.

See also sections §3.07[B] (Security Deposit) and §3.19[A] (Time of the Essence), *infra.*

[2] Failure to Meet Delivery Condition Prior to Delivery

An aircraft operating lease will typically set out a delivery condition which must be met in order for the airline to be obliged to take delivery of the lease. If it does not, the lessee should be free to reject the aircraft and demand the return of its deposit.

Lessors often worry that a lessee may find a minor non-conformity in delivery condition and use that as an excuse to refuse delivery in circumstances where the lessee's real reason is that it no longer wants the aircraft, or markets rents have dropped since it signed the lease agreement.

A New York case involving the sale of an aircraft which failed to meet the contractually stipulated delivery condition will not give such lessors much comfort. In *Austrian Airlines Oesterreichische Luftverkehrs AG v. UT Finance Corporation,*[54] Kaplan DJ was asked to rule on a contract which provided for the sale of an aircraft where the aircraft, as was stipulated by both parties, did not meet the required delivery condition in certain important respects. The airline sought to enforce the contract on the grounds that the contract provided for a reduction in price in case of non-conformity, and argued that industry practice meant that the defendant was acting unreasonably in refusing such reduction, its real grounds for refusal being the collapse in aircraft values after the terrorist incidents in the United States of America of 11 September 2001 involving aircraft.

Kaplan J was firm in disposing of the claim: the contract provided that the defendant 'may' but did not have to accept a reduction in price in lieu of precise conformity to the delivery condition. He held that any contrary industry practice does not apply in the case of clear contrary language in the contract. He also held that the

53. *See* Bunker D.H., *International Aircraft Financing, Volume 2: Specific Documents*, 2nd Edition, IATA, 2015, at 84–87.
54. 04 Civ 3854 (LAK) (2008).

defendant did not act in bad faith: it was entitled to take account of the decline in aircraft values 'to insist upon getting everything it bargained for'.[55]

Finally, in this case, the contract was governed by New York law, under which, pursuant to section 2-508(2) of the Uniform Commercial Code:

> [w]here the buyer rejects a non-conforming tender which the seller had reasonable grounds to believe would be acceptable with or without money allowance the seller may if he seasonably notifies the buyer have a further reasonable time to substitute a conforming tender.

Kaplan DJ held in *Austrian*[56] that the seller in the case had no such reasonable grounds.

In the context of a lease, not only does the above statute, dealing with sales, not apply, but pursuant to the judgment in *Austrian*, a lessee may well be justified, if the wording of the lease so permits it, in demanding precise conformity of the aircraft to the delivery condition set out in the lease even if its main reason is that it no longer wants the aircraft or that lease rents have indeed dropped since it first signed the lease. Lessors should beware!

[3] Effect of Acceptance of Delivery

In *ACG Acquisition XX LLV v. Olympic Airways,*[57] there was a dispute between the lessor and the lessee where the lessee had accepted delivery of an aircraft under lease after due inspection and signing an acceptance certificate (execution of which was stated in the lease to be conclusive proof of the lessee's examination and acceptance of the aircraft condition) but where the aircraft was soon after delivery declared unairworthy by the lessee's aviation authority.

The lease also contained an exclusion that the lessee accepted the aircraft 'as is, where is' and that lessor would have no liability and had given no representations as to condition, airworthiness, fitness for any use or purpose, or otherwise.[58]

On the facts, Hamblen J refused to grant summary judgment in favour of the lessor, holding that the lessee had a sufficiently arguable case of total failure of consideration. Although there is much to criticize in his judgment, it is instructive to note that he laid much emphasis on the fact that, regardless of all the above provisions, in addition to its being a condition precedent to the lessee's obligation to accept the aircraft that the aircraft be in the agreed delivery condition, the lease also provided that, on the delivery date:

55. *Ibid.*, at 36.
56. *Supra.*
57. [2010] EWHC 923 (Comm). This author hereby discloses that, at the time of writing, the claimant, ACG Acquisition XX LLC is a related party to, and managed by Aviation Capital Group Corp, the parent company of, his employer, ACG Aircraft Leasing Ireland Limited.
58. *Ibid.*, at para. 37.

> Lessor shall deliver the Lease Property 'as is, where is' and in the condition required by Schedule 2.[59]...[60]

This clause made the lessee's obligation to lease the aircraft conditional on the lessor's delivering the aircraft in a condition meeting the contractually required condition. This is not an unusual provision[61] – normally execution of the acceptance certificate by the lessee is proof of satisfaction of such requirement.

This problem could, in theory, be avoided in future by removing from the clause of the lease setting out the lessor's obligation to deliver the aircraft any reference to the aircraft's being in a particular condition: this cuts across the exclusion and the conclusivity of the acceptance certificate whereas the lessee's interests would be adequately protected by ensuring it is a condition precedent to its obligation to accept delivery of the aircraft that it meets the delivery condition without imposing a contractual obligation on the lessor to deliver in the delivery condition.[62]

The lessor is not an operator: it either delivers the aircraft new from the manufacturer to the airline or delivers to it at the end of the lease from the previous operator at the end of that operator's lease. Even if the aircraft is off lease for a period, the lessor relies on a third-party authorized maintenance provider for any maintenance work performed on the aircraft. The lessor is not in a position to assure any particular condition other than the extent to which it can protect itself contractually as against its lessees and its maintenance providers.

All it can reasonably do, it is submitted, is to afford the lessee a sufficient right of examination for the lessee to decide for itself whether the aircraft meets delivery condition or not. If it does, the lessee should sign the acceptance certificate, and take responsibility for its inspection of the aircraft. If it does not, it should reject the aircraft and demand its deposit back.

A lessee should be careful in what inspection rights it wants, for the broader its inspection rights on delivery, the broader shall the lessor's inspections rights be correspondingly upon redelivery since these are usually negotiated fairly as to match. It is thus more than a bit disingenuous for an airline to complain that freely negotiated inspection rights on delivery are unfair.

Further, in arguing against the enforceability of the conclusivity language in the acceptance certificate provided for in the lease, the airline sets itself up for the possibility that the similar conclusivity language in the redelivery certificate given to it by the lessor upon completion of its corresponding redelivery inspection at the end of the lease may not be upheld.

In other words, airlines would be wise to consider whether they want to be able to ignore agreed contractual limits on inspection rights of the lessee at delivery and to

59. Schedule 2 set out the agreed delivery condition of the aircraft, including that the aircraft be airworthy.
60. *Ibid.*, at p. 3.
61. *See*, e.g., Bunker D.H., *International Aircraft Financing, Volume 2: Specific Documents*, 2nd Edition, IATA, 2015, at 69–70.
62. *See* section §3.05 *supra*.

ignore conclusivity language in the acceptance certificate[63] signed by the lessee at delivery for, should such arguments prevail, lessors would have the ability to claim correspondingly broader rights of inspection at redelivery and to sue lessees post-delivery for defects found after completion of the redelivery inspection notwithstanding conclusivity language in the redelivery certificate signed by the lessor at redelivery.

It is worth repeating this important fact: the lessor is never the operator or maintenance provider. It buys the aircraft, typically new from the manufacturer, leasing it first to one airline, then to another, until it sells the aircraft or the aircraft reaches the end of its economic life. The airline taking delivery of a used aircraft will inspect the aircraft before accepting delivery – this is typically the same as the redelivery inspection from the previous lessee. Thus, it seems inequitable[64] that a subsequent airline lessee could hold a lessor liable for defects without allowing the lessor similar recourse to the previous airline lessee on whose maintenance both the lessor and the subsequent airline lessee have relied. Any airline wishing to make aggressive claims as the subsequent airline lessee should bear in mind that it will, at the end of the lease, be in the shoes of the previous airline lessee.

It is submitted that *Olympic*, being only a judgment on an interlocutory hearing, without a full hearing of the facts or of the reasons (summarized above) why the standard operating lease practice should be given effect to both for contractual certainty and for the protection not only of lessors generally but of lessees as well, and in any event being a judgment peculiar to the particular drafting of the lease in question, is not a good precedent and should not be followed at a full trial.

At the full trial of the *Olympic*[65] case, Teare J held for the lessor. While he accepted that the statement in the lease as to conclusivity of the acceptance certificate insofar as it required the lessee to accept delivery of the aircraft did not, of itself, preclude lessee from suing lessor for a breach of an undertaking as to delivery condition, the wording of the acceptance certificate was such that the lessor was justified in relying on it, and indeed did rely on it, such that the lessee was estopped from denying its statement that the aircraft was satisfactory to it.[66]

Teare J's judgment is particularly welcome to this author as being consistent with his views throughout this study and in recognizing that:

63. Whereby the lessee confirms to the lessor that it accepts delivery of the aircraft in the contractually agreed delivery condition or waives any non-compliance therewith.

64. It is conceded that there is not a perfect symmetry between a subsequent lessee's claims against a lessor after delivery and a lessor's claim against a previous lessee after redelivery. With the former, Hamblen J in *Olympic* considered the possibility that, notwithstanding the conclusivity language of the acceptance certificate, a lessee may not be bound in case of total failure of consideration, which could occur with delivery of an unworthy aircraft.

By contrast, where a lessor has accepted redelivery from a lessee which performed its obligations during the lease, and only after redelivery discovered that the aircraft was unairworthy, it would be much more difficult for the lessor to establish total failure of consideration on the part of the lessee, since some consideration at least would have passed (e.g., rent during the lease term), and thus that could not be used as a ground to defeat or to ignore the conclusivity language in the redelivery certificate, if any, given to the previous lessee.

65. *ACG Acquisition XX LLV v. Olympic Airways*, [2012] EWHC 1070 (Comm).

66. At 127 et seq.

> [i]t is also necessary to bear in mind that commercial men generally prefer certainty over doubt ... The reasonable man with knowledge of the background would be surprised if that statement did not have consequences and that Olympic, having formally stated that the aircraft complied in all respects with the condition required at delivery under Section 4.2 and Schedule 2 of the Agreement, was nevertheless free to allege the contrary.[67]

If the lessee's argument had prevailed, it is submitted that lessors might have responded by refusing to grant redelivery certificates[68] to lessees at the end of the lease, as they will need to preserve their ability to sue the previous lessee after redelivery where a subsequent lessee is able to sue the lessor or to escape its obligations under its lease by reason of the condition (for which the previous lessee was responsible) of the aircraft being discovered to be unairworthy after delivery.

On appeal, the Court of Appeal[69] upheld Teare J's judgment but found that he came to 'the right conclusion but for the wrong reason'.[70] The court held that, if the lease provisions did not provide that delivery of the Certificate of Acceptance is conclusive proof of compliance of the aircraft with the contractual requirements, then it is not possible to regard the certificate of acceptance as nonetheless giving rise to an estoppel by representation to the same effect. However, the court held that, in fact, the lease provisions and certificate of acceptance provided finality for the lessee's acceptance that the aircraft complied with the lease requirements.[71]

In the EU, Article 1 of the Council Directive 85/374/EEC of 25 July 1985, dealing with product liability, provides that a producer shall be liable for damage caused by defects in his product, which is defined to mean all movables.[72] Under Article 3(1), any person who imports into the EU a product for leasing shall be deemed to be a producer. The liability of the producer arising from this Directive may not, in relation to the injured person, be limited or excluded by a provision limiting his liability or exempting him from liability.[73] Thus, in theory, any provision in a lease, such as that in the *Olympic* case, relieving a lessor of liability may be void under this Directive.[74]

In practice, however, a lessor is unlikely to face liability pursuant thereto since damage under Article 1 is limited to mean damage by death, personal injury or damage to certain property (other than the movable complained of) used by the injured person mainly for his own private use or consumption.[75] The lessee itself is more likely to face economic loss than such personal injury or physical property damage.

67. At 159.
68. Whereby the lessor confirms to the lessee that it accepts redelivery of the aircraft in the contractually agreed redelivery condition, or waives any non-compliance therewith.
69. *Olympic Airlines S.A. (in special liquidation) v. ACG Acquisition XX LLC* [2013] EWCA Civ 369.
70. Tomlinson LJ, at 54.
71. At 45–47.
72. With the exception of primary agricultural products and game: Art. 2.
73. Article 12.
74. *See also* the discussion in section §3.11[B][3] *infra* with respect to third parties.
75. Article 9.

[C] Conclusions

The term of the lease should normally be sufficiently clear as not to raise legal issues but the consequences of acceptance or non-acceptance of delivery may give rise to dispute, as seen above.

Neither public nor private international air law appears to have much of a role, if any, in respect of disputes concerning the term of or delivery under a lease. As seen above, these are dealt with, rather, under the governing law of the lease, which is a national law, and the main legal challenge, thus far unsuccessful, in this respect has been to the conclusivity of the acceptance certificates required by lessors or lessees. For the reasons given above, this author favours recognizing the conclusive nature of such acceptance certificates as stated in the terms thereof.

Once the aircraft has been delivered to the lessee under the lease, the lessee's obligations commence, including the obligation to pay rent and other amounts due under the lease, which are examined next.

§3.07 PAYMENTS

The net payment obligation of the lessee together with its gross-up obligation in the case of withholding tax will be examined. As well as rent, the security deposit (and its recasting as a commitment fee) and maintenance reserves (and their recasting as supplemental rent) will be examined.[76]

[A] Rent

Rent is the principal consideration paid by the lessee to the lessor for the use of its asset.

It may be fixed throughout the lease term. It may be 'float to fix' whereby there is an assumed rent amount which then varies according to fluctuation in a reference interest rate between the time of signing the lease and the time of delivery when it is then adjusted to reflect such fluctuation and fixed from that point.[77] It may also be a floating rate rent, where the adjustment for interest rate fluctuations does not stop at delivery but continues through the lease term.

Rent is typically paid monthly in advance, but sometimes other rental periods are encountered, such as quarterly rent payments.[78]

The airline's obligation to pay rent for the lease term is typically stated to be an absolute obligation – this is the so-called hell or high water clause to the effect that,

76. *See* section 5 of the Supplement *infra.*
77. Great care is needed in accurately drafting rent escalation or other adjustment clauses. For a case involving a dispute as to an escalation clause, *see Various Airfinance Leasing Companies & Ors v. Saudi Arabian Airlines Corporation* [2021] EWHC 2330 (Comm).
78. Indeed, Beatson J refused to characterize a lease as a sham where no rent was paid where evidence was adduced that no payments were made in return for set off of amounts owed under a loan from lessee to lessor: *Blue Sky One Limited and others v. Blue Airways LLC and others* [2009] EWHC 3314 (Comm) at para. 130.

come 'hell or high water' the lease rent must be paid. The lease rent is stated to be a net amount so that it must be grossed up such that, if any withholdings are imposed, the net amount must still be received by the lessor. Rent is payable periodically (typically monthly) in advance.

Further, any rights of set off on the part of the lessee (but not the lessor) are generally given up such that, even if the airline has a claim against the lessor, it must bring a legal action while continuing to pay rent.

In addition, there will normally be statements in the lease that the airline accepts the aircraft 'as is, where is' and that no representations or warranties, express or implied, are given by the lessor as to the condition or suitability of the aircraft.[79] The airline's sole right is thus to inspect the aircraft before delivery and to refuse the aircraft if it does not meet the required delivery condition.

Bunker has argued[80] that, while 'hell or high water' clauses may be acceptable in the context of a finance lease, they may be unfair to lessees in operating leases. He argues[81] that a finance lease is akin to secured financing[82] where it is reasonable for the finance lessor to assure repayment of what is essentially a loan. By contrast, he points out that an operating lessor has real obligations to the lessee, such as repayment of security deposits and reimbursements from maintenance reserves.

Insofar as reimbursement from maintenance reserves goes, he makes a fair point: the lessee is an unsecured creditor of the lessor with respect to them. This author, however, would not agree that the 'hell or high water' clause has no just application at all in the case of operating leases. The security deposit is not due to be refunded until the end of the lease term, by which time the lessee should already have paid all its rent, thus having nothing to set off anyway, and, by definition, as from delivery, the lessee has already accepted the condition of the aircraft pursuant to the terms of the lease and the acceptance certificate. The logic of keeping this clause intact has come under renewed scrutiny in light of the Boeing 737 MAX grounding and it is important to remember that this is a matter of contractual negotiation.[83]

Notwithstanding Bunker's argument in favour of not applying the 'hell or high water' clause at least to claims for reimbursement of maintenance reserves, the practice for operating leases and operating leases alike[84] is indeed to apply it without restriction – and the courts have tended to uphold it. In such circumstances, the lessee should at least consider the credit of their lessors before entering into an operating lease.

---

79. *See* Bunker D.H., *International Aircraft Financing, Volume 2: Specific Documents*, 2nd Edition, IATA, 2015, at 77–84.
80. Bunker D.H., *International Aircraft Financing, Volume 1: General Principles*, 2nd Edition, IATA, 2015, at 157–160; Bunker D.H., *International Aircraft Financing, Volume 2: Specific Documents*, 2nd Edition, IATA, 2015, at 91–94.
81. *Supra.*
82. *See* Chapter 2 section §2.01 *supra.*
83. IBA Article, *Have operating lease agreements evolved with the industry?*, 26 Feb. 2020, at www.iba.aero/insight/have-operating-lease-agreements-evolved-with-the-industry-february-2020/ on 9 Sep. 2021.
84. *See* Clark T. (ed.), *Leasing Finance*, Euromoney, 1985, at 55 and Bunker, *supra.*

For example, in *Celestial Aviation Trading 71 Limited v. Paramount Airways Private Limited,*[85] before the English High Court, Teare J held that a lessee could not set off an obligation to pay lessor against an obligation on the part of lessor[86] to reduce a deposit held pursuant to a letter of credit rather than in cash but that, even if the deposit had been held in cash, he would have upheld the clause in the lease requiring the lessee to make all payments thereunder to the lessor regardless of any 'defence, set-off, counterclaim ... or other circumstance'.[87]

Further, an English case, *Trident Turboprop (Dublin) Ltd v. First Flight Couriers Ltd.*,[88] has upheld certain such protections for the lessor, but on narrow grounds. In that case, the airline refused to continue to pay rent and justified this citing the poor performance of the aircraft and that it had been induced to enter into the leases in question in reliance on non-fraudulent misrepresentation on the part of the lessor.

In this case, English law applied, and the lessor relied on a provision of the leases which contained an acknowledgement by the airline that the lessor had not and would not be deemed to have made any warranties or representations about the aircraft and under which the lessee gave up any rights it would otherwise have had in respect of any warranty or representation other than those set out in the leases.

The airline argued that such provisions were covered by the United Kingdom Unfair Contract Terms Act 1977 (UCTA) and, as such, because they both purported to exclude or restrict liability, would be subject to the UCTA reasonableness test unless they were outside UCTA for some other reason.

UCTA does not apply to international supply contracts. The court considered that the leases were international sale contracts because the parties' places of business were in different territories and possession of the aircraft was being transferred between the parties, thus satisfying section 26(3) of UCTA. However, the court held that even where this is not the case, section 26(4)(a) is satisfied if goods are carried from the territory of one State to the territory of another State on conclusion of the contract.

In *Air Transworld Limited v. Bombardier Inc,*[89] Cooke J of the English High Court determined on the facts that the exclusion of warranties in a contract for the purchase of an aircraft was reasonable but that the claimant was, in any event, not a consumer, and the contract was an international supply contract. The fact that the word 'condition' was not used in the exclusion of warranties provision was not material where the intention to exclude all liability for 'breach of condition (merchantability) and fitness for purpose'[90] was clear from the contractual wording.

In other cases, the reasonableness test for any exclusion of representations would apply and this may add uncertainty to the airline's absolute liability to pay the rent 'come hell or high water'.

85. [2009] EWHC 3142 (Comm).
86. An obligation which the judge held the lessee had not in any event established on the facts.
87. *Ibid.*, at para. 7.
88. [2009] 1 All ER (Comm) 16.
89. [2012] EWHC 243 (Comm).
90. At 19.

If the test applies, under section 11(1) of UCTA, the party seeking to uphold the limitation on liability must show that:

> the term shall have been a fair and reasonable one to be included having regard to the circumstances which were, or ought reasonably to have been, known to or in the contemplation of the parties when the contract was made.

If UCTA had applied here, it would have been open to the lessor to show that, in the circumstances, the limitation was fair and reasonable by reference not only to industry practice but to the fact that the airline was afforded a full opportunity to inspect the aircraft prior to taking delivery with the right to refuse to take delivery if the aircraft did not meet the contractually stipulated legal condition.

In the US, the US Court of Appeals for the Eighth Circuit held[91] that a contractual acceptance provision in respect of a tower for installation on a skyscraper could not, despite its conclusivity language, override section 2-608 of the Uniform Commercial Code which allows for revocation of acceptance where non-conformity substantially impairs its value to the buyer if the buyer has accepted it: (i) on the reasonable assumption that its non-conformity would be cured and it has not been seasonably cured; or (ii) without discovery of such non-conformity, if the buyer's acceptance was reasonably induced by the seller's assurances.

In the context of operating leases and sales of commercial aircraft, it is submitted that lack of representations or other assurances in the lease or otherwise coupled with full pre-delivery inspection rights should adequately protect a lessor. However, if the acceptance certificate sets out defects and an agreed course of dealing with such defects, based on which a lessee agreed to accept delivery, revocation should be allowed where the lessor fails to proceed as agreed with regard to rectification of such defects.

[B] Security Deposit

[1] Security Deposit Rationale

Assuming that the airline has no valid argument to the 'hell or high water' provisions of the lease, the lessor can, of course, sue the airline for failure to pay rent, or invoke other dispute resolution provisions of the lease. Litigation and arbitration are uncertain, however, and cost time as well as money.

In order to protect the lessor against the airline's failure to pay rent, the lease will normally include a requirement that the airline pays a security deposit to the lessor, which the lessor may apply to remedy any failure by the airline to pay rent, or indeed to remedy any other failure by the airline to perform its obligations under the lease.[92]

The amount of the security deposit is commercially negotiated and will normally be calculated by reference to a number of months' rent, typically (in this author's

91. *Trinity Products, Inc v. Burgess Steel, LLC*, 486 F 3d 325, 329 (8th Cir 2007).
92. *See* Bunker D.H., *International Aircraft Financing, Volume 2: Specific Documents*, 2nd Edition, IATA, 2015, at 84–88.

experience) two or three. Sometimes the airline will want the deposit to bear interest at an agreed rate.

The lease will oblige the airline to replenish any amount spent by the lessor from the security deposit in rectifying any failure to perform on the part of the airline.

The greatest concern which the lessor has is that, if the airline goes bankrupt, the trustee in bankruptcy or the liquidator may demand the security deposit back, as being funds belonging to the estate in bankruptcy, and that it may claim that the lessor is merely an unsecured creditor in respect of any claims for failure to perform on the part of the airline (a likely situation where the airline is bankrupt).

[2] Charge over the Security Deposit

It is prudent for a lessor to include a provision in the lease that a first priority charge is granted by the airline to the lessor as security for performance by the airline of its lease obligations.

Care must be taken by the lessor to comply with any laws governing the creation of charges by a company over any of its assets. These laws will be the laws of the jurisdiction of the lessee in the case of an aircraft operating lease. For example, in the United Kingdom, under section 860(1) of the United Kingdom Companies Act 2006, 'a company that creates a charge to which this section applies must deliver the prescribed particulars of the charge, together with the instrument (if any) by which the charge is created or evidenced, to the registrar for registration before the end of the period[93] allowed for registration'.

It is surprising how often this requirement to perfect the charge is overlooked in practice given that, under section 874(1) of the Act, failure to register particulars in time renders the charge void as against a liquidator or creditors of the company.

In re Charge Card Services Ltd., the English High Court[94] and later the Court of Appeal[95] held it conceptually impossible for a company to be granted a charge over its own indebtedness to the charger insomuch as:

> a man cannot have a proprietary interest in a debt or other obligation which he owes another.[96]

That this case has effectively been overruled and is no longer a binding precedent is clear from the House of Lords in *Morris and others v. Rayners Enterprises Incorporated and Another*[97] where Hoffmann LJ held *per curiam* that:

> [i]n a case in which there is no threat to the consistency of the law or objection of public policy, I think that the courts should be very slow to declare a practice of the commercial community to be conceptually impossible.[98]

93. In this instance, twenty-one days – *see* section 870(1).
94. [1987] Ch. 150 (High Court).
95. [1996] Ch. 245 (Court of Appeal).
96. *Ibid.*, at 258.
97. [1997] UKHL 44.
98. *Ibid.*, at para. 6.

Nevertheless, *In re Charge Card* cast a long shadow on creditors and some lessors continue to take additional steps to protect their interest, to which we shall next turn.

[3] Commitment Fee

A further innovation used by some lessors to protect their ability to retain the security deposit even in the case of the lessee's bankruptcy is to provide in the lease that the sum is referred to not as a security deposit but as a commitment fee paid as consideration for the lessor's taking the aircraft off the market. The commitment fee is stated to be the absolute property of the lessor. Thus, upon an airline's bankruptcy, the lessor would argue that this does not form part of the estate in bankruptcy.

In such instances, it is important to provide that, upon the redelivery of the aircraft in accordance with the lease, and satisfaction of the airline's obligations under the lease, an amount equal to the commitment fee (or, better still, an amount not referencing the commitment fee but calculated so as to be the same as it) will be paid to the lessee.

As a precaution, such provisions as to commitment fees generally go on to state that if contrary to the intent of the parties the commitment fee is held to be a security deposit, then a first priority charge is granted over it.

[4] Market Reality

Of course, the ability of a lessor to require such stringent language depends on the state of the market at the time of lease negotiation. At the time of writing, many lessees are raising concerns as to potential lessor bankruptcy with the consequent risk that the security deposit may not be returned to them. To the extent that the market favours lessees, it would not be surprising to see lessees require such security deposits to be placed in a pledged account or to have the lessor's obligation to return the security deposit, assuming of course that the lessee discharges its obligations under the lease, supported by a letter of credit.

[C] Maintenance Reserves

[1] Maintenance Reserves Rationale

Just as the lessor will rely on having a security deposit available to it in case the airline fails to pay rent, a lessor will typically want reserves paid to it to cover the cost of scheduled maintenance to the aircraft in the event that the airline fails properly to maintain the aircraft.[99] Depending on the creditworthiness or bargaining position of the airline, this may be negotiable.

99. *See* section §3.10[B][1] *infra.*

Typically, these reserves are split out by airframe, engines, landing gear, auxiliary power unit, and life-limited parts and are calculated by reference to expected usage of each and expected heavy maintenance charges based on such usage.[100] The reserves are then paid periodically (typically monthly)[101] in arrears based on actual usage during the preceding month. For example, the cost of an airframe C Check will typically be spread out over the cost of an expected C Check interval.

Once scheduled heavy maintenance (not all maintenance is reimbursable and the precise parameters of what is reimbursable are heavily negotiated) is performed, an airline will typically want prompt reimbursement of that expenditure.

The lessor will agree, upon being satisfied that the work was properly carried out, to reimburse an amount equal to the lesser of the actual cost of such heavy maintenance and the amount currently in the account for such reimbursement event; in other words, the airline can, for example, only claim reimbursement up to the amount of airframe reserves paid by it against the cost of an airframe C Check and reimbursement up to the amount of engine reserves paid by it against the cost of an engine shop visit.[102]

On the other hand, the lessor will be concerned as to any claims for liens imposed by the party performing the maintenance in respect of work owed by the airline in respect of other aircraft which are not related to the lessor. The last thing a lessor wants is to reimburse the maintenance payment and then find that its asset is not released because the repair shop is asserting a lien in respect of such other unrelated work.

---

100. Careful drafting is needed here. Note, for example, the English Court of Appeal case of *Sunrock Aircraft Corporation Limited v. Scandinavian Airline Systems Denmark-Norway-Sweden* [2007] EWHC Civ 882, where Thomas LJ held, *per curiam*, that an obligation to pay at the end of the lease an amount by reference to the 'maintenance status' of life-limited parts at the end of the lease by comparing them with such status as of delivery did not mean that one looked to their condition (as in, how close to replacement they were at the end of the lease bearing in mind their life-limited nature) but rather whether or not they needed replacement at such points in time.

    Thomas LJ held (at para. 23) that:

    > the obligation of the parties in respect of the … [life limited parts] was to make an adjustment for the difference in maintenance status by reference to a comparison between what was required at the next overhaul as at delivery and redelivery and the difference in the length of time as delivery and redelivery to that overhaul. The clause plainly did not oblige SAS to pay Sunrock a sum calculated by reference to the proportion of the [life limited parts] used during the period of the lease.

101. Bunker D.H., *International Aircraft Financing, Volume 2: Specific Documents*, 2nd Edition, IATA, 2015, at 88–90.
102. Lessees should also argue for return of all maintenance reserves held by lessors in the case of total loss where the lessor has been paid the stipulated loss value of the aircraft under the insurances: *see* IBA Article, *Have operating lease agreements evolved with the industry?*, 26 Feb. 2020, at www.iba.aero/insight/have-operating-lease-agreements-evolved-with-the-industry-february-2020/ on 9 Sep. 2021.

[2] *Charge over Maintenance Reserves*

Just as with the security deposit,[103] a lessor should ensure that the airline grants it a first priority charge over such maintenance reserves and should ensure that such charge is perfected in accordance with the laws of the jurisdiction of the lessee.

[3] *Supplemental Rent*

The maintenance reserves may be stated to be supplemental or additional rent which is the sole property of the lessor. In such event, the amount paid to the lessee upon carrying out certain heavy maintenance is not stated to be reimbursement of maintenance reserves or supplemental or additional rent but rather payment or contribution by the lessor of an amount equal to the lesser of the actual cost of the relevant heavy maintenance and the sum of all amounts of relevant supplemental rent (airframe, engine, etc.) minus all such sums previously paid by the lessor to the airline.

Again, in such event, it may be advisable to provide that if contrary to the intent of the parties the supplemental or additional rent is held to be maintenance reserves, then a first priority charge is granted over it. On the other hand, such a statement may be seen by a court as defensive and effectively as an admission that, notwithstanding the language of the lease, the sums involved are reserves. Much here will depend on what view the judge in question takes, something which is not readily predictable, particularly in the absence of case law on the point.

[4] *Limited Reimbursement Obligation*

As operational risk of the aircraft is the sole obligation of the lessee under an operating lease, the lessor will only want to reimburse the lessee from the maintenance reserves[104] for scheduled[105] heavy checks or maintenance work (as carefully negotiated in the lease) in respect of the airframe, engines, life-limited parts, landing gear, auxiliary power unit, and (if applicable) thrust reversers.

The reserves collected will normally, in this author's experience, be calculated by the lessor's and lessee's technical staff to be sufficient to cover the expected costs of such work and thus the lessor's counsel will need to be careful to make clear in the lease that the lessor will expect the lessee to bear the cost of any other repairs or work, including foreign object damage, operational misuse, mishandling, faulty maintenance, accidental or intentional damage, abuse, modification or alteration for whatever

103. *See* section §3.07[B][2] *supra*.
104. Or, in the case of supplemental rent, pay an amount equal to relevant supplemental rent paid in to the extent such payments have not already been made.
105. The lessor will not reimburse from reserves for unscheduled maintenance (such as to repair, for example, foreign object damage) since the quantum of the reserves will have been calculated according to an agreed estimate of scheduled maintenance costs which by definition cannot include unscheduled maintenance. For unscheduled maintenance, lessee may be able to claim on its insurances but will otherwise have to fund it itself.

reason or requirements of airworthiness directives, service bulletins, regulatory revisions, mandatory orders, and instructions issued by such aviation authorities as are referenced in the lease.

Failure to do so will risk unnecessary depletion of the maintenance reserves, possibly leaving the lessor with insufficient reserves to pay a contribution to the follow-on lessee for the first scheduled heavy checks or maintenance work during the term of the follow-on lease where the follow-on lessee will expect the lessor to contribute for that portion of the work that reflects the operation of the aircraft prior to its taking delivery of it.

In a tight economic environment, cash flow is a major concern for lessors and lessees alike. Many lessees ask that lessors pay in advance part of the estimated fees for performing maintenance work, to save the lessees from having to pay that portion themselves in advance and then await reimbursement from the lessors. Again, lessors' reactions to this will depend on the then-prevailing environment. If the market favours the lessees, the lessors will have little choice but to work with the lessees on a solution here.

A lessor who agrees with a lessee to pay directly to a maintenance performer will want to approve the workscope in advance; sometimes, the lessor will not insist on advance approval but may decline reimbursement if the workscope is unsatisfactory, and will want even more than usual to be satisfied in advance with the identity of the maintenance performer. It will also want to approve the maintenance contract and ensure that, if it pays in advance, such sums will only be applied to its property, and (if it can) it will want the maintenance performer to agree to limit its mechanics' lien (as to which, *see* section §3.10[B][2] *infra*).

While this may help the lessor to limit its financial risk, the lessor will need to bear in mind that, much though it needs to retain the ability to approve maintenance work and the identity of any proposed maintenance performer on its aircraft, the more closely it becomes involved in this regard, the more likely that it will be sued in the case of a later accident involving its aircraft under the controversial theory of negligent entrustment (*see* section §3.11[C] *infra*).

[D] Standby Letters of Credit and Guarantees

[1] Standby Letters of Credit

A lessor will sometimes accept, in lieu of a security deposit or maintenance reserves, a standby letter of credit or bank guarantee issued by a bank acceptable[106] to it.

A standby letter of credit is a particular type of letter of credit which:

> commits the issuer to honor the credit not upon evidence of performance by the beneficiary, as by presenting evidence of shipment of goods to the customer, but

106. Credit rating and reputation of the issuing bank will be keys here.

upon evidence or a mere declaration of the customer's default in the underlying transaction with the beneficiary.[107]

There are advantages and disadvantages for both lessor and lessee in using a standby letter of credit.

The advantage to the lessee in using a letter of credit instead of a cash security deposit or maintenance reserves is that it frees up cash for the lessee. It will typically pay a fee to the issuer (dependent on its credit standing) which may be lower than the cost of foregone cash flow associated with a cash security deposit or maintenance reserves.

The disadvantage to the lessee is that, if the lessor draws on the letter of credit, it may damage the lessee's creditworthiness whereas resolution of disputes involving application by the lessor of a cash security deposit or maintenance reserves can often be resolved *inter partes* without impacting the lessee's creditworthiness.

The advantage to the lessor in accepting a letter of credit is that it is accepting the creditworthiness of the issuing bank and, as the issuing bank is a separate entity from the airline, if the airline goes bankrupt, this should not in principle affect the obligation of the bank to pay the lessor. The bank takes the risk that it may not recover the amounts paid out by it under the letter of credit from the estate of the bankrupt airline. The general rule is thus that the letter of credit is not affected by the bankruptcy of the airline, which will be the applicant to the issuing bank, but there are exceptions[108] to this general rule which can limit the usefulness of accepting a standby letter of credit in lieu of cash.

In *re Metrobility Optical Systems, Inc.*,[109] a US court held that a tenant of real estate who had secured its obligations under the lease with a letter of credit could prevent a lessor from drawing on the letter of credit where the tenant was current in rent but the bankruptcy filing itself constituted an event of default under the lease. Section 365(e)(1) of the US Bankruptcy Code invalidates such *ipso facto* clauses in executory contracts.

Wunnicke et al. discuss[110] the many exceptions to the general rule, noting in particular that courts may set aside as an indirect preferential transfer a letter of credit where the applicant for the letter of credit has provided collateral to the issuing bank as security.[111]

In addition to the risk of falling within such exceptions, another disadvantage to the lessor is that it foregoes the ability to apply the cash security deposit and maintenance deposit to enhance its cash flow, bearing in mind that a lessor will not see much advantage to having such deposits and reserves in cash if it is required to keep them in separate accounts. Further, bank creditworthiness is not what it once was and

107. *Black's Law Dictionary*, 6th Edition, 1990.
108. Wunnicke B., Wunnicke D.B. and Turner P.S., *Standby and Commercial Letters of Credit*, 3rd Edition, Wolters Kluwer, 2009, 9.04.
109. 268 B.R. 326 (D.N.H) 2001.
110. *See* footnote 108.
111. *Kellogg v. Blue Quail Energy, Inc. (In re Compton Corp.)*, 831 F.2d 586 (5th Cir. 1987).

banks may delay in accepting demands for payment even if all the paperwork is in order.

A lot depends on the facts of each case to determine whether cash or a letter of credit is better - the economics of the deal will usually dictate the outcome.

[2] Guarantees

Occasionally, a lessor may accept a bank guarantee[112] in place of a standby letter of credit but it should take care to review the language to ensure that it constitutes an indemnity and not merely a guarantee. With a guarantee, the guarantor has the same range of defences available to it as the lessee has[113] whereas with a standby letter of credit, the bank is the primary obligor and must pay upon the happening of a stated event (usually a certificate from the lessor that an event of default has occurred) and:

> [f]or this reason, a lessor will often agree to accept an LC[114] instead of a cash deposit, but may be less willing to accept a bank guarantee.[115]

While a bank guarantee may be an acceptable substitute for a standby letter of credit, which is itself a substitute for a security deposit paid in cash, depending on the credit and the corporate structure of the lessee, the lessor may also require a guarantee from the parent company of the lessee, which (unlike a standby letter of credit and a bank guarantee) is not necessarily limited in amount and should cover all obligations of the lessee under the lease and its related documents. This is, in effect, a performance guarantee. It should also contain language clarifying that it is an indemnity and not merely a guarantee so that the guarantor is the primary obligor. (If the lessor itself is a special purpose or pass-through entity, the lessee may require such a guarantee from its parent for the same reasons.)

[E] Late Payment

The lease will normally set out a default rate of interest for late payment of obligations - this interest typically accrues as soon as the payment is late, even if a default has not yet been triggered due to the presence of a grace period.[116]

The default interest rate should not be so low as to provide an attractive form of financing to the lessee, or so high as to risk being unenforceable due to its being deemed to be a penalty or to its being held to transgress any applicable usury law.

---

112. As with letters of credit, credit rating and reputation of the issuing bank will be keys here.
113. *See* Bunker D.H., *International Aircraft Financing, Volume 1: General Principles*, 2nd Edition, IATA, 2015, at 303-306 and 314.
114. Letter of credit.
115. Bunker D.H., *Securing Aircraft Financing*, Annals of Air and Space Law, Volume XXIX, 2004, 147-174, at 168.
116. *See* Bunker D.H., *International Aircraft Financing, Volume 2: Specific Documents*, 2nd Edition, IATA, 2015, at 96.

In *BAE Systems Management Service (Two) Limited & Another v. Trident Aviation Leasing Services (Jersey) Limited and AS Enimex,*[117] the English Court of Appeal upheld a decision to award interest on damages at a rate of 8% where the lease itself did not provide for interest on damages and the default interest provisions of the lease (setting default interest at 3% above the Bank of England base rate) applied only to rent and other amounts payable under the lease. The courts have a broad discretion in England to award interest on damages.

[F] Conclusions

Disputes as to payment obligations under contracts are not uncommon and aircraft operating leases are no exception. The foregoing provisions of section §3.07 do not reveal any particular provisions of public and private air law and the disputes reviewed were generally governed by the governing law of the lease.

The cases reviewed reveal a willingness by the courts to uphold contractual restrictions on a lessee's right to set off its payment obligations against claims it has against the lessor and a willingness to uphold requirements to continue to pay rent after acceptance of delivery of the aircraft despite claims as to its poor performance.

With respect to characterization of maintenance reserves and security deposits as supplemental rent and commitment fees, and to payment thereof by way of a letter of credit or bank guarantee rather than cash, these are efforts, of course, to provide protection under the governing law of the lease against the bankruptcy of the lessee, which bankruptcy will be governed by the laws of the jurisdiction of the lessee.

If the lessee goes bankrupt, its liquidator is likely to argue in court that the security deposit and/or maintenance reserves should be treated as assets of the lessee's estate. In such event, the lessor, in order to enforce the contractual provisions characterizing them as supplemental rent and/or commitment fees, respectively, will have to show that the charge was duly perfected in accordance with the provisions of the laws of the jurisdiction of the lessee.[118]

Allied to payments is always the issue of taxes thereon and on the transaction generally, which are examined briefly next.

§3.08 TAXES

A detailed examination of taxes is beyond the scope of this work but it should at least be mentioned that the standard practice is for the lessee to bear the entire tax risk relating to the transaction, and to indemnify the lessor against such risk, with the exception of those taxes for which the lessor would have been liable anyway even in the absence of the transaction in question.[119]

117. [2010] EWCA Civ 107.
118. *See* section §3.07[B][2] *supra*.
119. *See* section 5 of the Supplement *infra*.

Thus, the lessor should remain liable for taxes on its corporate income in its home jurisdiction and in any other jurisdiction in which it would have been liable even if it had not entered into the lease in question. Subject to that exception, the lessee should be liable for all other taxes to which the lessor may be liable as a result of the operation and possession of the aircraft by the lessee.

The lessee will want to make further exceptions to its indemnity obligation clear, such as that it will not be liable for any taxes arising prior to the term of the lease, or as a result of the lessor's financing arrangements with respect to the aircraft.

Typically, tax indemnities take the form of an unlimited indemnification obligation first from which exceptions are then later made.

One point which the lessor should take care never to forget is that the lessee's tax indemnity is only as good as the lessee's credit: if the tax is one which as a matter of law falls on the lessor, it is no defence to the lessor's liability at law to pay such tax that, as a contractual matter *inter partes* under the lease, the lessee is obliged to indemnify the lessor: with or without performance of such indemnity obligation by the lessee, the lessor remains liable to the tax authority as a matter of law.

As for taxes which as a matter of law the lessee should pay, the lessor should take steps to ensure they are paid, particularly where non-payment may give rise to a tax lien[120] over the aircraft. This may be a particular risk in the case of a flag carrier or other airline supported by its government where the government may well be willing to allow taxes to go uncollected from the airline but which may then intervene and impose a lien on the aircraft which the lessor must be pay if it acts to repossess the aircraft.

Having thus examined the provisions of the lease involving payments, including taxes, in respect of the aircraft, the examination turns to operational issues in respect of the aircraft itself.

§3.09 MANUFACTURER'S WARRANTIES

Typically, the airframe and engine manufacturers will grant warranties to the initial buyer of the aircraft as a means of supporting their product for an initial period following purchase.[121] The lessor, where it is the buyer, will normally be the recipient of such warranties, as are set out in the purchase agreement pursuant to which it acquires title.

Where the lessor leases the aircraft to an airline, the airline will typically want the benefit of such warranties by means of an assignment of warranties for the term of the lease so that it can, if it encounters difficulties with the aircraft, cause the manufacturer to rectify any defects covered by the warranties.[122]

The lessor may wish to retain such warranties for itself but agree with the lessee to extend the benefit of such warranties to the lessee. That is, if the lessee encounters

120. *See* section §3.10[B][2][d] *infra*.
121. *See* Bunker D.H., *International Aircraft Financing, Volume 2: Specific Documents*, 2nd Edition, IATA, 2015, at 308.
122. *See* section 6 of the Supplement *infra*.

a problem with the aircraft, it should report it to the lessor which will then make a claim under the appropriate warranty.

More often, however, both lessor and lessee agree that the lessor will assign the benefit of such warranties to the lessee so that the lessee can make a claim directly against the manufacturer during the term of the lease. In such cases, care should be taken to ensure that the lessee assigns the benefit of such warranties back to the lessor upon termination or expiration of the lease term.[123]

Invariably, the manufacturer will require that its consent be given in order to recognize such assignment. In part, this is because the manufacturer will want to ensure that the terms set out in the warranties governing assignment are observed and so that it is aware at any given time which is the party entitled to the benefit of the warranties which it has granted.

Typically, the manufacturer warranties will set out a form of warranty assignment[124] which must be used, which will involve notifying the manufacturer of the assignment and obtaining the manufacturer's consent.

In English common law, legal *choses in action*[125] were not enforceable directly by an assignee against a debtor. In time, the courts of equity allowed the assignment of equitable *choses in action.*[126] Absolute assignments of equitable *choses in action* allow an assignee to sue in its own name. Non-absolute assignments of equitable *choses in action*, as well as assignments (whether absolute or partial) of legal *choses in action*, allow an assignee to sue but require the assignor to be joined to the action.[127]

In terms of assignments in commercial transactions, such as assignments of rights under warranties (or indeed lease agreements), English statute law provided for absolute assignments of legal *choses in action* to be enforceable directly by an assignee against a debtor if the statutory provisions were met: such provisions required the assignment to be absolute (not partial), in writing and with notice to the debtor.[128]

An assignment stated to be only for the term of the lease will be a partial, not an absolute, assignment. Care should be taken that the assignment itself be absolute with a covenant for reassignment to the lessor upon expiration or termination of the lease.

Regardless of the form of the assignment of manufacturer's warranties, it should be noted that the Cape Town Convention and Aircraft Protocol, while they do provide for registration of interests in respect of assignments, only do so in respect of assignments related to an 'international interest'.[129] As an 'international interest' is defined[130] as one granted under a security agreement, title reservation agreement,

123. Upon such termination or expiration, the lessor should also require that the lessee assign to it the benefit of any warranties which the lessee has obtained from parties carrying out maintenance and repair work on the aircraft during the term of the lease.
124. Also, *see* discussion on assignment in section §3.16 *infra*.
125. Such as enforcement of a debt claim.
126. Such as seeking an injunction or an order for specific performance.
127. Furmston, *supra*, at 455 et seq.
128. First introduced into England by section 25(6) of the Judicature Act 1873 as initially replaced by section 136 of the Law of Real Property Act 1925.
129. Article 1(b) of the Cape Town Convention (2001).
130. Article 2 of the Cape Town Convention (2001) and Art. III of the Aircraft Protocol.

leasing agreement, or contract of sale, one can see that assignments of manufacturer's warranties fall outside the scope of the Cape Town Convention.[131]

A lessee should inquire as to whether, under the terms of its purchase agreement, the lessor also has a right to certain training support from the manufacturer from which, as a non-operator, the lessor cannot benefit. The lessor should have no reason not to pass on the benefit of such training to the lessee.

The lessee, in turn, will owe certain covenants to the lessor in respect of the operation of the aircraft in its possession, and these will next be examined.

§3.10 COVENANTS

[A] Lessor's Covenants

The lessor's covenants in favour of the lessee are limited in number, but important in kind – quiet enjoyment of the aircraft by the lessee for the term (while it is meeting its obligations) and, where and as appropriate, reimbursement from maintenance reserves (and payment of any other contractually agreed maintenance or other contributions).[132]

[1] Quiet Enjoyment

The lessor typically grants the lessee a covenant of quiet enjoyment on its own behalf and on behalf of anyone claiming through it, in the absence of a default on the part of the lessee under the lease.[133] Thus, for example, a lessee will want the ability to sue the lessor for breach of covenant in the event that, despite adhering to its obligations under the lease, it is dispossessed of possession of the aircraft during the lease term due, for example, to repossession of the aircraft by a secured creditor of the lessor.

Typically, the lessee will seek a letter granting quiet enjoyment in similar terms from secured lenders of the lessor but, for example, it will have to take the credit risk of the lessor in respect of certain other creditors of the lessor, such as Eurocontrol.[134]

Where the Cape Town Convention applies,[135] even in the absence of such a covenant on the part of the lessor, and so long as it has not otherwise agreed in the lease,[136] the lessee shall, in the absence of a default within the meaning of Article 11 of the Cape Town Convention, be entitled to quiet possession and use of the aircraft in

131. Unlike assignments of the lessor's interest in the leasing agreement, which, accordingly, may be registrable under the Cape Town Convention (2001). *See* section §3.16 *infra*.
132. *See* section 7 of the Supplement *infra*.
133. *See*, for example, Bunker D.H., *International Aircraft Financing, Volume 2: Specific Documents*, 2nd Edition, IATA, 2015, at 75–76.
134. *See* section §3.10[B][2][b] *infra*.
135. *See* Chapter 2 section §2.05 *supra*.
136. Express subordination clauses are sometimes seen in leases, especially where a lessee airline subleases to an affiliate – the alternative approach being to grant quiet enjoyment but also for the owner to be granted an assignment of the lessee's airline's rights as sub-lessor under the sublease as security for performance of its obligations under the head lease.

accordance with the lease agreement as against the lessor.[137] However, this is so only so long as the lease in which it is contained remains registered as an international interest under the Convention:[138] that can be deregistered at any time by the lessor although the lessor would be most unlikely to have any motivation to do so while the aircraft remains on lease to the lessee thereunder.

A classic example of the type of situation which may constitute a breach of lessor's covenant of quiet enjoyment to the lessee in the lease may be where a leased aircraft is detained due to no fault of the lessee but due to the existence of sanctions against the lessor – for example, *see* the European Court of Human Rights case of *Bosphorus Airways v. Ireland,*[139] discussed further in section §3.10[B][2][c] *infra,* or due to the exercise of an in rem right over the aircraft, such as by Eurocontrol, discussed further in section §3.10[B][2][b] *infra.*

[2] Reimbursement from Reserves and Other Payments

Where the lessee pays maintenance reserves,[140] howsoever described, the lessor should, so long as there is no default on the part of lessee, agree to pay the lessee for the cost of scheduled maintenance work from (or calculated by reference to) those reserves. The lessor will normally want to ensure that the work has been satisfactorily performed and paid for before so doing but lessees may request the lessor to pay the maintenance performer directly.[141] These matters are negotiable.

Likewise, depending on the commercial terms agreed between the party, which should be identified in the letter of intent,[142] if the lessor will make an additional contribution for the first covered maintenance event during the lease term (to reflect that part of the period between that and the previous such event would predate possession of the aircraft by the lessee) or if the lessor will make a contribution towards the cost to the lessee of complying with airworthiness directives which will benefit the lessor after the end of the lease term, these should likewise be set out here.[143]

The obligation to return the security deposit[144] at the end of the lease term, assuming there is no default, may be set out here, or, depending on the drafting of the lease in question, in the provisions dealing with payments or return of the aircraft.

137. Article XVI(1) of the Aircraft Protocol.
138. Legal Advisory Panel of the Aviation Working Group, *Practitioner's Handbook to the Cape Town Convention and Aircraft Protocol,* Cape Town Paper Series, Volume 3, UNIDROIT, 2010, at 59.
139. Grand Chamber Judgment of the European Court of Human Rights, 362, 30 Jun. 2005.
140. *See* section §3.07[C] *supra.*
141. *See* Bunker D.H., *International Aircraft Financing, Volume 2: Specific Documents,* 2nd Edition, IATA, 2005, at 114–116 and 126–129.
142. *See* Chapter 2 section §2.03 *supra.*
143. *See* IBA Article, *Have operating lease agreements evolved with the industry?,* 26 Feb. 2020, at www.iba.aero/insight/have-operating-lease-agreements-evolved-with-the-industry-february-2020/ on 9 Sep. 2021.
144. *See* section §3.07[B] *supra.*

[B] Lessee's Covenants

The lessee's covenants are much more extensive than those of the lessor[145] – to maintain the aircraft as required by the lease, not to part with possession except as agreed, swapping of engines, registration, etc. are all areas which typically take up the bulk of a lease negotiation, especially for non-lawyers. Typical operational covenants by the lessee are set out at Annex 9.

[1] Maintenance

The airline will be required by the laws of its jurisdiction to maintain the aircraft or to cause the aircraft to be maintained in accordance with the requirements of the aviation authority of that jurisdiction.

Under Article 31 of the Chicago Convention (1944), every aircraft engaged in international navigation must have a certificate of airworthiness issued or rendered valid by its State of registration. Annex 6 to Chicago Convention dealing with operation of aircraft, sets out standards and recommended practices (SARPs) in respect of airworthiness of aircraft. The essence of Annex 6, according to ICAO, is that 'the operation of aircraft engaged in international air transport must be as standardized as possible to ensure the highest levels of safety and efficiency', recognizing that the SARPs are 'operating minima' which 'do not preclude the development of national standards which may be more stringent than those contained in the Annex'.[146]

Under Article 37 of the Chicago Convention (1944), ICAO shall 'adopt and amend from time to time, as may be necessary', SARPs.[147] This allows for the operating minima provided for in to be kept up to date. Under Article 38 thereof, a state 'which finds it impracticable to comply' with SARPs must give notice thereof to ICAO, and any failure to comply therewith must be endorsed on the relevant licence or certificate.[148]

Under Article 40 of the Chicago Convention (1944):

> No aircraft or personnel having certificates or licenses so endorsed shall participate in international navigation, except with the permission of the State or States whose territory is entered.

In the US, under section 44713 (Inspection and Maintenance) of Chapter 447 (Safety Regulation) of Subtitle VII (Aviation Programs) of the Title 49 (Transportation) of the US Code, maintenance is clearly the obligation of the airline:

> An air carrier shall make, or cause to be made, any inspection, repair, or maintenance of equipment used in air transportation as required by this part or regulations prescribed or orders issued by the Administrator of the Federal Aviation Administration under this part.

---

145. *See* section 8 of the Supplement *infra*.
146. http://www.icao.int/safety/airnavigation/NationalityMarks/annexes_booklet_en.pdf on 9 Sep. 2021.
147. *See* Huang J., *Aviation Safety and ICAO*, PhD Thesis, Leiden University, 2008.
148. Article 39 of the Chicago Convention (1944).

The key phrase here is 'cause to be made'. If the airline is not itself licensed to perform the required maintenance, it should contract with a licensed performer. Section 43.3 (Persons authorized to perform maintenance, preventive maintenance, rebuilding and alterations) of Part 43 (Maintenance, Preventive Maintenance, Rebuilding and Alteration) of Chapter I (Federal Aviation Administration, Department of Transportation) of Title 124 (Aeronautics and Space) of the Code of Federal Regulations set out the requirements for licensing in the US.

In the EU, the European Aviation Safety Agency oversees aircraft maintenance pursuant to Council Regulation (EC) 216/2008, Part M whereof deals with Continuing Airworthiness[149] and Part 145 whereof deals with maintenance organizations' approvals.

The lessor does not operate the aircraft itself: further, under the lease, the lessee has exclusive possession and control of the aircraft for the term of the lease. The lessor thus requires the lessee to be responsible for maintenance under the terms of the lease.[150]

It follows that, if the airline itself does not possess the requisite approvals to perform required maintenance, it must contract with a Maintenance, Repair and Overhaul (MRO) organization that does. The lease itself as a contractual matter may require the airline as lessee only to use a licensed and approved MRO and may provide further that the identity of the MRO is, in addition, subject to its approval.

Further, a lessor will typically also require in the lease a higher standard of maintenance than the legal minimum required pursuant to applicable law, in order to preserve the value of its asset, and also, as a contractual matter, may also require compliance with any stricter requirements of the US FAA or the European Aviation Safety Agency (EASA) than those of the state of registration. In particular, the lease may have restrictions on the age and status of components installed on the aircraft and contractual requirements as to the timing of compliance with airworthiness directives and manufacturer's service bulletins.[151]

This is partly because these are considered to be strict and should enhance the value of the aircraft but also because, at the time of signing the lease, the lessor probably does not know to which jurisdiction the aircraft will be next leased, and so wishes to maximize its chances that the aircraft will be acceptable to the aviation authority of the follow-on lessee.

The lessor needs to ensure that other provisions of the lease do not unintentionally cut across this requirement. For example, although it was an interlocutory hearing rather than a full trial, the English Court of Appeal refused in *Air Mauritius v. Caribjet Inc.*[152] for technical reasons leave to appeal by an airline where the lessor terminated the lease by reason of the airline's repeated failure to maintain the aircraft in an airworthy and safe condition as required by the lease. The airline had sought to avail

149. *See* Arts 3 and 4 thereof.
150. Bunker D.H., *International Aircraft Financing, Volume 2: Specific Documents*, 2nd Edition, IATA, 2015, at 110 et seq.
151. *See* Bunker, *supra*, at 110–125, 163–167, and 200–201.
152. Royal Courts of Justice, 18 Sep. 2007.

of a force majeure clause in the lease to relieve it of liability resulting, *inter alia*, from the unserviceability of the aircraft owing to unscheduled failure.

[2] Liens

The lessee will generally not be allowed to place the aircraft in a position where liens are imposed on the aircraft. Clearly, some exceptions to this are needed: permitted liens should include liens created by or through the lessor itself since this is within the lessor's, not the lessee's control. Likewise, some liens arise by operation of law or will be insisted on contractually by third parties providing maintenance services on the aircraft. The principal liens of concern in the context of aircraft operating leasing will be examined here.

Liens are naturally a major concern for lessor since they give rise to an in rem right to seize the aircraft and possibly to sell it:[153] this is not something covered by the insurances on the aircraft, so an aircraft lessor could lose its aircraft, without compensation, upon enforcement of a lien. Of course, if it was not a lien permitted under the lease, the lessor has a contractual right to sue the lessee but this is an in personam right which is likely to be of cold comfort since, having already suffered enforcement of a lien, it is likely that in such a situation the lessee will not have sufficient assets to pay on such a claim.

In addition to requiring the lessee not to allow unpermitted liens on the aircraft, the lessor should require the lessee to covenant only to use the aircraft lawfully.[154] Although it may be able to assert an 'innocent owner defence' if it can establish that it took 'all reasonable precautions to prevent illegal use of the aircraft',[155] a lessor may be subject to having its aircraft seized and declared a forfeit[156] if the lessee uses it for an illegal purpose such as drug running. Inclusion of a covenant will not likely deter a lessee who is willing to engage in criminal activity, and Bunker wisely advises lessor to be 'on guard against placing aircraft in the control of operators of questionable character'.[157]

[a] Mechanics' Liens

A mechanic's lien is 'a claim … for the purpose of securing priority of payment of the price or value of work performed and materials furnished'[158] and may, for these purposes, be treated as being essentially synonymous with an artisan's lien. An artisan's lien is:

---

153. *See*, e.g., section §3.10[B][2] *supra*.
154. *See* Annex 9 *infra*.
155. Bunker D.H., *Aircraft Financing and Drugs*, Annals of Air and Space Law, Volume XVI, 1991, at 37.
156. Under, e.g., section 141 of the English Customs and Excise Management Act 1979.
157. *Ibid.*, at 39.
158. Nolan J.R. and Nolan-Haley J.M., *Black's Law Dictionary*, 6th Edition, West Publishing co., 1990.

> a possessory lien given to a person who has made improvements and added value to another person's personal property as security for payment of the services performed.[159]

and may further be defined as being the:

> statutory right of an artisan to keep possession of the object that he has worked on until he has been paid for such labor.[160]

As the airline is responsible for maintenance of the aircraft while it is in the airline's possession, the airline may, if it is qualified to do so and permitted to do so under the lease, perform the maintenance itself or, if not, it may arrange for a qualified MRO organization to perform such maintenance work.[161] Lessors will typically require that such MROs be approved by it.

The MRO will generally have a mechanics' lien in respect of work undertaken by it in the event that it is not paid - simply put, it typically is not required to release the aircraft or aircraft engine or other part until it has been paid. Such mechanics' lien arises under applicable local statutory law and may differ in its details by jurisdiction.

Mindful of the need for the aircraft to be properly maintained, leases typically provide that, although the airline is generally forbidden from allowing liens to arise over the aircraft to arise, exceptions are made for 'permitted liens' which include mechanics' liens.

Great care must be taken with regard to the drafting of language in the lease dealing with permitted liens.

For example, if a lessee submits an aircraft engine to an MRO for maintenance, it may do so under the terms of a General Terms Agreement (GTA) between the airline and the MRO. Such GTA may provide for a contractual lien going beyond that provided for by the mechanics' lien which arises by operation of law. The MRO may provide, for example, in the GTA, that it shall have a lien over the engine until all sums due to it by the airline have been paid in full, whether or not relating to the engine in question.

The problem for the lessor is that, if the airline goes into bankruptcy or is otherwise unable or unwilling to pay the MRO, while the lessor understands that it will have to pay the MRO in respect of its engine, it will not want to have to pay the MRO for bills unpaid by the airline to the MRO which do not relate to its engine.

Such bills may relate to engines owned by the airline itself or by other lessors in respect of which the MRO cannot assert a lien since they are no longer in its possession. Thus, the MRO may try to assert, relying on the contractual language of the GTA, a lien over the lessor's engine in its possession covering the entire indebtedness of the airline.

Good local legal advice is crucial here. For example, depending on the jurisdiction, the MRO may only have a detention right without a sale right or it may have both or even neither. Generally speaking, it is advisable to put the MRO on notice early on, even before any dispute arises, that the engine belongs to the lessor and not to the airline. This may be sufficient to disapply the contractual lien provisions of the GTA

---

159. *Ibid.*
160. *Ibid.*
161. *See* section §3.10[B][1] *supra.*

(since the lessor is not a party to it) to the extent that they go beyond the statutory mechanics' lien.

Further, as the lessor is not a party to the GTA and thus not bound by its terms, the MRO may, depending on the jurisdiction, only be entitled to the value added by it to the engine in question – thus, it may not be entitled to seek the profit element of the contract price set out in the GTA. Of course, its ability to seek payment for other engines and for the profit element in respect of the engine in question is not extinguished, but it has only an unsecured claim for this against the airline (which may not be very valuable if the airline is in bankruptcy) and at least, in being reimbursed its cost in adding value to the engine in question, should not incur a loss in respect of that engine in having to release the engine to the lessor.

Naturally, this becomes a matter of discussion between the lessor and the MRO. Generally, the MRO will initially assert the widest lien possible, with the lessor advising it of the correct limits of such lien as against a non-contractual owner, having obtained local legal advice.

It is not unusual for the MRO then to point out that its contract is with the airline, not the lessor, and thus even if it releases the engine, it should release it back to the airline, not to the lessor, in the absence of proof of termination of the lease or a court order. In practice, however, these scenarios are provoked by the collapse of the airline and thus a pragmatic solution is found.

Taking the example of an aircraft engine MRO based in Germany, in a situation where German law applies, the mechanics' lien (*Werkunternehmerpfandrecht*) provided for pursuant to section 647 of the German Civil Code (*Bürgerliches Gesetzbuch* or *BGB*) only arises with respect to claims under a GTA or other contract between the MRO and the owner of the engine. Section 647 BGB provides:

> For its claims under the contract, the workman acquires a lien over the movable assets of the customer that he has produced or repaired if they have come into its possession during the production or for the purpose of repair.

The mechanics' lien pursuant to section 647 BGB lapses after return of the asset by the MRO to its contractual partner. The important point here, however, is that, where the airline, as a lessee, delivers an aircraft engine to a German MRO pursuant to its GTA with the MRO, the engines are not 'assets of the customer' but assets of the customer's lessor.

The German Federal Court of Justice (*Bundesgerichtshof*) has held that where an MRO performs work with respect to an asset that is not owned by the customer a bona fide acquisition of a workman's lien is thus precluded under German law. However, Dr Dirk Schmalenbach of Freshfields in Germany has advised that this position is disputed in legal literature and thus strongly recommends notification by a lessor to the MRO to the effect that the engine in question is owned by the lessor and only leased to the MRO's customer, thereby eliminating the risk that the MRO could argue to have acted in good faith and justifiably believed that the lessee was the owner of the engine when the engine came into the MRO's possession.[162]

Schmalenbach has pointed out that, while pursuant to the foregoing it is unlikely that the MRO would have a lien in such a situation (which would allow the MRO to seek the forced sale of the engine at auction[163] to cover unpaid fees) the MRO may assert a retention right (*Zurückbehaltungsrecht*) pursuant to section 1000 BGB against both the lessor and the airline with respect to the engine if the airline does not pay for the maintenance work undertaken by the MRO with respect to that engine. Section 1000 BGB provides:

> The possessor may refuse the return of the asset until he is reimbursed the outlays due to him. He is not entitled to the right of retention if he obtained the asset by an intentionally committed tort.

According to Schmalenbach, the retention right pursuant to section 1000 applies only to outlays with respect to the engine in question, not other amounts. Thus, the retention right does not entitle the MRO to refuse to return the engine until it has been reimbursed for amounts owed by the lessee for work on unrelated property.

An interesting point of law arose in an interim judgment of the Scottish courts in *Wilmington Trust Company, Orix Aviation Systems Limited v. Rolls Royce PLC, IAE International Aero Engines PLC*[164] where the lessor argued that IAE as MRO did not have possession of aircraft engines sufficient to claim a lien for work unpaid by the lessee, Mexicana, as the MRO had entered into a subcontract with Rolls Royce and had passed possession of the engines to Rolls Royce. The court held that as Rolls Royce held the engines to the order of IAE, IAE still had civil possession sufficient to assert a lien.

Particularly in situations where the MRO only has a detention right, and not a sale right, which covers only amounts due on the engine, both lessor and MRO will be motivated to reach a commercial agreement. The lessor will want its engine back and the MRO will want to receive at least some payment and to free up storage space. Typically, then, the resolution will be found within the range of the value added to that engine and the contractual price agreed in the GTA between the airline and the MRO with respect to that engine.

[b] Eurocontrol and Similar Liens

Eurocontrol[165] was established by the Eurocontrol Convention[166] which came into force on 1 March 1963. The Eurocontrol Convention established Eurocontrol as having

162. Electronic mail correspondence between Dr Schmalenbach and the author between 1 and 4 May 2009.
163. McBain G., *Aircraft Liens & Detention Rights*, General Editor, Sweet & Maxwell, 2007, Chapter on Germany, section 1.1.
164. [2010] CSOH 157.
165. The European Organisation for the Safety of Air Navigation.
166. The Eurocontrol International Convention relating to Cooperation for the Safety of Air Navigation signed in Brussels on 13 Dec. 1960.

international legal personality with the intention of creating a single European upper airspace. Eurocontrol at the time of writing has forty-one members.[167]

Eurocontrol describes its role as being to help its members to 'run safe, efficient and environmentally-friendly air traffic operations throughout the European region'[168] and describes itself as working with its partners 'to deliver a Single European Sky that will help overcome the safety, capacity and performance challenges facing European aviation in the 21st century'.[169]

Indeed, Eurocontrol is active in all areas of air traffic management safety, safety research, planning, management, operations, and regulation.

In November 1971, Eurocontrol introduced a route charges system. It set up the Central Route Charges Office (CRCO) which collects charges for flights on behalf of Eurocontrol members, the amount of the charges varying based on the distance flown and the weight of the aircraft. The proceeds are used to finance the safety activities of Eurocontrol. Such services are also offered to non-members by way of a bilateral agreement.

One of the controversial aspects of CRCO's powers has been its reliance on broad powers of the United Kingdom Civil Aviation Authority to act on its behalf with respect to unpaid charges. Under Regulation 11 of the United Kingdom Civil Aviation (Navigation Services Charges) Regulations 2000, where there is a default in payment of charges due thereunder, which includes charges due to Eurocontrol, the United Kingdom Civil Aviation Authority may detain:

(a) the aircraft in respect of which the charges were incurred (whether or not they were incurred by the person who is the operator of the aircraft at the time the detention begins); or
(b) any other aircraft of which the person in default is the operator at the time when the detention begins.

There are several points to note here. Under Regulation 11, no court order is needed but a court order for sale is required under Regulation 13. Further, the effect of this combined right of detention and sale is to provide an in rem lien over the aircraft. The operator, being the airline, remains liable in personam for the debt, but the owner is not liable in personam.

If the aircraft is detained while in the possession of the operator, the aircraft may be sold to cover the entire fleet debt of the operator to Eurocontrol, not just the debt on that aircraft, even though the operator does not own the aircraft.

If the owner has recovered possession of the aircraft from the operator prior to enforcement by Eurocontrol of its lien, then the lien may be enforced in respect of all debt on that aircraft to Eurocontrol, regardless of by whomsoever incurred.

The potential effect of this on a non-operator is apparent – it may easily stand to have nothing left after its aircraft is sold pursuant to exercise of this lien.

167. http://www.eurocontrol.int/about-us on 9 Sep. 2021.
168. http://www.eurocontrol.int/what-we-do on 9 Sep. 2021.
169. *Ibid.*

This scheme has been the subject of legal challenges on the grounds that it exceeds Eurocontrol's powers under the Eurocontrol Convention and breaches the human rights of aircraft owners (where the debts are incurred by their lessees) under the European Convention on Human Rights[170] (ECHR). Article 1 of the First Protocol[171] to the ECHR provides:

> Every natural or legal person is entitled to the peaceful enjoyment of his possessions. No one shall be deprived of his possessions except in the public interest and subject to the conditions provided for by law and by the general principles of international law.
>
> The preceding provisions shall not, however, in any way impair the right of a State to enforce such laws as it deems necessary to control the use of property in accordance with the general interest or to secure the payment of taxes or other contributions or penalties.

It is the view of the AWG, which represents major aircraft and engine manufacturers and lessors that:

> AWG submits that the exercise of powers of Fleet Lien is disproportionate, does not strike a fair balance between the general interest and the fundamental rights of property rights holders and places an individual and excessive burden on the latter.[172]

MacCarthy[173] has described this power as 'oppressive and arbitrary'.

The situation is different in other countries covered by Eurocontrol and the AWG has complained of this lack of common policy.[174] For example, it points out[175] that in *Société Outremer Finance Limited*,[176] the highest administrative court in France held that a right of detention came to an end upon termination of the lease and is unenforceable against a non-operator owner of the aircraft. Likewise, it points out[177] that, under Dutch law, a court order allowing detention and sale of an aircraft may only be granted where the debtor is the owner of the aircraft.[178]

Nevertheless, a challenge, arising out of the bankruptcy of Zoom Airlines Incorporated, to the fleet lien of Eurocontrol on the grounds that it breached Article 1 of the First Protocol to the ECHR failed in the English Court of Appeal in *Global Knafaim*

170. Convention for the Protection of Human Rights and Fundamental Freedoms signed at Rome on 4 Nov. 1950.
171. Done at Paris on 20 Mar. 1952.
172. Submissions to the English High Court, Queen's Bench Division Administrative Court, on behalf of the Aviation Working Group in *CGTSN Limited and Global Knafaim Leasing limited v. The Civil Aviation Authority and BAA Limited*, Case No. CO/12012/2008.
173. MacCarthy R.J., *The Problem of Unpaid Eurocontrol Charges*, in Butler G.F. and Keller M.R., executive editors, *Handbook of Airline Finance*, 1st Edition, Aviation Week:McGraw-Hill, 1999, at 400.
174. *Supra*, at 11.
175. *Ibid.*, at 12.
176. *Counseil d'Etat*, 2 juillet 2003, No. 254536.
177. *Ibid.*
178. Section 5/20 of the Dutch Act of Air Navigation (*Wet luchtvaart*) and Art. 276 of Book 3 of the Dutch Civil Code (*Burgerlijk Wetboek*).

Leasing Ltd and another *v. Civil Aviation Authority and others*,[179] despite Collins J expressing some sympathy for the lessor's case that the fleet lien under English law is unfair. He held that, since the power to exercise the fleet lien was discretionary, not mandatory, it could not be said that its exercise was disproportionate without examining the given fact of a case.[180]

Collins J cited[181] as authority the case of *Air Canada v. UK*,[182] where the European Court of Human Rights upheld as consistent with Article 1 of the First Protocol to ECHR the seizure of an aircraft when cannabis resin was found on board and its release only upon payment by the airline of a large fine. As with the Eurocontrol fleet lien, there is detention but no transfer of title. Of course, the power of sale pursuant to the Eurocontrol fleet lien goes further.

Collins J rejected an argument that the fleet lien breached Article 1(2) of the Geneva Convention (1948)[183] whereby contracting states undertook not to admit or recognize any right as taking priority over property and other rights recognized in Article 1(1) thereof, holding that it did not restrict seizure of property for unpaid taxes and the like but rather was aimed at restricting priority of other private rights.[184]

In relation to the Cape Town Convention (2001), Collins J noted[185] that Article 39(1) allows contracting states to declare categories of non-consensual rights and interests having priority over international interests registered and thus protected thereunder and to declare that nothing therein shall affect its right or that of an:

> intergovernmental organisation or other private provider of public services to arrest or detain an object under the laws of that State for payment of amounts owed to such entity, organisation or provider directly relating to those services in respect of that object or another object.

The Eurocontrol Convention (1960) was extensively revised pursuant to a Protocol thereto signed on 27 June 1997.[186] It has not yet come into force as it has been ratified by most but not yet quite all of the requisite number of states.

By its own admission, disagreement among the Member States has slowed down ratification. It is the understanding of this author that one of the areas of disagreement had been the concern of certain members as to revisions to the provisions on charges but it appears that these have been mostly overcome now as the Protocol is only a few ratifications short of coming into effect.

Aware of the legal challenges to the in rem debt system referred to above, the Protocol proposes to extend the United Kingdom system throughout the territory of all

179. [2010] EWHC 1348 (Admin).
180. At 25.
181. At 47.
182. (1995) 20 EHRR 150.
183. Convention on the International Recognition of Rights in Aircraft, signed at Geneva on 19 Jun. 1948.
184. At 20.
185. At 21.
186. For a discussion of the Protocol, *see* Van Antwerpen N., *Cross-Border Provision of Air Navigation Services with Specific Reference to Europe: Safeguarding Transparent Lines of Responsibility and Liability*. PhD Thesis, Leiden University, 2007, at 48 et seq.

Member States,[187] subject only to the proviso that local law should so permit, and for the first time provides that owners should have also have in personam liability for the unpaid route charges of their lessees.[188]

The only realistic tool which the lessor has at present to manage this risk is to obtain the Eurocontrol letter discussed above in section §3.05[B][8] *supra* and to have a system in place for regularly checking the status of the lessee's account with Eurocontrol.

Although the Eurocontrol lien is unusually broad in its scope, other similar liens may exist of which lessor should be aware, such as unpaid airport charges or navigation charges outside the Eurocontrol area.

An interesting Canadian case, like *Global Knafaim Leasing* arising in the aftermath of the collapse of Zoom Airlines Incorporated, is *Calgary Airport Authority v. AerCap Group Services Inc.*,[189] which came before the Alberta Court of Appeal. In that case, the relevant legislation[190] allowed for the seizure and detention of aircraft for unpaid landing and airport charges, etc., owed by the owner or operator of the aircraft.

In this case, the airport authority obtained a seizure and detention order not knowing that the lessor had already taken possession of the aircraft. A few minutes after such order was obtained, the lessor notified the aviation authority of the lease termination and had the aircraft registered in the name of its nominee. The airline was not in possession of the aircraft when the airport authority sought to enforce its order. Accordingly, the lessor was held not to be liable for the debts of the airline as the airline was not then the owner or operator of the aircraft, notwithstanding that the owner had not yet been changed on the aircraft register of the aviation authority.

The court denied that this would lead to a 'race to repossess the aircraft'[191] but the fact is that there is always a race in such a situation.

Indeed, in the related case of *Calgary Airport Authority and Others v. Zoom Airlines Incorporated,*[192] Kent J of the Alberta Queen's Bench, held that where the lessor had repossessed the aircraft prior to the court order allowing seizure of the aircraft, the aircraft should be released. In this, he expressly followed the Supreme Court of Canada's (SCC's) decision in *Canada 3000 Inc.; Re: Inter-Canadian (1991) Inc. (Trustee of)*,[193] where the court excepted from detention aircraft already repossessed by the titleholder.

In *Canada 3000 Inc.*, Binnie J made the observation, cited with approval by Collins J in *Global Knafaim Leasing Ltd*,[194] that:

> [i]t is difficult to endorse the indignation of the legal titleholders with respect to detention of their aircraft until payment is made for debts due to the service

187. Article 5(1) of Annex IV to the Protocol.
188. Article 5(4) of Annex IV to the Protocol.
189. 2009 ABCA 306.
190. Airport Transfer (Miscellaneous Matters) Act, S.C. 1992, c. 5, section 9.
191. *Calgary Airport Authority, supra,* at para. 37.
192. Unreported, Court of Queen's Bench of Alberta, Judicial District of Calgary, Case No. 0801-10295, 5 Sep. 2008.
193. 2006 SCC 24 (CanLII).
194. At 42.

> providers. They are sophisticated corporate players well versed in the industry in which they have chosen to invest. The detention remedies do not affect their ultimate title. Investors who have done their due diligence will recognise that detention remedies have deep roots in the transport business ... As long as the aircraft is owned or operated by a person liable to pay the outstanding charges, it may be the subject of an application to seize and detain it. The fact that there may be other persons, who are not liable to pay the outstanding charges but have property interests in the aircraft, is of no consequence.[195]

Binnie J cited as evidence of such deep roots of detention rights in the transport business the 1905 case of *The Emilie Millon*[196] where the English Court of Appeal upheld the power of the Mersey Docks and Harbour Board to detain a ship owned by one party for harbour and tonnage payments incurred in respect thereof by the operator, a different party.

Thus, clearly, in Canada and in the United Kingdom, the lessor is motivated to repossess the aircraft before a court order is issued in favour of third-party creditors of the lessee allowing seizure of its aircraft.

[c] Emissions Lien

Pursuant to Council Directive 2008/101/EC, the EU has amended Council Directive 2003/87/EC (the 'EU ETS Directive') so as to include aviation activities in the scheme for greenhouse gas emission allowance trading within the EU.[197] In 2014, Regulation (EU) 421/2014[198] effectively limited this to flights within the European Economic Area (EEA) by providing that, to:

> facilitate progress at the upcoming 39th Session [of the ICAO Assembly] in 2016, it is desirable to temporarily consider the requirements set out in Directive 2003/87/EC of the European Parliament and of the Council to be satisfied for the period until 31 December 2016 in respect of flights to and from aerodromes in countries outside the European Economic Area (EEA).[199]

195. At 71–74.
196. [1905] 2 K.B. 817.
197. For a detailed examination, *see* Piera A., *Greenhouse Gas Emissions from International Aviation: Legal and Policy Challenges*, Eleven International Publishing, 2015, at 34–35 and 119–252.
198. Regulation (EU) 421/2014 of the European Parliament and of the Council of 16 Apr. 2014 amending Directive 2003/87/EC establishing a scheme for greenhouse gas emission allowance trading within the Community, in view of the implementation by 2020 of an international agreement applying a single global market-based measure to international aviation emissions.
199. Pursuant to Art. 28(a)(8) of the EU ETS Directive, as inserted by Art. 1(1) of Regulation (EU) 421/2014, following 'the 2016 ICAO Assembly, the Commission shall report to the European Parliament and to the Council on actions to implement an international agreement on a global market-based measure from 2020, that will reduce greenhouse gas emissions from aviation in a non-discriminatory manner'. That ICAO Assembly, which took place in October 2016, resulted in agreement on growth in aviation carbon emissions after 2020 – *see* http://www.atag.org/our-news/press-releases.html?view = pressrelease&id = 97 on 9 Sep. 2021.

There have been proposed in the various Member States that a regulator may, in respect of breaches of the EU ETS Directive, exercise a fleet lien in respect of aircraft in a manner similar to the Eurocontrol right discussed *supra*.

In such event, the appropriate regulator would have, in addition to having the power to ban aircraft operators which failed to do so, the right to detain and sell any and all aircraft that are operated by an operator (regardless of whether or not it owns such aircraft) which has failed to pay civil penalties imposed on it for failing to submit an emissions plan or failure to report as to emissions or to provide requested information as set out in the proposal.

AWG contends that any enforcement of environmental legislation should not be taken:

> against parties that do not produce the environmental impacts (such as owners that do not operate aircraft) or the property of such parties (such as through liens on aircraft owned by a non-operating party).[200]

It is difficult at this stage to determine the effect, if any, on any such new lien right of the case of *Bosphorus Airways v. Ireland.*[201] In that case, pursuant to EC Council Regulation 990/93 imposing sanctions on Yugoslavia, the Irish government seized an aircraft which was leased by a Yugoslav owner to a Turkish airline and which had been sent by the airline to an Irish MRO for maintenance.[202] The airline claimed this was a breach of discretion by the Irish government under Article 1 of ECHR. The court held, however, that it was not, given that the Irish government had no discretion in the matter, being obliged to impound any aircraft to which Article 8 of Regulation (EC) 990/93 applied. The court held that there was a presumption that the EU *régime* offered equivalent protection to the one that State parties should offer under the ECHR, and that, as the protection of the airline's rights was not manifestly deficient, the presumption that ECHR had been complied with was not rebutted.

Perhaps not surprisingly, there has already been legislative action in the United Kingdom[203] whereby regulations extend the sale and detention rights to the case of emissions breaches by aircraft operators. Even bearing in mind that the United Kingdom has particular restrictions in setting aside legislation under British law as discussed in section §3.10[B][2][b] *supra*, it is still surprising that this new lien right was passed without some amendment to take account of the fact of leased aircraft (as opposed to aircraft owned by the operator) due to the likelihood that it would breach the ECHR.[204]

200. http://www.awg.aero/wp-content/uploads/2019/09/AWG_Statement-of-Principles_CLEAN-DOC-2.pdf on 9 Sep. 2021.
201. Grand Chamber Judgment of the European Court of Human Rights, 362, 30 Jun. 2005.
202. *See* section §3.10[B][1] *supra*.
203. Aviation Greenhouse Gas Emissions Trading Scheme Regulations 2010 (SI 2010/1996), as amended by Aviation Greenhouse Gas Emissions Trading Scheme (Amendment) Regulations 2011 (SI 2011/765).
204. Notwithstanding the English judgment in *Global Knafaim* discussed in section §3.10[B][2][b] *supra*.

Under these United Kingdom regulations, where an operator has not paid a penalty incurred by it for breach thereof within six months, or where it has had an operating ban imposed on it under Article 16(1) of the EU ETS Directive, the regulator may detain and then sell the aircraft[205] with the leave of the court.[206] Upon a sale of the aircraft, the proceeds are to be paid by first paying any customs dues, then, in order, expenses of the regulator, airport charges in respect of the sold aircraft, the unpaid penalties in respect of which the aircraft was detained, and any other unpaid penalties of the aircraft operator.[207]

Having done all that, the regulator must pay any residue left over from the proceeds of sale to 'the person or persons whose interests have been divested by reason of the sale',[208] which, in the case of a leased aircraft will be the lessor (or other owner)[209] or, in the case of an owned aircraft, will be the aircraft operator.

A court case has already been brought in English High Court (Administrative Court) challenging the EU ETS Directive. In *The Queen on the application of Air Transport Association of America, Inc., and Others v. The Secretary of State for Energy and Climate Change*,[210] the plaintiffs alleged that it violates, *inter alia*, Articles 1,[211] 15,[212] and 24[213] of the Chicago Convention (1944), Articles 3(4)[214] and 11(2)(c)[215] of the EU-US Open Skies Agreement,[216] and Article 2(2)[217] of the Kyoto Protocol.[218] The English High Court referred the case to the Court of Justice of the EU[219] for a preliminary ruling. Bartlik[220] has expressed 'serious doubts'[221] as to whether 'some regulations contained in the Emissions Directive are compatible with the Chicago Convention'[222] but the Court of Justice of the EU upheld the directive on the grounds

205. Regulation 42.
206. Regulation 44.
207. Regulation 45(1).
208. Regulation 45(2).
209. *See* Chapter 2 section §2.02 *supra*.
210. Claim Co/15376/2009.
211. Dealing with each state's sovereignty with respect to its airspace.
212. Article 15 sets out limits on airport and air navigation charges and provides that no charges shall be imposed simply for transit over the territory of a contracting State.
213. Article 24 provides an exemption for aircraft fuel from customs duties or other charges in international air transport.
214. Article 3(4) only allows certain restrictions on frequency and capacity including for environmental reasons but only to the extent consistent with Art. 15 of the Chicago Convention.
215. Article 11(2)(c) provides an exemption for aircraft fuel from customs duties or other charges in international air transport.
216. Done at Brussels on the 25 Apr. 2007 and at Washington on the 30 Apr. 2007, in duplicate. *See* Official Journal of the European Union, L 134/4, 25 May 2007.
217. Article 2(2) provides that the parties thereto shall 'pursue limitation or reduction of emissions of greenhouse gases … from aviation … fuels, working through the International Civil Aviation Organization …'.
218. Kyoto Protocol to the United Nations Framework Convention on Climate Change, done at Kyoto on 11 Dec. 1997.
219. Case Nos C-366/10, 2010/C 260/12.
220. Bartlik M., *The Extension of the European Union's Emissions Trading Scheme to Aviation Activities*, Annals of Air and Space Law, Volume XXXIV, 2009, 151–172, at 171.
221. *Ibid.*
222. *Ibid.*

that the EU institutions are not party to or bound by the Chicago Convention (1944) and that, in any event, the charges involved were not:

> in respect solely of the right of transit over or entry into or exit from an EU territory. While each take-off and landing requires the aircraft operators to surrender emissions allowances, this does not mean that the charge is in respect of the take-off and landing, but that account is being taken of the emissions generated by the relevant flight.[223]

Following the adoption by ICAO of the Carbon Offsetting and Reduction Scheme for International Aviation (CORSIA) during the 39th Assembly held in October 2016,[224] the European Commission is proposing to harmonize the ETS regime and CORSIA implementation mechanisms under the umbrella of the EU Green Deal, with the aim of achieving at least a 55% net reduction in greenhouse gas emissions by 2030.[225]

[d] Tax Liens

Certain jurisdictions may impose tax liens in respect of unpaid taxes on an aircraft.

For example, if an aircraft is sold while within that jurisdiction, a sales tax may be imposed, with a lien being imposed in rem over the aircraft in the event that the sales tax is not paid.

In order to avoid this, or the risk that there might be a liability to pay stamp duty on the bill of sale transferring title, without payment of which the seller may be unable to record its ownership in the aircraft, lessors are typically careful when selling or buying aircraft to ensure the lessee's cooperation.

For example, the seller and the buyer may, having investigated the legal situation in the lessee's jurisdiction, and having agreed which of them ultimately takes the tax risk, ask the lessee to cooperate either in confirming when the aircraft is over international waters or in a jurisdiction agreed by the seller and buyer as not giving rise to a sales tax or tax lien.

Thus, at the time of closing of the sale, the parties will typically pay attention to the exact time of the transfer of ownership of the aircraft and its location at that time. Such evidence can then be submitted to a tax authority subsequently seeking to impose a sales tax or assert a tax lien over the aircraft.

A similar risk may exist with respect to customs issues. In Russia, for example, there is a scheme for paying import duty in respect of temporarily imported aircraft on terms preferable to those applying for permanently imported aircraft. Violation of the temporary import régime may result in a fine for the airline of up to 200% of the

223. Bisset M., *Taxes and Charges under the Chicago Convention, in from Lowlands to High Skies: A Multilevel Jurisdictional Approach Towards Air Law*, Nijhoff, 2013, 67–76, at 75.
224. *See*, Resolution A39-3: *Global Statement of continuing ICAO policies and practices related to environmental protection – Global Market Based Measure* (GMBM) *scheme.*
225. *See* https//ec.europa.eu/clima/policies/eu-climate-action/delivering/aviation_en and http://www.eurocontrol.int/tool/european-union-emissions-trading-system-support-facility on 9 Sep. 2021.

customs value of the aircraft. In addition, however, the aircraft may be confiscated by court order, despite the fact that the importing airline is not the owner of the aircraft.[226]

A very disquieting development, particularly in the context of the lien over a lessor's aircraft for unpaid Eurocontrol charges on the part of the lessee[227] or breaches of emissions limits on the part of the lessee[228] is the German legislation providing that a lessor may in certain circumstances be liable for the non-payment of an air travel tax in Germany on the part of its lessee.

The German Air Travel Tax Act[229] of 2010 provides[230] for an air travel tax based on the number of passengers departing from a domestic German point of departure. Under section 6(1), the airline's tax representative is jointly and severally liable along with the airline for payment of the tax.

Under section 6(2) of the German Air Travel Tax Act, if a non-German airline fails to appoint such a tax representative, the owner of the aircraft is liable for the taxes owed in addition to the operator.

Further, section 6(2) makes an exception to section 219 of the German Fiscal Code[231] which restricts recourse to a person liable to a tax to a situation where enforcement action against the movable property in question is unsuccessful or is not likely to lead to the payment of the tax. By removing this restriction, section 6(2) of the German Air Travel Tax Act leaves open immediate action not only in rem against the aircraft operated in Germany but also in personam against the owner of the aircraft itself in a situation where a foreign airline fails to appoint a German tax representative and fails to pay the air travel tax.

Even if the tax is not yet due, in a situation where a foreign lessee has not appointed a German tax representative, the relevant customs office:

> may require security from the tax debtors up to the amount of the tax likely to accrue for two calendar months in the event there is reason to believe the tax will not be collected.[232]

In other words, the lessor may be required to make a payment on behalf of the airline even where the tax is not yet due. Of course, the lessor can, at least in theory, seek to recover this from the lessee pursuant to the tax indemnity provisions[233] of the lease, but such recovery right will be of least use when it is most likely to be needed – when the airline is insolvent and the German tax authority seeks payment of the tax from the lessor having failed to recover from the airline or having concluded that recovery is unlikely.

---

226. Muriel A. and Yanboukhtin A., *Confiscation of Leased Aircraft by Customs*, International Law Office, Aviation – Russia, 20 May 2009 at http://www.internationallawoffice.com/Newsletters/Detail.aspx?g=143720a3-4ebf-43e0-9f89-98796faf313c on 21 May 2009.
227. *See* section §3.10[B][2][b] *supra*.
228. *See* section §3.10[B][2][c] *supra*.
229. *Luftverkehrsteuergesetz*.
230. In section 4.
231. *Abgabenordnung. Fundstelle*: 2002, S. 3866.
232. Article 9.
233. *See* section §3.08 *supra*.

According to Steppler:

> [i]t is likely that several German carriers will challenge their tax assessments, because the financial repercussions will be unacceptable. The act is poorly designed and the concept behind the tax is badly suited to a global industry such as aviation.[234]

Not only German carriers are likely to find this unacceptable: the legislation is still new as of the time of writing but it is possible that lessors may react to this new *régime* by requiring foreign airlines which are their lessees to pay to them as lessors, on the analogy of maintenance reserves,[235] reserves against payment of the air travel tax or by requiring them not to operate into or out of Germany without first satisfying the lessors that tax representatives have been duly appointed in accordance with this legislation.

This author's objections to the above legislation are the same as those discussed *supra* in relation to Eurocontrol and emissions liens and indeed go beyond those: not only does this legislation extend a lien over a lessor's aircraft to pay unpaid air travel tax on the part of a non-German lessee, which is objectionable enough per se, it actually goes further by making the lessor, as owner, primarily liable along with the lessee, as operator.

It is difficult to escape the conclusion that, at least in Europe, legislators are making lessors stand, in effect, as surety for the credit of airlines in an increasingly wide range of areas, none of which falls within the control of the lessor.

Under section 8(3) of the German Air Travel Tax Act, the tax representative must inform the relevant customs office of its details, including its contact details, and, under section 8(4) must inform that authority of any change in its details. At the very least, therefore, as long as this legislation is in place, lessors would be well advised to require any of its lessees to covenant not to fly into or out of Germany without having such a tax representative in place and should, *ex abundanti cautela,* require that the tax representative likewise undertake to inform the lessor of any change in its details or if it ceases to act as the airline's tax representative in Germany.

In this author's opinion,[236] this German legislation may be subject to challenge as being contrary to Article 15 of the Chicago Convention (1944).[237] Article 1 of the German Air Travel Tax Act states as the object of taxation the following:

> The authorized carriage of a passenger from a domestic departure point in an aircraft or helicopter by an aviation enterprise to a destination is a taxable legal transaction under the Air Travel Tax Act.

234. Steppler U., *Air Travel Tax and Aircraft Lease Agreements*, International Law Office: Aviation - Germany. 1 Dec. 2010, at http://www.internationallawoffice.com/Newsletters/Aviation/Germany/Arnecke-Siebold-Rechtsanwlte/Air-travel-tax-and-aircraft-lease-agreements on 9 Sep. 2021.
235. Discussed in section §3.07[C] *supra.*
236. And in that of Steppler, *supra.*
237. And indeed it may well also be open to challenge as being contrary to Art. 1 of the ECHR discussed in section §3.10[B][2][b] *supra.*

Article 15 of the Chicago Convention (1944) requires states to charge the same for use of its airports to aircraft of other contracting states as to its own national aircraft, and indeed the German Air Travel Tax Act does not distinguish in terms of *quantum* as between national and non-national aircraft.

Where the problem may arise is rather in the first paragraph of Article 15 of the Chicago Convention (1944), which requires as follows:

> Every airport in a contracting State which is open to public use by its national aircraft shall likewise, subject to the provisions of Article 68, be open under uniform conditions to the aircraft of all the other contracting States ... .

The German Air Travel distinguishes among national and non-national airlines in requiring only the latter to appoint German tax representatives who, as explained above, also become debtors. Although from a tax collection point of view, this may make sense, as otherwise, they may not have a person resident in Germany who may be sued in Germany for non-payment, this puts a burden on the non-German airline not put on the German airline. It may be difficult for a non-German airline to find a German resident willing to be its tax representative. Further, if it fails to find one, its aircraft are subject to seizure even if they are leased: thus they may be subject to particular scrutiny or terms by lessors who do not face the same risk with respect to German airlines.

Although the Chicago Convention (1944) speaks of national aircraft rather than national airlines, it is this author's view, for the reasons given above, that this legislation prima facie risks conflicting with Germany's obligations under the Chicago Convention (1944).

[3] Chicago Convention and Registration

The Chicago Convention (1944) provides that aircraft shall have the nationality of their State of registration[238] and allows for such registration to be changed from the register of one State to another, while only allowing an aircraft to be registered in one State at a time.[239]

Beyond that, and the requirement for aircraft engaged in international traffic to bear their appropriate nationality and registration marks,[240] and certain reporting requirements to ICAO and other State parties as to such registration,[241] the Chicago Convention (1944) does not lay out rules for eligibility for or form of such registration, but rather provides, in Article 19:

> The registration or transfer of registration of aircraft in any contracting State shall be made in accordance with its laws and regulations.

238. Article 17.
239. Article 18.
240. Article 20.
241. Article 21.

This was a change from the Paris Convention (1919) which laid out more detailed requirements for eligibility for aircraft registration:

> No aircraft shall be entered on the register of one of the contracting states unless it belongs wholly to nationals of such State.
>
> No incorporated company can be registered as the owner of an aircraft unless it possess the nationality of the State in which the aircraft is registered, unless the president or chairman of the company and at least two-thirds of the directors possess such nationality, and unless the company fulfills all other conditions which may be prescribed by the laws of the said State.[242]

As noted, the Chicago Convention (1944) superseded the Paris Convention (1919) pursuant to Article 80 of the former.

For the most part, the decision to be made by a state is whether to implement an aircraft register by the owner of the aircraft and/or by the operator of such aircraft, with regulations in each case as to nationality criteria to be met in order for the aircraft to be eligible for registration.

In the context of the EU, the provisions of Regulation (EC) 1008/2008 provide that:

(1) Without prejudice to Article 13(3),[243] aircraft used by a Community air carrier shall be registered, at the option of the Member State whose competent authority issues the operating licence, in its national register or within the Community.
(2) In accordance with paragraph 1, the competent authority shall, subject to applicable laws and regulations, accept on its national register, without any discriminatory fee and without delay, aircraft owned by nationals of other Member States and transfers from aircraft registers of other Member States. No fee shall be applied to transfers of aircraft in addition to the normal registration fee.

For his part, Gillick[244] refers to certain countries, such as Aruba, Bermuda, Ireland and Mauritius as examples of the establishment of 'aircraft registries of convenience'. Stating that restrictive citizenship requirements for aircraft registration have impeded the free flow of airline and aircraft financing and have precluded cross-border mergers, he continues, in relation to those countries mentioned by him that:

> [i]n these countries, an owner or a lessee may, for a fee, place an aircraft on that country's registry and in so doing accomplish a particular objective that would not

242. Article 7.
243. Article 13(3) deals with leasing of aircraft by a European Union airline which are registered in a third country. *See* section §3.05[B][5] *supra*.
244. Gillick J.E., *The Impact of Citizenship Considerations on Aviation Financing*, in Butler G.F. and Keller M.R., executive editors, *Handbook of Airline Finance*, 1st Edition, Aviation Week: McGraw-Hill, 1999, at 41 et seq.

be possible if the aircraft were registered, for example, in the home country of the lessee.

Huang discusses whether an aircraft need have a 'genuine link' with the state of registration but correctly concludes that Article 19 of the Chicago Convention (1944) reserves the right to fix conditions for registration of aircraft 'exclusively to sovereign States'.[245] Without conceding any need under the Chicago Convention (1944) itself for a 'genuine link', this author also agrees with Huang's conclusion that:

> the fact that an aircraft is not owned by a national of the State of registry does not necessarily deprive it of a genuine link with that State.[246]

He continues that:

> the practice of ICAO has been not to focus on foreign ownership of aircraft but, rather, on the safety oversight capabilities of the States which register foreign-owned aircraft.[247]

Article 83*bis* discussed in section §3.15[H] *infra* should be seen in this light. However, this author disagrees with Huang that Article 83*bis*:

> may be regarded as one of the few lawful exceptions to the requirement of a 'genuine link' between an aircraft and its State of registry,[248]

at least insofar as he may be implying such requirement under the Chicago Convention (1944) itself. Nevertheless, Huang is correct that such requirements do indeed exist, albeit outside of the Chicago Convention (1944) itself.

One hundred and ninety-three states[249] are party to the Chicago Convention (1944) which, under Article 5, gives each contracting State the right to have its aircraft, not being engaged in scheduled international air services, the right, subject as set out therein, to make flights into, or in transit non-stop across, or to make stops for non-traffic purposes in, the territory of the other contracting states, as well as (subject to Article 7 on cabotage) to take on and to discharge passengers, cargo and mail without the need for prior permission. Under Article 6, special permission of a contracting State is needed to operate any scheduled international air service over or into the territory of another contracting State.

One hundred and thirty-one[250] states are party to the International Air Services Transit Agreement (1944) which extends, among the states party thereto, to scheduled as well as to non-scheduled international air services the privilege of flying through the airspace of another contracting State and making a stop there for technical purposes.

Only eleven[251] states are party to the International Air Transport Agreement (1944) which, *inter alia*, extends to the mutual exchange of the first five Freedoms of

245. Huang J., *Aviation Safety and ICAO*, PhD Thesis, Leiden University, 2008, at 34.
246. *Ibid.*
247. Huang J., *Aviation Safety and ICAO*, PhD Thesis, Leiden University, 2008, at 37.
248. *Ibid.*, at 42.
249. http://www.icao.int/MemberStates/Member%20States.Multilingual.pdf on 9 Aug. 2021.
250. *Ibid.*
251. *Ibid.*

the Air for scheduled as well as to non-scheduled international air services, as well as (subject to Article 7 on cabotage) to take on and to discharge passengers, cargo and mail without need for prior permission.

The International Air Services Transit Agreement, in Article 1(3) and 1(6), and the International Air Transport Agreement, in Article 1(3) and 1(5), refer to 'substantial ownership and effective control' of 'the airlines of another contracting State' by citizens of that other State. Likewise, many bilateral agreements have similar requirements.[252]

However, both of the above agreements refer to the ownership of the airline and not to the ownership of the aircraft: once the airline meets the ownership requirements thereunder, it does not matter whether the airline possesses the aircraft pursuant to ownership or pursuant to a lease.

As to whether the use of a 'flag of convenience' in connection with aircraft is or should be a concern with respect to safety, Abeyratne[253] makes a useful distinction:

> There are two broad groups of foreign registered aircraft that can be deemed to be operated under a flag of convenience: those done for fiscal purposes; and those done to take advantage of a system with no or minimal economic or technical oversight. The first group may not pose a problem if arrangements are made between concerned States to ensure proper oversight, for example through bilateral agreements under Article 83 bis ... It is the second group that creates a major security problem that needs to be addressed.

If 'fiscal purposes' can be taken to mean a lessor's or financier's preference for a particular registry based on its ability better to protect its interests there, this author agrees with Abeyratne.

Verhaegen[254] has expressed the concern that a state could offer to the state of the operator to act, in effect, as a flag of convenience, while transferring functions back to the state of the operator. This author fails to see the concern: under Article 83*bis*, the state of the operator will still have the responsibilities under the Chicago Convention (1944) in respect of those transferred functions just as if it were the state of registration all along.

[a] Owner-Only Registration

In the United States, for example, an aircraft may be registered only by and in the legal name of its owner.[255] The operator of the aircraft is not, therefore, relevant.

252. Bunker D.H., *International Aircraft Financing, Volume 1: General Principles,* 2nd Edition, IATA, 2015, at 275-278.
253. Abeyratne R., *Registration of Aircraft: Legal and Regulatory Issues,* Annals of Air and Space Law, Volume XXXIV, 2009, 173-206, at 189.
254. Verhaegen B.M., *The Entry into Force of Article 83 bis: Legal Perspectives in Terms of Safety Oversight,* Annals of Air and Space Law, Volume XXII, Part II, 1997, at 273-274.
255. http://www.faa.gov/licenses_certificates/aircraft_certification/aircraft_registry/register_aircraft/ on 9 Sep. 2021. There are certain exceptions for aircraft primarily based in the United States where the owner or lessee certifies that 60%. or more of the aircraft's flight hours within each six month period were between two points in the United States – *see* Balfour J. (ed.), *Air Transport in 34 Jurisdictions Worldwide* 2009, at 190.

This is, however, an oversimplification. Preston G Gaddis II points out that the term 'owner' is not defined in the Federal Aviation Act and that the definition in the Federal Aviation Regulations is unhelpful and confusing. Although non-binding, persuasive legal opinions issued by counsel to the FAA set out certain guidelines whereby an aircraft subject to a lease may be registered in the name of a lessee (in other words, the lessee is treated as the owner for registration purposes) in certain circumstances.[256]

It is beyond the scope of this work to go into such leases in detail as they are not true operating leases but, in essence, such leases are full pay out leases, finance leases, conditional sales contracts, leases with lessee purchase options under certain conditions (e.g., the option amount is not to exceed 10% of lessor's cost (if a new aircraft) or 10% of the current value (if previously acquired by the lessor) or in excess of 10% if non-refundably prefunded prior to lease expiry).

Pre-filing opinions of counsel to the FAA, although not binding, are advisable.

To be registered as an owner, under the Transportation Code and applicable Federal Aviation Regulations, an aircraft is only eligible for US registration if it is owned by either:[257]

(a) a citizen of the United States or a resident alien; or
(b) a US corporation (which does not meet the requirements of a citizen of the United States) if the aircraft is based and primarily used in the United States.[258]

One means of registering an owner who does not qualify as a US citizen is for the owner of an aircraft to transfer title to that aircraft to an owner trust, typically a large US bank under the terms of an owner trust agreement whereby the owner trustee holds title to the aircraft in trust for such non-US citizen as beneficiary. The owner trustee is, in effect, simply a *nominee* and all rights and obligations are pass-through for all legal accounting and tax purposes to the beneficiary.

Accordingly, the owner trustee will act as lessor in any leases and words will appear in the lease to the effect that the lessor is acting '*not in its individual capacity but solely as Owner Trustee*'. It is for this reason that a lessee may reasonably require the beneficiary to grant to it a guarantee of the lessor's obligations under the lease.

One advantage for the lessor in being registered as the owner is that, should it come to a hostile repossession of the aircraft, it need only worry about physical repossession of the aircraft (including its records) and will not need to worry about a lessee wrongly refusing to deregister the aircraft. This is discussed further *infra* in section §3.15[I] in the context of the Irrevocable Deregistration and Export Request

256. Gaddis II P.G., *Registering Lease Aircraft in the US*, Airfinance Journal, May 1988, 48–49. This author is grateful to Dr Donald H Bunker for drawing his attention to this article.
257. McBain G., *Aircraft Finance: Registration, Security and Enforcement*, General Editor, Sweet & Maxwell, Volume 3, 2000, at United States of America-3 (para. 1.2).
258. 49 USC 44102(a)(1).

Authorization and in section §3.15[H] in the context of Article 83*bis* of the Chicago Convention (1944).

Please *see* above[259] the discussion of the requirement to renew aircraft registration in the United States every three years.

[b] Owner or Operator Registration

In Ireland, an aircraft may only be registered there if it is owned by a citizen or company[260] of Ireland or other EU Member State[261] but, even if the aircraft is not owned by such a citizen, if it is chartered by demise, leased or on hire to, or in course of being acquired under a lease-purchase or a hire-purchase agreement by such a citizen or company, then the aircraft may be registered in the state but such registration shall be subject to any conditions the Irish Aviation Authority may deem fit.[262]

In Belgium, the rule is similar, with aircraft on an operating lease of at least six months being registrable in Belgium so long as the lessee would be qualified as an owner if it owned the aircraft.[263]

McBain[264] notes that the aircraft register and certificate may contain a brief note identifying the lessor or owner which, while having no legal effect provides a form of comfort to lessors. He goes on to note[265] that the Belgian Civil Aviation Administration sometimes registers an aircraft in the name of the lessor but that:

> the preference of lessor is generally to leave the registration in the name of the lessee in order to avoid a possible exposure to operational liabilities.

What remains unclear is the effect of identifying the lessor or owner by means of a note for potential liability as owner of the aircraft under, for example, as discussed in section §3.11[B] *infra*.

[c] Owner and Operator Registration

Under Japanese law, even if the operator of the aircraft is a Japanese airline, the aircraft may not be registered in Japan unless it is also owned by a Japanese citizen.[266]

---

259. In section §3.05[B][2].
260. Such company having a place of business in Ireland and having its principal place of business in Ireland other EU Member State and of which not less than two-thirds of the directors are citizens of Ireland or other EU Member State.
261. Section 7(1) of the Irish Aviation Authority (Nationality and Registration of Aircraft) Order, 2005 (S.I. 634 of 2005).
262. *Ibid.*, section 7(4).
263. McBain G., *Aircraft Finance: Registration, Security and Enforcement*, General Editor, Sweet & Maxwell, 2000 at Belgium, 1.2.2.
264. *Ibid.*, at Belgium, 1.4.
265. *Ibid.*, at Belgium, 1.2.4.
266. Advice of Katsu Sengoku, Esq, of Nishimura & Partners, Tokyo, Japan. *See also* Hames G. and McBain R., *Aircraft Finance: Registration, Security and Enforcement*, Volume I, Longman, 1 Feb. 2000, Japan: Section 1.2.

In principle, for a foreign lessor, this poses a problem, but there are ways of dealing with it. One typical structure is as follows. A non-Japanese leasing company (*'Servicer'*) has a purchase agreement with the aircraft manufacturer. Under it, the Servicer can nominate affiliates or subsidiaries to acquire title to the aircraft.

The Servicer may wish to use a subsidiary entity (*'Beneficiary'*) to acquire title. This Beneficiary will be consolidated in the Servicer's accounts.

In fact, the Beneficiary will not acquire title directly. Instead, the Servicer will use an owner trustee (*'Lessor'*) whereby Lessor holds title to the aircraft in trust for the Beneficiary. This means that the Owner Trustee is simply a *nominee* and all rights and obligations are pass-through for all legal accounting and tax purposes to the Beneficiary (hence words will appear in the lease to the effect that Lessor is acting *'not in its individual capacity but solely as Owner Trustee'*). This is a very common structure for holding title to aircraft in the United States, as discussed in Chapter 2 section §2.02 *supra*.

In order for an aircraft owned by the non-Japanese Lessor to be registrable in Japan, therefore, it is common for a Japanese special purpose company (*'Owner'*), set up by an established Japanese company (*'Manager'*), to buy the aircraft from the Lessor. The Owner will then agree to sell the aircraft back to the Lessor under a conditional sale agreement (*CSA*) for the same price. Under the CSA, the Owner retains title until payment of USD 1 by the Lessor to the Owner (all other amounts being netted off). Because of this nominal amount, the Lessor is treated as owner for tax and accounting and most legal purposes, but the Owner is treated as owner for purposes of registering the aircraft in Japan.

Thus, the Owner passes through all rights and obligations to Lessor, which passes through all rights and obligations to Beneficiary, which is ultimately controlled by Servicer.

Servicer manages the Beneficiary (which has no staff of its own). Manager manages the Owner (which has no staff of its own). Lessee should usually only need to deal directly with Servicer, as all the other parties are in the structure for legal and accounting reasons only.

Annex 2 sets out this basic structure.

Annex 4 sets out a complication to this structure for leases of aircraft to be registered in Japan where there is a lender who requires title to the aircraft to be placed in an entity controlled by it, as is the case in financing guaranteed by the Export Import Bank of the United States. This entity (the *'Head Lessor'*) enters into the structure set out in Annex 2 between the Owner and the Lessor, by entering into the CSA in place of the Lessor and by then finance leasing the aircraft to the Lessor which continues to lease the aircraft under an operating lease to the lessee.

What is interesting here is that there are four entities which may be considered the owner of the aircraft:

(1) the Owner, the Japanese special purpose company, as the registered owner on the aircraft registered maintained by Japan pursuant to the Chicago Convention (1944);

(2) the Head Lessor, the SPV controlled by the lender which may be considered the owner for all accounting and tax purposes by virtue of its rights as conditional purchaser under the CSA between it and the Owner, the Japanese special purpose company;
(3) the Lessor (as owner trustee) as lessee from the lenders' SPV under a finance lease; and
(4) the Beneficiary, the true economic owner of the aircraft, as a beneficiary of the owner trust pursuant to which the Lessor has its interest in the aircraft.

[d] Operator-Only Registration

Finally, the aviation authority may look to the identity of the operator of the aircraft, not the owner. For example, Austria requires for Austrian registration that the operator be an Austrian or EU citizen.[267]

[4] Possession and Replacement of Parts and Engines

The lessor will want to ensure that the lessee does not part with possession of the aircraft or parts or engines of the aircraft without good reason – removal may only be for maintenance, repair or (in the case of parts) required replacement (due to time expiry, etc.). Typically, the lessee will not be allowed to replace the engines on a permanent basis for any reason short of replacement of a destroyed engine.

Temporary replacement or pooling (or interchange) with other airlines of engines[268] and parts may be allowed as being reasonably required for airline operation but even then the lessor will have a legitimate interest in ensuring that in so doing the value of the aircraft is not reduced, even during the term. A lessor cannot assume that the lease will run its full term – if the lessee defaults, it will have to repossess its aircraft at short notice and thus will need to ensure the aircraft is in reasonable condition.

[a] Possession

The lessee should covenant not to part with possession of the aircraft or any engine or part thereof during the lease term except for authorized maintenance to an authorized maintenance provider[269] or to a sub-lessee pursuant to a sublease[270] permitted pursuant to the terms of the lease or consented to by the lessor.

267. Hames R. and McBain G., *Aircraft Finance: Registration, Security and Enforcement*, Volume I, Longman, 1 Feb. 2000, Austria: Section 1.2.
268. Pooling of engines by lessees can be a contentious issue for lessor. Industry practice is such that, no matter what the lease may provide, engines will be pooled as needed by operators: *see* Bunker D.H., *International Aircraft Financing, Volume 2: Specific Documents*, 2nd Edition, IATA, 2015, at 117–121.
269. *See* section §3.10[B][1] *supra*.
270. *See* section §3.15[E] *infra*.

[b] Replacement of Parts

Parts may, typically under a lease, only be replaced if they are worn out or expired and in need of replacement or repair – typically they will have to be repaired in accordance with the standards set out in the lease, being of a type at least as good as that replaced, and having at least the same value and utility as it.

If replaced, there is quite often an argument during the negotiations over whether replacement parts must be original manufacturer (OEM) parts or may be parts manufacturer approval[271] (PMA) parts, parts made by manufacturers other than the original manufacturer and typically cheaper.[272]

In a case from the United States, *US Bank National Association v. Southwest Airlines Co.*,[273] brought in the Southern District of New York (SDNY), the airline was held to have:

> stripped the Aircraft of their valuable Engines and Parts, and replaced them with comparatively inferior Engines and Parts thereby constructing three substantially degraded airplanes.[274]

despite provisions in the lease requiring substitute engines and parts having at least the same value and utility as those replaced and despite a provision that the lessee does not discriminate against the leased aircraft as compared with other aircraft in the airline's fleet.

As most leases do not allow substitution of engines except in case of destruction, this is typically a concern as to parts rather than engines. The court did not define 'value and utility' since the airline admitted the reduction in value of the aircraft due to its conduct, arguing only over quantum, but it does illustrate the importance of having requirements as to value and utility and to non-discrimination in the context of replacement parts.

Usually, there is not the debate, seen in connection with engines,[275] over title being retained regardless of their installation on other aircraft – leases typically provide that ownership of parts does pass on installation even though they also claim not to relinquish ownership to removed parts unless and until they are replaced with parts permitted under the terms of the lease. However, title to such a removed part would probably pass to the owner of the aircraft on which it is installed regardless of the lease language, leaving only a contractual claim against the lessee – this issue is more fully discussed in the next section §3.10[B][4][c].

271. An approval granted by the United States Federal Aviation Administration under 14 C.F.R. 2.303.
272. Thus saving the airline money but potentially reducing the value of the aircraft.
273. 2009 WL 2163594 (S.D.N.Y. 20 Jul. 2009).
274. *Ibid.*, at 10.
275. *See* section §3.10[B][4][c] *infra*.

[c] Replacement of Engines

Unlike other parts, engines are considered such a valuable part of the aircraft that, barring a total loss of the engine, the aircraft should be returned in principle at the end of the lease term with the same engines with which it was delivered.

Permanent replacement of engines generally does not, in this author's experience, typically cause a problem in engine leasing – if an engine is destroyed, for example, it will be replaced permanently by an engine and the lessor will want the lessee, even if the lease provides for automatic vesting of title upon installation, to provide a bill of sale establishing title. Permanent replacement of engines is not otherwise allowed.

Temporary replacement of engines is where, heretofore, problems have been faced by this author in practice, and owners of engines worry that should their engine temporarily be installed on another airframe, the owner of that other airframe may acquire title to that engine by operation of law pursuant to an applicable rule of national property law.[276]

Thus, making clear in drafting legal documentation that title to temporarily replaced or temporary replacement engines *does* not pass may be more important than making clear that title to permanently replaced or permanent replacement engines *does* pass.

Leaving aside the issue of the distinction of permanent and temporary replacement of engines, and turning to the broader issue in hand of the ability of the parties to determine transfer of title of engine ownership, we need to examine not only applicable national law but also its effect at the global level.

Drafting the contract so as to reflect the will of the parties is important, and, by having a governing law clause, the parties can ensure that the *lex loci contractus*, being the law governing the contract, either because the contract was concluded in a particular jurisdiction or in the contract the parties chose the laws of a particular jurisdiction to govern it, will recognize and enforce the contractual provision on engine title.[277]

Thus, Releaux and Tonnaer[278] suggest that contractual provisions can suffice and, to a limited extent they are correct. Typically, a legal opinion will be obtained by the lessor that the contract, including this provision, constitutes the legal, valid, and binding obligation of the lessee.

---

276. Engine owners often request the airframe owner to sign a letter recognizing the former's ownership rights in the installed engine. If the letter is so limited, this should not cause a problem. Issues arise where the requested letters go beyond this, requiring notification or consent to the former before the latter may exercise repossession rights over the aircraft so long as the engine is installed. This is interference in the airframe owner's ownership rights in the aircraft and contractual rights under the lease and should be resisted.
277. *See* Hanley D.P., *Contractual and Property Rights in Leased Aircraft Engines*, in Singamsetty S.S.P., editor in chief, *Air and Space Law: Contemporary Issues and Future Challenges*, Air and Space Books, 2011.
278. Reuleaux M. and Tonnaer H., *Financing Aircraft Engines: Pitfalls and Solutions*, Zeitschrift für Luft- und Weltraumrecht, Volume 56, 2007, at 2.2.

However, although this contractual drafting may suffice as a matter of contractual rights *inter partes*, it may not suffice as a matter of proprietary rights where we are dealing with involuntary transfers by operation of law and possibly with third-party rights. As Honnebier points out:

> [t]his is particularly the situation where one of the interested parties becomes a bankrupt. Only the validly created proprietary rights of the other party will be recognized and enforced in other states.[279]

In other words, the contractual rights may suffice where the lessee is solvent as it, in effect, compels them to maintain the lessor's proprietary rights or pay the consequences; but, in bankruptcy, the contractual rights may be worthless.

It is, therefore, necessary to look to the proprietary rights at a national level. The general rule for the governing law relating to the proprietary rights in corporeal movable assets is that the *lex situs* applies – that is, the law of the jurisdiction where the asset was located at the time of the creation of the interest.[280]

The proper law then, determining proprietary rights which may arise upon operation of law, including any accretion rights to engines, will be the *lex situs*, rather than the *lex loci contractus*. If it is in a jurisdiction which is a state party to the Geneva Convention (1948), then, under Article 1(1) of the Geneva Convention (1948),[281] the rights to property in aircraft which should be recognized are rights which 'have been constituted in accordance with the law of the contracting State in which the aircraft was registered as to nationality at the time of their constitution'.

Immediately before delivery, the aircraft will still normally be on the register of the prior operator. At delivery, a request to deregister from the register of the prior operator will be filed, with a request that the aviation authority sends a confirmatory cable to the aviation authority maintaining the register where the aircraft is next to be registered. The new lessee will then quickly file to register the aircraft in such a register.

According to Article 3(3) of the Geneva Convention (1948), if the law of a contracting State provides that the filing of a document for recording has the same effect as actually recording it, it shall (so long as the document is open to the public) have the same effect under the Geneva Convention (1948).

The important point to note is that, to the effect that documentary provisions on title transfer are given effect to not only as a contractual matter but as a matter of proprietary rights, thus covering involuntary transfers and binding third parties, it is not because the governing law of the contract and the contract itself so provide, but because the applicable *lex situs* also so provides.

The *lex loci contractus* is the law of the place of the contract. This can be either the law where the contract is formed or the law which the parties agree should govern the contract.[282] This only governs contractual in personam rights between the parties and

279. Honnebier B.P., *Clarifying the Alleged Issues Concerning the Financing of Aircraft Engines*, Zeitschrift für Luft- und Weltraumrecht, Volume 3, 2007, 33–44, at 1.3.
280. *Ibid.*, at 2.3, refers to it as a universal rule.
281. *See* section §3.15[D] *infra*.
282. *Black's Law Dictionary*, 8th Edition.

thus does not govern proprietary rights in rem, which prevail in case of involuntary transfers of title, transfers by operation of law and bankruptcies.

The *lex rei sitae* (more commonly referred to in common law jurisdictions as the *lex situs*) is the law of the jurisdiction where property is situated at the time of creation of a right in it or, more specifically in this context, at the time of transfer of title to it.

This is the general rule applicable to determining which substantive law to apply to the transfer of an interest in corporeal moveable property. Only corporeal assets have a fixed *situs*, and the *situs* of immovable property does not change. Moveable property by definition may have more than one *situs*, depending on where it is at a given time.

Under the Geneva Convention (1948), Article 1(1), the *lex registri* applies for these purposes. In other words, the law of the state of registration for the purposes of the Chicago Convention (1944) of the aircraft applies.

Releaux and Tonnaer interpret this to mean the substantive law only of the *lex registri* applies. Thus, if under the national property law (looked at in isolation) of the *lex registri*, accretion of title to engines to the airframes on which they are installed occurs by operation of law, then, under the Geneva Convention (1948), the right of the person claiming title to such engine will be recognized and upheld by the Geneva Convention (1948).

Honnebier, however, argues that the Geneva Convention (1948) does not refer to the substantive laws only – it refers to laws without qualification and this must be taken to mean all laws of the state of registration, including conflicts of laws rules. Certain laws automatically provide that references to their law include references to their conflicts of law rules, such that parties choosing New York law, for example, to govern a contract, need to take care to exclude its conflicts of law rules if they want to ensure that New York substantive law applies to the contract rather than some other law as a result of New York's determination that the substantive laws of the *lex situs* (where different) apply instead.

As stated above, given the universality of the *lex situs* rules in these cases, the *lex registri* would apply the *lex situs* with the effect that any accretion rules would have to occur under the *lex situs* rather than purely under the substantive laws of the *lex registri*.

The Geneva Convention (1948) thus sets out procedural, not substantive, law, further proof of which comes in the fact that it 'recognizes' rather than 'creates' rights.

Complicating the picture is the doctrine of *renvoi*, whereby a court determines that, in this context, when examining the rules of a given jurisdiction, one should examine all its rules, including its rules of private international law. This may result, for example, in a court holding that, under the *lex situs* of one jurisdiction (including its rules of private international law), the laws of another, such as the *lex registri*, shall apply. The problem is that the rules of that other jurisdiction may, under its private international law rules, provide for the law of the *lex situs* to apply, thereby creating a circular process.

This is not a theoretical concern: in *Blue Sky One Limited and others v. Blue Sky Airways LLC and others,*[283] Beatson J of the English High Court held that the validity of aircraft mortgages is 'to be determined by the *lex situs*, the law of the place where the aircraft were situated on 21 December 2006, the date the mortgages were executed' and rejected an argument that the *lex registri* should be used instead so as to conform to the Geneva Convention (1948).[284]

Renvoi was thus rejected and the domestic laws of the *lex situs*, excluding its rules of *renvoi* which would have looked to the *lex registri*, applied. He continued that in the case of 'a transfer of title to tangible movables, such as the aircraft in this case, the reference to the *lex situs* is to the domestic law of the place where the aircraft are situated on the relevant date, and not to its entire law including its choice of law rules; that is the doctrine of *renvoi* does not apply'. Gerber[285] has commented that this judgment, harsh in its effect:[286]

> could probably be criticized as focusing overly on the hypothetical problems that might occur while ignoring the reasonable justifications of the particular facts of this case.

In order to overcome differing interpretations of, and problems involving *renvoi*, rules of private international law, and the risk of application of national law to what are inherently internationally moveable assets, the Cape Town Convention (2001) and Aircraft Protocol thereto provided for an 'international interest' in aircraft objects (defined to include: (i) airframes which can carry at least eight persons including crew or goods in excess of 2,750 kg; (ii) aircraft engines having at least 1,750 lb of lift for jet engines or otherwise at least 550 rated take-off shaft horsepower; and (iii) helicopters which can carry at least five persons including crew or goods in excess of 450 kg).

Goode describes the 'international interest' as a creature of the Cape Town Convention (2001) which:

> in principle is not dependent on national law. It is therefore irrelevant that the international interest has no counterpart under the otherwise applicable law or that the latter does not recognise non-possessory security at all. Once the conditions of the Convention have been satisfied an international interest comes into existence, even if fulfillment of those conditions would not suffice to create an interest under national law or would require further formalities in order to be effective. In this sense, the international interest is an autonomous interest.

283. [2010] EWHC 631 (Comm), at 200–201.
284. Havel and Gomez describe this decision as 'notorious'. *See* Havel B. and Sanchez G., *The Principles and Practice of International Aviation Law,* Cambridge University Press, 2014, at 333.
285. Gerber D.N., *Aircraft Finance Issues: The Blue Sky Ruling; The New ASU and the 'Home Country Rule'; and Recent Developments at the FAA Registry,* a paper presented at the American Bar Association Air and Space Law Forum 2010 Annual Meeting in Seattle, Washington on 26 Oct. 2010.
286. The mortgage had been perfected under the laws of the *lex registri*, which laws, under the private international laws of the *lex situs* applied, but had not been perfected under the laws of the *lex situs*, and thus was held not to have been perfected.

> However, it is not wholly independent of national law, which continues to govern the question of whether an agreement exists between the parties at all ... .[287]

Goode continues that the creation of interests under national law is not precluded, and that 'in most cases' an interest arising under national law under a leasing agreement will constitute both an international interest and a domestic interest, but that 'usually' the international interest will give stronger rights than a purely domestic interest since the former overrides even unregistrable unregistered interests whereas the latter may not.[288]

The Cape Town Convention (2001)[289] supersedes, pursuant to Article XXIII of the Protocol, the Geneva Convention (1948) for signatories thereto to the extent that the Cape Town Convention (2001) applies.[290] International interests may be registered in respect of aircraft objects if the airframe is registered as part of an aircraft in a contracting State, if the engine is registered as part of an aircraft in a contracting State or otherwise the engine is located in a contracting State[291] or if the debtor (or lessee) is situated in a contracting State.[292]

Once registered, international interests (pursuant to Article 29(1) of the Cape Town Convention (2001)), have 'priority over any other interest subsequently registered and over an unregistered interest'. An 'unregistered interest' is defined in Article 1 to include non-consensual rights or interests.

The Geneva Convention (1948) does not create any rights or govern matters such as the transfer of title to engines.[293] It is a conflict of laws treaty that deals with recognition of rights, not a substantive treaty that creates rights.

Honnebier's[294] view of the background to this is that, immediately after World War II, a substantive treaty on rights in aircraft was not feasible, so the Geneva Convention (1948) was entered into as a provisional body of rules. Likewise, according to Rosales, the drafters of the Geneva Convention (1948) initially hoped to establish a substantive treaty mortgage or charge on aircraft, or at least a uniform recordation

287. Goode R., *The International Interest as an Autonomous Property Interest*, European Review of Private Law, Volume 1, 2004, at 24.
288. *Ibid.*
289. Article XXIII of the Aircraft Protocol.
290. Article XXIII of the Aircraft Protocol goes on to provide: 'However, with respect to rights or interests not covered or affected by the present Convention, the Geneva Convention shall not be superseded.'
291. Article IV(1) of the Aircraft Protocol.
292. Article 3(1) of the Convention.
293. As Honnebier puts it: 'the Convention takes no account of new developments in international financing practice, such as the fact that at present aircraft engines are financed and registered separately': *The Convention on International Interests in Mobile Equipment and the Aircraft Equipment Protocol Will Encourage European Property Law Reform*, Edinburgh Law Review, Volume 1, 2004, 115.
294. Honnebier B.P., *The European Air Transport Sector Requires an International Solid Regime Facilitating Aircraft Financing: The Cape Town Convention*, Tijdschrift Vervoer + Recht, 2007-5, at 4.2 and 4.3.

system but found that would be too radical a departure in the face of great divergence in national conceptions.[295]

The Geneva Convention (1948) only deals with four types of consensually created rights and does not deal with non-consensual rights such as accretion or accession of title to aircraft engines by operation of law at all. Both Honnebier, on the one hand, and Releaux and Tonnaer, on the other hand, agree, albeit for different reasons, as to the inadequacy of the Geneva Convention (1948) in this regard and the need for the solution set out in the Cape Town Convention (2001).[296]

The Cape Town Convention (2001) creates an international interest which can be registered in respect of aircraft engines over a certain size (*see supra*). This international interest under Article 29(1) has 'priority over any other interest subsequently registered and over an unregistered interest'.[297] An 'unregistered interest' is defined to include non-consensual rights or interests.

Thus, a duly registered international interest in an aircraft engine under the Cape Town Convention (2001) prevails over a non-consensual right or interest such as a transfer of title to an aircraft engine by operation of law by reason of its installation on another aircraft even if, under some applicable national property law, such installation would otherwise vest title to the engine in the owner of the aircraft.

There is some difference of legal opinion as to whether, for example, under the law of the Kingdom of the Netherlands,[298] title to engines passes to the airframe owner upon installation thereon. Honnebier[299] argues that under such law there is no accession of title engines to the title of the aircraft on which it is installed. He cites two cases which decided against such accession: *AAR Aircraft & Engine Group v. Aerowings*[300] and *Volvo Aero Leasing v. AVIA Air*[301] decided on the basis of the prevailing industry view.

The argument in favour of engine accession is based on Article 8:3a(2) of the Civil Code of the Netherlands, which provides that:

> [t]he airframe, engines, propellers, radio apparatus, and all other goods intended for use in or on the machine '(toestel)', regardless whether installed therein or

295. Rosales R., *Recordation of Rights in Aircraft and International Recognition: A Comparison Between the American and Canadian Situations*, Annals of Air and Space Law, Volume XVI, 1991, at 209–210.
296. For a fuller discussion, *see* Hanley D.P., *The Relationship Between the Geneva and Cape Town Conventions*, Cape Town Convention Journal, Volume 4, Issue 1, 2015, at 103–113.
297. Registration ensures that application of the principle of title preservation and overrides any contrary local law of contracting States. *See* French D., *Legal Considerations for Aircraft Engine Financiers*, Airfinance Journal, July 2008 Supplement, at 23.
298. Bearing in mind that within the Kingdom of the Netherlands there are three separate jurisdictions, the Netherlands, the Netherlands Antilles and Aruba, each with its own Civil Code and that, accordingly, jurisprudential results in one jurisdiction may not necessarily be followed in the others.
299. Honnebier B.P., *Clarifying the Alleged Issues Concerning the Financing of Aircraft Engines: Some Comments to the Alleged Pitfalls Arising under Dutch, German and International Law as Proposed*, Zeitschrift für Luft- und Weltraumrecht, Volume 3, 2007, at 33–44.
300. Court of Appeal, Den Bosch, The Netherlands, 15 Aug. 2002.
301. Summary Proceedings, Court of First Instance of Aruba, 25 Jun. 2003.

temporarily separated there from, are a component part '(bestanddeel)' of the aircraft.[302]

Nevertheless, even those who argue in favour of accession agree that accession will no longer be the case once the Netherlands ratifies the Cape Town Convention (2001).[303]

Finally, in this regard, the Cape Town Convention (2001)[304] has not yet been as widely adopted as the Geneva Convention (1948)[305] even though, for those states bound by it, the Cape Town Convention (2001) supersedes[306] the Geneva Convention (1948) to the extent of rights or interests covered by the Cape Town Convention (2001). As noted above, the Geneva Convention (1948) was only intended as provisional in nature given the inability of states to agree to substantive rules at that time. The Cape Town Convention (2001) is proof that agreement on substantive rules could be reached, thus obviating the need for the provisional solution set out in the Geneva Convention (1948).

In summary, it could be said that neither the Cape Town Convention (2001) nor the Geneva Convention (1948) deals explicitly with the transfer of title to engines by operation of law but that the Geneva Convention (1948) had no effect on such transfer whereas the provisions of the Cape Town Convention (2001), which is growing in importance as it is increasingly adopted by more and more states, take precedence over any such transfer under national property law rules so long as the proper registration in respect of the international interest in the engine is made.

As a contractual matter *inter partes*, engine lessors commonly ask aircraft lessors to sign recognition of rights agreements (RORAs), particularly as aircraft engine leasing increasingly develops as a commercial field alongside aircraft leasing. The idea behind the RORAs is that, if an aircraft lessor repossesses its aircraft at a time when the airline has installed on that aircraft an engine belonging to the engine lessor, the aircraft lessor agrees not to make any ownership claim against the engine even if by operation of law title to the engine automatically passes to the aircraft lessor.

Usually, this is not a contentious request, but disagreements over the extent of a RORA can occur where the engine lessor seeks to extend its terms beyond those originally contemplated.

For example, the engine lessor may ask that the provisions of its lease prevail over those of the aircraft lease, or it may ask that the aircraft lessor not take any action with respect to its engine without the engine lessor's consent.

These are unrealistic requests: an airframe lessor has no reason to agree that the engine lease will prevail over the aircraft lease. Further, if it needs to act quickly to

302. https://lincolngomez.com/2010/02/11/aviation-engines-doctrine-accession-gomez-bikker-arub/ on 9 Sep. 2021.
303. *See*, e.g., Crans B., *Aircraft Finance Below Sea Level*, Airfinance Journal Supplement, July 2008, at 39.
304. At the time of writing, eighty-three States are party thereto – *see* http://www.unidroit.org/status-2001capetown on 9 Sep. 2021.
305. At the time of writing, ninety-one States are party thereto – *see* http://www.icao.int/secretariat/legal/List%20of%20Parties/Geneva_EN.pdf on 9 Sep. 2021.
306. Pursuant to Art. XXIII of the Aircraft Protocol.

repossess its aircraft and remove it to a different jurisdiction, it cannot lose valuable time obtaining consent and negotiating terms for it with the engine lessor.

The most the aircraft lessor can agree to do is to notify the engine lessor where its engine is after an aircraft repossession and invite the engine lessor to collect its engine.

Engine lessors may argue that they may be in breach of their covenant of quiet enjoyment to the airline if the aircraft lessor repossesses their engine while the airline is still complying with the engine lease. Such argument is specious, as the interference in quiet enjoyment would not have been caused by or through the engine lessor.

They may alternatively argue that commercially they may not wish or be able to terminate their engine lease: that is reasonable enough but they must accept and understand that if they allow their engine to be installed on somebody else's aircraft, they must expect that it is subject to being repossessed along with the aircraft by the aircraft owner. If they wish to continue their engine lease, they can collect it from the engine owner and ship it back to the airline. In most if not all cases, however, the engine lessor will be grateful that its engine was safely removed from the jurisdiction in the event of a major default or collapse on the part of the airline.

[C] Conclusions

The lessee's covenant's examined in section §3.10[B] *supra* show a great interplay between, on the one hand, public and private international law as well as of national law (both law of the jurisdiction of the airline and law of the state of registration) and, on the other hand, aircraft operating leases, something reflected in the length of section §3.10[B] itself.

Many areas of public international law and national law, in particular, involved covering maintenance (where the lease requires, as seen, compliance as a contractual matter with legal requirements as to maintenance, and indeed imposes higher requirements), liens (which may take the form of an in rem lien under the Eurocontrol Convention (1960) or even result in personal liability on the part of the lessor in the case of breach by the lessee of its obligations), registration, where, as foreseen by the Chicago Convention (1944), registration may take various forms depending on national law, and replacement of parts and engines, where the Geneva Convention (1948) and the Cape Town Convention (2001) are discussed.

What has to be borne in mind throughout is that the provisions of the law as they apply to third parties apply without reference to the provisions of the lease, which only apply *inter partes*, and yet are most likely to become an issue for the lessor precisely because the lessee is in breach of its covenants under the lease (as well as its obligations at law).

Of course, the lessor will insist on an indemnity claim against the lessee, examined next in section §3.11 but the lessee, if it is in breach of its covenants, may well be in breach because it is insolvent and thus in no more a position to indemnify the lessor for the consequences of its breach than it was in a position to avoid the breach in the first place.

§3.11 INDEMNITIES

These are some of the most closely negotiated parts of the lease for the lawyers if not for the non-lawyers. Since the lessor will not want to take the credit risk of the lessee in respect of its indemnity obligations, the lessor will insist that such indemnity obligations[307] be covered, insofar as that is possible,[308] by insurance, as discussed further in section §3.12 *infra*.

[A] Damage to Aircraft or Other Loss to Lessor

The indemnity provisions will require the lessee to indemnify the lessor for damage to or loss of the aircraft and for loss which the lessor suffers as a result of any breach by the lessee of its obligations under the lease.[309] Such indemnities will be stated to survive termination of the lease. Of course, the lessor can sue the lessee for breach of contract in accordance with applicable law and the dispute settlement provisions of the lease.

This is, however, at heart, a risk assignment among the parties whereby the lessee undertakes such risk and insures against it.[310] The hull insurances[311] should, subject to deductibles, cover loss or damage to the aircraft.

[B] Liability for Damage to Third Parties

[1] Liability to Non-passengers

Under the Rome Convention (1952),[312] the operator shall, pursuant to Articles 1 and 2, be liable for damage to any person on the surface 'upon proof only that the damage was caused by an aircraft in flight or by any person or thing falling therefrom'. Under Article 2(3) thereof:

> the registered owner of the aircraft shall be presumed to be the operator and shall be liable as such unless, in the proceedings for the determination of his liability, he proves that some other person was the operator and, in so far as legal procedures permit, takes appropriate measures to make that other person a party in the proceedings.

The problem with this provision is that the Chicago Convention (1944), in Article 17, refers, in fact, to the registration of aircraft, not to the registration of owners.

307. *See* section 10 of the Supplement *infra*.
308. For example, neither hull nor liability insurances will cover the lessor in case an in rem lien is imposed against its aircraft in the circumstances discussed in section §3.10 *supra*.
309. Clark T. (ed.), *Leasing Finance*, Euromoney, 1985, at 55, and Bunker D.H., *International Aircraft Financing, Volume 1: Specific Documents*, 2nd Edition, IATA, 2015, at 138–141.
310. *See* Bunker, *supra*.
311. *See* section §3.12[B] *infra*.
312. Convention on Damage caused by Foreign Aircraft to Third Parties on the Surface signed at Rome on 7 Oct. 1952. Although in force, it has never, to the author's knowledge, been applied.

Article 19 of the Chicago Convention (1944) leaves it to the contracting states to determine what laws and regulations apply. As we have seen in section §3.10[B][3] *supra*, not all contracting states have an ownership-based register, although some may do. As discussed there, in the case of a Japanese registered aircraft financed by the Export Import Bank of the United States, there may be four different legal entities which may be considered the owner.

In such an instance, it may not be entirely clear which is the owner for the purposes of Article 2(3) of the Rome Convention (1952) if the aircraft registration system concerned does not provide for an ownership-based register. It is conjectured that a court may look to the state of registration and apply the laws of such jurisdiction to determine who is the owner but that party may not be the 'registered owner' as required by the words of Article 2(3) of the Rome Convention (1952).

Article 9 of the Rome Convention (1952) goes on to provide:

> Neither the operator, the owner, ... nor their respective servants or agents, shall be liable for damage on the surface caused by an aircraft in flight or any person or thing falling therefrom otherwise than as expressly provided in this Convention. This rule shall not apply to any such person who is guilty of a deliberate act or omission done with intent to cause damage.

The basic premise under the Rome Convention (1952) of holding the operator liable but assuming the owner is the operator unless the owner can rebut this assumption is echoed in various national laws, many of which provide for liability for damage on the part of the owner in the first instance and then go on to provide that, where the owner has leased the aircraft to an operator other than itself, such liability provisions shall be construed as if they referred to that operator rather than to the owner.[313]

The Rome Convention (1952) has been reviewed by an ICAO Council Special Group on the Modernization of the Rome Convention particularly in light of the risk of terrorist attacks using aircraft and the AWG has made submissions with regard thereto to the effect that the sole remedy of a person suffering damage should be to the operator given that lessors are essentially financial service providers, providing aircraft possession to airlines in return for a use fee without access costs where all operational risk is borne by the airlines.[314]

Arising out of such review, the Unlawful Interference Compensation Convention (2009) was negotiated,[315] the rules of which, under Article 44 thereof, prevail over

313. *See*, for example, section 97(7) of the New Zealand Civil Aviation Act 1990 (which requires a hiring out essentially on a dry lease basis of greater than twenty-eight days); section 64 of the United Kingdom Civil Aviation Act 1982 (which provides in much the same terms except that the period should be greater than fourteen days), and section 10(a) of the Australian Damage by Aircraft Act 1999 (which also provides in much the same terms but does not have any minimum term requirement for a lease).

314. Wool J., *Lessor, Financier and Manufacturer Perspectives on the New Third-Party Liability Conventions*, The Air & Space Lawyer, Volume 22, Issue 4, 2010.

315. Convention on Compensation for Damage to Third Parties, Resulting from Acts of Unlawful Interference Involving Aircraft, signed at Montréal on 2 May 2009.

those of the Rome Convention (1952), has not yet come into effect.[316] It provides simply for liability on the part of the operator.[317] Article 27 explicitly provides:

> No right of recourse shall lie against an owner, lessor, or financier retaining title of or holding security in an aircraft, not being an operator, or against a manufacturer if that manufacturer proves that it has complied with the mandatory requirements in respect of the design of the aircraft, its engines, or components.[318]

Further, Article 29.1 sets out an exclusive remedy:

> Without prejudice to the question as to who are the persons who have the right to bring suit and what are their respective rights, any action for compensation for damage to a third party due to an act of unlawful interference, however founded, whether under this Convention or in tort or otherwise, can only be brought against the operator and, if need be, against the International Fund and subject to the conditions and limits of liability set out in this Convention. No claim by a third party shall lie against any other person for compensation for such damage.

Wool[319] writes that with this approach:

> for the first time, a major international air law instrument recognizes and advances the integrated industry principle. Previous air law instruments have equated airlines with the industry as a whole. The liability of others was beyond the scope of such instruments, meaning that they were left to applicable law.[320]

Abeyratne agrees with Wool that:

> [a] special and unique feature of the Convention is ... that ... any action ... can only be brought against the operator ... .[321]

Similarly, the related General Risks Convention (2009),[322] the rules of which, under Article 25 thereof also prevail over those of the Rome Convention (1952), has not

316. Eleven countries have signed so far at the time of writing – *see* http://www.icao.int/secretariat/legal/List%20of%20Parties/2009_UICC_EN.pdf on 9 Sep. 2021.
317. Article 3.
318. Thus effectively resolving the lack of clarity as to the owner is for the purposes of Art. 2(3) of the Rome Convention. An earlier draft had provided that claims against the operator would be an exclusive remedy and shielded all other entities. Germany expressed concerns about exonerating entities involved in the operational process – *see* International Conference on Air Law (Montreal, 20 Apr.–2 May 2009), *Draft Convention on Compensation for damage to Third Parties, Resulting from Acts of Unlawful Interference Involving Aircraft*, presented by Germany, ICAO DCCD Doc. No. 7, 13/03/09, at 4.2 and 4.3. Also, *see* section §3.11[B][2] *infra*.
319. Wool J., *Lessor, Financier, and Manufacturer Perspectives on the New Third-Party Liability Conventions*, The Air & Space Lawyer, Volume 22, Issue 4, 2010.
320. *See also* the discussion in section §3.11[B][2] *infra*.
321. Abeyratne R.I.R., *The Unlawful Interference Compensation Convention of 2009 and Principles of State Responsibility*, Annals of Air and Space Law, Volume XXXV, Part I, 2010, 177–211, at 186.
322. Convention on Compensation for Damage Caused by Aircraft to Third Parties, signed at Montréal on 2 May 2009.

yet come into effect.[323] It likewise provides simply for liability on the part of the operator.[324] Article 13 explicitly provides:

> Neither the owner, lessor or financier retaining title or holding security of an aircraft, not being an operator, nor their servants or agents, shall be liable for damages under this Convention or the law of any State Party relating to third party damage.

A previous submission by the AWG to ICAO[325] sets out a very useful comparative overview of liability *régimes* under various national laws, dividing them into three groups:

(1) liability only where there is fault on the part of the owner;[326]
(2) strict liability on the part of the owner, except where it was not in possession or control of the aircraft (this exception is often by way of a subsequent amendment to a strict liability régime which did not recognize the difference between owners and operators); and
(3) strict liability on the part of the owner, regardless of its possession or control of the aircraft.[327]

As of the time of writing, it is unlikely that either the Unlawful Interference Compensation Convention (2009) or the General Risks Convention (2009) will come into force soon.[328]

[2] Liability to Passengers

The Warsaw Convention (1929) (under Article 1 thereof) or the Montreal Convention (1999) (under Article 1 thereof) may apply to an accident occurring between embarkation and disembarkation during international carriage by aircraft for reward, in each case as defined in the relevant convention.

If either Convention does apply, then, under Article 24 of the Warsaw Convention (1929), any action for damages 'however founded' may only be brought 'subject to the conditions and limits set out' in the Convention. Article 29 of the Montreal Convention (1999) provides likewise.

323. Thirteen countries have signed so far at the time of writing – *see* http://www.icao.int/secretariat/legal/List%20of%20Parties/2009_GRC_EN.pdf on 9 Sep. 2021.
324. Article 3.
325. http://www.awg.aero/pdf/SPECIAL%20GROUP%20ON%20THE%20MODERNIZATION%20OF%20THE%20ROME%20CONVENTION%20OF%201952.pdf on 4 May 2009.
326. *See* for example, section 146 para. 1 of the Austrian Aviation Act 1946.
327. *See* for example, section 11-1 of the Norwegian Aviation Act 1993; Arts 117 and 119 of the Greek Civil Aviation Code (making owner and operator jointly and severally liable for damage to persons on the surface); and Art. 127 of the Danish Aviation Act 1927.
328. Lee J.W., *The Regime of Compensable Damage in the Modernized Rome Conventions: A Comparison Between Article 3 of the General Risks Convention of 2009 and Article 17 of the Montreal Convention of 1999*, Annals of Air and Space Law, Volume XXXV, Part I, 2010, 213–230, at 229.

The Warsaw Convention (1929) and Montreal Convention (1999) refer to 'any action', and the references are not limited to any action against the airline as carrier and thus, this author argues, they properly apply to any action against anyone, whether founded in contract or tort.[329]

In *Sidhu v. British Airways*,[330] the court held that:

> 'it matters not whether the plaintiff brings his claim in contract ..., or in tort, as in the present case ...' and that 'the plaintiffs have no rights save under the Convention'.

The US Supreme Court concluded similarly in *El Al Israel Airlines Ltd v Tseng*[331] to the effect that:

> the Warsaw Convention precludes a passenger from maintaining an action for personal injury damages under local law when her claim does not satisfy the conditions of liability of the Convention.

Thus, if either Convention applies, it is submitted that the passenger's sole recourse is pursuant to the conditions and limits of the applicable Convention. The question which then falls to be considered is whether such recourse, against the carrier, excludes any recourse against a non-carrier, such as a lessor in the case of a leased aircraft.

It may, it is conceded, be argued that Article 24(1) of the Warsaw Convention (1929) in providing that:

> [i]n the cases covered by Articles 18 and 19 action for damages, 'however founded' may only be brought subject to the conditions and limits set out in the Convention.

and Article 24(2) thereof in providing that:

> [i]n the cases covered by Article 17 the provisions of the preceding paragraph also apply ... .

mean that only actions involving liability of the carrier are covered by this provision, since each of Articles 17, 18 and 19 begin: 'The carrier is liable ...', thus leaving to be examined the possibility, or otherwise, of actions outside of the terms of the Warsaw Convention against other parties, such as manufacturers and lessors.

Nevertheless, it is submitted that these references to '[i]n the cases covered by ...'. should be construed as references to the nature of the damage incurred, rather than to mean the plaintiff is nevertheless free to bring a claim against parties other than the carrier airline.

329. Article IX of the Guatemala City Protocol to the Warsaw Convention signed at Guatemala City on 8 Mar. 1971 did not come into force but expressly provided that the Warsaw Convention (1929), as amended, provided an exclusive remedy 'for any action for damages, however, founded, whether under this Convention or in contract or tort or otherwise ...', language not repeated in Art. VIII of the Montreal Additional Protocol No. 4 to the Warsaw Convention signed at Montreal on 25 Sep. 1975 or in Art. 29 of the Montreal Convention (1999).
330. 1 Aviation and Space Law Reports 217–219 (1994).
331. 525 U.S. 155 (1999).

In one case, *In re: Air Crash over the Taiwan Strait on 25 May 2002,*[332] an action was brought in the United States against both the airline, China Airlines, and the manufacturer, Boeing. The defendants brought a motion to have the action dismissed on the grounds of forum non conveniens, which was granted.[333]

What is of interest here is that China Airlines had waived the liability limits set out therein vis-à-vis plaintiffs whose claims were governed by the Warsaw Convention but the plaintiffs argued that this did not affect their right to proceed against Boeing. Morrow J. held that:

> The court finds, however, that the pendency of the Warsaw Convention cases, while not mandating retention of the actions in this forum, weighs slightly in favor of such a result.

In other words, there was no discussion that plaintiffs whose cases were governed by the Warsaw Convention could *only* proceed against the airline, without recourse to any other party such as, in this case, the manufacturer.

In *Ellis v. AAR Parts Trading, Inc.,*[334] discussed below in section §3.11[F], in the context of domestic US law, the issue was not discussed but it should be noted that the ill-fated flight here was a domestic flight[335] within the Philippines, not an international one.

Likewise, in a case[336] involving a crash by the Indonesian carrier Adam Air, the Northern District of Illinois granted a motion by defendant lessors and manufacturers to dismiss on grounds of forum non conveniens without discussing this issue but, as with Ellis, the flight involved was a domestic flight.

Not only in case law but also in the literature, it is remarkable how little discussion there has been on this issue. In an interesting review of *Ellis* and other US cases involving potential lessor liability, Clark and Richardson[337] do not discuss the effect of the Warsaw Convention or the Montreal Convention at all. Alexander H., in his article *Does the Montreal Convention 1999 Provide an Exclusive Remedy in the International Carriage of Goods and Passengers?*[338] does not discuss at all the issue of recourse against parties other than the carrier. Likewise, Tory A Weigand, in his article *Accident, Exclusivity, and Passenger Disturbances under the Warsaw Convention*[339] does not discuss the issue.[340]

332. 2002, 331 F. Supp. 2d 1176, 1187 (C. D. Cal 2004).
333. *See* sections §3.11[C][1] and §3.18[B] *infra* for further discussion on forum non conveniens.
334. 828 N.E. 2d 726, 730 (Ill. App. Ct. 2005).
335. Leaving aside any issue of passengers connecting form or to international flights – an issue not discussed in the case.
336. *In re Air Crash Disaster Over Makassar Strait, Sulawesi*, No. 09-cv-3805, MDL 2037, 2011 WL 91037 (N.D. Ill. 11 Jan. 2011).
337. Clark R.W. and Richardson T.M., *Is Lessor More?*, 75 Journal of Air Law & Commerce 2010, 69.
338. Annals of Air and Space Law, Volume XXXIV, 2009, at 379–436.
339. Weigand Published, 3/30/01.
340. *See also* Chassot L., *Les sources de la responsabilité du transporteur aérien international: entre conflict et complementarité*, Schulthess, Geneva, 2012, which expressly only deals with liability of operators.

Dempsey and Milde[341] do not expressly deal with lessors in this regard, although they do state that:

> Warsaw does not regulate the liability of aircraft manufacturers, of the airport authorities or air navigation services providers, or to (sic) domestic travel.[342]

It seems reasonable to assume that they are only talking of airlines in their treatment of Article 29, where they discussed the US Supreme Court finding in *El Al Israel Airlines v. Tseng*[343] that:

> the 'cardinal purpose' of the Warsaw Convention was to establish uniformity of law governing international aviation liability.[344]

Indeed, the title of the work makes clear that its focus is not on liability of parties other than air carriers.

Even if such argument[345] is correct, it is submitted that it does not apply to cases where the Montreal Convention applies. Unlike Article 24 of the Warsaw Convention (1929), the equivalent Article 29 of the Montreal Convention (1999) provides quite categorically:

> In the carriage of passengers, baggage and cargo, any action for damages, however founded, whether under this Convention or in contract or in tort or otherwise, can only be brought subject to the conditions and such limits of liability as are set out in this Convention ... .

The formulation 'any action for damages, however founded, whether under this Convention or in contract or in tort or otherwise' was introduced first in Guatemala

341. Dempsey P.S. and Milde M., *International Air Carrier Liability: The Montreal Convention of 1999*, McGill University Centre for Research in Air & Space Law, 2005.
342. *Ibid.*, at 71–72.
343. 525 U.S. 155 (1999).
344. *See also* Tompkins Jr G.N., *The Continuing Development of Montreal Convention 1999 Jurisprudence*, Air and Space Law, Volume 35, Issue 6, 2010, at 433–440, for a discussion on the differing judgments following *Tseng* in the United States on this issue, some of which, he argues, at 434, seek 'to disregard or rationalize a restrictive interpretation of the Supreme Court's decision' in *Tseng*. It must be borne in mind that these cases concern actions against carriers, and not against non-carriers such as lessors. He writes, at 436, that eventually:

> this issue of exclusivity and pre-emption may find its way to the US Supreme Court and be resolved finally in the United States. Until that time, we shall have to live with the courts in the Seventh and Ninth Federal Judicial Circuits, which seem to be determined to disregard the clearly expressed intent of the Parties in Article 29 as to the exclusivity and pre-emptive effect of MC99.

345. That claims against lessor are not precluded by the Warsaw Convention (1929) or the Montreal Convention (1999) where it applies.

City Protocol 1971[346] in Article IX[347] and repeated in Montreal Protocol No. 4[348] in Article VIII.

The language is not restricted to 'any action for damages against the carrier' but to 'any action for damages', period. Where the Montreal Convention applies, this author sees no grounds from the text for any claim being brought against the lessor of the aircraft involved on the grounds that the lessor is not the carrier. Given the different wording, case law under the Warsaw Convention on this issue is not relevant to interpretation of the Montreal Convention.

Further, Article 37[349] of the Montreal Convention (1999) provides:

> Nothing in this Convention shall prejudice the question whether a person liable for damage in accordance with its provisions has a right of recourse against any other person.

In support of his view, this author refers to Article 31(1) of the Vienna Convention (1969)[350] which provides that:

> A treaty shall be interpreted in good faith in accordance with the ordinary meaning to be given to the terms of the treaty in their context and in the light of its object and purpose.

Article 31(2) of the Vienna Convention (1969) makes clear that the context includes the preamble and annexes in addition to the text of the main body itself. The preamble to the Montreal Convention (1999) does not talk of carriers at all but of 'protection of the interests of consumers' and the 'need for equitable compensation'.[351]

Article 32 of the Vienna Convention (1969) allows recourse to supplementary means of interpretation, 'including the preparatory work of the treaty and the circumstances of its conclusion' in three cases only:

---

346. Protocol to Amend the Convention for the Unification of Certain Rules Relating to International Carriage by Air Signed at Warsaw on 12 Oct. 1929 as Amended by the Protocol Done at The Hague on 28 Sep. 1955, Signed at Guatemala City on 8 Mar. 1971.
347. Unfortunately, in his article on the Montreal Convention, one of the participants in the conference which produced the Guatemala City Protocol did not discuss the reasons for the different wording from that of the Warsaw Convention. *See* Mercer A., *The Montreal Convention 1999: The Challenges of a New, Modern Liability Regime for International Civil Aviation – An Airline Perspective on Certain Features*, Civil Aviation Summit, 29–30 Mar. 2005.
348. Additional Protocol No. 4 to Amend the Convention for the Unification of Certain Rules Relating to International Carriage by Air Signed at Warsaw on 12 Oct. 1929 as Amended by the Protocol Done at The Hague on 28 Sep. 1955, Signed at Montreal on 25 Sep. 1975.
349. This provision has no equivalent in the Warsaw Convention but was copied from Art. 30A of the Montreal Protocol No. 4 (1975) thereto.
350. Vienna Convention on the Law of Treaties, done at Vienna on 23 May 1969.
351. It is true that Art. 29 appears within Chapter III of the Montreal Convention which is headed 'Liability of the Carrier ...' but is entirely consistent with a channeling of claims against the carrier in the first instance. Likewise, Art. 43 allowing servants and agents of a carrier to avail of the conditions and limits of liability of the Montreal Convention is, it is submitted, no more than clarifying the liability of the master or principal as a matter of *respondeat superior* in a master–servant or principal–agent relationship. On the other hand, it is conceded that this could be argued as consistent with the view that express extension beyond the carrier itself is necessary as it was done in the case of servants and agents.

(1) in order to confirm the meaning resulting from the application of Article 31;[352]
(2) to determine the meaning when the interpretation according to Article 31 ... leaves the meaning ambiguous or obscure;[353] or
(3) 'to determine the meaning when the interpretation according to article 31 ... leads to a result which is manifestly absurd or unreasonable'.[354]

It is submitted that, following these provisions, nothing in the context suggests that the words 'against the carrier' should be implied after the words 'any action for damages' in Article 29 of the Montreal Convention (1999). Article 29 is clear on its face, in its context, and does not lead manifestly to an absurd or unreasonable result: the plaintiff brings its claim against the carrier under Article 29, or not at all, and the carrier, in turn, is not restricted from bringing a claim against any other parties.[355] Thus, recourse should not be had to supplementary means of interpretation.

In considering a case involving the interpretation of Article 35 of the Montreal Convention (1999) (providing for a two year limitation period for bringing claims thereunder), in *UPS Supply Chain Solutions f/k/a Menlo Worldwide Forwarding, Inc. v. Qantas Airways Limited at al.*,[356] O'Scannlain J of the US Ninth Circuit Court of Appeals held, in response to an argument that the drafters of the Montreal Convention (1999) did not intend to overrule precedents under the equivalent provision of the Warsaw Convention (1929), that:

> We are not allowed to consider the treaty's drafting history, however because its text is unambiguous.[357]

O'Scannlain J cited as authority for his decision the following:[358]

> The interpretation of a treaty, like the interpretation of a statute, begins with its text. Medellin v Texas, 552 U.S. 491, 506 (2008). And, where the text of a treaty is clear, a court has 'no power to insert an amendment' based on consideration of other sources. Chan v Korean Air Lines, Ltd., 490 U.S. 122, 134 (1989).[359]

This is consistent with the judgment of the US Court of Appeals, Second Circuit, in *Fishman Fishman v. Delta Airlines Inc.*[360] which held that:

> In interpreting the Warsaw Convention, we look first to the literal language of the treaty and go no further if that language is reasonably susceptible to no more than one interpretation ... Because the language of Article 29 is susceptible to at least

352. Article 32. Note this is only to confirm, not to overturn.
353. Article 32(a).
354. Article 32(b).
355. Article 37.
356. US Court of Appeals, 9th Circuit, No. 08-55281, 2 Oct. 2010.
357. At 2501.
358. The United States is not a party to the Vienna Convention (1969) but, among others, the International Court of Justice has confirmed that this convention includes provisions which are considered as customary law. Hence, the United States may also be bound by them.
359. At 2496.
360. Numbers 1818, 2038, Dockets 96-9345, 96-9457 (1998).

> two plausible interpretations, we turn to the negotiating history of the Convention to resolve the ambiguity.[361]

Nevertheless, courts do not interpret treaties in precisely the same manner as private contracts.

In the United States, the Supreme Court has held:

> Treaties are construed more liberally than private agreements, and to ascertain their meaning we may look beyond the written words to the history of the treaty, the negotiations, and the practical construction adopted by the parties.[362]

In the United Kingdom, Lord Wilberforce[363] in the House of Lords in *Fothergill v. Monarch Airlines Ltd*[364] noted that the courts of the United States are more liberal in referring to *travaux préparatoires* than those of the United Kingdom and commented:

> there may be cases where such travaux preparatories can profitably be used. These cases should be rare, and only where two conditions are fulfilled: first, that the material involved is public and accessible, and, secondly, that the travaux preparatories (sic) clearly and indisputably point to a definite legislative intention.[365]

Even if, pursuant to Article 32 of the Vienna Convention or otherwise, recourse is had to supplementary means of interpretation of Article 29 of the Montreal Convention (1999), we find nothing substantial in the *travaux préparatoires*[366] therefore discussing the significance of the difference in wording on this point between the Warsaw Convention and the Montreal Convention or anything to suggest that the words 'against the carrier' should be implied after the words 'any action for damages' in Article 29 of the Montreal Convention.

This author submits, therefore, that the better reading of the Montreal Convention (1999), construed in accordance with the Vienna Convention (1969), is to limit a passenger's recourse, in circumstances where the damage complained of is covered by the Montreal Convention (1999), to the airline, and to the airline alone, while allowing the airline then to bring a claim where appropriate against other parties such as manufacturers or lessor. In other words, the passenger cannot in such circumstances claim directly against the manufacturer or the lessor.

He acknowledges, nevertheless, that this is a disputed (perhaps minority) view; for a contrasting view, *see* the discussion of Wool in section §3.11[B][1] *supra*. Specifically, in the context of contrasting it with Article 29 of the Montreal Convention

361. At 3-31.
362. *Air France v. Saks*, 470 U.S. 392, 405, 105 S.Ct. 1338, 1345, 84 L.Ed.2d 289 (1985), at 1345.
363. Cited with approval by Lord Phillips, *per curiam*, in *KLM Royal Dutch Airlines v. Morris*, [2001] EWCA Civ 790.
364. [1981] AC 251; [1980] 2 All ER 696; [1980] 3 WLR 209; [1980] 2 Lloyd's Rep 295, (33 ICLQ 797).
365. *Ibid.*, at 75.
366. International Civil Aviation Organization, *International Conference on Air Law, Montreal, 10–28 May 1999, Minutes*, 1999, at 103.

(1999), Wool writes of Article 29.1 of the Unlawful Interference Compensation Convention (2009)[367] that:

> [t]his provision, while superficially similar to parallel clauses in other air law instruments, is in fact quite new. It channels liability to the operators. It prevents actions by third-party victims against others.[368]

Thus, by contrast, Wool does not believe that Article 29 of the Montreal Convention (1999) is so limited. Likewise, Neenan[369] writes that unlike certain other conventions:

> the Montreal Convention and its predecessors do not create a positive obligation on a plaintiff to bring their action only against the carrier; they neither state that no other person shall be liable nor do they state that the right for compensation can only be exercised against the carrier.[370]

Further, this proposition is not always made by defendants in cases where it could be: for example, *In re Air Crash Over the Mid-Atlantic on 1 June 2009*[371] where the US District Court for the Northern District of California granted the defendant manufacturers' motions to dismiss all claims arising from the 2009 accident of Air France Flight 447 over the Atlantic Ocean on grounds of forum non conveniens.

Support for this author's view is, however, expressed by Mendelsohn[372] who argues for just such an approach on the basis of the decision in *Tseng*:[373]

> In short, victims enjoy full recoveries quickly and under the absolute liability standards of Montreal 1999. And afterwards, the professionals can litigate for as long as they wish over the issue of who was partially, mostly or completely at fault.[374]

Whalen[375] points out that, by the addition of the words 'or in contract or in tort or otherwise' to Article 29 of the Montreal Convention (1999), the drafters were 'unwilling to leave Article 24 alone',[376] and thus differentiated it from the Article 24 of the Warsaw Convention (1929). The effect is that:

367. Discussed in section §3.11[B][1] *supra*.
368. Wool J., *Lessor, Financier, and Manufacturer Perspectives on the New Third-Party Liability Conventions*, The Air & Space Lawyer, Volume 22, Issue 4, 2010.
369. Neenan P., *The Effectiveness of the Exclusivity Provision in Foreign Serious Accidents: Does the Montreal Convention Channel Liability Against the Carrier?*, LLM Thesis, Leiden University, 2011.
370. *Ibid.*, at 53.
371. MDL Docket No. 10–2144-CRB (NDCal. 4 Oct. 2010).
372. Mendelsohn A.I., *Foreign Plaintiffs, Forum Non Conveniens and the 1999 Montreal Convention*, paper presented to the IATA Legal Symposium held in February 2011 at Vancouver, British Columbia, Canada.
373. *Supra*.
374. *Ibid.*, at 9.
375. Whalen T.J., *The New Warsaw Convention: The Montreal Convention*, Air & Space Law, Volume XXV, Issue 1, 2000.
376. *Ibid.*, at 20.

> [t]he Delegates also unwittingly may have made a fundamental change in the litigation posture of Warsaw cases in the United States.[377]

A fortiori the same case can be made for the innovation of the words 'In the carriage of passengers, baggage and cargo, any action for damages' in Article 29 of the Montreal Convention(1999).

A case[378] against a lessor currently before the California state courts may help to cast some judicial light on the matter and, however, decided, is, given the stakes, likely to be appealed through the federal courts unless settled before then.

No matter how it is decided, it should not be assumed that other courts will follow its approach. Although writing apparently on the assumption that the Warsaw Convention (1929) only deals with claims against the carrier, and in the context of who has the right to bring such claims, Myburgh writes:

> While Civilian jurisprudence has consistently tended to the view that the Convention was intended to operate as an exclusive code, thereby restricting rights of action to the consignor and consignee named in the air waybill exclusively, courts in Common Law jurisdictions have, for the most part, traditionally adopted a non-exclusive reading of the Convention.[379]

As a matter of policy rather than of textual interpretation, this author also submits that his interpretation of the Montreal Convention (1999) is more consistent with the trend towards operator-only liability discussed in section §3.11[B][1] *supra* in the context of the Unlawful Interference Compensation Convention (2009)[380] and the General Risks Convention (2009).[381] Certainly, it would result in disallowing a claim against a lessor by a plaintiff who could claim instead from the carrier airline: this would not, in this author's view, lead to an unjust result.[382]

---

377. *Ibid.*
378. *Hassanati v. International Lease Finance Corporation*, No. BC452279 (Cal. Super. Ct. 10 Jan. 2011).
379. Myburgh P., *Title to Sue under the Warsaw Convention: Construing a Dinosaur Text in the Digital Age*, New Zealand Business Law Quarterly, Volume 6, 2000, 305–313, at 306.
380. *See* International Civil Aviation Organization, *Report of the Rapporteur: Draft Convention on Compensation for Damage Caused by Aircraft to Third Parties*, Legal Committee – 33rd Session, Montreal, 21 Apr.–2 May 2008, in Annals of Air and Space Law, Volume XXXIV, 571–586.
381. *See* International Civil Aviation Organization, *Report of the Rapporteur: Draft Convention on Compensation for Damage Caused by Aircraft to Third Parties, in Case of Unlawful Interference*, Legal Committee – 33rd Session, Montreal, 21 Apr.–2 May 2008, in Annals of Air and Space Law, Volume XXXIV, 549–570.
382. In this regard, there is a fascinating discussion in Bunker D.H., *The Law of Aerospace Finance in Canada*, McGill University, Montréal, 1988, at 62, about how the International Institute for the Unification of Private Law, in its preliminary draft uniform rules with respect to international leasing (which drafts eventually became the Cape Town Convention (2001) discussed in sections §3.14[D][2] and §3.15[C] *infra*), at Art. 7 thereof, proposed that a lessor would be excluded from liability in tort and contract while merely in its capacity as lessor where it is essentially performing a financial function (injection of necessary capital for purchase of the equipment).

    Although Bunker notes that such rules were initially aimed solely at finance not operating leases, and although the Cape Town Convention (2001) did not distinguish between operating and finance leases, the principle is the same: the operating lessor performs essentially a financial function (injection of necessary capital for purchase of the equipment but also

This is consistent with the views of Mauritz,[383] who writes:

> As financiers[384] of aircraft are generally not involved in the operational aspects of the flight of the aircraft, the chances of their implication in liability suits are evidently more remote than those of the operators of aircraft. However, owners of aircraft may be implicated in certain cases, for instance for supplying a defective aircraft or aircraft components or for improper maintenance, if they are obliged to provide such a service under the conditions of the lease. More alarmingly, they may even be implicated for the mere fact that they are perceived as the so-called deepest pocket from which to seek compensation.
>
> These distinctions between operators and owners of aircraft imply that the legislature should clearly exclude the category of owners from his absolute or strict liability regime if the owners are not the same entities as the operators of aircraft.[385]

Support for this view is given by Germany in its presentation[386] in Montréal in 2009 on the draft Unlawful Interference Compensation Convention (2009) then under discussion, where it made clear that it objected to a proposed complete exoneration of all parties other than the operator, noting, for example, that such a provision would encompass manufacturers and thus breach European law on products liability,[387] with the result that the EU Member States would be prevented from ratifying the Convention.[388] Germany drew a distinction, however, between entities involved in the operational process, such as manufacturers and airlines, on the one hand, and parties not involved in the operational process, on the other hand, such as aircraft lessors and financiers, since they are not involved in the operational process and thus cannot 'contribute to damage'.[389]

Such an argument, ultimately, as noted, adopted in the Unlawful Interference Compensation Convention (2009), cannot be distinguished from that of a claim of a passenger for injury where the Montreal Convention (1999) applies: the lessor is no more an operator under either situation.

---

assumption of residual value risk. It is (except in the rather different case of airline lessors) never an operator or maintenance performer itself.

383. Mauritz A.J., *Liability of the Operators and Owners of Aircraft for Damage Inflicted to Persons and Property on the Surface*, PhD Thesis, Leiden University, 2003.
384. *Ibid.*, note that Mauritz adds: 'Under leasing agreements, the term "owner" can refer to a number of potential entities engaged in the financing of aircraft, such as lenders, investors, and lessors of aircraft. Lessors on their part can be divided into financial and operational lessors, although the latter category is strictly speaking not a financier due to the nature of the lease.'
385. *Ibid.*, at 45. It is conceded, however, that Mauritz is writing prescriptively *de lege ferenda* rather than descriptively *de lege lata*.
386. International Conference on Air Law (Montreal, 20 Apr.–2 May 2009), *Draft Convention on Compensation for Damage to Third Parties, Resulting from Acts of Unlawful Interference Involving Aircraft*, presented by Germany, ICAO DCCD Doc. No. 7, 13/03/09. Also, *see* section §3.11[B][1] *supra*.
387. *See* section §3.11[B][3] *infra*.
388. *Ibid.*, at 4.2.
389. *Ibid.*, at 4.3.

The report[390] of the rapporteur on the draft Unlawful Interference Compensation Convention (2009) rightly discusses this as an 'integrated approach to the industry' which:

> channels all claims to the aircraft operator' for the good reason that leaving out non-operators from the protections of the convention would undermine the protection that the Convention gives to aircraft operators because of the potential that these other actors have for recovery from the carriers through interlocking agreements, subrogation and other recovery means.

In the context of the United States, the provisions of the US Federal Aviation Act[391] discussed further in section §3.11[C][2] *infra*, to the effect that a 'lessor ... is liable for personal injury, death or property damage ... only when a civil aircraft is in the actual possession or control of the lessor ...' are also consistent with the Warsaw Convention and the Montreal Convention (1999) on this point.

For these reasons, efforts to found liability based on the tort of negligent entrustment will, of necessity, involve an argument that the Warsaw Convention and Montreal Convention (1999) do not apply - either on the basis that the relevant convention does not apply at all on technical grounds[392] or on the grounds (even if doubted by this author) that even if they do apply, they do not limit recourse against the owner or lessor.

A further reason for arguing that they do not apply is that the whole *raison d'être* of negligent entrustment theory, discussed next, is to bring cases within the US judicial system which would not otherwise be justiciable there.[393]

If the Warsaw Convention (1929) or Montreal Convention (1999) applied, not only would the exclusive remedy provisions thereof limit a passenger's claim to one against the carrier, but US jurisdiction might well become impossible anyway.

Under Article 28 of the Warsaw Convention, a claim thereunder must be brought:

> at the option of the plaintiff, in the territory of one of the High Contracting Parties, either before the Court having jurisdiction where the carrier is ordinarily resident, or has his principal place of business or has an establishment by which the contract is made or before the Court having jurisdiction at the place of destination.

Article 33(1) of the Montreal Convention (1999) repeats in essence this provision and Article 33(2) thereof adds a fifth jurisdiction, and thus a greater possibility of bringing an action within the jurisdiction of the US courts,[394] for cases of death or personal injury, allowing additionally the plaintiff to choose to bring an action:

390. International Civil Aviation Organization, *Report of the Rapporteur: Draft Convention on Compensation for Damage Caused by Aircraft to Third Parties, in Case of Unlawful Interference*, Legal Committee - 33rd Session, Montreal, 21 Apr.–2 May 2008, in Annals of Air and Space Law, Volume XXXIV, 549–570, at 563.
391. 49 USC S. 44112.
392. For example, a purely domestic point to point flight with no connecting international passengers.
393. *See* the discussion of forum non conveniens in sections §3.11[C][1] and §3.18[B] *infra*.
394. Discussed in section §3.11[C] *infra*.

> in the territory of the State Party in which at the time of the accident the passenger has his or her principal and permanent residence and to or from which the carrier operates services for the carriage of passengers by air ... .[395]

Thus, for example, if an action based on negligent entrustment or any other theory were brought against a lessor in the United States simply by virtue of the lessor being incorporated or resident there, where there is no other connection to the United States, that action should not be allowed to proceed in a case where the Warsaw Convention, arguably, or Montreal Convention, clearly, applies both because the exclusive remedy should be against the carrier and because the United States is not one of the jurisdictions allowed thereunder.

[3] Product Liability

Product liability[396] concerns the liability of the manufacturer of goods for damage caused by those goods and is not of direct relevance to the situation of the lessor of an aircraft. Nevertheless, it is of indirect relevance in the context of the foregoing discussion on the nature of the exclusivity of the remedies set out in the Warsaw Convention and the Montreal Convention and thus will be examined here in brief.

Council Directive 85/374/EEC of 25 July 1985 deals with product liability and provides that 'a producer shall be liable for damage caused by a defect in his product'.[397] Product is defined to mean all movables[398] and thus includes aircraft. A producer means not only the manufacturer of the product but also 'any person who imports into the Community a product for sale, hire, leasing or any form of distribution in the course of his business'.[399]

Thus, if the Warsaw Convention (1929) or the Montreal Convention (1999) can be construed, as argued in section §3.11[B][2] *supra*, in such a manner as to exclude recourse against a lessor where there is recourse to the operator thereunder, there will be a conflict with this Directive on product liability. It is clearly undesirable for states to have conflicting international legal obligations.

That is not to say that this is a reason to give anything other than their plain meaning to the words of the Warsaw Convention and the Montreal Convention where they are unambiguous but, although Brownlie[400] points out that '[j]urists are in general

395. Dempsey P.S. and Milde M., *International Air Carrier Liability: The Montreal Convention of 1999*, McGill University Centre for Research in Air and Space Law, 2005, suggest at footnote 485 on p. 219 that the requirement for such service may be satisfied by code-sharing or wet lease arrangements.
396. Defined by Nolan J.R. and Nolan-Haley J.M., *Black's Law Dictionary*, 6th Edition, West Publishing Co., 1990, as referring to the 'legal liability of manufacturers and sellers to compensate buyers, users and even bystanders, for damages or injuries suffered because of defects in goods purchased, noting that liability may also be imposed ... occasionally ... upon a lessor ...'.
397. Article 1.
398. Article 2.
399. Article 3(1).
400. Brownlie I., *Principles of Public International Law*, Oxford, 1982.

cautious about formulating a code of "rules of interpretation"'[401] for treaties, he points out that the International Law Commission and the Institute of International Law consider the 'intention of the parties as expressed in the text'[402] as being the best guide to the parties' intent.

Further, as noted, the Vienna Convention (1969)[403] provides, in Article 31(1) that:

> A treaty shall be interpreted in good faith in accordance with the ordinary meaning to be given to the terms of the treaty in their context and in the light of its object and purpose.

If, on the other hand, the Warsaw Convention (1929) or the Montreal Convention (1999) can indeed be construed in such a manner[404] as not to preclude any action against a manufacturer where there is recourse to the operator thereunder, there is a different problem. If there is recourse to any party other than the operator, then these conventions do not distinguish between such other parties, in other words, they do not distinguish between manufacturers and lessors. This would lead to a different result than claims brought under the Unlawful Interference Compensation Convention (2009) or the General Claims Convention (2009),[405] which do distinguish between manufacturers, who have an operational role, and lessors, who do not.

It also appears from this analysis that there is a prima facie conflict between the Unlawful Interference Compensation Convention (2009) and the General Claims Convention (2009), on the one hand, precisely because they make this distinction, and the Council Directive 85/374/EEC, because it does not.[406]

Recommendations for dealing with the varying approaches of these actually or potentially conflicting legal provisions are made in Chapter 4 section §4.02 *infra*.

[4] A Note on Public International Air Law Instruments

In the realm of public international air law,[407] there are some conventions which are worth briefly examining for any relevance to aircraft operating leasing and in particular indemnities with respect to liability to third parties.

---

401. At 624.
402. *Ibid.*
403. Vienna Convention on the Law of Treaties done at Vienna on 23 May 1969.
404. This is the opposite of the position taken by this author in section §3.11[B][2] *supra*.
405. *See* section §3.11[B][1] *supra*.
406. This would not be the first such conflict between the Montreal Convention (1999) and European Union law: *see* Dempsey P.S. and Johansson S.O., *Montreal v. Brussels: The Conflict of Laws on the Issue of Delay in International Air Carriage*, Air and Space Law, Volume 35, Issue 3, 2010 which discusses Commission Regulation (EC) 261/2004 and the Montreal Convention (1999) where they point out, at 208, that, under Art. 27 of the Vienna Convention (1969), if an 'international convention provides that its remedies are exclusive, then any inconsistent domestic law of ratifying States addressing the same subject is void'.
407. *See Public International Air Law Instruments*, Annals of Air and Space Law, Volume XXX Part I, McGill University, 2005, at 5-322.

[a] Tokyo Convention (1963)

Under Article 1(b) of the Tokyo Convention (1963),[408] the Convention applies to 'acts which, whether or not they are offences' may or do jeopardize the safety of the aircraft or of persons or property therein ...' Under Article 1(2), the Tokyo Convention only applies where such acts are 'done by a person on board any aircraft ... while that aircraft is in flight or on the surface of the high seas or of any other area outside the territory of any State'.[409]

Abeyratne[410] states that as the Tokyo Convention (1963) provides that the state of registration[411] has jurisdiction for offences committed on board aircraft, and as more carriers are entering into lease agreements, these developments 'necessitate a closer look at the requirements of registration and nationality as dictated to by the Chicago Convention', presumably in the context of how such state of registration may differ in the case of leased and owned aircraft due to Article 83*bis*.

Having undertaken just such a closer look, this author has concluded that there is little material relevance being inferred by reason simply of an aircraft being leased rather than owned and thus being registered in a different State than would otherwise be the case.

ICAO set up[412] a panel of experts on lease, charter, and interchange of aircraft. The panel's recommendations ultimately led to Article 83*bis* of the Chicago Convention (1944).[413] It considered recommending amending Article 3 of the Tokyo Convention (1963) to provide that, in the case of an aircraft leased without crew to a lessee having its principal place of business in a state other than the state of registration of the aircraft, that other State should 'also be competent to exercise jurisdiction'.[414] Various amendments to this effect were discussed but misgivings were expressed and ultimately, although the relevant:

> Tokyo Conference had before it a text prepared by an ICAO Legal Subcommittee, [it] rejected the idea of making criminal jurisdiction depend upon a private-law transaction such as a lease.[415]

Article 11 of the Tokyo Convention requires contracting states to take 'all appropriate measures' to restore control of an aircraft to its lawful commander when:

> a person on board has unlawfully committed by force or threat thereof an act of interference, seizure or other wrongful exercise of control of an aircraft in flight ... .

408. Convention on Offences and Certain Other Acts Committed on Board Aircraft, signed at Tokyo on 14 Sep. 1963.
409. Note the reference to 'any State', not 'any Contracting State'.
410. Abeyratne R.I.R., *Aviation in Crisis*, Ashgate, 2004, at 101.
411. Article 3(1).
412. Pursuant to ICAO Council decision C-Min 87/13 paras 17–24 of 7 Apr. 1976.
413. *See* section §3.15[H] *infra*.
414. Fitzgerald G.F., *The Lease, Charter and Interchange of Aircraft in International Relations: Amendments to the Chicago and Rome Conventions*, Annals of Air and Space Law, Volume II, 1977, 103–137, at 120.
415. *Ibid.*, at 136.

The person must be established to be on board the aircraft, the act complained of must be unlawfully committed 'by force or threat thereof' and, most of all, while the aircraft is 'in flight'.[416]

Article 10 of the Tokyo Convention (1963) provides that the aircraft commander and other crew members are not responsible to any person against whom they take actions under the Tokyo Convention (1963), such as under Articles 5–9 therefore allowing him or crew members authorized by him to restrain and deliver to competent authorities a person whom he has 'reasonable grounds'[417] to believe has committed an offence as contemplated by the Tokyo Convention (1963).

Article 10 is where leasing is of relevance as Article 10 also provides that the owner, operator and person on whose behalf the flight is performed shall have no such liability either.

In *Eid v. Alaska Airways, Inc.*,[418] the US 9th Circuit Court of Appeals upheld the requirement of Article 6(1) of the Tokyo Convention (1963) that the aircraft commander had reasonable grounds to restrain and hand over suspects to the competent authorities and that it was a for a jury to decide whether he had indeed acted on such reasonable grounds to determine whether the airline was entitled to the protection of Article 10. Following this logic, a lessor would also have to show that the aircraft commander acted on reasonable grounds in order to avail of the protections of Article 10 in that a claim was made against the owner.

However, mere failure to establish the protection of Article 10 does not equate to liability on the part of the lessor for the actions of the aircraft commander provided, in the case of a dry lease, by the lessee. Nevertheless, while it may be fair to impute a reasonableness test in order for the aircraft commander's employer to be relieved of responsibility, it is the author's view that for a lessor to rely on the protection of Article 10, it should not have to show that the aircraft commander acted reasonably since it has no control whatsoever over the commander.

[b] Hague Convention (1970)

Article 1(a) of the Hague Convention (1970)[419] makes it an offence punishable under Article 2 by 'severe penalties' where any person on board an aircraft in flight:

> unlawfully, by force or threat thereof, or by any other form of intimidation, seizes, or exercises control of, that aircraft, or attempts to perform such act ... .[420]

416. As defined in Art. 1(3).
417. Article 6(1).
418. 621 F.3d 858 (9th Cir. 2010).
419. Convention for the Suppression of Unlawful Seizure of Aircraft, signed at The Hague on 16 Dec. 1970.
420. Under Art. II of the Protocol Supplementary to the Convention for the Suppression of Unlawful Seizure of Aircraft, signed at Beijing on 10 Sep. 2010, which is not yet in force, this will, when it does come into force, be replaced by language referring to the situation where a person 'unlawfully and intentionally seizes or exercises control of an aircraft in service by force or threat thereof, or by coercion or by any other form of intimidation, or by any technological means' or, *inter alia*, attempts or credibly threatens to do so.

A contracting State must establish its jurisdiction over offences covered by the Hague Convention (1970) not only when the aircraft in question is registered in such state[421] or located within its territory[422] but also:

> when the offence is committed on board an aircraft leased without crew to a lessee who has his principal place of business or, if the lessee has no such place of business, his permanent residence, in that State.[423]

Nevertheless, it is submitted that, apart from this provision, as with the Tokyo Convention (1963), the Hague Convention (1970) has little or no applicability to the lessor–lessee relationship.

[c] Montreal Convention (1971)

Under the Montreal Convention (1971),[424] a person commits an offence under Article 1(b) thereof if he:

> destroys an aircraft in service or causes damage to such an aircraft which renders it incapable of flight or which is likely to endanger its safety in flight ... .

Article 4(2) provides that the Montreal Convention (1971)[425] shall apply:

> irrespective of whether the aircraft is engaged in an international or domestic flight, only if:
>
> aa) the place of take-off or landing, actual or intended, of the aircraft is situated outside the territory of the State of registration of that aircraft; or
>
> ba) the offence is committed in the territory of a State other than the State of registration of the aircraft.

The Beijing Convention (2010)[426] will, now that it is in force,[427] prevail,[428] as between states party thereto, over the Montreal Convention (1971), but, as it is not yet in force,[429] the Montreal Convention (1971) remains in force for all states party thereto.[430]

421. Article 4(1)(a).
422. Article 4(1)(b).
423. Article 4(1)(c).
424. Convention for the Suppression of Unlawful Acts against the Safety of Civil Aviation, signed at Montreal on 23 Sep. 1971.
425. Article 5(2) of the Beijing Convention (2010) reads likewise.
426. Convention on the Suppression of Unlawful Acts Relating to International Civil Aviation done at Beijing on 10 Sep. 2010.
427. It is not yet in force: *see* http://www.icao.int/secretariat/legal/List%20of%20Parties/Beijing_Conv_EN.pdf on 9 Sep. 2021.
428. Pursuant to Art. 24(a) thereof.
429. For a detailed examination, *see* Pier A. and Gill M., *Will the New ICAO-Beijing Instruments Build a Chinese Wall for International Aviation Security?*, Vanderbilt Journal of Transnational Law, Volume 47, Issue 1, January 2014, at 145–237.
430. In any event, Art. 1(b) of the Beijing Convention 2010 is the same as Art. 1(b) of the Montreal Convention 1971.

In the context of leasing, Article 5(d) of the Montreal Convention (1971) obliges contracting states to establish jurisdiction:

> when the offence is committed against or on board an aircraft leased without crew to a lessee who has his principal place of business or, if the lessee has no such place of business, his permanent residence, in that State.[431]

[C] Negligent Entrustment

In the context of liability to third parties, such as passengers or third parties on the ground, with whom there is no contract, aircraft lessors need to be mindful of a relatively new theory of tort liability whereby a lessor may be liable for injury or damage caused by a lessee while in possession of an aircraft pursuant to an operating lease between it and the lessor. This is the theory of negligent entrustment – the lessor negligently entrusted an unsuitable entity with possession of a potentially dangerous asset, an aircraft, with resulting liability for damage caused by that unsuitable entity.

There are two primary theories of liability, one seeking to impose liability based on delivery of a defective or improperly maintained aircraft. The second theory is much broader and seeks to impose liability where the lessor is alleged to have delivered an aircraft on lease to an airline that 'was not capable of operating and maintaining the aircraft in a safe and appropriate manner',[432] thus, essentially attempting to make the lessor vicariously liable for the negligent act of the airline.

A classic example of the second theory is an adult allowing a minor to use his or her car, where an accident occurs and the adult knows or has reason to know that the driver, whether due to inexperience or otherwise, is likely to use it in a manner involving an unreasonable risk of harm to third parties. The instinctive answer to this might be to say that there is surely a difference between the case of a minor who does not yet have a driving licence and one who does have a licence.[433]

[1] Extension to Aircraft Operating Leases

Applied to an aircraft, a lessor would argue that the theory was not intended for complex commercial transactions where the lessor is not an operator and relies on the lessee's possession of all necessary licences and certificates issued by the lessee's aviation authority.[434]

431. Article 8(1)(d) of the Beijing Convention 2010 reads likewise except for non-substantive gender neutralizing changes in language.
432. Byrnes T.P. and Kass G.R., *Aircraft Lessor Liability*, Joint Presentation to 26th Annual Conference of the International Society of Transport Aircraft Trading, Scottsdale, Arizona, held on 17 Mar. 2009.
433. *Ibid.*
434. *Ibid.*

As has been noted by Byrnes T.B. and Kass G.R.,[435] this puts the lessor in the difficult position of either defending the lessee's maintenance practices as sufficient or else having to justify its failure to uncover insufficient maintenance practices. They suggest dealing with this in the language in the lease dealing with lessor's inspection rights but this author doubts that this will be sufficient for plaintiffs' counsel – they will, it is submitted, either argue that the wording in the lease leads to an inspection right sufficient to uncover insufficiencies or, if such wording is not there, blame lessor for failing to include such language.

A leading plaintiff's counsel, Don Nolan, is quoted as stating that a lessor 'having in the lease reserved to itself rights of inspection, and requiring that maintenance and safety be followed ... can face responsibility for loss of life'.[436] One can only imagine his reaction to a lessor which did not reserve in its lease inspection rights and did not require the lessee to follow all applicable rules relating to safety and maintenance. In a press release, his firm has stated that lessors have a duty 'to provide oversight to ensure that passengers fly on airplanes that are adequately equipped, safely maintained, and operated by properly trained pilots'.[437] It is submitted that such a duty is, in fact, the duty of the airline with operational control of the aircraft and the aviation authority granting it its requisite licences and certificates.

The reason behind the extension of the theory of negligent entrustment has a lot to do with a desire on the part of plaintiffs' counsel, it is submitted, to get emotionally powerful if legally weak arguments in front of reputedly more generous American juries than compelling legal scholarship.

An argument against the dismissal of action from US courts on grounds of forum non conveniens often involves an argument that foreign plaintiffs 'often face insurmountable procedural or practical problems that effectively preclude redress in their home countries'[438] such as 'a 10-year plus backlog of cases, lack of access to qualified aviation attorneys in their home jurisdiction, inadequacies in their justice system, and the high cost of prosecuting claims ...'.[439]

On the other side is the argument that 'only those matters sufficiently related to the United States'[440] remain in those courts. A three-step analysis is applied to considering motions to dismiss on grounds of forum non conveniens: the degree of deference to be given to the plaintiff's chosen forum, the adequacy of an alternative forum and the balancing of interest of the parties.

Even allowing for the argument that a defendant cannot seriously argue that its home jurisdiction is not a convenient forum,[441] the other arguments raised above against dismissal can be dealt with by examination of the adequacy of the alternative

435. *Ibid.*
436. Quoted in Chicago Lawyer Magazine, May 2008.
437. Press release of Nolan Law Group, 10 Mar. 2008.
438. Verna M.P., *Convenience Has Nothing to Do with FNC Motions*, The Air and Space Lawyer, Volume 22, Issue 1, 2008, at 9.
439. *Ibid.*, at 10.
440. Dameris T.T., Weiner D.J. and Crane A.R., *The United States Is No Longer the Courthouse for the World*, The Air and Space Lawyer, Volume 22, Issue 1, at 13.
441. Verna, *supra*, at 11.

forum at the hearing. It is hard to escape the conclusion that the real attraction of the US courts is indeed the intention:

> to gain advantage in settlement discussions from the substantial damages awards that may be obtained from American juries.[442]

To this author, it is thus hard to escape the conclusion that the initiation of proceedings against an American lessor is largely with a view to finding any American party at all to an action in an attempt to get a case before such a jury which would not otherwise be eligible – were that not the case, lessors would routinely be sued in courts other than the those of the United States. Indeed, this author agrees with Dameris et al. who state that:

> it is disingenuous to assert that these claims are brought here for any reason other than strategic gamesmanship.[443]

As Olson succinctly puts it:

> Both parties of the two sides of aviation litigation today can rightly be considered to engage in so called forum shopping; the plaintiffs at the stage of selecting the forum where to initiate the action and similarly the defendants by seeking to remove the case to a jurisdiction where local law treats passenger claims less favorable.[444]

[2] US Federal Law

Under the US Federal Aviation Act,[445] a lessor:

> is liable for personal injury, death or property loss or damage on land or water only when a civil aircraft is in the actual possession or control of the lessor… .

This is a federal statute and not all state laws in the United States accept it as pre-empting any state law to the contrary. Without such pre-emption, it is open to a plaintiff to bring suit in the courts of a US state under this theory of negligent entrustment, thus forcing a lessor to defend the suit on its merits.

Sterns[446] points out that the language here is disjunctive: 'possession or control', not 'possession and control'. He continues:

> The obvious intent of this section was to protect those who passively either provide capital for the operation of aircraft by airlines, or who provide the aircraft

442. *Esheva v. Siberia Airlines*, 499 F. Supp. 2d, 498 (S.D.N.Y 2007) in Dameris et al., *supra*, at 13.
443. Dameris et al., *supra*, at 16.
444. Olson U., *Interpretation of the Montreal 99 Convention in a Forum Non Conveniens Case*, https://www.mcgill.ca/iasl/files/iasl/Session_7_Olson.pdf on 9 Sep. 2021.
445. 49 USC S. 44112.
446. Sterns G.C., *Lessor Liability; or Absence Thereof: Federal Immunity or Not for Lessors of Commercial Aircraft*, paper presented at McGill Institute of Air & Space Law Conference on International Aviation Liability & Insurance, Montreal, Canada, 6–7 May 2011.

itself as a business investment similar to the investment of capital and who are not involved in the day to day operations or control of the aircraft.[447]

Wickersham[448] points out that the financier, in this case including the lessor, never has zero control[449] and never (in the absence of possession) has complete control of the aircraft.

One state which rejects the pre-emption theory is Illinois,[450] where both an aircraft manufacturer, The Boeing Company (Boeing), and an aircraft leasing company, AAR Parts and Trading Co. (AAR), are headquartered and thus are attractive targets for plaintiffs. Another such state is Florida, where, in the case of *Vreeland v. Ferrer, et al.*,[451] the Florida Supreme Court held, with Lewis J writing for the majority, that federal pre-emption is narrowly construed, that there is no express pre-emption in the federal statute in question[452] and that the words 'on land or water' in section 44112 mean that the provision only applies for damage caused to persons or property on the surface, not to passengers.[453]

[3] AAR Cases

Air Philippines (PAL) acquired a Boeing 737-700 aircraft on a finance lease from AAR and, after some years of operation, it crashed causing tragic loss of life. There was no allegation of a defect in the aircraft at the time of delivery. Plaintiffs' counsel sued AAR in Illinois in a case referred to by Holland and Knight[454] as an 'aberration' and a 'perfect storm'.

In *Ellis v. AAR Parts Trading, Inc.*,[455] the Illinois courts rejected forum non conveniens arguments as to Illinois jurisdiction and in *Layug v. AAR Parts Trading, Inc.*,[456] they held that AAR's argument:

> with regard to the issue of control of the aircraft is without merit as that was a distinction that had no bearing on the issue of preemption in the applicable case law. Accordingly, the Court here finds that the Plaintiff's state law claims are not preempted by the Federal Aviation Act.

Ultimately, however, PAL's insurers settled the claim without admission of liability and plaintiffs' counsel, The Nolan Group,[457] in claiming victory, described the

---

447. *Ibid.*, at 4.
448. Wickersham D.K., *When Should Courts Pierce the Veil Protecting Aircraft Financiers*, University of California, Los Angeles, May 2007.
449. For instance, they have contractual rights to monitor and in certain situations to repossess the aircraft.
450. *See Retzler v. Pratt & Whitney Co.*, 309 Ill. App. 3d 906 (1st Dist. 1999).
451. Supreme Court of Florida, No. SC10–694, 8 Jul. 2011.
452. At 9.
453. At 22 et seq.
454. https://www.hklaw.com/en/insights/publications/2011/07/florida-supreme-court-finds-no-federal-preemption on 9 Sep 2021.
455. 357 Ill. App. 3d 723, 828 N.E.2d 723 (2005).
456. No. 00 L 9599, 2003 WL 25744436 (Ill. Cir. Ct., Cook Cty. 16 May 2003).
457. http://www.nolan-law.com/the-crash-of-air-philippines-541/ on 9 Sep. 2021.

problem as one of dumping of older aircraft in the third world as the American fleet became younger and called for increased safety oversight by lessors.

To the extent that the settlements in the AAR have an effect on future cases or settlements, the direct effect on lessors will be limited with the primary effect being rather that the lessees, who, under their leases, bear the responsibility and cost of insuring the lessors against liability claims (as to which, *see* section §3.05 *supra*), will have the costs of this increased risk passed onto them by their insurers by way of higher insurance premiums.

Even if the AAR cases had not been settled, they may well be limited to their facts as the only causal connection to Illinois was the presence there of the defendant. Apart from AAR and Boeing, Illinois is not a noted aviation centre and so future attempts to replicate the fact pattern there are likely to be limited. Further, the flight in question was a domestic flight and, for reasons discussed in section §3.11[B] *supra*, the plaintiffs would not have wished to assert that the Warsaw Convention (1929) or Montreal Convention (1999) applied.

The theory as applied to an aircraft operating lessor makes as much sense as suing a car salesman or a car rental company for selling or renting a car to a customer based on no more than payment by the customer and production by him/her of a valid driving licence – if one is forced to look behind a valid qualification, where does the duty stop? And of what use then is the licence?

Under Article 33 of the Chicago Convention (1944), certificates and licences issued by a state of registration must be recognized as valid by other contracting states so long as the minimum standards established pursuant thereto are met. To the extent that contracting states do not, and even may not, look behind such certificates and licences, why should operating lessors be obliged to do so?

In the EU, under Commission Regulation (EC) 1071/2010, amending Commission Regulation (EC) 474/2006, certain airlines are banned from operating within the EU on safety grounds.

In the United States, a foreign air carrier must obtain a foreign air carrier permit under the Federal Aviation Act.[458] Under 14 Code of Federal Regulations Part 129, the carrier must meet the safety standards contained in Part 1 (International Commercial Air Transport) of Annex 6 (Operations of Aircraft) to the Convention on International Civil Aviation (Chicago Convention). If the civil aviation authority of the carrier is found to be meeting its minimum safety obligations under the Chicago Convention (1944), the Federal Aviation Administration of the United States will forward a positive recommendation to the US Department of Transportation for issuance of a foreign air carrier permit.

If the lessee in question is not on the European banned list or has a foreign air carrier permit for the United States, and the lessor is an EU or US lessor, there appear to be no justifiable grounds for requiring the lessor to look behind the licences and certificates issued to the lessee by its aviation authority.

458. 49 USC 41302.

What of other carriers? Should a lessor not lease to such carriers at all? Or should it only not lease if it is an EU- or US-based lessor, as the case may be? To what liability should a lessor be exposed for deciding to proceed with a lease in such a situation? An increased role for ICAO has been proposed[459] in determining implementation of SARPs[460] but, even if ICAO determines a state not to be in compliance, on what legal basis should this affect a lessor's decision whether or not to lease to such a carrier? All that can be said is that these matters are still unclear at the time of writing.

An operating lessor, having by definition an interest in the residual value of the aircraft after the lease, will always be concerned that its aircraft is well maintained well beyond minimal airworthiness in order to maintain the residual value of its aircraft - in so doing, it will indirectly contribute to the overall safety of passengers who fly on it - this can be ensured by providing for covenants as to maintenance on the part of the lessee in the lease - but a lessor is not a regulatory authority with the power and means to ensure safety but rather only has its remedies for breach of a contractual covenant under the lease. Even inspection rights, which might disclose a breach of such covenant as to maintenance, under the leases are limited by lessees - they may, so long as there is no default, be limited to once a year visual inspections only with limited rights to open panels.[461]

It is submitted that the arguments in favour of extending the theory of negligent entrustment to operating lessors are intellectually dishonest (a point made by Byrnes and Kass)[462] and are simply a means to an end of getting cases into a more generous US court system. They could in any event simply be avoided by the lessor's relocating to less generous jurisdictions.[463]

Even if negligent entrustment is determined to be in principle applicable to operating leases of aircraft, for the reasons discussed *supra* in section §3.11[B][2], the impact should be limited to claims falling outside the scope of the Montreal Convention (1999) or, possibly, the Warsaw Convention (1929).

[4] Liability Insurance and Indemnities

Particularly in light of the issues discussed in sections §3.11[B] and §3.11[C] *supra*, a prudent lessor will naturally want to be covered against potential claims being brought against it by third parties when it does not have possession of the aircraft, whether due to lease to a lessee or sale to a purchaser, by providing in the contract that the lessee (for the term of the lease) or the purchaser (typically until the earlier of two years after

459. *See*, e.g., Blumenkron J., *Implications of Transparency in the International Civil Aviation Organization's Universal Safety Oversight and Audit Programme*, Annals of Air and Space Law, Volume XXXIV, 2009, 31–70, at 69.
460. *See* section §3.10[B][1] *supra*.
461. *See* the discussion in Bunker D.H., *International Aircraft Financing, Volume 2: Specific Documents*, 2nd Edition, IATA, 2015 at 104–105.
462. Byrnes T.P. and Kass G.R., *Aircraft Lessor Liability*, Joint Presentation to 25th Annual Conference of the International Society of Transport Aircraft Trading, Scottsdale, Arizona, held on 17 Mar. 2009.
463. A point noted by Wickersham, *supra*, at 40.

the sale or until the next heavy check) indemnifies the lessor against any claims brought against it and by then requiring the lessee or purchaser to obtain insurance whereby such indemnity obligation is insured, with the lessor named as an additional insured.

Bunker describes the indemnity provisions of aviation transactions as 'probably the most frustrating and misunderstood subjects of transaction negotiations'.[464] He explains their need as being based on a 'straightforward insurance and risk-assignment concept' with one party, the lessee, agreeing to 'assume responsibility through indemnification and lay off the risk through insurance'.[465]

Sometimes, particularly in sale contracts, but occasionally also in leases, a party will suggest eliminating the indemnity clause altogether but leaving the obligation to obtain such liability insurance coverage. The reason for such a suggestion is that, if for some reason the insurer refuses to pay or its limit of coverage is insufficient, the indemnifying party is still liable to pay and may not have the funds to do so.

The problem with such an approach is that the lessee or purchaser must have an insurable interest: it insures against its obligation to pay out under an indemnity clause. In the absence of an indemnity clause, it would be open to an insurer to refuse to pay under the insurances on the basis that the lessee or purchaser had no 'insurable interest' (its indemnity obligation) against which it was taking out insurance coverage.

Even if such an insurable interest can be established, the insurance coverage will most likely be narrower if it does not expressly cover the scope of the indemnity language in the lease or sale agreement.[466]

A prudent lessor, therefore, should not agree to drop indemnity provisions where it wishes to rely on insurance coverage to be provided by a lessee or purchaser.

[D] Conclusions

Not having operational control of the aircraft, the lessor naturally requires indemnities from the lessee to cover any claims brought against the lessor for actions which may not be attributable to it. Whether or not the lessor can enforce such a right of indemnification in practice will, in theory, depend on the solvency and adequacy of assets of the lessee against which to enforce a judgment, and, in practice, on the adequacy of insurances, examined next, in place.

The relative length of section §3.11 is proof of the great level of interplay between, on the one hand, public, but more particularly, private international air law and national law, as seen above, and, on the other hand, the practice of aircraft operating leasing.

The lessor must guard against not only damage to its own property, but also against claims brought against it for injury to or damage to the property of third parties,

464. Bunker D.H., *International Aircraft Financing, Volume 2: Specific Documents*, 2nd Edition, IATA, 2015, at 141.

465. *Ibid.*

466. Wielinski P., et al., *Contractual Risk Transfer: Strategies for Contract Indemnity and Insurance Provisions*, International Risk Management Institute, Inc., 2000 at XI.B and XI.C.9.

the legal *régimes* for which may differ, not only depending on whether the case is purely domestic or has an international dimension but also depending on whether the third party is a passenger or a non-passenger on the ground.

The foregoing analysis has led this author to three principal conclusions in connection with the issue of lessor liability to third parties.

The first is that, on its face, the Montreal Convention (1999) is intended as an exclusive remedy so that claims that may be brought thereunder must be brought only against the carrier thereunder, to the exclusion of claims brought against the carrier or any non-carrier, such as a lessor, outside of the terms thereof. Any claim against a non-carrier must, under the terms of Article 37 the Montreal Convention (1999), only be brought by the carrier, having been found liable under this l convention, against a non-carrier, such as a lessor.[467]

The second is that, regardless of whether his view as to the exclusivity of the Montreal Convention (1999) is correct or not, in the area of private international law, there are differences of approach as to the liability of non-carriers which cannot in his view be rationally justified, and he returns to this theme with his recommendations in Chapter 4.[468]

The third is that attempts to extend liability to lessors are not so much about ensuring justice for plaintiffs, who have recourse against the carrier, which carries liability insurances, and are more about creative attempts by plaintiffs' counsel to find whatever routes they can into plaintiff-friendly courts in the United States in the hope of increasing the quantum recovered by way of damages. Whether the operator or the lessor is sued, both are covered under the same liability insurances: thus, the real issue, in this author's view, is about obtaining a judgment which will maximize the insurance payout.

§3.12 INSURANCES

These are closely linked to the indemnities, discussed in section §3.11 *supra*, and to the concept of risk allocation inherent in the aircraft operating lease.[469]

Invariably, the lease will require the airline to take out hull and liability insurances in respect of the aircraft for the duration of the lease term, and sometimes for a certain period thereafter.

The lessee has an insurable interest in the aircraft by virtue, *inter alia*, of the fact that it has operational control of the aircraft and thus stands to lose financially if the aircraft is damaged; further, it will typically be liable to indemnify the lessor for damage

467. In the event of such a claim, the lessor would defend itself by reference, *inter alia*, to the conclusivity of the acceptance certificate signed by the lessee in respect of the aircraft at delivery, as discussed in section §3.06[B][c] *supra*.

468. Adding to the complexity, under the UNIDROIT Convention on Financial Leasing discussed in Chapter 2 section §2.01 *supra*, while a lessor shall not be liable to third parties for death, injury or damage caused by the property in its capacity as lessor (Art. 8(1)(b)), there is expressly no statement as to liability in any other capacity, such as owner (Art. 8(1)(c)). As the lessor will in many cases be the owner, this distinction is curious.

469. *See* sections 9 and 11 of the Supplement *infra*.

to the aircraft under the lease and can insure against such contractual indemnification obligation.[470]

Insurances are generally divided into hull and liability insurances. Hull insurances provide coverage to the owner of the aircraft in case of damage to or loss of the aircraft – this is a commercial risk which a lessor generally will not want to take but is not a matter of concern under public or private international air law.[471]

[A] Liability Insurances

Liability insurances, on the other hand, which provide limited cover for damage or injury to third parties are indeed such a concern. The Warsaw Convention (1929)[472] and Montreal Convention (1999)[473] cover carrier liability for death, injury, or damage of or to passengers, baggage, and cargo in international carriage.

Chrystal[474] has noted that, as airline marketing departments are reluctant to dwell on safety as it is a sensitive issue, it is not surprising that the subject of aviation insurance maintains a low profile in the aviation industry. Airlines want passengers to concentrate on excellence of service, not on the likelihood of a crash or adequacy of insurance in the event of one. The subject of insurance is nonetheless an important one.

The Warsaw Convention (1929) does not set out any specific requirements that airlines be insured for liability. Article 50 of the Montreal Convention (1999), by contrast, does require that State parties 'shall require their carriers to maintain adequate insurance covering their liability' thereunder and 'may be required by the State Party into which it operates to furnish evidence' thereof. Under Article 55 of the Montreal Convention (1999), the provisions of the Montreal Convention (1999) prevail, for parties thereto, over those of the Warsaw Convention (1929). Nevertheless, what constitutes 'adequate' insurance coverage is not spelt out in the Montreal Convention (1999). Peña[475] sees this as complex and concludes that it is a matter left to each contracting State to the Montreal Convention (1999) to determine under its national law.

The Rome Convention (1952) provides for liability of the operator of an aircraft for damage to persons on the surface caused by an aircraft in flight or anything falling therefrom.[476] The liability falls on the operator but, under Article 2(3), the registered owner is presumed to be the operator unless he proves some other person was the

---

470. Margo R.D., *Aviation Insurance*, 3rd Revised Edition, Butterworths Law, 1999, at 147.
471. For a discussion of insurance issues from the perspective of a lessor or financier, *see* Bisset M. and Sharman R., *Aviation Insurance: Issues in Law and Practice from the Lessor/Lender Perspective*, Clyde & Co., 2014.
472. At Art. 1, as amended by Art. I of the Hague Protocol thereto.
473. At Art. 1.
474. Chrystal P., *The Aviation Insurance and Reinsurance Markets-Defying the Odds*, in Butler G.F. and Keller M.R., executive editors, *Handbook of Airline Finance*, 1st Edition, Aviation Week: McGraw-Hill, 1999, at 297 et seq.
475. Peña S.F., *Defining Insurance Coverage Adequacy under the Montreal Convention of 1999*, Annals of Air and Space Law, Volume XXXIV, 2009, 343–378, at 369.
476. Article 1.

operator and 'in so far as legal procedures permit, takes appropriate measures to make that other person a party to the proceedings'.

As with claims brought under the Warsaw Convention (1929) or Montreal Convention (1999),[477] Article 9 of the Rome Convention (1952) provides that, where the Rome Convention (1952) applies, the remedies set out therein are an exclusive remedy.

The phrase 'registered owner' may be problematic. The Chicago Convention (1944) provides, in Article 17, for registration of aircraft, not owners of aircraft, and leaves the details to national law.[478] Article 21 of the Chicago Convention (1944) requires contracting states to supply information concerning registration and ownership of the aircraft to ICAO and it may be implied that this is the registered owner intended by the Rome Convention (1952) but this is not clear. As further discussed in section §3.10[B][3] *supra* there may potentially be four or so parties who may be described as owners of the aircraft for various purposes.

In any event, Article 11 of the Rome Convention (1952) sets out the limits of liability and Article 15 sets out the requirements as to insurance (or other acceptable security, such as cash deposit or bank guarantee). Article 15(5) allows a state overflown by an aircraft to require that the aircraft carry on board a certificate of insurance setting out details of coverage unless such certificate is instead filed with a designated authority of the overflown State or with ICAO. Article 15(5) was deleted by Article VI of the Montreal Protocol 1978 and replaced with a simpler requirement that evidence of insurance or guarantee by other security adequate to cover liability under Article 11 be provided to an overflown state upon request – thus the certificate of insurance need not be kept on the aircraft. Article 15(7) provides that states may refer any dispute over the adequacy of financial responsibility of an insurer or bank guarantor to submit it to ICAO for arbitration but this was removed by Article VI of the Montreal Protocol 1978.

National legislation (two examples are given below: one from a developed country, the United Kingdom, the other from a developing country, Nigeria)[479] may set out further details on required liability insurance, and, in the case of the EU, such legislation will have to comply with the requirements of Commission Regulation (EC) 785/2004 (discussed below).

An important point to note is that aircraft operating leases will typically require airlines to maintain liability insurances in excess of the minimum amounts required under national law.[480]

To take an example from a developed country, the United Kingdom, the Civil Aviation (Insurance) Regulations 2005 (S.I. 2005 No. 1089) implement Commission

477. *See* section §3.11[B][2] *supra*.
478. Article 19.
479. *See also* Mauritz A.J., *Liability of the Operators and Owners of Aircraft for Damage Inflicted to Persons and Property on the Ground*, PhD Thesis, Leiden University, 2003, at 119–140, for a discussion of the national liability *régimes* and insurances requirements of additional jurisdictions.
480. *See* Bunker D.H., *International Aircraft Financing, Volume 2: Specific Documents*, 2nd Edition, IATA, 2015, at 129–134 and 182–183.

Regulation (EC) 785/2004 and provide for minimum liability coverage based, *inter alia*, on minimum take-off weight, cargo payload, and passenger capacity. According to public records,[481] the estimated minimum liability insurance required for commercial operations of a Boeing 737-800 aircraft[482] in 2016 was GBP 341,070,425.83 (at the time of writing, approximately USD 471,799,039.33).[483] Typically, in this author's experience, a lessor will require substantially higher minimum liability coverage in the range of USD 600,000,000–USD 750,000,000 for each occurrence. This is consistent with the advice given by Aon Group Limited, Aviation, a leading provider of aviation insurance broking:

> Minimum liability limits are often stipulated by domestic law. These minimum limits can be surprisingly low and should not be viewed as recommendations.[484]

By way of example from a developing country, in Nigeria, the Civil Aviation Act, 2006 requires minimum liability coverage in case of death or injury of passengers of USD 100,000 per passenger, as compared with SDR 250,000 (at the time of writing, approximately USD 356,374.75)[485] per passenger as required in the EU by Article 6(1) Commission Regulation (EC) 785/2004. In the case of the Boeing 737-800 aircraft referred to above, Boeing[486] estimates a typical passenger capacity of 189 passengers in one class configuration. The Nigerian regulations, therefore, would only require minimum liability coverage in respect of passengers of approximately USD 18,900,000, and are silent as to other minimum liability coverage (e.g., in respect of non-passengers, cargo or property damage).

Typically, the lease will require the lessee to maintain the lessor and other additional insureds on its liability insurances for two years after the expiration of the lease, or until the next heavy check of the aircraft to occur after such expiration. The lessor has an insurable interest if:

> he would suffer prejudice on the occurrence of the event insured against. Thus where an insured is obliged by law or by contract to indemnify third parties or passengers for damage to property or personal injury (including death), the insured would have an insurable interest in respect of his potential liability.[487]

Such potential liability is discussed in section §3.11 *supra*.

481. http://www.caa.co.uk/application.aspx?catid = 60&pagetype = 65&appid = 1 at 30 Aug. 2016.
482. Bearing manufacturer's serial number 28229 and UK aircraft registration number G-CDZI.
483. http://www.xe.com on 9 Sep. 2021.
484. The Aon Aviation Guide: *The Banker's & Lessor's Guide to Insurance Aspects of Aircraft Financing*. Aon Group Limited, Aviation, 2nd Edition, 2000.
485. http://www.xe.com on 9 Sep. 2021.
486. http://www.boeing.com/commercial/737family/pf/pf_800tech.html on 9 Sep. 2021.
487. Margo R.D., *Aviation Insurance in the United Kingdom: Law and Practice*, DCL Thesis, McGill University, Montréal, 1979, at 106.

[B] Hull Insurances

Agreed Value and Total Loss are key concepts with respect to hull insurances and are examined here.

The lessor has an insurable interest in the hull insurances insofar as it is the owner of the aircraft. According to Margo:[488]

> an insured will have an insurable interest if he is so related to the subject-matter of the insurance that he will suffer prejudice if it is lost or damaged by the occurrence of the risks insured against.

The lessor need not be the owner of the aircraft to have an insurable interest in the hull insurances. Likewise, financiers have an insurable interest therein:

> In the case of hull insurance, ownership is not the only basis for acquiring an insurable interest. Such interest may be based on contract such as in the case of a mortgage, or even on mere lawful possession.[489]

While the lessor need not be the owner, ownership is in itself sufficient for this purpose: Margo notes that such ownership may be 'sole, joint, absolute, limited, legal or equitable'.[490]

[1] Agreed Value

One other tool by which the owner can protect itself is to require that the lessee insure the aircraft for the term of the lease on an agreed value basis rather than a replacement basis, naming the owner as the sole loss payee[491] in the event of an actual or constructive total loss of the aircraft. This agreed value is fixed at the outset of the lease and is normally (in this author's experience) slightly greater than the then-current market value.

In order to manage its insurance costs, the lessee may negotiate with the lessor to reduce this agreed value by an agreed percentage every year during the lease term. If the aircraft is a total loss, the insurer will then pay to the owner the then agreed value of the aircraft under the hull insurance policy regardless of the then market value of the aircraft.

The lessor should ensure that any aggregate limits on the coverage available will be sufficient to pay it out in the event of simultaneous calamitous damage to multiple aircraft in the lessee's fleet (such as for example by a bombing of the lessee's home base).

---

488. *Ibid.*, at 105.
489. *Ibid.*, at 106.
490. *Ibid.*, at 110.
491. As to which, *see* McBain G., *Aircraft Finance: Registration, Security and Enforcement*, General Editor, Sweet & Maxwell, 2000, Volume-1 at Insurance-10 (para. D-25). Another approach is to provide for payments to the contract parties as their interests appear so that payment for buyer furnished equipment, such as in-flight entertainment systems, belonging to the airline is made to the airline.

[2] Determination of Total Loss

A total loss of an aircraft occurs if it is so damaged as to be beyond economical repair, having regard to its value.[492]

The timing of the occurrence of an event of total loss is normally clear in the case of a crash. However, if the aircraft simply disappears or is hijacked, it may be difficult to determine when exactly the aircraft should be deemed to be a total loss. Under the terms of hull insurance policies, such a decision is normally left to the judgment of the insurer.

This raises the issue of unacceptable uncertainty for the owner and it is therefore normal[493] to find in leases that the lessee is obliged to pay the agreed value to the lessor once the disappearance or hijacking has continued for more than a certain period.[494] Thus, the lessee will be obliged to pay the agreed value at the expiration of such period whether or not the insurer has at that time agreed that the disappearance or hijacking constitutes a total loss.

Of course, this is largely a theoretical protection for the lessor since, in practice, the airline will not likely have the funds to pay the agreed value of a commercial aircraft to the lessor other than through payment on its behalf by its insurers.

Leases may sometimes provide for separate agreed values for the airframe and for each engine in the event that the airframe but not the engines are destroyed or vice versa.

[C] Deductibles

Other insurance risks of which the lessor should be aware are deductibles, which is the first amount of damage the insurer will not bear (e.g., it may only pay for damage above USD 250,000). Although the lease will require the lessee to pay this, if the lessee is bankrupt, the lessor will end up paying it.

[D] Reinsurance and Cut-Through Clause

Where a lessor requires in a lease that a lessee obtain reinsurance coverage for the insurance coverage required by the lease, it is standard practice to demand a 'cut-through' clause.

Reinsurance basically insures the insurances: in many jurisdictions, insurance must be placed with a local insurance company. Lessors may have concerns about the jurisdictional risk of the local insurance company or about its credit – hence they may require reinsurance, which pays out in the event that the primary insurer has to pay out.

---

492. Margo, *supra*, at 186.
493. *See* Bunker D.H., *International Aircraft Financing, Volume 2: Specific Documents*, 2nd Edition, IATA, 2015, at 135.
494. This period is most often in the range of 90–180 days.

Originally, the idea was to ensure that the primary insurer would have funds with which to meet its obligations – if called upon to pay under its insurance policy, it could make a corresponding claim on its reinsurers under its reinsurance policy.

By means of a 'cut-through' clause, the lessor, or other insured parties, can ensure that the reinsurers will pay directly to it rather than to the primary insurer for further payment to it – this makes sense as it cuts out the 'middle man' and spares the lessor from the uncertainties and possible delays of litigation in a potentially unfriendly or undeveloped jurisdiction.

In an English High Court case, *Grecoair v. John Tilling and Others,*[495] Langley J refused to allow a lessor of an aircraft to Angola Air Charter Ltda. to proceed directly against the reinsurers where the aircraft was involved in a crash in circumstances where it could have proceeded against the insurers in the normal fashion and left it to the insurer to pursue the reinsurers. In this case, the lease provided only for the lessee to obtain insurances and did not deal with the need for reinsurances or a 'cut-through' clause therein. The primary insurances did provide for a 'cut-through' clause in respect of reinsurances on other aircraft, but for the aircraft in question, the insurances provided that the provisions of the relevant lease with respect to insurances were incorporated.

[E] Termination of Insurances

If the lessee fails to pay the premium on renewal for any reason, the insurances may be terminated by the underwriter. In such an event, the lessor will be left without hull coverage, which could be disastrous in the case of damage *to* the aircraft. Accordingly, a prudent lessor will insist on obtaining a broker's letter of undertaking whereby the lessee's insurance broker undertakes to inform the lessor if for any reason the insurances are not renewed or the insurance premium is not paid.[496]

Further, the liability coverage will lapse, leaving not only the lessee but, potentially, the lessor liable for any damage caused *by* the aircraft.[497] Such termination may also cause the air transport licence[498] of the airline to be revoked[499] as it is generally a condition of such licence that required liability insurances be in place.[500]

The lessor may also want to consider taking out contingency insurance which takes effect if the primary insurance fails to respond or proves inadequate for any reason.[501] However, such insurance will not cover a situation where the primary

495. [2004] EWHC 2851 (Comm).
496. McBain G., *Aircraft Finance: Registration, Security and Enforcement,* General Editor, Sweet & Maxwell, 2000, Volume 1, at Insurance-18 (para. D-33).
497. *See* section §3.11[B] *supra.*
498. *See* section §3.05[B][5] *supra.*
499. This author has experience of just such a case with a European airline which flew after termination of its insurances took effect – its air transport licence was revoked upon proof to the relevant aviation authority thereof.
500. *See,* for example, Art. 4(h) of European Commission Regulation (EC) 1008/2008
501. Aon Aviation Guide, *The Banker's & Lessor's Guide to Insurance Aspects of Aircraft Financing,* 2nd Edition, 2000, at 90.

insurance is terminated – hence the importance of obtaining the broker's letter of undertaking referred to above.

In *Oxford Aviation Services Limited v. Godolphin Management Company Limited,*[502] Cooke J of the English High Court held that a bailee pursuant to a draft agreement for hire (as to which, *see* section §3.20 *infra*) had to account to the bailor for the loss of its aircraft where the agreement provided for the bailee to arrange insurances, notwithstanding the assertion by the bailee (rejected by Cooke J) that the bailor had agreed to arrange its own insurances.

[F] Conclusions

Private international air law is largely concerned with the protection of second and third parties and thus is not concerned with hull insurances which protect only those with an ownership interest in the aircraft. The discussion in section §3.11 shows how the private air law instruments[503] discussed, where they require liability insurances, do not set out themselves the required minimum amounts of coverage, leaving those to national or, where relevant, European law.

In practice, the aircraft operating lease will provide still higher levels of liability coverage again than those required by law, which constitutes a de facto additional level of protection for third parties.

Just because a lessee is required by law to insure the aircraft, or else risk losing its right to operate, a lessor cannot assume that a lessee will do so and should take steps to ensure that the lease contract provisions as to insurance are being complied with at all times.

§3.13 REDELIVERY

Redelivery in required redelivery condition, consequences of delay and/or failure so to redeliver are of vital consequence to the aircraft operating lessor.[504]

The main components of redelivery are timely redelivery in the condition required by the lease agreement, with physical delivery of the aircraft, together with all records, and, often, deregistration of the aircraft.[505]

[A] Redelivery in Redelivery Condition

At the end of the lease, the lessee must redeliver the aircraft to the lessor in the redelivery condition set out in the lease. Disputes between lessors and lessees are not infrequent here since, if upon tender for redelivery, the lessor successfully asserts that

502. [2004] EWHC 232 (QB).
503. *See also Private International Air Law Instruments*, Annals of Air and Space Law, Volume XXX, Part I, McGill University, 2005, at 323–655.
504. *See* section 12 of the Supplement *infra*.
505. *See* section §3.15 *infra*.

the aircraft is not in the required redelivery condition, not only must the airline incur additional cost in order to meet the redelivery conditions, but rent will continue to accrue, with the lease sometimes providing for an increase, in this author's experience, of one and a half to two times the normal rent if the delay in redelivery continues beyond a certain agreed time period.

[B] Timely Redelivery

The lessor needs timely redelivery of the aircraft in the agreed condition as it will plan on having a follow-on lessee ready to take the aircraft and that follow-on lessee may not accept delivery if the aircraft is delayed or does not meet its contracted delivery condition, which should normally match the redelivery condition from the previous operator, thereby causing loss to the lessor. A 'time of the essence' clause in the lease is most advisable here.[506]

A lessee may sometimes assert that a lessor is unreasonably arguing, rather than accepting redelivery, so as to continue the lease, particularly where the lessor does not have a follow-on operator ready to take the aircraft or, in the words of Thomas LJ, that the lessor is engaged in what is '[s]imply a clever attempt to obtain more money for the use of the aircraft'.[507]

There is also the case to consider where the lessee refuses or fails to redeliver the aircraft at the end of the lease for whatever reason. It is possible for such a refusal or failure to constitute the tort of conversion. Cresswell J reviewed conversion in the case of *Kuwait Airways Corporation v. Iraqi Airways Company.*[508]

He outlined the basic threefold features of the tort of conversion as: (1) whether the defendant's conduct was inconsistent with the rights of the owner (or other person entitled to possession); (2) whether the conduct was deliberate rather than accidental: and (3) whether the conduct was 'so extensive an encroachment on the rights of the owner as to exclude him from use and possession of the goods'.[509] Importantly, he held that it does not matter whether the defendant still had the goods in his possession or whether he acted 'in the genuine and reasonable belief that the goods were his'.[510]

He went on to cite[511] with approval Lloyd LJ in *Ministry of Defence v. Ashman*,[512] who held that the owner of the property did not need to establish that he would have let the property to somebody else or used it himself and stated the principle, rejecting the defendant's claim that user damages should not exceed the value of the benefit to the defendant, that:

506. *See* section §3.19[A] *infra.*
507. *Sunrock Aircraft Corporation Limited v. Scandinavian Airlines System Denmark-Norway-Sweden* [2007] EWCA Civ 882 at 24(vi).
508. [2004] EWHC 2603 (Comm).
509. *Ibid.*, at paras 220–223.
510. *Ibid.*
511. *Ibid.*, at para. 450.
512. (1993) 25 HLR 513, at 845.

> [w]hen goods are converted and some (but not all) of the goods are returned months or years later, the claimant may be awarded by way of damages a sensibly/reasonably calculated amount of money to provide just compensation in respect of the period between the date of conversion and the date of return.[513]

Beatson J cited the judgment in *Kuwait Airways* with approval in *Blue Sky One and others v. Blue Sky Airways LLC and others*,[514] but he also noted[515] that under the *English Tort (Interference with Goods) Act 1977*,[516] an order to deliver up the asset to its true owner would not be made if damages were an adequate remedy and noted further that:

> [w]hile in some circumstances a contract concerning a ship or aircraft will be specifically enforceable, it is clear that this is not the invariable position. The court must still ask whether damages would be an adequate remedy ... .[517]

Damages may not constitute an adequate remedy where the lessor is already contractually committed to deliver the aircraft to a follow-on operator or buyer. Simply to award the lessor the market value of the aircraft may risk harming the lessor unfairly by requiring it to post a loss on its books in respect of that aircraft through no fault of its own where the book value of the aircraft is above the fair market value.[518]

An important point to note in transactions with a head lease and sublease structure is that, in the event of a late redelivery, there may be difficulty recovering damages for a lost sale by the owner which might not be present if the owner and lessor were the same. Even though the aircraft was owned by a company in the same group as the lessor, the English High Court held in *Pindell Limited and BBAM Aircraft Holdings 98 (Labuan) Limited v. AirAsia Berhad*[519] that, where the owner lost a sale of the aircraft due to the late redelivery by the lessee to the lessor, such loss was too remote to allow recovery. It is not clear how the court would determine a case on similar facts but where the lessor was also the owner and the lease contained clear language providing for indemnification in such event. It is submitted that, in such event, the lessor should be allowed recovery due to the direct contractual relationship between the lessor and lessee and the express agreement to such indemnification in the contract.

[C] Non-compliance with Redelivery Condition

Although a lessor will require strict compliance with the redelivery condition and procedures, under English law, this may only be possible to the extent that the aircraft is diminished in value as a result of such non-compliance. In *Sunrock Aircraft*

513. *Ashman*, at para. 462.
514. [2009] EWHC 3314 (Comm), at para. 306.
515. *Ibid.*, at para. 309.
516. Which act put the common law tort of conversion on a statutory footing.
517. *Ibid.*, at para. 313.
518. Alternatively, the court could award the lessor damages in the amount of the book value.
519. [2010] EWHC 2516.

Corporation Limited v. Scandinavian Airlines System Denmark-Norway-Sweden[520] before the English Court of Appeal Thomas LJ held, per curiam, that it is:

> common ground that the measure of damages for redelivering a hired chattel in damaged condition was the cost of repairs, unless it was unreasonable to effect the repairs; if it was unreasonable to effect the repairs, then the measure was the diminution of value.[521]

In this case, where scab patches were not repaired on an aircraft prior to redelivery, in breach of the lease, only nominal damages were awarded when the lessor's expert witness conceded that such breach was immaterial to the value of the aircraft. It follows from this case that specific performance would, as an equitable remedy, most likely not be available either.

A lessor planning to lease the aircraft to a follow-on lessee rather than to sell it, it is submitted, could reasonably claim the cost of repairs even if there is no diminution in the overall value of the asset. The reason is that bearing in mind that the delivery conditions in the follow-on lease should normally mirror the redelivery conditions of the prior lease, the follow-on lessee may well refuse to take delivery of the aircraft until the non-conformity is rectified and thus the lessor would be required to perform the necessary repair or remedial work itself.

It is entirely reasonable that in such circumstances the prior lessee, who was responsible for the non-conformity, should perform the repair or remedial work and, in addition, pay rent to the lessor for the duration involved to the extent that it goes beyond the expiry date agreed in the prior lease. Indeed, as noted, leases often provide that the rent for any period beyond the originally contracted period should be at a higher rate since this period was not initially agreed to by the parties but is, in effect, forced on the lessor due to the lessee's failure to redeliver the aircraft in good time in the agreed condition. The lessor's justification for this is that it risks losing the follow-on lessee if the prior lessee causes a delay in delivery to the follow-on lessee.

[D] Residual Value Guarantee

In an operating lease, the owner is normally not only the legal owner of the asset but also the economic owner. In the legal context, 'ownership' can be defined to mean a '[c]ollection of rights to use and enjoy property, including the right to transmit it to others'.[522] In the economic context, the 'economic owner' of an asset can be defined to mean 'the party who has the risks and rewards of ownership'.[523]

In the case of the aircraft operating lessor, its rights and rewards consist of leasing the asset for rent and in due course selling it. One of the risks of economic ownership,

520. [2007] EWCA Civ 882.
521. *Ibid.*, at 32.
522. *Black's Law Dictionary*, 1990, 6th Edition.
523. *Balance of Payments and International Investment Position Manual*, International Monetary Fund, 2007 at http://www.imf.org/external/pubs/ft/bop/2007/pdf/chap5.pdf on 23 Mar. 2009.

however, is the risk that the residual value of the aircraft will be lower than forecast by the lessor. In order to manage this risk, an owner will occasionally accept a residual value guarantee, either from the manufacturer of the asset (where the owner buys new), if market conditions are such that the manufacturer deems it commercially necessary at the time of sale to grant such support or from a third-party guarantee provider in return for a fee.

Typically, the guarantee will spell out a required minimum condition of the aircraft at the time the guarantee is invoked, in order to ensure that market demand and not poor maintenance is the reason for the lower than expected value. Further, the guarantor may structure the guarantee such that, if the owner cannot sell the aircraft in the required condition for the guaranteed amount at the contracted time, the guarantor will either have the option to purchase the aircraft itself for the guaranteed amount or allow the sale at a lower price to a third party to proceed, with the guarantor making up the shortfall in sale price. Given the requirement as to minimum condition, a residual value guarantee is not an effective tool to manage the risk of failure of the airline to redeliver in the agreed redelivery condition.

[E] Records

Not only the aircraft but all relevant records must be returned in accordance with the requirements of the lease agreement. It is easy to overlook the importance of records but they should be considered as part of the aircraft.

In an Irish High Court case, *Cityjet Limited v. Irish Aviation Authority*,[524] Kelly J held that even where a United Kingdom certificate of airworthiness was in place in respect of an aircraft, the Irish Aviation Authority was entitled to refuse to issue an Irish certificate of airworthiness in respect of the aircraft due to *lacunae* in the aircraft records. This would be of particular importance to lessors seeking to change the state of registration of an aircraft at the end of one lease and the start of another.[525]

It is advisable that, during the term, the lessor keep copies of relevant documentation so that, in the event of difficulties with the documentation on redelivery, reconstructing the documents should not be too onerous and any *lacunae* therein should not defeat an attempt to change the state of registration of its aircraft.

[F] Conclusions

Redelivery condition is a frequently disputed issue between lessors and lessees. The foregoing review does not reveal any provisions of public or private air law instruments

524. 2005 [IEHC] 206.
525. An important point here hinged on the fact that, at the time in question, the relevant part M of European Commission Regulation 1702/2003 had not yet come into force, and pursuant to Art. 2(12) of which, relevant national rules were to prevail until it did come into force. Part H 21A.183(2) thereof provides that a European Union Member State must issue a certificate of airworthiness so that, Part M having come into effect on 28 Sep. 2005, such a case would be decided differently now.

therewith. This is not surprising as this is a dispute *inter partes* which generally involves contractual requirements to meet a condition better than simply the minimum required in order to obtain a certificate of airworthiness.

Cases have been dealt with under the governing law of the lease and this author, respectfully disagreeing with the decision, is concerned by the refusal of the court in the *SAS*[526] case to require precise compliance with the contractually agreed redelivery condition.

§3.14 EVENTS OF DEFAULT

Default, events of default, grace periods, cross default, bankruptcy, illegality are all matters which both lessor and lessee will want to negotiate closely due to their potentially serious consequences.[527]

It is established in English law[528] that the parties to a commercial contract are entitled to agree as between themselves what breaches of a contract by one party entitle the other party to terminate it: this was upheld by the House of Lords in *Mardorf Peach & Co., Ltd. v. Attica Sea Carriers Corpn of Liberia, The Laconia.*[529] The consequences of an event of default in terms of the lessor's remedies are examined in section §3.15 (remedies) *infra*: here we are concerned with what triggers such remedy rights. Typical events of default are set out at Annex 10.

Leases often distinguish between 'Default' and 'Events of Default'[530] defining the former as any breach of the agreement, but the latter, which trigger the lessor's remedies, only where any grace period provided for has expired or determination or notice by lessor provided for has been made or served. Sometimes 'Events of Default' are termed 'Termination Events' as some events are not attributable to a breach by the lessee but to some external event beyond its control, such as government action. Alternatively, both terms may be used, the former for actions within the lessee's control and the latter for those outside it.

The rationale here is in part to avoid triggering cross-default provisions in other leases and other contracts of the lessee due to the existence of a default under a given lease for reason beyond the lessee's control. That rationale is often defeated by such cross-default provisions referring to events of default 'however defined' or by referring both to events of default and termination events.

In situations where the Cape Town Convention (2001) applies, Article 11(1) thereof provides that:

---

526. *See* section §3.13[C] *supra*.
527. *See* section 13 of the Supplement *infra*.
528. Furmston, *supra*, at 497.
529. [1977] AC 850, [1977] 1 All E R 545.
530. Although Bunker does not so distinguish the definitions, dealing only with 'Events of Default', he does discuss those events which may become events of default: *see* Bunker D.H., *International Aircraft Financing, Volume 2: Specific Documents*, 2nd Edition, IATA, 2015, at 145 et seq.

> [t]he debtor and the creditor may at any time agree in writing as to the events that constitute a default or otherwise give rise to the rights and remedies specified ... .

Thus, courts applying by the Cape Town Convention (2001) should honour express agreements in lease agreements as to what constitute events of default at least insofar as such events give rise to the remedies as set out in the Cape Town Convention (2001).

[A] Payment

For scheduled payments, such as rent, and maintenance reserves, a short grace period, typically of a week or less, may be negotiated. A lessee does not want to be declared in default just for being a day late, which may be due to the vagaries of electronic banking, but where the amounts are fixed (in the case of rent) or known in advance to the lessee (in the case of maintenance reserves calculated in advance by reference to lessee's own operation of the aircraft), the grace period should not be long as the lessee should know each month to have funds ready for timely payment.

[B] Breach of Other Obligations

Other obligations, even payment obligations, which are unscheduled, such as indemnity payments, are generally allowed a slightly longer grace period before failure to pay constitutes an event of default.

[C] Insurance

Given the importance of insurances, as discussed in depth in sections §3.11[C][4] and §3.12 *supra*, typically it is an immediate event of default should the required insurances not be in place at any time during the lease term. There is no grace period.[531]

In such event, the lessor should require the aircraft to be taken immediately out of service by the lessee with the lessee to provide insurance cover to cover the aircraft on the ground.[532] Of course, in such event, the lessor should not want to take the risk that the lessee will not or cannot comply and should consider having its own contingent insurance in place.

[D] Bankruptcy

The applicable law in the case of the bankruptcy of an airline will be the law of the state having jurisdiction over the airline, not the governing law of the lease. All obligations

531. *See* Bunker D.H., *International Aircraft Financing, Volume 2: Specific Documents*, 2nd Edition, IATA, 2015, at 133–134 and 145.
532. *Ibid.*

of the bankrupt airline may be[533] stayed while the liquidator liquidates the assets of the airline and then distributes what is left to the creditors in accordance with that law.

The aircraft under an operating lease, of course, is an asset of the lessor, not the airline. Nevertheless, the owner may face certain restrictions in repossessing its aircraft in the case of bankruptcy. There follows an examination, by way of example, an examination of a national bankruptcy code (focusing principally on the United States). For states party to the Cape Town Convention (2001) the bankruptcy *régime* set out in Article XI of the Aircraft Protocol thereto will apply and this too will be examined below.

By way of comparison, with respect to finance leases covered thereunder, the UNIDROIT Convention on Financial Leasing (1988)[534] provides[535] that a lessor's real rights in an aircraft shall be valid against the lessee's trustee in bankruptcy and creditors provided that where the law of the state of registration of the aircraft[536] so requires, any public notice requirements are first complied with.[537] The foregoing shall not, however, affect the provisions of any other treaty requiring the lessor's real rights to be recognized[538] – thus the provisions of the Cape Town Convention (2001) prevail where they apply.

[1] US Bankruptcy Code

For example, section 1110 of the US Bankruptcy Code has special provisions relating to aircraft. Under section 1110, the automatic stay under section 362 against repossession, unless the court finds cause to grant relief, applies to aircraft lessor only for the first sixty days after the official commencement of a bankruptcy case. During that period, the debtor must cure any pre-bankruptcy defaults and enter into a court-approved agreement to perform all obligations under the pre-petition lease.

By the end of the sixty-day period, if all defaults are not cured and a court-approved agreement is not in place, section 1110 overrides the automatic stay such that, immediately upon the debtor's default and without a court order, the lessor is entitled to retake possession of its aircraft and to enforce any of its rights or remedies in accordance with the provisions of the underlying lease.

In the context of the section 1110 stay period, Dempsey and Gesell[539] have noted, somewhat drily but accurately, that:

> [t]ypically, during this period, the company negotiates at a feverish pace with aircraft lessors and lenders, urging that they give the airline additional time to make good on outstanding indebtedness, and re-open the financial terms to place the airline in a position to emerge from bankruptcy successfully.

533. Especially in the United States – *see* section §3.14[D][1] *infra.*
534. *See* Chapter 2 section §2.01 *supra.*
535. Article 7(1)(a).
536. Article 7(3)(b).
537. Article 7(2).
538. Article 7(4).
539. Dempsey P.S. and Gesell L.E., *Air Commerce and the Law*, Coast Aire, 2004, at 389–390.

This is essentially the same concept as proposed by Alternative A on bankruptcy proposed in Article XI of the Aircraft Protocol to the Cape Town Convention (2001).[540] Other jurisdictions may prefer allowing a court greater flexibility as regards repossession by a lessor upon an airline lessee insolvency. This will always be governed by the laws of the jurisdiction of the airline and thus may vary widely, too widely to be examined in detail in this work. Such states, wishing to adopt the Cape Town Convention (2001), but wishing to retain such flexibility, may opt for Alternative B.[541] To date, only Mexico has elected for Alternative B.[542]

[2] Cape Town Convention (2001)

The Cape Town Convention (2001) and Aircraft Protocol provide in Article XI of the Aircraft Protocol for two alternatives, A and B, in the case of airline bankruptcy. A contracting State may elect either A in its entirety, B in its entirety or neither.

[a] Alternative A

Under Alternative A, upon the occurrence of an insolvency-related event, the insolvency administrator shall either cure all defaults or give possession of[543] the aircraft to the lessor by the end of whatever time period is stated by the contracting State in its declaration (or such earlier date on which the lessor would have been entitled to repossession in the absence of Article XI). This is similar in concept to the US section 1110 procedure.

[b] Alternative B

Under Alternative B, the insolvency administrator must, upon the lessor's request, indicate to the lessor within the time period stated by the contracting State in its declaration whether it will cure all defaults or allow the creditor to take repossession.

However, the court has broad discretion in requiring additional steps and the court may (not shall) allow the lessor to repossess the aircraft 'upon such terms as the court may order'.

Wool and Littlejohns have criticized Alternative B as follows:

> Alternative B is unsatisfactory to creditors because it does not impose a time limit for actual assumption of the agreement or return of the aircraft – the only time limit imposed on the airline or its insolvency administrator is to notify its initial decision.[544]

540. *See* section §3.14[D][2] *infra.*
541. *See* section §3.14[D][2] *infra.*
542. *Ibid.*
543. *See* section §3.15[A] *infra* for what is meant by giving possession.
544. Wool J. and Littlejohns A., *Cape Town Treaty in the European Context: The Case for Alternative A, Article XI of the Aircraft Protocol*, Airfinance Annual, 2007/2008.

As of the date hereof, only Mexico has opted for the more debtor-friendly Alternative B.[545]

It should be noted that, just as any sovereign State may choose to adopt or not adopt the Cape Town Convention (2001), it may, if it chooses to adopt it, choose Alternative A or Alternative B as it in its sole discretion decides. That said, there are certain implications to its choices.

If it decides to adopt the Cape Town Convention (2001), and if it chooses Alternative A, then certain officially supported export credit enhancements, by way of a lower minimum rate of interest for such financing, may be available.[546] In addition to the other requirements, it is necessary in order to obtain such a lower rate, that:

> [t]he operator of the aircraft (or the borrower/buyer or lessor if, in the view of the Participant providing the official support, the structure of the transaction so warrants) is situated in a State which appears on the list of States which qualify for the reduction of the minimum premium rates.[547]

and such state shall have made the 'qualifying declarations' set out in Annex 1 to the Sector Understanding on Export Credits for Civil Aircraft – Final Text.[548]

In addition, the state shall have:

> [h]ave implemented the Cape Town Convention, including the qualifying declarations, in its laws and regulations, as required, in such a way that the Cape Town Convention commitments are appropriately translated into national law.[549]

In other words, by adopting the Cape Town Convention (2001), and making the qualifying declarations thereunder, including Alternative A, all of which are intended to give greater certainty to enforcement of the lease in accordance with its terms, the very concern of this work, a state can ensure[550] that its airlines can benefit from cheaper financing, or that lessors to its airlines can so benefit, which benefits can be passed on by way of lower lease rental.

In the context of the EU, the Cape Town Convention (2001)[551] and the Aircraft Protocol[552] provide for the accession thereto not only of states but of regional economic integration organizations. The EU is a party thereto.[553] The declaration made by it are complex due to the division of competencies between the EU and its Member States[554] but, for these purposes, it is sufficient to note that the EU declined to make a declaration regarding remedies on insolvency, leaving it to each Member State to decide.[555]

545. http://www.unidroit.org/status-2001capetown-aircraft?id = 1598 on 9 Sep. 2021.
546. Organisation for Economic Co-operation and Development, *Sector Understanding on Export Credits for Civil Aircraft – Final Text*, 20 Dec. 2010, section 35(b).
547. *Ibid.*, section 1.
548. Set out for convenience at Annex 11 hereto.
549. *Ibid.*, section 37(c).
550. At least in theory.
551. Article 48.
552. Article XXVII.
553. http://www.unidroit.org/status-2001capetown-aircraft on 9 Sep. 2021.
554. UNIDROIT, *Seminar Report: The European Community and the Cape Town Convention*, Rome, 26 Nov. 2009.
555. *Ibid.*, at 6.

[3] Non-insolvency Restructuring and the Cape Town Convention (2001)

In order to avoid the downside to an insolvency restructuring, an airline may wish to consider instead, where it is available to it, a scheme of arrangement, which need not necessarily be insolvent but is seeking by means of the scheme to avoid becoming insolvent and instead rehabilitating the company. Such a scheme of arrangement is provided for in Part 26 of the United Kingdom Companies Act 2006.

Non-English companies can take advantage of the English scheme of arrangement if there is a 'sufficient connection' with England, it seems that if the lease is subject to English law and English courts' jurisdiction, as many leases are, this is sufficient.

The AWG, which represents most lessors, set up the independent Cape Town Convention Academic Project,[556] hosted by the Law Faculty of Cambridge University. Professors Louise Gullifer and Riz Mokal of the Project provided a legal opinion to the AWG that both restructuring plans and schemes of arrangement under the United Kingdom Companies Act 2006 come within the Cape Town Convention (2001) Alternative A provisions.[557]

In their opinion, the scheme of arrangement offered by Malaysian Airlines[558] complied with these provisions. The scheme 'offered each holder of a Lease the option ... to terminate the Lease, recover the aircraft object, and receive a termination payment calculated at 115% of what the Lease holder would receive in a liquidation. If the Lease holder chose instead to continue the Lease, then upon the Scheme's being approved by the requisite statutory majority of Lease holders and sanctioned by the Court, Lease holders would receive substantially reduced rents'.[559] By offering this option to lessors to enjoy the benefits of their Cape Town Convention (2001) Alternative A rights rather than partake in the scheme, if they so choose, the scheme complied with the Cape Town Convention (2001). Thus, the best way to preserve a non-insolvency scheme of arrangement from challenge by lessors on the grounds of non-compliance with the Cape Town Convention (2001) is to ensure a termination option along the lines outlined above. Although the basic point of the Cape Town Convention (2001) is to protect creditors' interests, this is one way in which the Cape Town Convention (2001) may work to the benefit of airlines, since the AWG promotes the advice of the Cape Town Convention Academic Project to its members.

---

556. http://ctcap.org on 9 Sep. 2021.
557. Gullifer L. and Mokal R., *UK Restructuring Plan and Scheme of Arrangement Proceedings: Expert Opinion on Status under the Cape Town Convention*, 23 Nov. 2020, revised 29 Apr. 2021, at http://awg.aero/wp-content/uploads/2021/04/CTC-status-of-RPs-and-Schemes-Expert-Report-Revised-29-Apr-2021.pdf on 9 Sep. 2021.
558. *Re MAB Leasing Limited* [2021] EWHC 152 (Ch).
559. In the comparable Irish High Court case, *Nordic Aviation Capital Designated Activity Company v. The Companies Act 2014 to 2018 (Approved)* [2020] IEHC 445, Barniville J held that it 'would be appropriate to leave over to a future case a determination of the potentially controversial issues which could arise in terms of the potential application of the Cape Town Convention (2001) and the Aircraft Protocol to schemes of arrangement' under the equivalent Irish legislation, since no creditors objected to the scheme.

This advice is consistent with a judgment of the High Court of Malaysia,[560] cited with approval by the High Court of Ireland,[561] that termination, as opposed to modification of the terms of, a lease, triggering the right to possession of the aircraft, is not inconsistent with the provisions of Alternative A of Article XI of the Aircraft Protocol to the Cape Town Convention (2001).

[4] Conclusions

What constitutes an event of default is not dealt with in the public or private air law instruments and is generally a matter for the governing law of the lease. This includes the occurrence of a bankruptcy or insolvency event in respect of the lessee. However, whether or not, and for how long, or subject to what conditions, a lessor's rights may be stayed before he can enforce them in the case of the bankruptcy of an airline will depend on the law of the jurisdiction of the airline. As the aircraft will likely be in the hands of the airline, and thus its liquidator or other trustee in bankruptcy, this may lead to legal claims not only in the dispute resolution venue set out in the lease[562] but also the bankruptcy courts of the jurisdiction of the airline.

An event of default in and of itself only has contractual implications under the lease to the extent that it triggers remedy rights on the part of the lessor, which remedy rights are next examined.

§3.15 REMEDIES

In addition to a claim for unpaid rent or other payments,[563] a lessor's main concern on a default will be to obtain repossession of the aircraft and its documents, to deregister the aircraft from the aircraft register on which the lessee placed it, and to export it from the lessee's country as soon as possible, ideally before any declaration of bankruptcy in respect of the lessee.[564] Complications with liens, and borrowed engines, can turn this into a very difficult area for lessors.

Under English law, where the lessor terminates the leasing of the aircraft pursuant to a default by the lessee and seeks to exercise its rights, a breach by the

560. *AirAsia X Berhad v. BOC Aviation Limited* (WA-24NCC-467-10/2020).
561. *Arctic Aviation Assets Designate Activity Company & ors v. Companies Act*, 2014 (Approved) [2021] IEHC 268.
562. *See* section §3.18 *infra*.
563. A detailed examination of such debt claims is beyond the scope of this work and are generally of less importance to the lessor, who accepts the lessee's credit risk when the lessor agree to lease its aircraft to it, than the ability quickly to repossess the aircraft and to remarket it. One straightforward example of a summary debt claim may be seen at *AerCap Ireland Ltd & Ors v. Hainan Airlines Holding Co Ltd* [2020] EWHC 2025 (Comm). Nevertheless, the author draws the reader's attention to the possibility of seeking a third party debt order whereby a debtor of the airline is directed to pay such debt to the lessor in (partial) satisfaction of the airline's debt. *See*, for example, the failed attempt to obtain a final such order against the IATA clearing house in *Ross Leasing Ltd & Ors v. Nile Air* [2021] EWHC 2201 (Comm).
564. *See* section 13 of the Supplement *infra*.

lessee, under a lease worded in accordance with industry practice, involves a repudiation by the lessee and a breach by it of all obligations remaining unperformed: the loss suffered by the lessor is treated in law not as being caused by the lessor's decision to treat the lease as discharged but by the lessee's breach which led the lessor to take such a step.[565]

Under English law, a lessor also has a duty to mitigate its damages: otherwise, any amount of damages which it receives must be reduced accordingly. This was confirmed in *BAE Systems*[566] which also confirmed that:

> [t]he duty to mitigate arises only when a breach of contract has been committed, not before. It is not open to a person who has broken his contract to say that the other party should have acted before the breach in a way that would have reduced his loss when the breach eventually occurred.[567]

For comparison, it should be noted that, with respect to finance leases covered thereunder, the UNIDROIT Convention on Financial Leasing (1988)[568] allows for recovery of unpaid rentals together with interest and damages[569] but restricts repossession to where the lessee's default is 'substantial'[570] and to claim for acceleration of payment of future rentals.[571] Further, the lessor can only recover damages if it has taken all reasonable steps to mitigate its loss.[572]

[A] Repossession

In the event the airline defaults in its obligations under the lease, the lessor may be entitled to exercise certain remedies under applicable law. The applicable law providing such remedies could be the law of the jurisdiction where the aircraft is located, the law of the jurisdiction where the aircraft is registered, the law where the airline is located, and/or the governing law provided for in the lease. In each case, the parties will need to consult with legal counsel in each of those jurisdictions in order to verify the situation in that jurisdiction.[573]

The Cape Town Convention (2001)[574] provides:

> References to the applicable law are to the domestic rules of the law applicable by virtue of the rules of private international law of the forum State.[575]

565. *BAE Systems Management Service (Two) Limited & Another v. Trident Aviation Leasing Services (Jersey) Ltd & AS Enimex* [2010] EWCA Civ 107.
566. *Supra.*
567. *Ibid.*, per Moore-Bick LJ, at para. 16.
568. *See* Chapter 2 section §2.01 *supra.*
569. Article 13(1).
570. Article 13(2).
571. Article 13(4) and (5).
572. Article 13(6).
573. The jurisdictional questionnaire discussed in Chapter 2 section §2.04 *supra* may identify remedies available in respect of the jurisdiction concerned.
574. *See* section §3.15[C] *infra.*
575. Article 5(3).

The Cape Town Convention (2001) goes on to provide that a court has jurisdiction to grant an order of repossession of the aircraft[576] if it is:

(a) a court chosen by the parties;[577]
(b) a court of a contracting State on the territory of which the lessee is situated, being relief which, by the terms of the order granting it, is enforceable only in the territory of that contracting State;[578] or
(c) a court of the State of registration of the aircraft.[579]

In addition, the lessor will normally[580] want to set out certain agreed contractual remedies in the lease, including the contractual right to terminate the leasing of the aircraft under the lease and to take repossession of the aircraft. Article 10(a) of the Cape Town Convention (2001) provides that, subject to the right of a contracting State under Article 54(2)[581] to require that leave of the court first be obtained, in the event of default under a lease, the lessor may terminate the leasing agreement and take possession and control of the aircraft.[582]

Physical repossession alone of the aircraft is not, however, enough. The lessor will want to put the aircraft into revenue service with a new lessee with a minimum of delay. In order to do so, it needs not only the aircraft with all engines and parts but all aircraft documents, as the new lessee will not otherwise accept delivery of the aircraft. It needs to fly the aircraft away from the airport where it is located at the time of repossession (and thus may need to deal with unpaid landing and parking fees), export the aircraft from the jurisdiction of the previous lessee (and thus may need to deal with excise taxes and export duties) and to deregister the aircraft, where relevant, from the aircraft register of the jurisdiction of the previous lessee.

How exactly a hostile repossession will proceed is hard to gauge in advance. To give one view:

> 'It's pretty exciting walking through customs with $30,000 in cash strapped to your stomach', says one lessor. 'But you need it when you are repossessing an aircraft.'[583]

576. Under Art. 13(1)(b) of the Cape Town Convention.
577. Under Art. 43(2)(a) of the Cape Town Convention.
578. Under Art. 43(2)(b) of the Cape Town Convention.
579. Under Art. XXI of the Aircraft Protocol to the Cape Town Convention.
580. *See* Bunker D.H., *International Aircraft Financing, Volume 2: Specific Documents*, 2nd Edition, IATA, 2015, at 151–159.
581. According to Krupski, Art. 54(2) was added in order to accommodate civil law jurisdictions that are generally hostile to non-judicial remedies such as self-help. *See* Krupski J.A., *Conflict of Laws in Aircraft Securitization*, Annals of Air and Space Law, Volume XXIV, 1999, at 144.
582. In other words, absent a declaration under Art. 54(2), self-help is allowed.
583. Segal S., *Repossessions and Remarketing after the Repo Man*, Airfinance Journal, December 2008/January 2009, at 28.

Although self-help[584] remedies may be possible in certain jurisdictions to a greater or lesser degree,[585] often some kind of court order will be required in the case of a legal hostile repossession. This will typically involve seeking an interim order, often on an ex parte basis, granting the lessor repossession of its asset pending resolution of the underlying dispute in substantive proceedings. This is because it is unlikely that the lessor can afford to await the outcome of substantive proceedings in a situation where it almost certainly is not being paid rent.

In order to protect a lessee in case it should later win in the substantive proceedings, the lessor is often required to post a bond in an amount which will be paid should the lessee ultimately be successful. This amount may, according to the jurisdiction, be fixed by the judge or may be determined by reference to the value of the asset in question[586] (even though the lessee has no ownership interest therein and even though its losses would be calculated by reference to lost revenue rather than by reference to the underlying value of the asset which it is renting).

By way of example, in Brazil,[587] which has ratified the Rome Convention (1933),[588] the amount of the bond is at the court's discretion but in practice is usually between 10%–20% of the 'value of the cause', which was taken to be the amount of the overdue debt. The Rome Convention (1933) is discussed in detail in section §3.15[B] *infra*. Further, a preliminary injunction is normally insufficient to allow export of the aircraft from Brazil. Although the lessor can take possession of the aircraft, therefore, until the order is final, the aircraft cannot be effectively remarketed.[589]

Lessors should be aware that, where the grounds for seeking forfeiture or repossession of the aircraft relate solely to a money claim for unpaid amounts under the lease, such as rent, it is open to a lessee, under English common law, to seek equitable relief against forfeiture on the grounds that the right to forfeit is essentially to secure payment of that money as contrasted, with, say, an obligation to keep the leased property in good repair. This right was confirmed by Teare J of the English High Court in *Celestial Aviation Trading 71 Limited v. Paramount Airways Private Limited.*[590]

The effects of repossession of an aircraft may go beyond simply the aircraft itself:[591] if the aircraft repossessed is the only aircraft operated by the airline, it may

584. That is, remedies exercised directly by the lessor without first obtaining a court order.
585. Crans B. and Nath R., *Aircraft Repossession and Enforcement: Practical Aspects*, Wolters Kluwer, 2009.
586. Basch K. and Iezzi I., *Summary of Repossession Procedure in Brazil*, a paper presented to the American Bar Association Air and Space Law Forum annual meeting in Seattle, Washington on 11 Oct. 2010.
587. *See* section §3.15[B] *infra*.
588. The Convention for the Unification of certain Rules relating to the Precautionary Arrest of Aircraft, signed at Rome on 29 May 1933.
589. Basch K. and Iezzi I., *Summary of Repossession Procedure in Brazil*, a paper presented to the American Bar Association Air and Space Law Forum annual meeting in Seattle, Washington on 11 Oct. 2010, at 4.
590. [2009] EWHC 3142 (Comm), at paras 22 et seq. This case is discussed in detail in Chapter 2 section §2.01 *supra*.
591. This author has personal experience of just such a situation involving the loss of its air transport licence where the last aircraft in its fleet was repossessed by the lessor after defaulting under the lease. Such revocation led to the liquidation of the airline.

stand to lose its air transport licence.[592] For example, in the context of the EU, European Council Regulation 1008/2008 provides:

> An undertaking shall be granted an operating license by the competent licensing authority of a Member State provided that: ...
>
> cc) it has one or more aircraft at its disposal through ownership or a dry lease agreement;[593]

The consequences for the lessee in such a situation could be terminal for the airline. Without an air transport licence, the airline may well be faced with liquidation: a situation with which this author has experience[594] in the French courts.

The Federal Court of Australia has held[595] that the reference in Alternative A of Article XI of the Aircraft Protocol to the Cape Town Convention (2001) to giving possession of the aircraft to the lessor does not mean there is an obligation to give such possession in accordance with the terms of the lease agreement, with the estate in bankruptcy bearing the costs of redelivery. This judgment was cited with approval by the Irish High Court.[596]

[B] Rome Convention (1933)

The Rome Convention (1933)[597] has not been widely ratified, being in force in only nineteen states,[598] but may impede a lessor's ability to seek repossession prior to obtaining a final judgment. Under Article 3(1) thereof, the following aircraft are exempt from arrest unless the owner dispossessed of his aircraft by an unlawful act [599]

(a) aircraft exclusively appropriated to a state service, including the postal service, but excluding commercial service;
(b) aircraft actually in service on a regular line of public transport, together with the indispensable reserve aircraft;
(c) every other aircraft appropriated to the carriage of persons or goods for reward, where such aircraft is ready to start on such carriage, unless the arrest is in respect of a contract debt incurred for the purposes of the journey which

592. *See* section §3.05[B][5] *supra*.
593. Article 4.
594. *Me Raymond Dupont acting as appointed liquidator of SAS Noor Airways v. Aviation Capital Group Acquisition XX LLC*, Case 119083, Commercial Court of Saint Nazaire, 2011.
595. *VB Leaseco Pty Ltd (administrators appointed) v. Wells Fargo Trust Company, National Association (trustee)* [2020] FCAFC 168.
596. *Arctic Aviation Assets Designate Activity Company & ors v. Companies Act*, 2014 (Approved) [2021] IEHC 268.
597. Sand P., *The International Unification of Air Law*, Law and Contemporary Problems, Volume 30, Issue 2, 1965, 400–424, at 405.
598. It should be noted that the Rome Convention (1933) does not apply in cases of bankruptcy – *see* Art. 7.
599. Article 3(2).

the aircraft is about to make, or of a claim which has arisen in the course of the journey.

Under Article 4, if the airline is not entitled to the protection of Article 3 or does not invoke such protection, the airline shall have the right to immediate release. Upon posting security sufficient to cover:

> the amount of the debt and costs and if it is appropriated exclusively to the payment of the creditor, or if it covers the value of the aircraft if this value is smaller than the amount of the debt and costs.

This author has successfully obtained,[600] in the courts of Ontario, Canada, the precautionary arrest of an aircraft where the Rome Convention (1933) did not apply – many variables are in play: persuading the court to accept jurisdiction, persuading the court to post a bond which is not prohibitively high[601] and, perhaps most importantly, persuading the judge to issue the order on an ex parte[602] basis.[603]

The reason for this is simple to grasp – Rochus Mönter,[604] in his most interesting account of his legal actions on behalf of a lessor against a Mexican airline which refused either to pay the lessor rent or to return the aircraft to the lessor, observes that, without the benefit of an ex parte basis for a precautionary order in California, the delinquent airline could easily have evaded sequestration of the aircraft by the simple expedient of not flying it into California.

Prior to his successful detention, this author witnessed such simple expedient. Having successfully obtained a court order on an ex parte basis, he received confirmation from a private detective hired by his aircraft lessor employer that the nationality and registration mark of an aircraft departing the airline's home base at a particular time matched the scheduled departure time for a flight to a city where an ex parte detention order had been obtained upon posting a reasonable bond. Unfortunately, somehow, word got to the airline, and the flight was diverted to another jurisdiction: it is not known how the passengers were accommodated or the reason for the diversion explained to them. In any event, ultimately, the aircraft was successfully arrested, and possession granted to the lessor – this still did not resolve payment of the unpaid rent and other amounts or deregistration of the aircraft.[605]

600. *Mitsui & Co., Ltd. and Tombo Aviation Inc v. Viacao Aerea Sao Paulo S.A. – VASP*, Court File No. 99-CV-170574, Superior Court of Justice, Ontario, 1999.
601. Depending on the jurisdiction, for example, in Brazil (*see* section §3.15[B] *supra*), the judge may not have discretion and the amount of the bond may be calculated by reference to the value of the asset in dispute, even though in the case of an operating lease, the lessee has no ownership interest in the aircraft, only a leasehold interest.
602. That is to say, without notice to the other party, the airline.
603. *See also* an account of an ex parte order freezing a leased aircraft at Dublin Airport pending enforcement of an arbitration award, *Aircraft prevented from leaving Dublin airport after court order*, 10 Feb. 2021, at www.breakingnews.ie/ireland/aircraft-prevented-from-leaving-dublin-airport-after-court-order-1079003.html on 9 Sep. 2021.
604. Mönter R., *Today's Challenges of Leasing Aircraft into Mexico!*, Air And Space Law, Kluwer Law International, Volume XXXIII, Issue 6, November 2008, 430–443, at 437.
605. As to which, *see* section §3.15[F] *infra*.

[C] Cape Town Convention (2001)

The Rome Convention (1933) is superseded by the Cape Town Convention (2001) pursuant to Article XXIII of the Aircraft Protocol thereto insofar as aircraft, as defined in the Aircraft Protocol,[606] are concerned and states are party thereto, except for states which make a declaration to the contrary pursuant to Article 24 of the Aircraft Protocol.

If the Cape Town Convention (2001) and Aircraft Protocol apply, then, so long as the lessor acts in a commercially reasonable manner,[607] it may, if the lessee has agreed to it, take possession of the aircraft or apply for a court order authorizing it to take possession or control of the aircraft. Under Article 54(2) of the Cape Town Convention (2001), a state may require leave of the court for such taking of repossession or control.

Under Article 13 of the Cape Town Convention (2001), a contracting State shall ensure that a lessor may, pending final determination of a claim, and if the lessee has so agreed, obtain speedy relief as to possession, control and custody of the aircraft, subject to such terms as the court thinks necessary to protect the lessee or other interested parties.

It remains to be seen how the provisions of the Cape Town Convention (2001) and the Aircraft Protocol will be interpreted by the courts.

[D] Geneva Convention (1948)

The Geneva Convention (1948), has already been discussed in section §3.10[B][4][c] *supra* in the context of engines. Under the Geneva Convention (1948), which has been ratified by ninety-one states,[608] the contracting states undertake to recognize property rights in aircraft provided that such rights have been constituted in accordance with the laws of the state of registration of the aircraft applicable at the time of their creation and are recorded in a public record of such state of registration[609] and include the right to possess an aircraft under a lease of six months or more.[610] Some states continue to adopt the Geneva Convention (1948) notwithstanding the advent of the Cape Town Convention (2001).

The remainder of the Geneva Convention (1948) largely deals with the rights of secured creditors and is of little practical use to operating lessors. Honnebier has commented that the Geneva Convention (1948) is merely a conflict of laws treaty rather than a substantive law treaty, and from the outset has been simply regarded as a 'provisional body of rules'.[611]

---

606. As to which, *see* Art. 1(2) of the Aircraft Protocol.
607. Article 9(3) of the Aircraft Protocol.
608. http://www.icao.int/secretariat/legal/List%20of%20Parties/Geneva_EN.pdf on 9 Sep. 2021.
609. Article 1(a).
610. Article 1(c).
611. Honnebier B.P., *Clarifying the Alleged Issues Concerning the Financing of Aircraft Engines: Some Comments to the Alleged Pitfalls Arising under Dutch, German and International Law, as Proposed*, Zeitschrift für Luft- und Weltraumrecht, Volume 3, 2007, at 33–44 *See* section §3.10[B][4][c] *supra*.

Pursuant to Article 23 of the Aircraft Protocol to the Cape Town Convention (2001), the Geneva Convention (1948) is superseded by the Cape Town Convention (2001) and the Aircraft Protocol as it relates to aircraft as defined in the Aircraft Protocol except in relation to parties thereto which make a declaration to the contrary.[612]

[E] Subleasing

In the context of repossession, a lessor should be careful in consenting[613] to any proposed subleasing by the lessee of its aircraft.[614] The sublease term should not extend beyond the term of the head lease and the rent thereunder should not be less than that under the head lease. Most importantly in the context of repossession, however, is that the lessor should be clear up front as to what will happen to the sublease should the head lease terminate.

Either the sublease should be explicitly stated to be subordinate to the head lease (such that, should the head lease terminate, the sublease automatically terminates too, thus entitling the lessor to repossession from the sub-lessee) or the head lessee[615] should assign its rights, but not its obligations, to the lessor as security for the performance by the lessee of its obligations under the head lease.

The effect of this will be that, if the lessee defaults, the lessor can terminate the head lease, but can take over the sublease so as to enjoy the rights of the sub-lessor thereunder. Notice of the assignment should be given to the sub-lessee and an acknowledgement thereof and consent thereto obtained from the sub-lessee.

In return for this, the lessor normally grants a letter of quiet enjoyment to the sub-lessee confirming that, so long as the sub-lessee performs under the sublease in favour of the lessor, pursuant to the assignment, the lessor will not interfere with the sub-lessee's quiet enjoyment of the aircraft for the term of the sublease.

Annex 1 sets out the interplay of the assignment by way of security and the letter of quiet enjoyment in a typical operating lease structure.

[F] Deregistration

Simply obtaining possession of the aircraft alone may not of itself by a sufficient remedy for the lessor in respect of the aircraft itself.

612. *See* Hanley D.P., *The Relationship Between the Geneva and Cape Town Conventions*, Cape Town Convention Journal, Volume 4, Issue 1, 2015, at 103–113.
613. Whether such consent is a general subleasing right set out in the lease or a specific consent to a specific subleasing request by the lessee.
614. Indeed, a prudent lessor should carefully review which subleases by the lessee will require its prior consent since this will involve the lessee parting with possession of the lessor's property to a third party. This will vary by case: a lessor may require its specific prior consent to any sublease, or a lessee may negotiate for such consent to be dispensed with for subleases to other airlines within its corporate group or to certain specified other airlines acceptable to the lessor.
615. This is also the sub-lessor under the sublease.

The aircraft must be registered pursuant to Article 17 of the Chicago Convention (1944). Under Article 19 of the Chicago Convention (1944), however, it is up to each contracting State to decide what laws and regulations will govern registration of aircraft. *See* the discussion in section §3.10[B][3] *supra*.

Where the aircraft is registered in the name of the owner, the owner[616] will control deregistration and thus should not face any difficulty in this regard.

Where the aircraft is, however, registered in the name of the lessee as an operator, and the lessee refuses to deregister the aircraft, the lessor will be unable to deliver the aircraft to another lessee on terms whereby that lessee can operate the aircraft. To deal with the likelihood of such a refusal on the part of the lessee, the lessor may demand a deregistration power of attorney, which is next examined.

[G] Deregistration Power of Attorney

In cases where the aircraft is registered in the name of the lessee as operator of the aircraft, in order to protect the lessor in the case where the lessee is in breach of the lease and refuses to deregister the aircraft despite being required to do so under the lease, the lessor frequently demands a deregistration power of attorney to be executed by the lessee in favour of the lessor authorizing the lessor to deregister the aircraft from the aircraft register.

In practice, such powers of attorney are of limited practical use. Notwithstanding any language therein to the effect that they are irrevocable, under many legal systems they are irrevocable at any time and aviation authorities are loath to rely on them alone to deregister an aircraft in the face of opposition from the local operator.

Further, under English law, powers of attorney must be executed as a deed. This fact is frequently forgotten, especially where the power[617] is granted in the body of the lease itself. English law regarding due execution of a deed must be followed carefully.

In an English High Court case,[618] a document purporting to be executed as a deed was disallowed since, following common practice, the signature pages thereto had been pre-placed and the final text added later, in breach of the requirement that the signature and attestation form part of the same physical document such that the deed was signed in its final form.

[H] Article 83*bis* Transfer

One possible step which may be open to a lessor who is wary of leasing to an operator based on a country with an operator-only registration system for aircraft may be to

616. Assuming it is, or is related to, the lessor – *see* Chapter 2 section §2.02 *supra*.
617. This may take the form of a specific power of attorney to deregister or the form of a broader power of attorney to take all steps necessary to allow the lessor to exercise its remedies thereunder.
618. *R. (on the application by Mercury Tax Group and another) v. HMRC* [2008] EWHC 2721.

effect a transfer under the widely adopted Article 83*bis*[619] of the Chicago Convention (1944) which provides that:

> when an aircraft registered in a contracting State is operated pursuant to an agreement for the lease ... of the aircraft ... by an operator who has his principal place of business ... in another contracting State, the State of registry may, by agreement with such other State, transfer to it all or part of its functions and duties as State of registry in respect of that aircraft ... .[620]

This is also popularly referred to as an Annex 6 delegation or transfer since what is transferred are the obligations of the state of registration under Annex 6 of the Chicago Convention (1944), dealing with International Standards and Recommended Practices(SARPs) relating to the operation of aircraft. Areas which may be covered by such a transfer are rules of the air,[621] aircraft radio equipment,[622] certificates of airworthiness[623] and licences of personnel.[624]

If it is possible to achieve such a transfer, then the risk of the lessee's wrongly refusing to deregister the aircraft can be managed but it should be borne in mind that such transfers are done between states and thus require two willing states, either of which can refuse the transfer or impose such conditions as it may see fit.

For example, the United Kingdom will not normally agree to such a transfer for a period exceeding six months in duration.[625] Such a period would not be long enough for most operating leases and is more often availed of in practice where a lessee itself wishes to sublease an aircraft for a summer or winter season.

Dempsey[626] gives the hypothetical example that Ireland could delegate to Germany the responsibility to oversee the airworthiness of aircraft owned by Irish leasing companies but operated by Lufthansa. Although Dempsey indeed gives a good example, in fact, there is no such delegation between Ireland and Germany. One reason why Article 83*bis* is not more widely availed of[627] may be that the state of the aircraft operator has no motivation to accept such responsibility, even though it would have no ability to avoid such responsibility if, in this example, the lessor and Lufthansa agreed

619. Article 83*bis* has been adopted by 177 contracting States of the Chicago Convention – *see* http://www.icao.int/secretariat/legal/List%20of%20Parties/83bis_EN.pdf on 9 Sep. 2021.
620. Leloudas and Haeck express concern that the reference to the principal place of business rather than to the place of incorporation of the operator 'means that the State of the operator is unable to maintain control of the airline and the aircraft': Leloudas G. and Haeck L., *Legal Aspects of Aviation Risk Management*, Annals of Air and Space Law, Volume XXVII, 2002, 149–169, at 163. This author, however, sees no reason why an operator having its principal place of business in a state would not be subject to the jurisdiction of that State, and has seen no evidence of this issue causing any problem in practice.
621. Article 12 of the Chicago Convention.
622. Article 30 of the Chicago Convention.
623. Article 31 of the Chicago Convention.
624. Article 32(a) of the Chicago Convention.
625. United Kingdom Civil Aviation Authority Official record Series 4, Air Navigation Order 2005 General Exemption, 30 Sep. 2005.
626. Dempsey P.S., *Public International Air Law*, McGill University, 2008, 118.
627. A full list of Art. 83*bis* agreements registered with ICAO may be found at http://cfapp.icao.int/dagmar/main.cfm?UserLang=_e (as of 9 Sep. 2021).

that the aircraft should be registered in Germany rather than Ireland for the term of the lease.[628]

Although Ireland and Germany have not entered into any such agreements, there is no reason, in principle, why they should not as, for example, Ireland and Italy have entered into such agreements and also Italy and Germany have likewise entered into such agreements. It is a matter of both states being willing: no State can be forced into such an agreement.

ICAO[629] has made clear that the concept of registration implies responsibility of the state of registration for the safety of aircraft registered with it, wherever they may be operated.[630] Article 83*bis* was developed in response to safety concerns arising out of the growing trend for aircraft leasing. The aim is to offer:

> a solution under public international law that aims at facilitating safety oversight, taking into account the need of airlines for flexible commercial arrangements in the use of their aircraft.[631]

As of 20 November 2002, twenty-five transfer agreements had been registered with ICAO, twelve of them by Italy (and six of those to Germany) and eight of them by Ireland.[632] Thus, the take-up rate has not, apparently, been very high.[633]

A note of diffidence to such arrangements may, perhaps, be noted in recital 8 to Regulation (EC) 1008/2008,[634] which provides:

> In order to avoid excessive recourse to lease agreements of aircraft registered in third countries, especially wet lease,[635] these possibilities should only be allowed in exceptional circumstances, such as a lack of adequate aircraft on the Community market, and they should be strictly limited in time and fulfil safety standards equivalent to the safety rules of Community and national legislation.

Certainly, this shows a greater concern with wet leasing than with dry leasing but the regulation does not discuss what greater comfort, if any, may be taken in the case of dry leases of aircraft registered in third countries where there is a transfer of oversight pursuant to Article 83*bis*.[636]

---

628. At the time of writing, ICAO has established a task force to examine ways of encouraging greater uptake, such as by way of examining signing authority requirements for such agreements and possibly allowing a web-based method for states to upload such agreements directly onto the ICAO register of agreements: ICAO Letter LE4/70-IND/14/9 of 31 Jul. 2014.
629. *Guidance on the Implementation of Article 83bis* of the Convention on International Civil Aviation, ICAO, 2003. Agreements can be looked up at http://www.icao.int/applications/dagmar/main.cfm?UserLang= but no overall list or number of agreements is available there.
630. *Ibid.*, at 4–5.
631. *Ibid.*, at 5.
632. *Ibid.*, at 23.
633. That said, although the website does not disclose precisely how many have been registered with ICAO, the ICAO website shows at least 100 having been registered. *See* http://cfapp.icao.int/dagmar/main.cfm?UserLang=_e (as of 9 Sep. 2021).
634. Regulation (EC) 1008/2008 of the European Parliament and of the Council of 24 Sep. 2008 on common rules for the operation of air services in the Community.
635. *Sic.*
636. It should be noted here that a party to the Chicago Convention which is nevertheless not a party to Art. 83*bis* is not bound by any such delegation among States.

The model transfer agreement[637] and sample transfer agreements set out by ICAO refer to SARPs laid down in Annexes to, rather than to Articles of, the Chicago Convention (1944), but generally show full transfer of oversight in respect of Annex 1 (personnel licensing), Annex 2 (rules of the air), Annex 6 (operation of aircraft), as referred to above, but reserving oversight or having only a limited transfer in respect of Annex 8 (airworthiness).

In this context, according to Abeyratne:[638]

> [t]echnically, Article 83 bis is calculated to tighten and ensure the more efficient operation of aircraft in terms both of safety and of commercial expediency ... .

It is not, therefore, a case of having to choose between one and the other. He helpfully goes on to point out[639] that an incentive to a state considering whether or not to conclude an agreement under Article 83*bis* is the assurance that the state to which safety oversight is delegated has the capability of fulfilling its responsibilities in respect of the aircraft involved: such state has access to the results of audits carried out under the ICAO Safety Oversight Audit Programme.

Although there is no reason under the terms of Article 83*bis* why a delegation under Article 83*bis* need be limited to specific aircraft, in practice, they are: *see*, for example, the Memorandum of Understanding (with two Schedules) between the Irish Aviation Authority (Ireland) and the Ente Nazionale per l'Aviazione (Italy) on the Implementation of Article 83*bis* of the Convention on International Civil Aviation for the Transfer of Surveillance Responsibilities (Operations, Maintenance and Continuing Airworthiness) of Aircraft Operated under Dry Lease Contract[640] dated 14 October 2000.

It is specific to fifty-three aircraft listed by aircraft type, registration mark and manufacturer's serial number and Italian operator. Under its terms,[641] consistent with the ICAO model transfer agreement referred to above, there is full transfer, in respect of the aircraft covered by the agreement, of oversight in respect of Annex 1 (personnel licensing), Annex 2 (rules of the air), and Annex 6 (operation of aircraft), but only a limited transfer in respect of Annex 8 (airworthiness): oversight is retained by the state of registration except for maintenance surveillance in respect of leased aircraft. Further, each party agrees[642] to the other only to authorize leasing contracts of aircraft which are in compliance with the terms of the agreement.

Even before Article 83*bis* took effect, on 20 June 1997, ICAO urged states of registration unable adequately to fulfil their responsibilities adequately in instances where aircraft are leased 'in particular without crew' by an operator of another state to delegate to the state of the operator, subject to acceptance by the latter, those functions of the state of registration that can more adequately be discharged by the latter, it being

637. Set out as Annex 12 hereto.
638. Abeyratne R.I.R., *Aviation Trends in the New Millenium*, Ashgate, 2001, 25.
639. *Supra*, 27.
640. http://cfapp.icao.int/dagmar/main.cfm?UserLang=_e on 9 Sep. 2021.
641. At Part IV (Transferred Responsibilities) thereof.
642. Under Part VI (Lease Authorisation) thereof.

understood that pending entry into force of Article 83*bis*, such delegation would only be a matter of practical convenience and would not affect the provisions of the Chicago Convention (1944).[643] Further, even after such entry into force, any such delegation will only have force against third states if it has been communicated to the ICAO Council and made public or communicated directly to such third states.[644]

Under the multilateral Article 83*bis* agreement drawn up in the Chicago Convention (1944), entitled *Agreement on the Practical Application of the Provisions of Article 83bis of the Convention on International Civil Aviation*, registered with ICAO on 22 April 1996 by the Russian Federation, and entered into among the Russian Federation, Armenia, Azerbaijan, Belarus, Georgia, Kazakhstan, Kyrgyzstan, Republic of Moldova, Tajikistan, Turkmenistan, Ukraine and Uzbekistan, the parties thereto did, in fact, agree to apply the provisions of Article 83*bis*, *inter se*, prior to its coming into force.

This is the only example of a multilateral Article 83*bis* agreement registered with ICAO – all the others showing on the ICAO database at the time of writing are bilateral in nature.[645]

In the absence of a delegation under Article 83*bis*, the state of registration may set certain requirements where aircraft on its registered are leased to operators in another State. For example, in Ireland, the aviation authority must be satisfied that, where aircraft registered in Ireland are to be leased to operators elsewhere, the AOC of the operator must extend to the leased aircraft, the operator's facilities and maintenance arrangements must be acceptable to it, and deregistration will be required in any instance where such requirements are not met, in order to avoid Ireland's being in breach of its obligations as the state of registration under Article 20 of the Chicago Convention (1944).[646] Of necessity, this will require an examination of each case individually whereas an Article 83*bis* delegation can be as broad as the terms of delegation set out therein.

[I] Irrevocable Deregistration and Export Request Authorization

Given the difficulties faced by lessors in enforcing deregistration powers of attorney, the Cape Town Convention (2001) and Aircraft Protocol introduced[647] a new form of Irrevocable Deregistration and Export Request Authorization (IDERA), the form of which is set out in the Annex to the Aircraft Protocol. The form set out in the Annex must be used and not altered. Under Article 13(3) of the Aircraft Protocol, the person

643. *Annex 6 to the Convention on International Civil Aviation: Operation of Aircraft*, ICAO, 8th Edition, 2001, at 3-1, and *Annex 8 to the Convention on International Civil Aviation: Airworthiness of Aircraft*, ICAO, 10th Edition, 2005, at II.1.1.
644. Article 83*bis*(b).
645. http://cfapp.icao.int/dagmar/main.cfm?UserLang=_e on 9 Sep. 2021.
646. Aeronautical Notice of the Irish Aviation Authority, Nr SP1A, Issue 2, 31 Mar. 2000 (Arrangements for Maintenance of Irish Registered Commercial Transport Aircraft Leased to Overseas Operators) pursuant to Art. 18 of the Irish Aviation Authority (Airworthiness of Aircraft Order) (S.I. No. 324 of 1996) and Part VIII of the Irish Aviation Authority (Operations) Order (S.I. 19 of 1999).
647. Article 13(2) of the Aircraft Protocol.

in whose favour the IDERA is granted is the only person who may procure the deregistration and export remedy set out in Article 9(1) of the Aircraft Protocol and may do so only in accordance with the terms of the IDERA 'and any applicable safety laws and regulations'.

Article 13(3) goes on to provide that the authorization may not be revoked without the consent of the party in whose favour it is made and Article 13(4) provides that the relevant registry authority 'shall expeditiously co-operate with and assist the authorized party in the exercise of the remedies ...'.

The provisions regarding the IDERA therefore systematically attempt to resolve each of the shortcomings of the deregistration power of attorney and seek to remove the discretion of the aviation authority.

So far, the only instance of which this author is aware involving an attempted use of an IDERA involves an aircraft registered in Ireland. Apparently, the Irish Civil Aviation Authority refused to deregister an aircraft on the Irish register but operated by a Mexican operator and subject to an Article 83*bis* transfer to the Mexican authority on the grounds that the party authorized by the IDERA had not first secured repossession of the aircraft and removed all Irish registration marks, on grounds relating to the reference to 'applicable aviation safety laws and regulations' in Article 13. This has not at the time of writing been fully confirmed[648] or finally resolved but, if true, would be remarkable, given that nothing in the Cape Town Convention (2001) or the Aircraft Protocol links enforcement of the IDERA to prior repossession of the aircraft.

It is at least consistent with the general rules relating to deregistration where the Irish Aviation Authority requires proof, *inter alia*, of removal of registration marks[649] but even here it should be pointed out that the regulations governing cancellation of registration do not provide for such requirements.[650]

It is unclear what is the Irish Aviation Authority's concern as to safety laws and regulations since, pursuant to the Article 83*bis* transfer, oversight of compliance with Articles 12 (Rules of the Air), 30 (Aircraft Radio Equipment), 31 (Certificates of Airworthiness) and 32(a) (License of Personnel) of the Chicago Convention (1944) are transferred from the state of registration and '[t]he State of registry shall be relieved of responsibility in respect of the functions and duties transferred'. There are no other safety obligations imposed on the state of registration by the Chicago Convention (1944) and no other grounds in the Cape Town Convention (2001) for not deregistering upon presentation of a valid IDERA.

If the above report is true, this author submits that the Irish aviation authority may be mistaken in law, at least to the extent that a full transfer of oversight was made. The only plausible explanation is that if the registration marks remain on the aircraft,

648. *See*, however, the proceedings of *The Cape Town Convention after Three Years* participatory seminar on advanced contract, registration and transaction practices held at Freshfields, London on 18 Mar. 2009, Session III: Legal Opinions, Closings and Opinions.

649. https://www.iaa.ie/commercial-aviation/aircraft-registration-2/how-to-deregister-(and-export)-an-aircraft-1 on 9 Sep. 2021.

650. Section 18(1) of the Irish Aviation Authority Nationality and Registration of Aircraft order 2005 (S.I. No. 634 of 2005).

and the Irish aviation authority did not transfer oversight of airworthiness, it could remain liable as the state of registration but that is a liability, not a safety, issue.

If this view is followed in future cases, it will greatly limit the value of the IDERA.

Both in the case in question and in previous cases in which this author has been involved, the operator had refused to divulge the whereabouts of the aircraft to the owner and was refusing to pay the owner for it. In such cases, repossession is not possible, and deregistration[651] is one of the few practical remedies open to the owner. It may not restore possession to the owner but at least it prevents the airline from operating the owner's aircraft for reward while failing to pay the owner for the use of its asset.

[J] Indemnity Claim

A lessor may, upon default by the lessee, in practice, be willing to take repossession of its aircraft and to remarket it – it may not be worth the cost in terms of money and time to pursue the lessee for unpaid rent. That said, a lessor will not wish to waive its right to make such a claim. Except for claims regarding the inadequate condition of the aircraft of redelivery, such money claims are largely beyond the scope of this work but there is one point worth noting here.

Leases typically give the lessor the right to obtain indemnification from the lessee not only for unpaid rent but for any other losses incurred by the lessor. The lessor, certainly under English law, has a duty to mitigate its loss but, having done so, if it leases the aircraft out at a lower rent than from the defaulting airline, will reserve the right to claim the difference under the defaulted lease and the replacement lease for what would have been the balance of the term of the defaulted lease.

Further, it may mitigate its loss by deciding to sell the aircraft, rather than leasing it (if it cannot do so on reasonable terms) or leaving it producing no income off the lease on the ground, in which case, the lessor will likely reserve the right in the lease to pursue the airline for indemnification of the diminution in value of selling the aircraft in the condition as when repossessed from the defaulting lease as compared with the sale of the aircraft with no such diminution of value or sale of the aircraft with the lease attached as if there had been no such diminution.

In this regard, parties should note the English High Court case of *Protea Leasing Limited v. Royal Air Cambodge and others,*[652] where Moore-Bick J held that even if the lessor acted in a commercially reasonable manner in response to a difficult situation facing it, and even if it had done a great deal of work to the aircraft and had attempted to sell or lease the repossessed aircraft, nevertheless, the lessor is obliged to give credit to the lessee for the value of the aircraft in repossession, not the price for which it was eventually sold (if lower):

651. By the owner itself *qua* owner in case of registration in the case of owner registration or by the owner pursuant to enforcement of a deregistration power of attorney, as discussed in section §3.15[G] *supra*, or IDERA, in the case of operator registration.
652. [2002] EWHC 2731 (Comm).

> If [the lessor] dealt with the aircraft in a manner which prevented it from realizing their full value, it cannot in any event pass the resulting loss on to [the lessee] by giving credit only for the price actually obtained.[653]

In *Credit Suisse AG v. Arabian Aircraft & Equipment Leasing Co Ec and others,*[654] the English Court of Appeal upheld an appeal by the defendants against a High Court ruling allowing the lessor to claim against the lessee for diminution in the value of the aircraft on the grounds that the lease provision providing for such right was stated to be an alternative remedy to its other contractual remedies allowing, *inter alia*, for claims based on a lower lease rental being obtained by the lessor after repossession and yet the claim had originally been brought based on those other remedies and the particulars of claim had not been amended by the lessor to allow for a claim based on this alternative remedy.

[K] Voluntary Restructuring[655]

The paragraphs above deal with the enforcement by the lessor of the contractual and legal remedies available to it in the event of the occurrence and continuation of an event of default under the lease. The COVID-19 pandemic crisis exposed the limitations of this approach, admittedly under extreme circumstances. The contractual and legal remedies available to a lessor presume that the lessor wishes to recover swift possession of the aircraft from the defaulting lessee airline so as to be able to put it into revenue production elsewhere with a minimum of delay and expense. However, for this to be a viable option for a lessor, there needs to be an alternative market into which to place the aircraft. During the worst of the COVID-19 pandemic crisis, such an alternative market can scarcely have been said to exist.

Even in more normal times, it is usually desirable, where possible, to pursue less drastic outcomes than the arrest and hostile repossession of an aircraft. Where an airline is unable to meet its contractual obligations under a lease, its lessor should consider what alternatives may be open to it short thereof.

For example, a rent and/or maintenance reserves holiday, with or without interest running, may be allowed for a particular period of time. A temporary or permanent rent and/or maintenance reserves reduction may be agreed upon. An early return of the aircraft on a voluntary basis under the lease may also be agreed upon.

In the absence of an alternative market into which to place the aircraft, the lessor may conclude that it is preferable, even if the airline cannot pay full rent, for the airline at least to maintain possession of the aircraft at its risk, storing, insuring and maintaining the aircraft at its own expense in accordance with the terms of the lease, and paying rent on an hourly or similar basis in the event that it does actually operate the aircraft for revenue. If that is not possible, a lessor may prefer to pursue a debt claim and seek an order for specific performance, if damages are determined not to be an

653. *Ibid.*, at 67 et seq.
654. [2013] EWCA Civ 1169.
655. *See also* section §3.14[D][3], *supra.*

adequate remedy, rather than to take repossession of an aircraft which it cannot place elsewhere, but the legal wisdom of such a path must be balanced against the financial ability of the airline to pay and the possible reputational risk to the lessor in the market. A lessor would be prudent at least to consider the wisdom of pursuing, in a given situation, a mutually acceptable restructuring or other resolution before resorting to unilateral legal action.

Similarly, for a lessee, this author has written elsewhere[656] as to why, in his view, airline claims for relief from a lessor in circumstances such as those during the COVID-19 pandemic crisis, whether pursuant to a force majeure, frustration or other claim are unlikely to succeed, and as to why the lessor's contractual and legal remedies remain intact.

In support of this view, in *Wilmington Trust SP Services (Dublin) Ltd & Ors v. Spicejet Ltd*,[657] the English High Court refused to hold that the grounding of Boeing 737 MAX aircraft for a period of only about 10% of the lease term did not give rise to compelling reasons to order a full trial allowing for a claim of frustration instead of proceeding to summary judgment for a debt claim. In the same year, in *Iris Helicopter Leasing Limited v. Elitaliana SRL and Point Holding SpA* [2010] EWHC 2516, the English High Court allowed summary judgment for a debt claim where a helicopter was seized by customs for non-payment of import tax on the grounds that the lease provided for assumption of risk on delivery of the helicopter to the lessee outside of Italy and clearly provided that the lessee was responsible to pay any such tax. It is interesting to note that Jacob J distinguished this case from one involving the COVID-19 pandemic crisis:

> It is not even like one of the cases which concerns the impact of the Covid pandemic on commercial operations, where commercial operations were no longer viable and may be prohibited by authorities for a period of time. In the present case, the demand for services is still there. All that has happened is that there is a seizure which means that the aircraft is unavailable for any services at all.[658]

Likewise, in *Salam Air SAOC v. Latam Airlines Group SA*,[659] the same court had, in the previous year, refused to grant an injunction based on the argument of frustration due to the COVID-19 pandemic to prevent a lessor from drawing on standby letters of credit.

[L] Conclusions

The ability to enforce remedies for breach of contract is a key to its being an enforceable contract: if a contract may be breached without the breach giving rise to remedies, or to remedies which cannot be enforced, it is not a contract which may be relied upon.

656. Hanley D.P., *COVID-19 and International Aircraft Financing Law*, Air & Space Law Volume 45, Special Issue, 2020, 155–172.
657. [2021] EWHC 1117 (Comm).
658. Paragraph 62.
659. [2020] EWHC 2414 (Comm).

Most often, the breach under an aircraft operating lease will be by the lessee. Depending on the breach, the lessor may wish to sue for unpaid rent or for other damages. It may wish to terminate the leasing of the aircraft – and thus terminate the contractual relationship between the parties – and recover possession of its aircraft.

The Cape Town Convention (2001) generally upholds the agreement of the parties as to agreed events of default and agreed remedies upon the occurrence of such events of default. Exercise of such remedies may be tempered in the case of bankruptcy of the lessee[660] or by, for example, provisions of private air law instruments such as the Rome Convention (1933) where this is in force.

Even if physical possession of the aircraft and its records is achieved, the aircraft must still be deregistered, if it is registered in the name of the lessee, and this author makes certain recommendations in Chapter 4 as to Article 83*bis* of the Chicago Convention (1944) and the IDERA under the Cape Town Convention (2001) whereby this can be more readily achieved.

Termination of the leasing of the aircraft for breach is one way by which the contractual relationship between the lessor and the lessee may be ended. Another way to terminate the relationship, not involving a breach, is for the leasing of the aircraft to continue, but for the lessor to assign its interest in the aircraft, together with the lease thereof, to another lessor, which assignment is examined next.

In light of the COVID-19 pandemic, the lessor may want to consider even more than usual a voluntary resolution with its lessee to a conflict, especially where there may not be an alternative market for the aircraft.

§3.16 ASSIGNMENT

Assignment by a lessor upon a sale or upon a financing of the aircraft by the lessor will here be examined in turn.[661]

If a lessor decides to sell to a third party the aircraft, subject to the lease to the lessee,[662] the buyer will want an assignment in its favour of the lessor's interest in the lease, in addition to acquiring title to the aircraft.

If a lessor raises finance on a secured basis, with security for repayment of the loan consisting of the lessor's ownership of the aircraft and rights under the lease of that aircraft, the lessor's lender will require, in addition to a mortgage or other security over the aircraft, an assignment of the lessor's rights, but not its obligations, under the lease.

Where the lessor's interest in the lease itself is registrable as an 'international interest' under the Cape Town Convention (2001),[663] an assignment thereof, being an assignment related to an 'international interest'[664] is likewise registrable thereunder[665]

660. Discussed in section §3.14 *supra.*
661. *See* section 14 of the Supplement *infra.*
662. The lessor cannot sell the aircraft free of the lease due to the quiet enjoyment right of the lessee under the lease discussed in section §3.10[A][1] *supra.*
663. Articles 2(2) and 16(1)(a).
664. Article 1(b) of the Cape Town Convention.

and thereby gains priority over any other interest subsequently registered and over an unregistered interest.[666]

Assignments are either absolute, in the case of a sale, or by way of security, in the case of a financing, each of which will next be examined.

[A] Absolute Assignment

An absolute assignment normally takes place upon the sale of the aircraft by the lessor, subject to the lease, to a third party. Such an assignment is, in practice, rare, since the lessor cannot assign its obligations without the consent of the lessee, only its rights.[667]

Where both the lessor's rights and obligations are assigned, this is typically pursuant to a novation, if the lease is governed by English law, or an assignment and assumption, if the lease is governed by New York law, whereby the assignor transfers both its rights and obligations under the lease and the assignee assumes both the assignor's rights and obligations thereunder.[668]

A lessee will often require that any such assignee be reasonably experienced in aircraft leasing, that it have a minimum net worth or have its obligations guaranteed by another party having such minimum net worth and, sometimes, that it not be a competitor of the lessee.[669] As the lessee must be a party to a novation or an assignment and assumption, it is in a good position to ensure that its legal position is adequately safeguarded through legal representation.

[B] Assignment by Way of Security

By way of contrast to an absolute assignment, under an assignment by way of security, a lessor assigns only its rights, not its obligations, to a third party by way of security by the performance by it of some obligation owed by it to such third party.

Under English law,[670] in order for such an assignment to be a statutory assignment,[671] notice of such assignment must be served on the lessee and, once such notice has been given, it is a legal assignment such that the assignee can directly enforce the

665. Article 16(1)(b).
666. Article 29(1).
667. Also, *see* section §3.09 *supra*.
668. This process can be greatly simplified by using the Global Aircraft Trading Scheme developed by the Aviation Working Group. The basic concept is to place the lessor's interest into an owner trust, with the owner trustee holding on behalf of the beneficiary, the economic owner. When that owner sells its interest in the aircraft subject to and with the benefit of the lease, the owner trustee holds the lease henceforth for the benefit of the buyer, but the lessor, as owner trustee, does not change, hence obviating the need for a lease novation, whilst respecting the lessee's rights in respect of such transfer under the lease. For further details, *see* www.awg.aero/project/gats/ and https://e-gats.aero on 9 Sep. 2021.
669. Thereby addressing the need for caution on the part of the lessee addressed in Bunker D.H., *International Aircraft Financing, Volume 2: Specific Documents*, 2nd Edition, IATA, 2015, at 168–169.
670. First introduced into England by section 25(6) of the Judicature Act 1873 as initially replaced by section 136 of the Law of Real Property Act 1925.
671. *See* section §3.09 *supra*.

assignor's rights under the lease as against the lessee without joining the assignor to the action.

On the other hand, if notice is not given, the assignment can, under English law, only amount to an equitable assignment, such that the assignee can still enforce its rights under the assignment but can only do so by joining the assignor to any action against the lessee.[672]

Although it is the giving of notice which makes an assignment a legal assignment under English law, in practice, an acknowledgement of such notice is typically requested of the lessee. The reasons are not only evidentiary, in relation to the receipt of the notice, but because sometimes additional obligations are therein undertaken.[673] In the English High Court, Moore-Bick J held in *Protea Leasing Limited v. Royal Air Cambodge Company Limited*[674] that, correctly drafted, assignment language could be construed such that:

> [i]n the absence of any notice of default ... the right to recover rent and other payments due under the lease remained vested in [the assignor].[675]

As consideration for providing such notice, the lessee typically requests a letter of quiet enjoyment from the assignee to the effect that, so long as the lessee performs its obligations under the lease, the assignee will not interfere in the lessee's quiet enjoyment or possession of the aircraft.

Even with such a letter of quiet enjoyment, lessees are sometimes justifiably nervous that such assignments by way of security may negatively affect them – they do take a limited credit risk of the lessor in respect of reimbursement of maintenance reserves and security deposit.

Such lessees may take some comfort from the English Privy Council case of *The Nippon Credit Bank Limited v. Air New Zealand Limited,*[676] an appeal against a decision of the Court of Appeal in New Zealand. This involved an aircraft lease where 'upon redelivery' the lessor was to reimburse the lessee for certain modification work undertaken by the lessee airline to extend the range of the aircraft. The lessor had sold the aircraft and assigned the lease to another company, which in turn granted a mortgage over the aircraft and granted an assignment over its rights under the lease in favour of its creditor bank. At the time of redelivery, the new owner defaulted under its loan and the bank sought to enforce the assignment of the lessor's rights under the lease.

Air New Zealand argued that it had a workman's lien for the modification work and that its obligation to return the aircraft was conditional upon its being paid the reimbursement amount. The bank argued that it had a proprietary interest in the aircraft, that there was no lien, and that the obligation to return was unconditional: the

672. *See* section §3.09 *supra*.
673. Typically, including to the effect that the lessee is still to discharge its obligations to the assignor until it receives a notice from the assignee that the assignor has defaulted under its secured obligations, whereupon henceforth the lessee is to discharge its obligations to the assignee.
674. [2002] EWHC 2731 (Comm).
675. *Ibid.*, at 213.
676. [1997] UKPC 60.

airline should, in its view, return the aircraft and claim against the liquidator of its debtor for the reimbursement amount.

On the drafting of the lease, the court held, by a majority, that no lien arose outside of the lease, such that this case involved the proper construction of the lease terms. Accordingly, Air New Zealand was entitled to be paid the reimbursement amount at the time it redelivered the aircraft. It is submitted that the dissenting judgment of Hoffmann L and Saville L make for better law: they pointed out that nothing in the lease made the redelivery of the aircraft conditional upon receipt of the reimbursement payment and that there was no basis (whether in law or by way of trade practice) for implying any form of lien.

[C] Conclusions

Assignments by the lessor may be absolute assignments or assignments by way of security in favour of the lessor's financiers. Lessees should be careful to ensure that their obligations are not increased – or their credit exposure to their lessor increased – as a result thereof and should insist on having their legal expenses in that regard covered by the lessor.

Assignments are generally dealt with under the governing law thereof, which in practice tend to follow the governing law of the underlying instrument the subject thereof, in this case, the lease.

The Cape Town Convention (2001) provides protection for assignees where the assignment is registered on the international registry, as discussed above.

§3.17 GOVERNING LAW

Most commonly, aircraft operating leases are expressed to be governed by English or New York law.[677] However, some may be governed by other laws, for instance, Québec, Ontario or California law are occasionally encountered in practice also. The preference for England and New York is due to the existence of 'well-developed commercial legal precedents'[678] in those jurisdictions.[679]

In transactions where the Cape Town Convention (2001) applies, and if the relevant contracting State has made a declaration to that effect,[680] then, the parties to a lease agreement:

> may agree on the law which is to govern their contractual rights and obligations, wholly or in part.[681]

677. Bunker D.H., *International Aircraft Financing, Volume 2: Specific Documents*, 2nd Edition, IATA, 2015, at 173–174.
678. *Ibid.*
679. *See* section 15 of the Supplement *infra*.
680. Under Art. 71(1).
681. Article 9(2).

Unless they further agree to the contrary, such law shall be construed as a reference to:

> the domestic rules of law of the designated State or, where that State comprises several territorial units, to the domestic law of the designated territorial unit.

It thus appears, although it is not made explicit, that, where the Cape Town Convention (2001) applies, if it is intended that the rules of private international law of a jurisdiction should be disapplied to a lease contract so that only the substantive laws of that jurisdiction are applied,[682] this need not be made explicit in the governing law clause of the lease.[683] Nevertheless, there is no harm in doing so in order to put the matter beyond doubt.

Within the EU, Regulation (EC) 593/2008[684] and Regulation (EC) 864/2007[685] apply.

Regulation (EC) 593/2008 (Rome I) applies to 'contractual obligations in civil and commercial matters'[686] but excludes various agreements including 'agreements on the choice of court'.[687] Article 3(1) recognizes the freedom of choice of the contract parties to choose the governing law of the contract.

This freedom is limited only by Article 3(3), whereby if all other relevant elements are in a country other than that the laws of which have been chosen, the chosen law will not prejudice provisions of the law of the other country which cannot be derogated from. Article 3(4) provides likewise for where all other relevant elements are within one or more EU Member States. Further, Article 9(9) provides for overriding mandatory provisions 'regarded as crucial by a country for safeguarding its public interests'.

Regulation (EC) 864/2007 (Rome II) applies to 'non-contractual obligations in civil and commercial matters',[688] such as torts/delicts,[689] including product liability.[690] Article 14(1)(b) allows parties pursuing a commercial activity freedom of choice to choose the governing law, subject to Article 14(2) ad 14(3), which reflect Article 3(3) and 3(4) of Rome I respectively.

---

682. Thus, avoiding the risk that the substantive laws of a different jurisdiction might instead be applied due to the application of the rules of private international law of the desired jurisdiction. *See* the discussion of the doctrine of *renvoi* in section §3.10[B][4][c] *supra*.
683. The governing law clause examined in Bunker D.H., *International Aircraft Financing, Volume 2: Specific Documents*, 2nd Edition, IATA, 2015, at 173, does not provide for an explicit exclusion of the rules of private international law.
684. Regulation (EC) 593/2008 of the European Council and of the Parliament of 17 Jun. 2008 on the law applicable to contractual obligations (Rome I).
685. Regulation (EC) 864/2007 of the European Parliament and of the Council of 11 Jul. 2007 on the law applicable to non-contractual obligations (Rome II).
686. Article 1.1.
687. Article 1.2(e).
688. Article 1(1).
689. Chapter II.
690. Article 5. McBain G., *Aircraft Finance: Registration, Security and Enforcement*, General Editor, Sweet & Maxwell, 2000.

Article 16 provides for overriding mandatory provisions of the law of the forum which apply irrespective of the law otherwise applicable to the non-contractual obligation.

Where Rome I and Rome II may apply, therefore, it would be better, if the parties wish for greater certainty, for the governing law clause to make clear that it extends not only to contractual but to non-contractual obligations also.

Even outside the EU, in cases not covered by Rome I or Rome II, public policy exceptions typically apply to the choice of governing law. To take just two examples, in Canada, a choice of law will generally be upheld unless 'contrary to public policy, or if ... made for the purpose of avoiding a mandatory provision ...'[691] and, in China, a choice of law will be upheld 'unless the choice would violate the fundamental principles of Chinese law or the public interest ...'.[692]

The jurisdictional questionnaire[693] and legal opinion[694] should make clear that the courts of the jurisdiction covered thereby will enforce a choice of governing law as set out in the lease and will not seek to impose the laws of another jurisdiction and should make clear any exceptions or qualifications in that regard.

§3.18 DISPUTE RESOLUTION

[A] Contractual Agreement

Goode comments that:

> the typical international contract is likely to involve points of contact with several states, and this gives considerable opportunity to the plaintiff and his advisers to engage in forum shopping and to select the state whose law and procedural rules are most favorable to the claim.[695]

It is for this reason that an aircraft operating lease will typically set out a dispute resolution clause, providing for exclusive[696] or non-exclusive jurisdiction to be granted to stated courts, or providing instead for settlement of disputes by arbitration.[697] The choices made, and any other requirements, such as the advisability of having an agent for service of process within the jurisdiction, should be guided at least in part by the result of the jurisdictional questionnaire.[698]

691. McBain G., *Aircraft Finance: Registration, Security and Enforcement*, General Editor, Sweet & Maxwell, 2000, Canada-34.
692. *Ibid.*, at China-22.
693. *See* Chapter 2 section §2.04 *supra*.
694. *See* Chapter 2 section §2.05 *supra*.
695. Goode CBE QC Sir Roy, *Commercial Law*, 2nd Edition, Penguin Books, 1995.
696. *See Airbus S.A.S. v. Generali Italia S.P.A. & Ors* [2019] EWCA Civ 805 which upheld the provision of a manufacturer's airframe warranties agreement providing for exclusive jurisdiction of the English courts to settle disputes thereunder.
697. *See* section 15 of the Supplement *infra*.
698. *See* Chapter 2 section §2.04 *supra*.

For transactions where the Cape Town Convention (2001) applies, Article 54(1) provides that, save as provided in Articles 55 and 56, the courts of a contracting State chosen by the parties shall have jurisdiction in respect of any claim brought thereunder:

> whether or not the chosen forum has a connection with the parties or the transaction. Such jurisdiction shall be exclusive unless otherwise agreed between the parties.

Article 55(1) allows such chosen forum as well as the courts of the contracting State in which the aircraft is registered and those of the contracting State in which such aircraft is situated jurisdiction to grant orders for:

(a) the preservation of the aircraft object and its value;
(b) possession, control or custody of the aircraft object;
(c) immobilization of the aircraft object;[699]

as well as to:

(a) procure the deregistration of the aircraft; and
(b) procure the export and physical transfer of the aircraft object from the territory in which it is situated.[700]

Thus, the agreed forum has jurisdiction to order the deregistration of an aircraft even if the aircraft is registered elsewhere and to order the export and physical transfer of the aircraft even if it is located elsewhere.

In the unlikely event that no dispute resolution mechanism is chosen in the lease, it is not automatic that the courts of the jurisdiction whose law is chosen as the governing law will have jurisdiction: in other words, simply agreeing, for example, that a lease be governed by English law is not the same thing as submitting to the jurisdiction of the English courts, where the English courts would not otherwise have jurisdiction. Thus held the English Court of Appeal in *Novus Aviation Limited v. Onur Air Tasimacilik AS.*[701] That case involved a wet lease, which, as discussed in Chapter 1 section §1.02[A] *supra*, is often negotiated under great time pressure and thus may not be properly negotiated.

In *Novus*, the lease provided that it was to be 'governed and construed with English law' but there was no jurisdiction clause. Wilson LJ held *per curiam*, on appeal, here that the burden of relying on the governing law provision to determine the correct jurisdiction is a heavy one and that too much importance should not be placed on the governing law clause. On the other hand, given, *inter alia*, language differences, the English courts were clearly in a better position to construe the lease than Turkish ones. Neither party was a native English speaker – English was chosen since neither party

699. Article 20(1).
700. Article 15(1), as referenced in Art. 20(7), itself as referenced in Art. 55.
701. [2009] EWCA Civ 122.

spoke the other's language. The only connection to England was the governing law clause. Provided that the judge did not treat the governing law clause as equivalent to a submission to jurisdiction clause, which he did not do here, he was entitled, however, in this finely balanced case, to conclude that England was an appropriate forum.

The lessor should also consider, based on the jurisdictional questionnaire, discussed in Chapter 2 section §2.04 *supra*, whether it is better to provide for submission to binding arbitration, particularly where the lessee's jurisdiction is a party to the New York Convention on the Recognition and Enforcement of Foreign Arbitral Awards:[702] recognition of foreign courts' judgments is not governed by any treaty.

Thus, if the jurisdictional questionnaire indicates a reluctance on the part of courts in the lessee's jurisdiction to enforce foreign courts' judgments, but such jurisdiction is a party to this convention, submission to arbitration coming within the scope of such convention may be preferable as a dispute resolution provision in the lease.

[B] Third Parties and Forum Non Conveniens

We have examined *supra* in section §3.11[B] liability of the lessor for damage to third parties. In this context, we consider the situation where a third-party claim[703] is brought against the lessor in a particular forum on the basis that the lessor and the lessee have agreed that that particular forum is to have jurisdiction to hear disputes arising out of or in connection with the aircraft lease agreement.

In *Gambra v. International Lease Finance Corp.*,[704] the plaintiffs in an air crash litigation case involving Flash Airlines of Egypt failed to defeat a forum non conveniens motion where they named the aircraft lessor as the defendant and relied on the choice of jurisdiction clause in the lease between that lessor, based in California, and the lessee airline. The only connection to California was the fact that the lessor was based there and the relevant submission to the jurisdiction clause in the lease. The lease provided that:

> Lessor and Lessee hereby … irrevocably waive any claim that any such suit, action or proceeding brought in any such court has been brought in an inconvenient forum.[705]

Plaintiffs argued that they were entitled to rely on this clause as third-party beneficiaries of the lease. On the terms of the lease, the court rejected this argument, holding that:

> the forum selection clause does not govern the claims of plaintiffs against the defendants in these cases. The lease governs the obligations of ILFC and Flash with

702. Signed at New York on 10 Jun. 1958.
703. That is, a claim brought by a party other than a party to the contract.
704. 377 F. Supp. 2d 810 (C. D. Cal. 2005).
705. *Ibid.*, at 821.

> respect to the subject aircraft, not the liability of either of them to those passengers and crew aboard the subject aircraft.[706]

Condon & Forsyth[707] note that this case provides 'valuable guidance' on how to draft aircraft leases so as to minimize the risk that their terms may be used to defeat forum non conveniens motions.[708]

In *Esheva v. Siberian Airlines,*[709] a similar case brought in the courts of the SDNY where the only US connection was the fact that the lessor, Airbus Leasing II, Inc., of the aircraft to the airline involved in the crash, was based in the United States and the lease between it and the airline had a jurisdiction clause submitting to such jurisdiction, the court had no hesitation in rejecting the plaintiffs' attempt to defeat a forum non conveniens motion.

The court held that there was a 'compelling argument' that the lessor had been added to the proceedings 'solely to provide some American nexus to the litigation' and that the contractual relationship between the lessor and lessee 'had no ... relevance to the motion'.[710]

[C] Conclusions

Parties should be guided by the jurisdictional questionnaire[711] in deciding whether to provide for litigation or arbitration to resolve disputes and in choosing the forum for dispute resolution. Where the Cape Town Convention (2001) applies, such choice of the parties will be upheld, but it is not binding on third parties.

As part of their decision-making process, parties should also consider more broadly the track record of the courts of such jurisdiction,[712] and their level of expertise and experience, in determining complex cross-border litigation involving high-value assets, such as commercial aircraft.

706. *Ibid.*, at 822–823.
707. Condon & Forsyth Newsletter, *Attempts by Plaintiffs to Defeat Forum Non Conveniens Motions by Alleging Aircraft Owner or Lessor Liability*, Newsletter, Winter 2008, at 2.
708. In an update in its Spring 2008 newsletter, Condon and Forsyth, *49 U.S.C. Section 44112(B): Limits on the Liability of Aircraft Owners and Lessor*, Condon & Forsyth Newsletter, Spring 2008, at 7, the authors note that although the California court dismissed the case to France on grounds of forum non conveniens, the French court itself dismissed the case on the basis that none of the defendants was domiciled in France and the incident did not occur in France.
709. 499 F. Supp. 2d 493 (S.D.N.Y. 2007).
710. *Ibid.*, at 499, No. 4.
711. *See* Chapter 2 section §2.04 *supra*.
712. In that regard, it may be noted that the European Court of Human Rights held in *Euroatlantic Airways – Transportes Aéreos, S.A. v. Portugal* [2015] ECHR 1077, that a period of some five years and six months for the Portuguese courts (including appeals) to rule on a wet-lease dispute infringed the rights of the applicant under Art. 6(1) of the ECHR which provides that 'In the determination of his civil rights and obligations ..., everyone is entitled to a ... hearing within a reasonable time by a ... tribunal ... .'

§3.19 MISCELLANEOUS

This so-called boilerplate language is often glossed over by lawyers for both sides but should be carefully examined since a judge will take care to read them should a dispute end in litigation.[713]

[A] Time of the Essence

Leases will typically contain a provision that time is of the essence to performance of the parties' obligations thereunder. Thus, the lessee should accept delivery by the final date provided therefor, should pay rent and reserves when due, and should redeliver the aircraft in a timely manner in the required contractual condition, failing which, the lessor should be free to exercise its remedies as set out in the lease and any other remedies available to it at law.

In *Celestial Aviation Trading 71 Limited v. Paramount Airways Private Ltd,*[714] Hamblen J of the English High Court[715] was asked to rule on the plaintiff's submission[716] that equity does not intervene to relieve a party from the termination of a contract for a failure by that party to perform an obligation by a fixed date where the parties have made time of the essence expressly or by necessary implication, where the plaintiff cited an authority, albeit in connection with real estate, *Union Eagle Ltd. v. Golden Achievement Ltd.,*[717] where Hoffman LJ, for the Privy Council, reaffirmed the principle that:

> in cases of rescission of an ordinary contract of sale for land for failure to comply with an essential condition as to time, equity will not intervene.

While Hamblen J accepted in *Celestial* the *Union* judgment insofar as land was concerned, he did not accept in this case, involving an aircraft, that the:

> mere inclusion of a time of the essence clause provision necessarily excludes the relief jurisdiction.[718]

Unfortunately, he did not give his reasons for making such a distinction. It should be concluded that such clauses should continue to be included since, even if their inclusion is not treated as conclusive, their omission may tempt a court to grant relief to a dilatory lessee even more readily.

In a New York case, *Austrian Airlines Oesterreichische Luftverkehrs AG v. UT Finance Corporation,*[719] Kaplan J of the US District Court, SDNY, refused to hold that a willingness to discuss extending a deadline for delivery of an aircraft meant that the

713. *See* section 16 of the Supplement *infra.*
714. [2010] EWHC 185 (Comm).
715. Queen's Bench Division, Commercial Court.
716. *Ibid.*, at paras 76–80.
717. [1997] AC 514, at 523.
718. *Ibid.*, at 79.
719. 04 Civ 3854 (LAK) (2008).

deadline could be ignored and held that the plaintiff had failed to show that the defendant had waived its right to timely delivery. The legal analysis here then was not of whether or not to uphold the clause but whether or not the defendant had waived its right to rely on it.

[B] No Waiver

Leases should contain a clause to the effect that no delay by lessors in enforcing their rights thereunder constitute a waiver of such rights, and any such waiver must be in writing signed by the lessor.

Although such inclusion is standard practice, in itself, it is not enough to protect the lessor, at least under English law. In *Tele2 International Card Company SA v. Post Office Ltd.*,[720] the English Court of Appeal, holding that such clauses were of no particular benefit to the party seeking to rely on them except perhaps to emphasize that a right will only be waived if so communicated to the other party, found in favour of a party in breach where the other party knew of the breach but did nothing for a year, reasoning that its normal continued performance without complaint constituted such a communication. As a result, some English law firms recommend that, as soon as a party becomes aware of a breach, it write to the other side at once, informing them thereof and reserving expressly its rights.[721]

Indeed, simply reserving rights may not of itself be sufficient. In *Tigris International N.V. v. China Southern Airways Limited*,[722] the English Court of Appeals held *per curiam* that:

> the mere reservation of rights under contract will not preclude a waiver or estoppel where the remaining circumstances justify a finding to that effect.[723]

[C] Entire Agreement

Leases will typically contain a provision that the terms thereof set out the entire agreement of the parties with respect to the subject matter thereof. The idea is to exclude extrinsic evidence of agreements or representations not set out in the lease itself which may contradict or impede enforcement of the lease upon the terms set out therein.

Typically, such clauses will also go on to provide that amendments to the lease may only be made in writing signed by both lessor and lessee.

In *Lithoprint (Scotland) Ltd. v. Summit Leasing Ltd. & Others*,[724] Milligan J of the Scottish Court of Session held that a side letter entered into prior to execution of a lease

720. [2009] All ER (D) 144 (Jan).
721. *See*, e.g., Thomson K., *Waving Goodbye to Your Rights*, Banking Update, Linklaters, 14 Jun. 2009.
722. [2014] EWCA Civ 1649.
723. Per Lewison LJ, at 195.
724. [1998] ScotCS 36 (23 Oct. 1998).

and not referred to in the lease could, even if it did not come within such requirements of a lease, nevertheless be upheld as a collateral agreement in its own right, particularly where it did not contradict the terms of the lease. He also noted[725] that in commercial contracts, the argument for admitting collateral agreement is stronger than in other cases and that it is easier to import collateral agreements where standard forms are used.[726]

[D] Waiver of Sovereign Immunity

In addition to providing for representations and warranties in the lease that the airline is not entitled to claim sovereign immunity, it may be advisable to include a separate clause to the effect that, if the airline is or ever becomes entitled to claim such immunity, it waives such rights in respect of any claim brought against it by the lessor under or in connection with the lease or the aircraft.

Under public international law, a sovereign State originally enjoyed absolute immunity 'for all activities whether governmental or commercial'.[727] It was thus held by the English Court of Appeal in *The Cristina* that:[728]

> the courts of a country will not implead a foreign sovereign ... whether the proceedings involve process against his person or seek to recover from him specific property or damages.

A development to public international law in this regard is the European Convention on State Immunity (1972)[729] which provides for certain exceptions in that a contracting State cannot claim immunity from the jurisdiction of the courts of another contracting State, *inter alia,* in the case of a counterclaim where it institutes the proceedings,[730] or has expressly consented to jurisdiction,[731] if it has on the territory of the state of the forum an establishment through which it engages, in the same manner as a private person, in an industrial, commercial or financial activity, and the proceedings relate to that activity of the office,[732] and, of particular interest in the case of an aircraft lease:

> A Contracting State cannot claim immunity from the jurisdiction of a court of another Contracting State if the proceedings relate to:
>
> aa. its rights or interests in, or its use or possession of, immovable property; or

725. *Ibid.*, at 8.
726. Such is not generally the case with operating leases of commercial aircraft, such leases typically being fully negotiated.
727. Clark T. (ed.), *Leasing Finance*, Euromoney, 1985, at 80.
728. [1938] A.C. 485.
729. Signed at Basle on 16 May 1972.
730. Article 1.
731. Article 2.
732. Article 7.

ba. its obligations arising out of its rights or interests in, or use or possession of, immovable property and the property is situated in the territory of the State of the forum.[733]

At the national level, for example, in the United States, under the Foreign Sovereign Immunities Act of 1976, a foreign State, defined in section 1603 to include its political subdivisions, agencies and instrumentalities, shall:

> [s]ubject to existing international agreements to which the United States is a party at the time of enactment of this Act ... be immune from the Jurisdiction of the courts of the United States and of the States except as provided in sections 1605 to 1607 of this chapter.[734]

The main exceptions of concern in the context of this work are as follows:

> A foreign state shall not be immune from the Jurisdiction of courts of the United States or of the States in any case
> (1) in which the foreign state has waived its immunity either explicitly or by implication, notwithstanding any withdrawal of the waiver which the foreign state may purport to effect except in accordance with the terms of the waiver;
> (2) in which the action is based upon a commercial activity carried on in the United States by the foreign state; or upon an act performed in the United States in connection with a commercial activity of the foreign state elsewhere; or upon an act outside the territory of the United States in connection with a commercial activity of the foreign state elsewhere and that act causes a direct effect in the United States.[735]

A lessor would argue that even in the case where a lessee falls within the definition of a 'foreign state' for the purposes of this statute, entering into an aircraft lease for the purposes of leasing a commercial aircraft constitutes a 'commercial act' for the purposes of section 1605(a)(2) of this statute also. Nevertheless, obtaining an express waiver provides an additional strong argument under section 1605(a)(1).

In *Kuwait Airways v. Republic of Iraq,*[736] the Canadian Supreme Court unanimously allowed a claim by Kuwait Airways against the Republic of Iraq to proceed to enforce a judgment of the English courts against the latter, despite the assertion of sovereign immunity by the latter, where the acts complained of consisted of the seizure of aircraft of the former by Iraqi Airways Company during the 1990 Gulf War. The Canadian Supreme Court held that Iraq had funded, controlled and supervised the litigation on behalf of Iraqi Airways and that this involvement by Iraq fell within the 'commercial activity' exception to the international law doctrine of State immunity. The Court held this on the basis that, even though the original appropriation of the aircraft by Iraqi Airways Company was a sovereign act, the subsequent retention and use of the aircraft by Iraqi Airways Company constituted commercial acts and thus fell within an exception to the claim for sovereign immunity.

733. Article 9.
734. Section 1604.
735. Section 1605(a).
736. 2010 SCC 40.

[E] Conclusions

It is all too easy to overlook these 'boilerplate' provisions, but it is important to read them and to consider them in the context of each transaction as they have been the subject of litigation and of international agreements.

Indeed, each of the time of the essence, no waiver, entire agreement, and waiver of sovereign immunity provisions has been the subject of litigation, as has been demonstrated above.

§3.20 EXECUTION

Formalities as to execution, filings that must be made, and other formalities which have to be observed, are all matters that should not be forgotten at this final stage. Reference should be had to the jurisdictional questionnaire and to the legal opinion to ensure that formalities for lease execution are known and have been met.

There is one interesting English High court case involving the lease of a light aircraft. In that case, *Oxford Aviation Services Limited v. Godolphin Management Company Limited,*[737] Cooke J held that, on the facts, an agreement for hire or bailment existed on the basis of a draft unexecuted delivery for hire, where the parties had had a history of dealing with one another.

The jurisdictional questionnaire[738] obtained at the outset of a leasing transaction should, at the outset, and the legal opinion[739] at the time of signing of the lease should clarify any issues regarding requirements for execution, witnesses, notarization and the like together with confirmation that no stamp duty will be imposed as a result of the place of execution of the lease or otherwise.

Disputes may exist as to the proper interpretation of any contract but no lawyer will want to tell his or her client that there is no contract to enforce at all for want simply of due execution.

737. [2004] EWHC 232 (QB).
738. *See* Chapter 2 section §2.04 *supra*.
739. *See* Chapter 2 section §2.05 *supra*.

CHAPTER 4
Conclusion

§4.01 OVERALL CONCLUSIONS

This part will attempt to synthesize the practical and theoretical lessons learned from the foregoing to show that the basic concept of the aircraft operating lease is intact but that, given the number of courts which may, rightly or wrongly, apply any number of legal provisions which override the provisions of the lease, one is dealing here more with art than with science. Certain recommendations will also be made.[1]

It is essential, in this author's view, that practitioners understand aircraft operating leases, and the issues associated therewith, not only in the context of practice but also in the context of relevant legislation and case law and, above all, in the overall context of public and private international air law.

Further, relevant provisions of public and private international law have been shown to be available to practitioners, and possibly of aid to their client's legal position, if only they are aware of them. In particular, the provisions of the Cape Town Convention (2001) on events of default and remedies come to mind.

Certain problems for practitioners in the field of the aircraft operating lease arising from certain provisions of, or *lacunae* in, public and private international air law have been identified examined and certain proposals are made in section §4.02 *infra* in respect thereof by way of remedy.

Before then, it is worthwhile here to review the principal parts of the aircraft operating lease in light of the research and analysis set out in Chapter 3 *supra*. Dividing the lease in the same manner as in Chapter 2 section §2.06 *supra*, the following broad conclusions can be drawn.

1. *See* section §4.02 *infra*.

[A] Pre-delivery

This covers the parties, recitals, definitions, representations and warranties, and conditions precedent.[2]

These generally reveal any do not any tension between the practice and law of aircraft leasing and are generally not the focus of the public or private air law and other instruments but are still influenced by and reflective of them. Perhaps this is not surprising, as, at this point, the aircraft has not yet been tendered for delivery to the airline, and thus legal disputes are less likely. Further, the rights of third parties are not yet involved.

For example, the parties to the transaction will be determined by reference, *inter alia*, to applicable double tax treaties, and options regarding the State of registration of the aircraft. Likewise, the conditions precedent listed, showing which licences and approvals the lessee must have in place, will reflect the relevant legal provisions of the jurisdiction of the state of the lessee and, where different, the state of registration of the aircraft. These in turn are driven, at least in part, by the provisions of the public and private air law instruments to which such states are party.

[B] Post-delivery

This covers term and delivery, payments, taxes, manufacturer's warranties, covenants, indemnities, and insurances.[3]

Not surprisingly, this area sees more disputes, involving as it does, the condition and operation of the aircraft at and after delivery, and significant payment obligations.

Challenges to the provisions of leases dealing with conclusivity of the acceptance certificate seem inconsistent with challenges requiring precise conformity to delivery condition: it seems inconsistent that a court would, on the one hand, entitle a lessee to precise conformity to contracted delivery condition, while on the other hand allowing the lessee to disregard contractual agreements as to conclusivity of acceptance of delivery. Nevertheless, case law examined in Chapter 3 section §3.07 *supra* has shown how national legislation may provide for tests of reasonableness which override contractually agreed conclusivity. These challenges reveal a tension between law and practice, but not a particular relation to public and private international air law.

This is not so of the covenants, touching, as they do, on such critical issues as maintenance, liens, registration, and replacement of parts and engines, all of which are, to a greater or lesser extent, the subject of provisions of the public and private air law instruments.

Maintenance, being closely related to safety, is of concern to public international air law as well as national law. As discussed in Chapter 3 section §3.10[B] *supra*, the lease does not, and cannot, reduce the minimal requirements of such laws and will, if anything, set higher contractually required minima. Thus, the lease provisions reflect,

2. *See* Chapter 3 sections §3.01–§3.05 *supra*.
3. *See* Chapter 3 sections §3.06–§3.12 *supra*.

but are not in tension with, such laws, something which should give comfort to those concerned that the increase in aircraft leasing may be of concern from a safety perspective. Indeed, this should be considered a public benefit of leasing.

Liens are a great concern to lessor, since the lessor may stand to lose title to its aircraft for debts incurred by its lessee, and these risks are increasing most noticeably within the EU as a result of the Eurocontrol and emissions liens. Proposals to give the lessor the tools to manage such increased risks are made in section §4.02 *infra*.

The role of the Chicago Convention (1944) and the variety of national laws passed as to registration are reflected in the discussion in Chapter 3 section §3.10[B] *supra*, as is the more active role of the Geneva Convention (1948) and the Cape Town Convention (2001) on the issue of title to replacement parts and engines, discussed also in Chapter 3 section §3.10[B] *supra*.

The insurance provisions, as the maintenance provisions, reflect the legally required minimum coverage, which they do not and cannot reduce, but if anything, the lease provisions increase such required coverage beyond the minima, which gives increased protection to third parties who suffer damage. This is a benefit of leasing in that the airline may not otherwise, and is not otherwise legally required, to have such increased insurance coverage. The indemnity provisions, which are closely linked to the insurance provisions, are very intimately bound up with the provisions of the Warsaw Convention (1929), the Montreal Convention (1999) and other private international air law instruments. These instruments, concerned as they are with protection of third parties, are not concerned with the contractual allocation of risk as between the private parties to an aircraft leasing contract. Nevertheless, they should be coherent and fair as regards the liability of the lessor, and certain observations and recommendations in this regard are made in section §4.02 *infra*.

[C] Post-lease Term

This covers redelivery, events of default, remedies, assignment, governing law, dispute resolution, miscellaneous, and execution.[4]

Disputes as to redelivery tend to be based on factual issues and national law rather than international law.[5] The Cape Town Convention (2001) deals with protection of contractually agreed remedies[6] in case of default.[7] The Cape Town Convention (2001) likewise deals with enforcement of duly registered assignments[8] and of dispute resolution provisions.[9]

The other public and private air law instruments are not, otherwise, as much in evidence in this part, which, given that the issues dealt with here do not affect third parties, is not surprising.

4. *See* Chapter 3 sections §3.13–§3.20 *supra*.
5. *See* Chapter 3 section §3.13 *supra*.
6. *See* Chapter 3 section §3.15 *supra*.
7. *See* Chapter 3 section §3.14 *supra*.
8. *See* Chapter 3 section §3.16 *supra*.
9. *See* Chapter 3 section §3.18 *supra*.

It is a fact that this work focuses more on areas of potential breach by lessees than by lessors. Although he freely admits to working for an aircraft leasing company, this emphasis reflects, not a bias towards lessor, but the simple fact that most undertakings in a lease are on the part of the lessee. The lessor's obligations are essentially limited to certain reimbursement obligations (maintenance reserves and security deposit) and its covenant of quiet enjoyment to the lessee. The lessee's obligations are many and varied, as is natural given that the lessee has operational possession and control of the aircraft during the lease term. Simply put, there is a lot more scope for breach on the part of the lessee under the operating lease than on the part of the lessor.

§4.02 RECOMMENDATIONS

This author believes that operating leasing of aircraft should be encouraged for reasons of public benefit for the reasons set forth in the following paragraphs.

The public international air law safety objectives of the Chicago Convention (1944) would be enhanced by encouraging airlines to meet maintenance and redelivery requirements of operating leases, which typically go beyond the SARPs made under the Chicago Convention (1944) as well as going beyond FAA or EASA or other local aviation authority requirements. The fact that the lessor's motives in having such high maintenance standards are primarily to preserve its equity in, and value of, its aircraft in no way cuts across the public benefit that flows therefrom.

Further, the public protection of the private international air law instruments would be enhanced by encouraging airlines to take out liability insurance for greater amounts, as typically required by leases, thus providing greater coverage than required under national law or private international air law[10] – and ultimately therefore providing greater protection for passengers and third parties.

Both the legally required minimum liability insurance requirements and the legally required minimum maintenance requirements are precisely that – *minima*. States have, therefore, an interest in encouraging airlines to observe their contractual obligations to meet a higher standard than the legally required *minima*. This is not only because enforcing higher contractually required minimum requirements on insurance and maintenance benefits the lessor in terms of increasing insurance coverage of any potential liability on its part and because it is likely to maximize the residual value of the aircraft, although those benefits to the lessor are real. Rather, states should enforce such contractual requirements precisely because they provide increased protection to the public by way: (i) of increasing safety, by making an accident less likely to occur in the first place, in the case of contractually required maintenance obligations in excess of the legally required minimum; and (ii) if an accident should nevertheless occur, by providing that more insurance coverage will be available for compensation to the public than is required by law.

10. Bearing in mind that no minimum insurance requirements are set out in the Montreal Convention.

In order to encourage, therefore, aircraft operating leasing, this author sets out below certain recommendations in respect of both public and private international air law as well as in connection with the practice of aircraft operating leasing.

[A] Article 83*bis* of the Chicago Convention (1944)

It is submitted that encouraging greater use of transfers of safety oversight under Article 83*bis* of the Chicago Convention (1944) is desirable from a lessor's point of view since the lessor's ability to register the aircraft in its name in a suitable jurisdiction will enable it to deregister[11] as required in the event of exercise by it of its remedies under the lease will encourage compliance by airlines with their lease obligations.

Even if this of itself does not ensure return of possession of the aircraft to the lessor, the ability on the part of the lessor to ensure deregistration means that, at least, it can prevent the lessee from operating the aircraft while not paying for it under the lease or otherwise breaching its lease obligations and thus greater use of Article 83*bis* would be of benefit to lessors.

States may not particularly care about a private debt due by an airline to a lessor, for example, for unpaid rent, or about a reduced residual value, as a result of failure to maintain as required by the lease, seeing these as private disputes between private parties. But states should care about promoting principles of public and private international law and in particular about safety.

One potential way in which greater use of Article 83*bis* could be achieved rather than by cumbersome bilateral negotiations[12] would be for an agreement to be developed whereby states that are party thereto may agree freely thereunder to allow Article 83*bis* delegations *inter se*, at least for aircraft dry leased from non-operators, thus addressing safety and regulatory concerns as to wet leases and as to dry leases from other airlines.

By analogy with the International Air Services Transit Agreement (1944) and the International Air Transit Agreement (1944), whereby the Chicago Convention (1944) foresees certain arrangements subject to the consent of the states concerned, and such consent is, by the parties thereto, granted on a global basis, this author proposes that states which are satisfied with each other's safety standards could consider voluntarily entering into a multilateral agreement Article 83*bis* agreement whereby they would agree in advance that any aircraft[13] on the register of any one Member State could be the subject of a delegation of all or any of the responsibilities of such state of registration to the Member State of the operator.

---

11. And consequently deny then lessee the ability wrongly to prevent a deregistration.
12. *See* Annex 12 for the model agreement set out at *Guidance on the Implementation of article 83 bis* of the Convention on International Civil Aviation, ICAO, 2002, at 9-14.
13. The types could be restricted or not, as the states may choose.

The model ICAO agreement set out at Annex 12 *infra* could be adapted for such multilateral use. The main consideration would be for notification[14] of the delegation rather than the multilateral agreement itself to deal with the responsibilities transferred, the aircraft covered, and the lease terms thereof. Thus, a new multilateral agreement would not need to be entered into each time.

That said, no such multilateral agreement has been entered into as of the date hereof. The multilateral agreement entered into among states of the Russian Federation[15] simply provided for application of the provisions of Article 83*bis* among the parties to such multilateral agreement prior to its coming into effect under the Chicago Convention (1944).

With owned aircraft, an airline need only comply with the requirements of its national aviation authority. With a leased aircraft the subject of an Article 83*bis* transfer, in addition thereto, the requirements of such aviation authority of the operator will also have to be approved by the state of registration, and the lessor will further require under the lease compliance with FAA and/or EASA requirements as well as additional contractual requirements.

The fact that Article 83*bis* has not been widely availed of so far is no reason not to consider the benefits of its being more widely used.

[B] Cape Town Convention (2001) and IDERA

It is submitted that the public goals which can be achieved by greater reliance on Article 83*bis* transfers may equally,[16] and perhaps more realistically, be achieved by states becoming party to the Cape Town Convention (2001) and by giving effect to the provisions therein relating to IDERA.[17] However, in order for this to be effective, aviation authorities, and national courts need correctly to interpret the Cape Town Convention (2001) with respect thereto.

It is to be hoped that in due course it will be clear from judicial precedent or from other authoritative guidance that safety is not in any way at issue in allowing deregistration of an aircraft pursuant to an IDERA without providing proof first of the removal of the nationality and registration marks of the aviation authority to whom the deregistration request has been made.

Restrictions on enforceability of IDERAs set out therein should be properly limited to safety concerns, *proprement dit*. Requirements that the aircraft first be

14. Under Art. 83*bis*(b) of the Chicago Convention (1944), notification of the delegation to bind another State party must be made to the ICAO Council and be made public or be directly notified to such other State party itself.
15. *See* Chapter 3 section §3.15[H] *supra*.
16. This author does not, however, share the unqualified preference of Fitzgerald for the Cape Town Convention over Art. 83*bis* of the Chicago Convention in this context. With the latter, the option is not towards flags of convenience but is always, if it occurs at all, to transfer safety oversight away from the state of registration (which may not be where the aircraft physically is) to the state of the operator (where the aircraft usually is). *See* Fitzgerald P.P., *In Defense of the Nationality of Aircraft*, Annals of Air and Space Law, Volume XXXVI, 2011.
17. In order to allow reliance on the IDERA, States must, of course, first become party to the Cape Town Convention.

repossessed and nationality marks removed should not be imported as additional requirements contrary to the clear wording of the Cape Town Convention (2001). To do so would be to limit the value of the IDERA, to restrict the lessor from the legitimate exercise of its rights under the Cape Town Convention (2001), and to push the lessor back on other solutions, such as greater reliance on Article 83*bis*.

The IDERA is not the only reason why wider adoption of the Cape Town Convention (2001) is desirable. Although it may not be a *panacea* as some of its promoters may sometimes suggest, it does have real benefits in terms of providing for contractual certainty in allowing the parties to agree, for example, what constitutes a default, and in terms of allowing the parties certain contractual freedom to agree on remedies in the case of default.[18] Of course, where it applies, it is incumbent on the parties to an aircraft operating lease to take advantage of the Cape Town Convention (2001) by carefully reading it and by adapting the lease into which they enter to take account of its provisions, such as by expressly assenting in the leases to certain remedies provided for in the Cape Town Convention (2001).

[C] Eurocontrol Liens, Emissions Liens, and Similar Liens

Although such liens seem unjust to this author, liens in respect of Eurocontrol liabilities and emissions breaches[19] seem to be a fact of life for lessors which will not go away. These liens are not simple rights of detention but extend beyond those to rights of sale of the lessor's aircraft for the unmet obligations of the airline.

A particularly worrying development is that discussed above in the case of Germany, where Germany seeks to impose not only a lien on the aircraft but also a personal liability on the lessor as owner of the aircraft, for non-payment of travel tax by non-German airlines which have failed to appoint a German tax representative. This extension of liens in itself is objectionable in principle but imposing personal liability in addition represents a particularly unwelcome step by Germany.

Its justification for such a step is particularly difficult to understand in light of Germany's acceptance of a distinction between those having an operational role, such as airlines, and those not having an operational role, such as lessors, in the context of the Unlawful Interference Compensation Convention (2009).[20] Surely, it cannot be argued that lessors have an operational role in the context of collection and payment by airlines of an air travel tax based on the numbers of passengers carried by the airline as an operator.

This author surmises that the real reason for the distinction is not a jurisprudential but a practical, opportunistic one. Governments may be willing to limit recourse for

18. Contracting States can obtain further benefits from entering into the Cape Town Convention (2001) not only in relation to the IDERA but the other provisions of the Cape Town Convention (2001) discussed throughout this work. Further, by making qualifying declaration thereunder, as discussed in Chapter 3 section §3.14[D] *supra*, they can obtain for their airlines a reduction to the minimum premium rates of finance provided for in the Sector Understanding on Export Credits for Civil Aircraft – Final Text, set out at Annex 11 *infra*.
19. *See* Chapter 3 sections §3.10[B][2][b] and §3.10[B][2][c] *supra*.
20. *See* Chapter 3 section §3.11 *supra*.

damage to third parties against lessors for the principled reason that they do not have operational control but also for the practical reason that the interests of third parties are protected in practice by requiring the airline to have a minimum of third-party liability insurance in place to protect such third parties by ensuring payment of compensation in the event of damage, thus rendering at least somewhat academic the question of recourse to other parties such as a lessor.[21]

On the other hand, governments may be keen to extend recourse for themselves for unpaid Eurocontrol charges and air travel taxes as well as breaches of emission limits against lessors,[22] not because they have any greater operational control against airlines in this context than they do in the context of damage to third parties – they clearly do not – but precisely because there are no insurances in place to cover a simple credit default by an airline.

If the airline goes bankrupt or otherwise fails to pay, the government cannot claim on an insurance policy. Instead, it effects a similar result by simply turning the lessor into a sort of insurer of the airline's payment obligation. If the airline fails to pay Eurocontrol charges, the lessor's aircraft may be seized. If the airline breaches emissions limits, the lessor's aircraft may be seized. If the airline fails to pay a German air travel tax, the lessor's aircraft may be seized and/or the lessor may be sued as if it were the debtor. It is such a convenient system for governments that it is hard to see how, once entrenched, it would not be extended to cover many other areas of an airline's obligations. In other words, why stop there?

If such is really the case, with private lessors effectively and involuntarily being conscripted as enforcement agents of the European authorities, and effective guarantors of their lessee's performance of an increasing number of obligations owed to such authorities, at least those authorities must give the lessors the tools with which to act as such enforcement agents and guarantors effectively.

If performance by lessees of obligations relating to Eurocontrol and emissions and now also air travel tax is to be enforced by lessors it must, therefore, be by way of the lessors having effective and timely remedies available to them if their lessees fail to comply. Such remedies will be set out in the lease: it is important for European states, therefore, in particular, since they are notably the ones increasingly looking to lessors, to allow lessors to enforce expeditiously their remedies under leases in the case of default by lessees.

One way in which this can be achieved is, as advocated above, by greater reliance on Article 83*bis* transfers and IDERAs – but it need not be limited to these. Even without such greater reliance, states should ensure that their courts quickly enforce lease obligations, and contractual remedies for breach thereof, insofar as possible in accordance with their terms. This is the simplest tool for helping lessors, with whom they have burdened the consequences for non-compliance, to ensure that their lessees pay their Eurocontrol charges and respect their emissions limits.

21. *See* Chapter 3 section §3.12[A] *supra*.
22. *See* Chapter 3 sections §3.10[B][2][b], §3.10[B][2][c] and §3.10[B][2][d] *supra*.

The alternative, if nothing is done, such that lessors are frustrated or unduly frustrated in enforcing their contractual remedial rights in case of breaches by lessees, will ultimately lead lessors to prefer jurisdictions which do not impose such onerous obligations on lessors and to avoid, or to charge a higher rent or otherwise impose protections to try to manage such increased risks in those jurisdictions which do impose such onerous obligations.

[D] Standardization of Documentation

One practical way in which courts can be encouraged quickly to enforce lease obligations is to ensure that they take account of relevant law including public and private international law. To encourage market efficiency, reduce transaction costs[23] and documentation turnaround time, it is submitted that increased standardization of the provision of aircraft operating leases is desirable, with the parties being free, of course, to adapt the terms.

The parties should have confidence that such standard forms will be enforced in accordance with their terms by national courts and, as case law builds up, greater certainty can be achieved with a greater number of judicial precedents interpreting similarly or identically worded lease provisions.

Bunker[24] rightly expresses the difficult nature of such an endeavour:[25]

> Any attempt to standardize contract forms and internationalize contractual relationships is very difficult and confusing since the laws of the different interests are bound to be different, particularly between a civil law and a common law jurisdiction.[26]

The difficulty is mitigated somewhat in the case of the aircraft operating lease by the fact that the governing law of the cross-border aircraft operating lease is almost always a common law one such as England or New York, as noted in Chapter 1 section §1.03 *supra*.

Further, there is precedent for such standardization, notably the International Swap and Derivatives Association Master Swap Agreement of 1992, the London insurance brokers standard aircraft insurance clauses AVN 67B and AVN 67C, not to mention shipping charters which have long used standard form documentation, IATA

23. According to Clark and Wool, reduction of transaction costs by overcoming national laws inconsistent with aircraft leasing and financing transactions is also expressly one of the motivating factors behind the development of the Cape Town Convention (2001). *See* Clark L. and Wool J., *International Aviation Finance Laws Revisited: A Report on the Development of the Proposed Unidroit Convention on International Interests in Mobile Equipment Applied to Aircraft*, Annals of Air and Space Law, Volume XXIII, 1998, at 272.
24. Bunker D.H., *The Law of Aerospace Finance in Canada, Institute and Centre of Air and Space Law*, McGill University, 1988.
25. A caution echoed by Simon Hall in Clark T. (ed.), *Leasing Finance*, Euromoney, 1985, at 73.
26. *Ibid.*, at 61.

standard form ground handling agreements and, since 2002, the Master Short-Term Emergency Engine Lease Agreement.[27]

IATA, representing airlines as operators of aircraft,[28] and the AWG, representing manufacturers, lessor, and financiers as direct or indirect suppliers of aircraft,[29] have been working jointly[30] not only on the Master Short-Term Emergency Lease Agreement but also on standard forms of aircraft purchase and sale agreements, airframe and engine warranty assignments and engine RORA.

It is to be hoped that ultimately their cooperation will extend to the much more document-intensive aircraft operating lease and that the result of such cooperation will carefully take account of applicable principles of public and private international air law as discussed in this work with a view to ensuring insofar as possible that courts will enforce them in accordance with their terms.

[E] Lessor's Civil Liability for Acts of the Airline

It is submitted that the tort theory of negligent entrustment as applied to aircraft lessors is unfair as, if this theory is followed, it applies a higher standard to lessors than the Chicago Convention (1944) applies to states which are party thereto. This is because the theory of negligent entrustment, if followed to its logical conclusion, requires lessors to look behind certificates and licences granted by aviation authorities whereas, under Article 33 of the Chicago Convention (1944), contracting states themselves cannot do so. Under Article 33, states must, rather, recognize certificates of airworthiness and personnel licences provided that the requirements under which they were issued are equal to or above minimum standards established under the Chicago Convention (1944).

The theory of negligent entrustment also goes against the General Claims Convention (2009) and against this author's reading of the Montreal Convention (1999) in terms of the exclusive remedy for claimants thereunder being against the airline. Even if this author's reading of the Montreal Convention (1999) is wrong, it is submitted that the Montreal Convention (1999) should then be conformed to the trend set out in the General Claims Convention (2009).

There is no justification for difference in treatment of claims brought against a lessor by passengers and those brought by parties on the ground – if anything, there is a greater argument in the other direction since a passenger will or should know who his carrier is whereas a party on the ground may not know who is operating an aircraft overhead.

27. Wilson F.S., *Mastering Engine Leasing: The Master Short-Term Engine Lease Agreement Will Serve as Models for Future Standardization in the Aviation Industry*, Airfinance Journal, Sep. 2007.
28. *See* http://www.iata.org on 9 Sep. 2021.
29. *See* http://www.awg.aero on 9 Sep. 2021.
30. In the interests of full disclosure, this author here discloses that he is a member of the joint working group on behalf of the Aviation Working Group.

There may be a justification for difference in treatment of claims by passengers against an airline, where a contract exists between the parties, on the one hand, and claims for injury or damage brought by non-passengers against an airline, where no contract exists between the parties, on the other hand. Such a distinction, however, cannot be made regarding claims brought against a lessor of aircraft. Claims for injury or damage against a lessor, whether brought by passengers or by non-passengers alike, are brought in the absence of a contract between the plaintiff and the lessor.

The General Claims Convention (2009) and the Unlawful Interference Compensation Convention (2009), which are not in force, both recognize the difference between parties having operational control of the aircraft, where there may be a liability for damage caused, and parties not having operational control, where there may be no such liability. Given that operational control is a matter of fact which does not vary depending on under which instrument of private international air law a claim is brought, this author can see no reason why claims brought under the Montreal Convention (1999) should be distinguished in this regard.

This issue is not something that can be addressed by contractual drafting in the leases, as those only apply *inter partes*. Although indemnity provisions in the lease backed up by insurance coverage in large measure keep the problem from becoming one often encountered in practice, nevertheless, that is no reason for complacency – any one claim if not covered by insurances for any reason could have catastrophic consequences for a lessor given the large amounts that may be awarded against it.

If this author's view is correct, and the Montreal Convention (1999) prevents any claims which could be brought thereunder against the operator from being brought against the lessor, then this author has identified a prima facie inconsistency in the EU with Council Directive 85/374/EEC, which expressly allow claims to be brought against manufacturers and lessors in terms not stated to be subject to the Montreal Convention (1999).

If, on the other hand, he is wrong, such that such claims may be brought against lessors, then, as stated above, it is hard to see why a claimant should be able to sue a lessor thereunder where the Montreal Convention (1999) applies but not thereunder where the General Claims Convention and the Unlawful Interference Compensation Convention (2009) apply.

His view is that, however politically unrealistic it may be to think that it will necessarily happen, the Montreal Convention (1999) and Council Directive 85/374/EEC should at an opportune time amended so as to follow the system set out in the General Claims Convention and the Unlawful Interference Compensation Convention (2009). Broadly, his proposal is that, for passengers and non-passengers alike, the only recourse in such a situation should be to the airline or other party with operational control of the aircraft. This would be without recourse to the right of the airline or any such other party to claim, in turn, from parties not having operational control of the aircraft. Even if his proposal does not meet favour, at least there should be a consistency of approach in this area.

Nevertheless, even if lessors are found to be liable in US courts for claims brought in respect of the operation of aircraft by airlines, as a practical matter, they will find ways to manage the risk, primarily by way of insurance, but also by way of leasing via non-US jurisdictions such as Ireland, using a head lease-sublease structure or even by way of placing ownership into a subsidiary incorporated outside the United States.

[F] Lessor's Criminal Liability for Acts of the Aircraft Commander and Crew (Tokyo Convention (1963))

Following the same line of logic as in section §4.02[E] *supra*, this author proposes that the Tokyo Convention (1963) be amended so as to make clear that, in order to be relieved of responsibility under Article 10 of the thereof, a lessor[31] should not have to show that the aircraft commander whose acts are the subject of proceedings acted on reasonable grounds under Article 6(1). That said, he recognizes that, as noted in Chapter 3 section §3.11[B][4][a] *supra*, a previous attempt to amend the Tokyo Convention (1963) failed but he proposes that, if and when the Tokyo Convention (1963) is amended anyway, this point be taken into consideration.

Regarding the failed proposal to amend Article 3 of the Tokyo Convention (1963) to provide that, in the case of an aircraft leased without crew to a lessee having its principal place of business in a state other than the state of registration of the aircraft, that other State should 'also be competent to exercise jurisdiction',[32] this author believes that such an amendment would be consistent with Article 83*bis* of the Chicago Convention (1944). Why should criminal jurisdiction depend on the nature of the airline's possession of the aircraft? If a passenger commits a crime aboard a flight operated on board an aircraft operated by Alitalia, owned by Alitalia, and registered in Italy, the Italian authorities have jurisdiction. Why should they not have jurisdiction simply because the same passenger commits the same crime on board the same aircraft operated by the same airline on the same route simply because Alitalia leases the aircraft instead of owns it, and the aircraft is registered in Ireland, pursuant to Article 83*bis* delegation? To make a distinction here is to allow a private commercial transaction to determine criminal jurisdiction.

[G] Hell or High Water

The 'hell or high water' clause, discussed in Chapter 3 section §3.07[A] *supra*, has been criticized[33] in the context of the operating lease. Absent any legal or policy consideration to the contrary, and he has not encountered any, this author believes that this is a matter of negotiation among the parties to the contract. If the parties agree to it, it should, in such instance, be enforced. However, there seems no reason why, at least in a market where airlines have the upper hand, concessions could not be obtained from

31. Or any other party not having operational control of the aircraft or being vicariously liable for the acts of the operating airline's employees.
32. Fitzgerald G.F., *The Lease, Charter and Interchange of Aircraft in International Relations: Amendments to the Chicago and Rome Conventions*, Annals of Air and Space Law, Volume II, 1977, 103–137, at 120.
33. *See* Chapter 3 section §3.07[A] *supra*.

the lessor, provided always that the lessor's financiers are still willing to provide the financing necessary to the lessor to fund the transaction.

[H] Conclusivity of Acceptance

As discussed in Chapter 3 section §3.06[B][3], the lease provides for acceptance of the aircraft by the airline, as evidenced by its execution of the certificate of acceptance to be conclusive that the aircraft is satisfactory in all respect to the lessee. Coupled with limits on inspection rights and exclusions of warranties by the lessor, the idea is to place the entire risk on the lessee.

To the extent that airlines dispute this after delivery, and especially to the extent that they are successful in defeating their own lease provisions, freely negotiated by them with the benefit of professional legal representation, the airlines should be at least aware of one unintended consequence of success in overturning such provisions. In arguing against the enforceability of the conclusivity language in the acceptance certificate provided for in the lease, the airline not only sets itself up for the possibility that the similar conclusivity language in the redelivery certificate given to it by the lessor upon completion of its corresponding redelivery inspection at the end of the lease may not be upheld but also to the possibility that the lessor will not be bound by limits on inspection on redelivery if the lessee is not bound by limits on inspection on delivery.

Success on this point might be welcome to an airline in a given case but such success would have implications for all airlines under all leases going forward, truly a case of being careful about what one wishes. It is a different matter as to whether a lease can be differently negotiated from the outset, and it may be that airlines may seek some protection or, at least, sharing of risk in future in the case of complete grounding of an aircraft type as was the case for a period with the Boeing 737 MAX.

[I] Jurisdictional Rankings

Arising originally out of a desire to monitor compliance by countries with their qualifying declarations under the Cape Town Convention (2001)[34] in the context for eligibility for cheaper export credit finance, the AWG has developed a Cape Town Convention Compliance Index,[35] which ranks, using various metrics, state parties thereto by their actual adherence to their treaty obligations. The various member of the Legal Advisory Panel to the AWG, and the practitioners and academics contributing to the work of the Cape Town Convention Academic Project,[36] set up by the AWG as a founding sponsor but run independently by the International Institute for the Unification of Private Law (UNIDROIT) and the Faculty of Law at Cambridge University, are to be thanked for their important contribution to transparency in this area. The

34. *See* section §3.14[D][2] *supra*.
35. https://ctc-compliance-index.awg.aero on 9 Sep. 2021.
36. https://ctcap.org on 9 Sep. 2021.

Academic Project in particular provides many freely available resources, not only of judicial cases but also of administrative cases, as well as hosting the Cape Town Convention Journal.

In addition to this focus on compliance with the Cape Town Convention (2001), there are other rankings of jurisdictions available in terms of their attractiveness to lessors and financiers in enforcing their rights. One worth mentioning in particular is the Pillsbury Worldwide Aircraft Repossession Index.[37] This distinguished law firm is also to be thanked for making this work freely available.

These various rankings are, of necessity, subjective but worthy of consideration in view of their sources and may contribute to the work of rating agencies and corporate risk officers by encouraging transparent adherence to the rule of law.

§4.03 CLOSING WORDS

In the foregoing pages, this author has endeavoured to provide not only the legal framework within which aircraft operating leases are considered judicially but also the commercial environment within which they are negotiated in the first place. That commercial environment is never static, and parties are largely free to negotiate as they will. Particularly in the aftermath of the unprecedented COVID-19 pandemic crisis, it may be that certain lease provisions, particularly as regards allocation of risk as between the parties, which previously were effectively considered immutable may change, whether out of consideration of the experience of lessors and airlines during the crisis, or the commercial necessity of securing the income stream from a lease or the operation of an aircraft in a changed environment. Only time will tell how the industry will evolve, but it has shown itself flexible and quick to rebound in the past, and it is to be hoped that it will continue to do so going forward.

Aircraft leasing is assuming an ever-increasing importance in international aviation to the point where it cannot be presumed that the operator of the aircraft is the owner. Recent public and private air law instruments show an emerging awareness of this importance but there remain areas of policy to be considered before aircraft leasing can be said to be systematically integrated into the systems of public and private international air law.

Public international air law is of most relevance to aircraft operating leasing in its desire to protect third parties, whether in the air or on the ground, from injury or damage by means of safety, which finds its connection with such leasing most clearly in the area of maintenance. There is no tension here between public good and private interest as it is in all the parties' interests to ensure high maintenance standards for aircraft: the former acting in order to avoid accidents, the latter acting in order to maximize the residual value of the aircraft at the end of the lease.

Private international air law is of most relevance to aircraft operating leasing in its desire to provide for recourse to adequate compensation for second and third parties for injury or damage if, God forbid, despite all safety efforts, an accident occurs. There

37. https://www.pillsburylaw.com/en/news-and-insights/wari.html on 9 Sep. 2021.

is an apparent tension here between some of the private air law instruments and the allocation of risk as between lessor and lessee in the aircraft operating lease. Nevertheless, this author asserts that the public benefit is always met by providing full recourse to the operator, requiring the operator to carry ample liability insurance. This is without limitation to the operator's right of recourse against the lessor, which should be governed by the terms of the lease. The tension is largely only apparent as the lessor requires in the lease that the lessee procure liability insurance in excess of the minimum coverage legally required. This benefits both the public good and private interest.

The area where the tension is real and not apparent is in the area of liens: the lessor cannot cover this by insurance, and yet is increasingly at risk in the case of lessee default. If it is to discourage such default, with the public good that Eurocontrol debts are paid and emissions limits met, it must be allowed to make use of the enforcement tools set out in the lease.

In closing, it is to be hoped that those involved with policy matters in this area will consider the issue of leased aircraft in an integrated rather than a piecemeal manner and that those practitioners in the area of aircraft operating leases will be aware of how the current public and private air law instruments may affect the interpretation and enforcement of the leases which they negotiate. This will be not only for the benefit of private interests but also for the public good.

Annexes

Annex 1

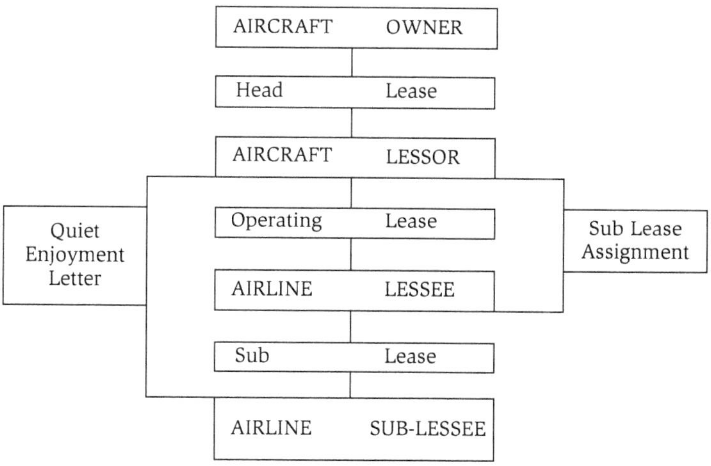
AIRCRAFT OWNER
Head Lease
AIRCRAFT LESSOR
Quiet Enjoyment Letter
Operating Lease
Sub Lease Assignment
AIRLINE LESSEE
Sub Lease
AIRLINE SUB-LESSEE

Annex 2

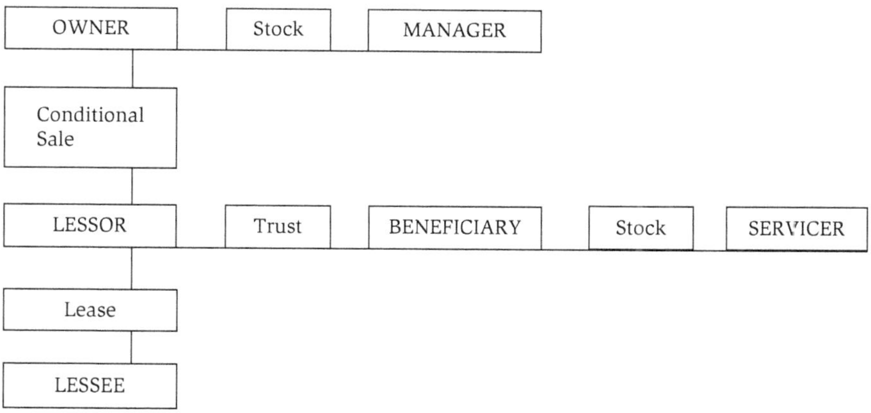
OWNER
Stock
MANAGER
Conditional Sale
LESSOR
Trust
BENEFICIARY
Stock
SERVICER
Lease
LESSEE

Annex 3

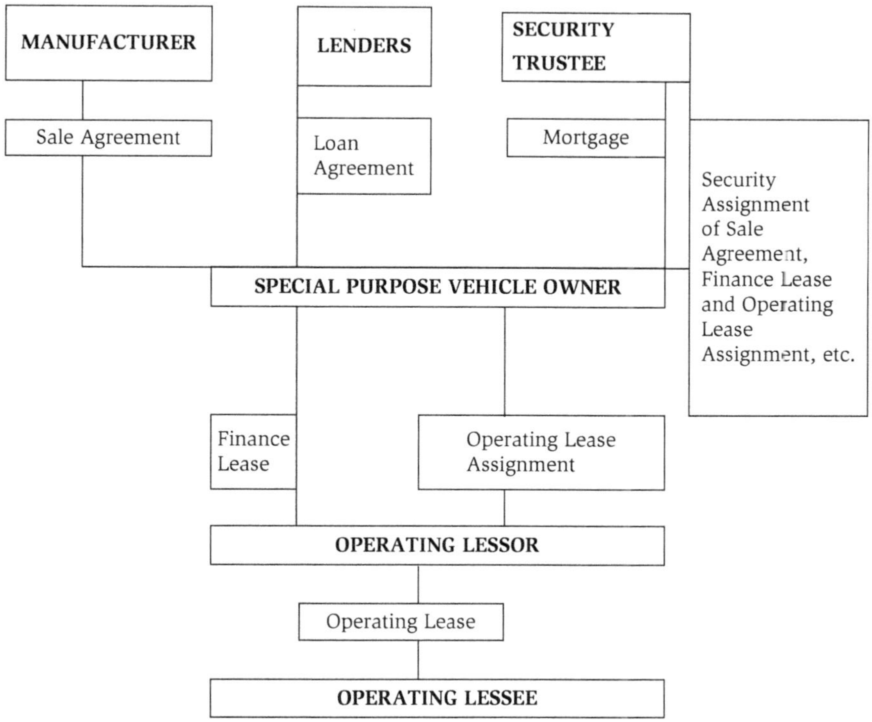

MANUFACTURER
LENDERS
SECURITY TRUSTEE
Sale Agreement
Loan Agreement
Mortgage
Security Assignment of Sale Agreement, Finance Lease and Operating Lease Assignment, etc.
SPECIAL PURPOSE VEHICLE OWNER
Finance Lease
Operating Lease Assignment
OPERATING LESSOR
Operating Lease
OPERATING LESSEE

Annex 4

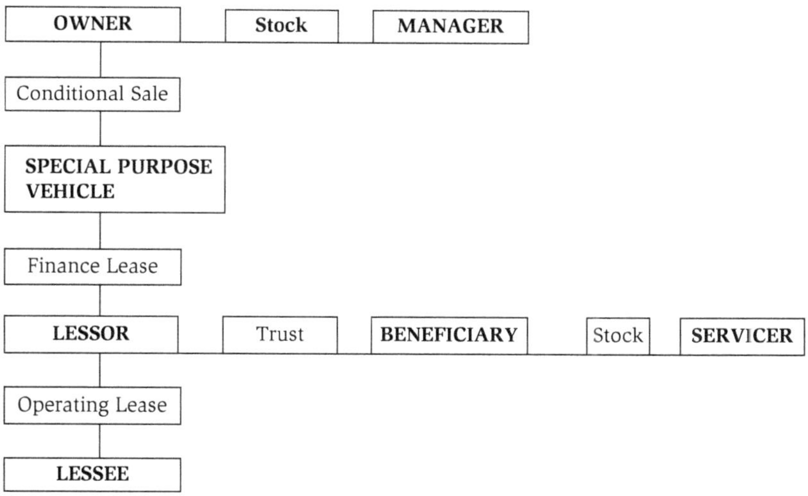
OWNER
Stock
MANAGER
Conditional Sale
SPECIAL PURPOSE VEHICLE
Finance Lease
LESSOR
Trust
BENEFICIARY
Stock
SERVICER
Operating Lease
LESSEE

Annex 5

TYPICAL JURISDICTIONAL QUESTIONNAIRE PROVISIONS*

(a) Description of property rights in aircraft.
(b) Description of results of previous attempts to repossess aircraft.
(c) Judicial attitudes towards foreign lessors and financiers.
(d) Summary of aircraft registration laws and regulations.
(e) Documents and procedures required for aircraft registration.
(f) Adherence to Chicago Convention.
(g) Possibility for registration of foreign-owned aircraft if leased to local operator.
(h) Registration in name of owner or operator.
(i) If operator registration, noting of interests of owner and lenders.
(j) Details of aviation authority.
(k) Adherence to all Annexes to Chicago Convention.
(l) Details of last aviation authority inspection of operator's operations.
(m) Inspection of foreign-registered aircraft.
(n) Summary of aircraft mortgage laws and regulations.
(o) Details of operation of any aircraft mortgage registry.
(p) Registration of any security assignments.
(q) Details of formalities of execution of mortgage and security assignments.

* *See* Chapter 2 section §2.04 *supra*. Although current transaction specific advice should be sought from legal counsel, general guides with respect to the subject matter of jurisdictional questionnaires by country may be found at, *inter alia*, Balfour J. (ed.), *Air Transport in 34 Jurisdictions Worldwide 2009*, Getting the Deal Through, 2009; Bushell S. (ed.), *Dispute Resolution in 50 Jurisdictions Worldwide 2008*, Getting the Deal Through, 2008; Crans B. and Nath R., Aircraft *Repossession and Enforcement: Practical Aspects*, Wolters Kluwer, 2009; McBain G., *Aircraft Finance: Registration, Security and Enforcement*, General Editor, Sweet & Maxwell, 2000; McBain G., *Aircraft Liens & Detention Rights*, General Editor, Sweet & Maxwell, 2007, and Shawcross and Beaumont, *Air Law*, 4th Edition, Butterworth, 1991.

(r) Adherence to Geneva Convention on International Recognition of Rights in Aircraft.
(s) Adherence to Cape Town Convention and related Aircraft Protocol.
(t) Details of claims ranking ahead of mortgage and security assignments.
(u) Effect of bankruptcy on mortgage and security assignments.
(v) Enforceability of pledge of stock in offshore special purpose vehicle owner.
(w) Enforceability of lease remedies, including repossession, in case of default or bankruptcy.
(x) Requirements to sell aircraft locally in case of enforcement of mortgage.
(y) Procedures for, and obstacle to, deregistration of aircraft in case of default.
(z) Enforceability of operator deregistration irrevocable power of attorney.
(aa) Possibility of undertaking from aviation authority not to deregister without owner consent.
(bb) Possibility of undertaking from government not to expropriate and to co-operate with repossession.
(cc) Taxes or filing fees for aircraft registration or filing of mortgage or other agreements.
(dd) Taxes to repossess, deregister, export aircraft or exercise remedies under mortgage, security assignments or lease.
(ee) Withholding or income taxes on payments under lease.
(ff) Stamp duty or other tax on execution, enforcement or bringing into jurisdiction of any documents.
(gg) Will the owner or lender be required to file tax returns or have liability to tax simply due to their involvement in the lease?
(hh) Is airline subject to government control?
(ii) Can airlines assert sovereign immunity?
(jj) Enforceability of submission to foreign jurisdiction.
(kk) Will foreign judgment be enforced without review of merits?
(ll) Adherence to New York Convention on the Recognition and Enforcement of Foreign Arbitral Awards.
(mm) Will the choice of governing law be upheld?
(nn) Procedures for appointing an agent for service of process.
(oo) Is the owner or are lenders subject to suit locally?
(pp) Necessity of permit to import or export aircraft under lease.
(qq) Exchange control or other consents.
(rr) Any other necessary permits, consents, registrations or filings.
(ss) Requirement for local insurance.
(tt) Restrictions on reinsurance and enforceability of "cut-through" clause.
(uu) Strict liability of owner or financiers for damage by operator.
(vv) Liens for air navigation and airport charges.
(ww) Any provisions required to be in or not in transaction documents.
(xx) Any other relevant information.

Annex 6

TYPICAL LESSEE LEGAL OPINION PROVISIONS*

(a) Corporate status of lessee.
(b) Corporate authority of lessee.
(c) Legal validity and enforceability of lessee's obligations.
(d) Ranking of obligations.
(e) Lessee's governmental approvals.
(f) Necessary filings and registrations.
(g) Withholding taxes.
(h) Limitation on interest rates.
(i) Documentary taxes.
(j) Lessor's rights on lease termination.
(k) No violation of laws.
(l) No deemed residence by lessor.
(m) Validity of choice of law.
(n) Validity of submission to jurisdiction.
(o) No immunity.
(p) Enforcement of foreign judgment.
(q) No owner liability for lessee operation.
(r) Protection from expropriation.
(s) Exchange control.
(t) Judgment in US dollars.
(u) Insolvency events.
(v) Cut-through clause in insurances.

* *See* Chapter 2 section §2.05 and Chapter 3 section §3.05[A][5] *supra* and also Bunker D.H., *International Aircraft Financing, Volume 2: Specific Documents*, 2nd Edition IATA, 2015, at 185–186 and 342.

Annex 7

TYPICAL REPRESENTATIONS AND WARRANTIES OF LESSEE*

(a) Corporate status of lessee.
(b) Power and Authority to enter into the lease and related documents.
(c) Valid execution and delivery of lease and related documents.
(d) Legal validity and enforceability of lessee's obligations.
(e) Non-conflict of lessee's lease obligations with its other legal, contractual or other obligations.
(f) All necessary authorizations, consents and registrations being in place for lessee to discharge its obligations.
(g) No Immunity with respect to lessee's lease obligations.
(h) Most Financial Statements are accurate.
(i) No obligation to operate the aircraft to countries subject to United Nations Security Council sanctions.
(j) Lease obligations ranking *pari passu* with lessee's other unsecured and unsubordinated obligations.
(k) Choice of law and submission by the Lessee to jurisdiction set out in the lease are being valid and binding.
(l) No Default (as defined in the lease) has occurred and is continuing.
(m) Listing of any necessary filings and registrations to perfect interest of lessor and financing.
(n) No litigation or arbitration which could have a material adverse effect upon lessee.
(o) All necessary tax returns and payments having been made.

* *See* Chapter 3 section §3.04 *supra*, section 2 of the Supplement *infra*, and also Bunker D.H., *International Aircraft Financing, Volume 2: Specific Documents*, 2nd Edition, IATA, 2015, at 56–62 and Clark T. (ed.), *Leasing Finance*, Euromoney, 1985, at 62–64.

(p) No material adverse change in the financial condition of lessee has occurred since the date of its most recent financial statements to date.
(q) No default in the payment of any sums due by lessee to any air traffic control or airport authority.

Annex 8

TYPICAL CONDITIONS PRECEDENT TO BE SATISFIED BY LESSEE*

(a) Copy of constitutional documents of lessee to be delivered to lessor.[1]
(b) Copy of board resolution approving transaction to be delivered to lessor together with the power of attorney and certified specimen signature of those signing lease and acceptance certificate on behalf of lessee.[2]
(c) Lease and related documents to have been duly executed by lessee and delivered to lessor.
(d) Legal opinions to have been delivered to lessor.[3]
(e) Copies of necessary approvals, licences, consents and registrations to be delivered to lessor.[4]
(f) Proof that all insurances required under lease are in place and broker's letter of undertaking delivered to lessor.[5]
(g) Eurocontol letter, if required under lease, and letter from aviation authority undertaking not to deregister the aircraft except by direction of lessor, to have been delivered to lessor.[6]
(h) Deregistration power of attorney and, if applicable, IDERA to have been delivered to lessor.[7]

* *See* section 3 of the Supplement *infra* and also Bunker D.H., *International Aircraft Financing, Volume 2: Specific Documents*, 2nd Edition. IATA, 2015, at 62–66 and Clark T. (ed.), *Leasing Finance*, Euromoney, 1985, at 53–54.
1. *See* Chapter 3 section §3.05[A][2] *supra*.
2. *See* Chapter 3 section §3.05[A][3] *supra*.
3. *See* Chapter 3 section §3.05[A][5] *supra*.
4. *See* Chapter 3 section §3.05[A][4] *supra*.
5. *See* Chapter 3 section §3.05[B][1] *supra*.
6. *See* Chapter 3 section §3.05[B][7] *supra*.
7. *See* Chapter 3 section §3.15[I] *supra*.

(i) Acceptance of appointment by lessee's agent for service of process to have been delivered to lessor.[8]

(j) All payments required to be made under the lease prior to delivery having been made.[9]

(k) No default or event of default under the lease having occurred which default or event of default is still continuing.[10]

(l) All representation and warranties made by lessee under the lease being correct by reference to facts and circumstances existing as of the proposed delivery date.[11]

8. *See* Chapter 3 section §3.18[A] *supra.*
9. *See* Chapter 3 section §3.07[A] and §3.07[B] *supra.*
10. *See* Chapter 3 section §3.14 *supra.*
11. *See* Chapter 3 section §3.04 *supra.*

Annex 9

TYPICAL OPERATIONAL COVENANTS OF LESSEE*

(a) Provide information regarding aircraft.
(b) Operate aircraft lawfully.
(c) Pay taxes and other charges in respect of aircraft.[1]
(d) Only sublease aircraft or part with possession as permitted by lease or otherwise by lessor (typically such sub-lessee to be approved by lessor for a term not to exceed lease term, for no less a rent, and sublease either to be subordinate to lease or lessee (as sub-lessor) to assign its rights under sub-lease to lessor as security for performance by it of its obligations under lease).[2]
(e) Allow lessor inspection rights as agreed (usually without interference to commercial operation, and limited in number per year as long as there is no default; cost of inspection may be borne by lessor or lessee depending on whether inspection show compliance or non-compliance with lease).
(f) Protect lessor's title to the aircraft and allow only permitted liens (as defined in the lease) over the aircraft.[3]
(g) Preserve its corporate existence and remain in business as an airline.
(h) Keep aircraft records as required by the lease.[4]
(i) Maintain aircraft registration and other filings as required by lease.[5]
(j) Maintain and repair the aircraft as required by lease.[6]

* *See* section 9 of the Supplement *infra* and also Bunker D.H., *International Aircraft Financing, Volume 2: Specific Documents*, 2nd Edition, IATA, 2015, at 100–125 and 130–131 and Clark T. (ed.), *Leasing Finance*, Euromoney, 1985, at 59–62 and 64–66.
1. *See* Chapter 3 section §3.08 *supra.*
2. *See* Chapter 3 section §3.15 *supra.*
3. *See* Chapter 3 section §3.10[B][2] *supra.*
4. *See* Chapter 3 section §3.13[E] *supra.*
5. *See* Chapter 3 section §3.10[B][3] *supra.*
6. *See* Chapter 3 section §3.10[B][1] *supra.*

(k) Only remove engines and parts from aircraft as permitted by lease.[7]

(l) Only install removed engines and parts on other aircraft as permitted by lease.[8]

(m) Only install other engines and parts on aircraft as permitted by lease.[9]

(n) Not discriminate against aircraft as compared with other aircraft in lessee's fleet.

(o) Not operate the aircraft for training purposes.

7. *See* Chapter 3 section §3.10[B][4][b] and §3.10[B][4][c] *supra*.
8. *Ibid.*
9. *Ibid.*

Annex 10

TYPICAL EVENTS OF DEFAULT*

(a) Failure to pay any amount due within applicable grace period (a longer grace period may be allowed for unscheduled payments than for scheduled payments; although remedies will not be exercisable until end of grace period, default interest typically applies as soon as payment is late without a grace period).[1]
(b) Failure to insure or to return the aircraft in time in required condition or other breach of material covenant as stated (certainly no grace period is allowed in respect of breach of insurance obligations).[2]
(c) Failure to remedy breach of any obligation other than as referred to in (a) or (b) within applicable grace period.[3]
(d) Any representation or warranty proving untrue.[4]
(e) Any cross default under other agreements as specified (this is negotiable and may be distinguished as to other agreements with lessor and other agreements with third parties).
(f) Any necessary approvals or consents not being obtained, or lapsing or being revoked.[5]
(g) Any insolvency event as stated in the lease.[6]
(h) Any bankruptcy event as stated in the lease.[7]

* *See* section 13 of the Supplement *infra* and also Bunker D.H., *International Aircraft Financing, Volume 2: Specific Documents*, 2nd Edition, IATA, 2015, at 145–163 and Clark T (ed.), *Leasing Finance*, Euromoney, 1985, at 66–69.
1. *See* Chapter 3 section §3.14[A] *supra*.
2. *See* Chapter 3 section §3.14[C] *supra*.
3. *See* Chapter 3 §3.14[B][1] *supra*.
4. *See* Chapter 3 §3.04 *supra*.
5. *See* Chapter 3 §3.05[B] *supra*.
6. *See* Chapter 3 §3.14[D] *supra*.
7. *Ibid*.

(i) Lease or lessee's obligations thereunder becoming unlawful or unenforceable.
(j) Suspension or cessation of business by lessee.
(k) Denial of rights of lessor by lessee.
(l) Change of ownership or control of lessee.
(m) Failure by lessee to accept delivery of aircraft when properly tendered by lessor.
(n) Material adverse change in the condition of lessee.

Annex 11

OECD SECTOR UNDERSTANDING ON EXPORT CREDITS FOR CIVIL AIRCRAFT, ANNEX I (QUALIFYING DECLARATIONS) [TAD/ASU (2011)1]

1. For the purpose of Section 2 of Appendix II, the term "qualifying declarations", and all other references thereto in this Sector Understanding, means that a Contracting party to the Cape Town Convention (Contracting Party):
   a) Has made the declarations in Article 2 of this Annex, and
   b) Has not made the declarations in Article 3 of this Annex.
2. The declarations for the purpose of Article 1 a) of this Annex are:
   a) Insolvency: State Party declares that it will apply the entirety of Alternative A under Article XI of the Aircraft Protocol to all types of insolvency proceeding and that the waiting period for the purposes of Article XI (3) of that Alternative shall be no more than 60 calendar days.
   b) Deregistration: State Party declares that it will apply Article XIII of the Aircraft Protocol.
   c) Choice of Law: State Party declares that it will apply Article VIII of the Aircraft Protocol.
3. And at least one of the following (though both are encouraged):
   a) Method for Exercising Remedies: State Party declares under Convention Article 54 (2) that any remedies available to the creditor under any provision of the Convention which are not expressed under the relevant provisions thereof to require application to a court may be exercised without leave of the court (the insertion "without court action and" to be recommended (but not required) before the words "leave of the court");
   b) Timely Remedies: State Party declares that it will apply Article X of the Aircraft Protocol in its entirety (though clause 5 thereof, which is to be encouraged, is not required) and that the number of working days to be used for the purposes of the time-limit laid down in Article X (2) of the Aircraft Protocol shall be in respect of:

1) The remedies specified in Articles 13 (1) (a), (b) and (c) of the Convention (preservation of the aircraft objects and their value; possession, control or custody of the aircraft objects; and immobilisation of the aircraft objects), not more than that equal to ten calendar days, and
2) The remedies specified in Articles 13 (1) (d) and (e) of the Convention (lease or management of the aircraft objects and the income thereof and sale and application of proceeds from the aircraft equipment), not more than that equal to 30 calendar days.

4. The declarations referred to in Article 1 b) of this Annex are the following:
   a) Relief Pending Final Determination: State Party shall not have made a declaration under Article 55 of the Convention opting out of Article 13 or Article 43 of the Convention; provided, however, that, if State Party made the declarations set out under Article 2 d) of this Annex, the making of a declaration under Article 55 of the Convention shall not prevent application of the Cape Town Convention discount.
   b) Rome Convention: State Party shall not have made a declaration under Article XXXII of the Aircraft Protocol opting out of Article XXIV of the Aircraft Protocol; and
   c) Lease Remedy: State Party shall not have made a declaration under Article 54 (1) of the Convention preventing lease as a remedy.
5. Regarding Article XI of the Aircraft Protocol, for Member States of the European Union, the qualifying declaration set out in Article 2 a) of this Annex shall be deemed made by a Member State, for purposes hereof, if the national law of such Member State was amended to reflect the terms of Alternative A under Article XI of the Aircraft Protocol (with a maximum 60 calendar days waiting period). As regards the qualifying declarations set out in Article 2 c) and e) of this Annex, these shall be deemed satisfied, for the purpose of this Sector Understanding, if the laws of the European Union or the relevant Member States are substantially similar to that set out in such Articles of this Annex. In the case of Article 2 c) of this Annex, the laws of the European Union (Regulation (EC) 593/2008 on the Law Applicable to Contractual Obligations) are agreed to be substantially similar to Article VIII of the Aircraft Protocol.

Annex 12

MODEL AGREEMENT BETWEEN [STATE 1] AND [STATE 2] ON THE IMPLEMENTATION OF ARTICLE 83 *BIS* OF THE CONVENTION*

WHEREAS the Protocol relating to Article 83 *bis* of the *Convention on International Civil Aviation* (Chicago, 1944) (hereinafter referred to as "the Convention"), to which [State 1] and [State 2] are parties, entered into force on 20 June 1997;

WHEREAS Article 83 *bis,* with a view to enhanced safety, provides for the possibility of transferring to the State of the Operator all or part of the State of Registry's functions and duties pertaining to Articles 12, 30, 31 and 32 *a)* of the Convention;

WHEREAS, in line with Doc 9760 *(Airworthiness Manual),* Volume II, Part B, Chapter 10, and in light of Doc 8335 *(Manual of Procedures for Operations Inspection, Certification and Continued Surveillance),* Chapter 10, it is necessary to establish precisely the international obligations and responsibilities of [State 1] (State of Registry) and [State 2] (State of the Operator) in accordance with the Convention;

WHEREAS, with reference to the relevant Annexes to the Convention, this Agreement organizes the transfer from [State 1] to [State 2] of responsibilities normally carried out by the State of Registry, as set out in Sections 3 and 4 below;

The Government of [State 1], represented by its [Civil Aviation Authority], and The Government of [State 2], represented by its [Civil Aviation Authority],

Hereinafter referred to as "the Parties", have agreed as follows on the basis of Articles 33 and 83 *bis* of the Convention:

* Guidance on the Implementation of Article 83*bis* of the Convention on International Civil Aviation, ICAO, 2002, at 9–14.

ARTICLE I – SCOPE

Section 1. [State 1] shall be relieved of responsibility in respect of the functions and duties transferred to [State 2], upon due publicity or notification of this Agreement as determined in paragraph *b)* of Article 83 *bis*.

Section 2. The scope of this Agreement shall be limited to [types of aircraft] on the register of civil aircraft of [State 1] and operated under leasing arrangement by [operator], whose principal place of business is in [State 2]. The list of aircraft concerned, identified by type, registration number and serial number, is reproduced in Attachment 1, which also indicates the term of each leasing arrangement.

ARTICLE II – TRANSFERRED RESPONSIBILITIES

Section 3. Under this Agreement, the Parties agree that [State 1] transfers to [State 2] the following functions and duties, including oversight and control of relevant items contained in the respective Annexes to the Convention: Annex 1 -	*Personnel Licensing,* issuance and validation of licences.
Annex 2 -	*Rules of the Air,* enforcement of compliance with applicable rules and regulations relating to the flight and manoeuvre of aircraft.
Annex 6 -	*Operation of Aircraft* (Part I – *International Commercial Air Transport – Aeroplanes),* all responsibilities which are normally incumbent on the State of Registry. Where responsibilities in Annex 6, Part I, may conflict with responsibilities in Annex 8- *Airworthiness of Aircraft,* allocation of specific responsibilities as defined in Attachment 2.

Section 4. Under this Agreement, while [State 1] will retain full responsibility under the Convention for the regulatory oversight and control of Annex 8 – *Airworthiness of Aircraft,* the responsibility for the approval of line stations used by the [operator], which are located away from its main base, is transferred to [State 2]. The procedures related to the continuing airworthiness of aircraft to be followed by the [operator] will be contained in the operator's maintenance control manual (MCM). Attachment 2 hereunder describes the responsibilities of the Parties regarding the continuing airworthiness of aircraft.

ARTICLE III – NOTIFICATION

Section 5. Responsibility for notifying directly any States concerned of the existence and contents of this Agreement pursuant to Article 83 *bis b)* rests with [State 2] as the State of the Operator, as needed. This Agreement, as well as any amendments to it, shall also be registered with ICAO by [State 1] as the State of Registry or [State 2] as the State of the Operator, as required by Article 83 of the Convention and in accordance with the *Rules for Registration with ICAO of Aeronautical Agreements and Arrangements* (Doc 6685).

Section 6. A certified true copy [in each language] of this Agreement shall be placed on board each aircraft to which this Agreement applies.

Section 7. A certified true copy of the air operator certificate (AOC) issued to [operator] by [State 2], in which the aircraft concerned will be duly listed and properly identified, will also be carried on board each aircraft.

ARTICLE IV – COORDINATION

Section 8. Meetings between [State 1-CAA] and [State 2-CAA] will be held at [three-] month intervals to discuss both operations and airworthiness matters resulting from inspections that have been conducted by respective inspectors. For the sake of enhanced safety, these meetings will take place for the purpose of resolving any discrepancies found as a result of the inspections and in order to ensure that all parties are fully informed about the [operator's] operations. The following subjects will be among those reviewed during these meetings:

- Flight operations
- Continuing airworthiness and aircraft maintenance
- Operator's MCM procedures, if applicable
- Flight and cabin crew training and checking
- Any other significant matters arising from inspections

Section 9. Subject to reasonable notice, [State 1-CAA] will be permitted access to [State 2-CAA] documentation concerning [operator] in order to verify that [State 2] is fulfilling its safety oversight obligations as transferred from [State 1].

Section 10. During the implementation of this Agreement, and prior to any aircraft subject to it being made the object of a sub-lease, [State 2], remaining the State of the Operator, shall inform [State 1]. None of the duties and functions transferred from [State 1] to [State 2] may be carried out under the authority of a third State without the express written agreement of [State 1].

ARTICLE V – FINAL CLAUSES

Section 11. This Agreement will enter into force on its date of signature, and come to an end for aircraft listed in Attachment 1 at the completion of the respective leasing arrangements under which they are operated. Any modification to the Agreement shall be agreed by the parties thereto in writing.

Section 12. Any disagreement concerning the interpretation or application of this Agreement shall be resolved by consultation between the Parties.

Section 13. In witness thereof, the undersigned directors of civil aviation of [State 1] and [State 2] have signed this Agreement. For the	For the
Government of [State 1]	Government of [State 2]
[Signature]	[Signature]
[Name, title, place and date]	[Name, title, place and date]

Attachments:	Attachment 1 -	Aircraft Affected by this Agreement
	Attachment 2 -	Responsibilities of [State 1] and [State 2] Regarding Airworthiness

----

Attachment 1

AIRCRAFT AFFECTED BY THIS AGREEMENT

Aircraft type	Registration number	Serial number	Leasing term
[A320]			[date]
[B737]			[date]
[E120]			[date]
[IL62]			[date]

Attachment 2

RESPONSIBILITIES OF [STATE 1] AND [STATE 2] REGARDING AIRWORTHINESS

ICAO Doc	Subject	Responsibilities of the State of Registry ([State 1])	Responsibilities of the State of the Operator ([State 2])
Annex 8, Part II, Doc 9760, Volume II, Part B, Chapter 8	Mandatory continuing airworthiness information	Ensure that [State 2-CAA] and the [operator] receive all applicable mandatory continuing airworthiness information	Ensure that the [operator] complies with mandatory continuing airworthiness information transmitted by [State 1-CAA].
Annex 6, Part I, 5.2.4	Operation of aircraft in compliance with its Certificate of Airworthiness (C of A)		Assume State of Registry's responsibility as defined in 5.2.4 of Annex 6, Part I.
Annex 6, Part I, 8.1.2	Operator's maintenance responsibilities	Approve maintenance organizations used by [operator], except for line stations away from [operator's] main	Approve line stations away from the operator's main base.
Annex 6, Part I, 8.2.1 to 8.2.4	Operator's maintenance control manual (MCM)		Ensure that guidance is contained in the MCM, approve the MCM and transmit a copy to [State 1-CAA].
Annex 6, Part I, 8.4.1 to 8.4.3	Maintenance records	Inspect maintenance records and documents every six months	Ensure that records are kept in accordance with 8.4.1 to 8.4.3 of Annex 6, Part I, and inspect in accordance with the requirements of the AOC.

ICAO Doc	Subject	Responsibilities of the State of Registry ([State 1])	Responsibilities of the State of the Operator ([State 2])
Annex 6, Part I, 8.5.1 and 8.5.2	Continuing airworthiness information	Ensure that the airworthiness requirements of [State 1] are known to both [State 2-CAA] and [operator].	Ensure that the airworthiness requirements of [State 1] and [State 2] are complied with and adequate procedures are incorporated in the MCM.
Annex 6, Part I, 8.6; Doc 9760, Volume II, Part B, Chapter 10, Attachment 10-A	Modifications and repairs	Ensure that they have been previously approved by the States of Design and of Manufacture.	Ensure that the requirements are contained in the MCM and approve the MCM.
Annex 6, Part I, 8.7 and 8.8	Approved maintenance organization and maintenance release	Approval of the [operator's] base maintenance organization and procedures in accordance with 8.7 and 8.8 of Annex 9, Part I, and communication to [State 2-CAA] of related procedures to be included in the MCM.	Approval of the [operator's] line maintenance arrangements away from base. Ensure that procedures are contained in the MCM and approve the MCM.

Supplement: Sample Aircraft Lease Agreement

LEASE AGREEMENT [MSN]

This **LEASE AGREEMENT [msn]**, [date of Lease], (this "Agreement") is between:

(1) [NAME OF LESSOR], ______________, having its principal place of business at [Address of Lessor] ("Lessor"), and
(2) [NAME OF LESSEE], a company organized and existing under the laws of the State of Organization having its principal place of business at *[to be supplied by Lessee]* ("Lessee").

RECITALS:

(A) Lessor is the owner of the [mfgr] Model [model] aircraft bearing Manufacturer's serial number [msn] and related Leased Property.
(B) Lessor wishes to lease the Leased Property to Lessee, and Lessee agrees to lease the Leased Property from Lessor, upon and subject to the covenants, terms and conditions set out in this Agreement.

NOW, THEREFORE, in consideration of the foregoing and for other good and valuable consideration whose receipt and sufficiency are acknowledged, Lessor and Lessee agree as follows:

1. DEFINITIONS AND INTERPRETATION[1]

1.1 Definitions

In this Agreement the following expressions shall, unless the context otherwise requires, have the following respective meanings:

Actual Cost	as it applies to any maintenance work or rectification of discrepancies on the Aircraft, means the actual cost of replacement parts and/or the cost of labor associated with such work, rectification or replacement at Lessee's in-house labor rates (if the work is performed by Lessee) or at third party costs charged to Lessee (if the work is performed by third parties) and shall in no event include late charges, mark-ups, freight charges, interest, exchange fees or other similar amounts.
AD	any airworthiness directive, consigne de navigabilité or other requirement of the FAA, EASA or the Aviation Authority applicable to the Airframe, any Engine, any Part or the Aircraft Documents.
Additional Rent	collectively, Airframe Additional Rent, APU Additional Rent, Engine Additional Rent, Engine LLP Additional Rent and Landing Gear Additional Rent.
Affiliate	in relation to any Person, any other Person controlled directly or indirectly by that Person, any other Person that controls directly or indirectly that Person or any other Person under common control with that Person. For this purpose "control" of any Person means ownership of a majority of the voting power of such Person.
Agreed Maintenance Performer	Lessee or any other reputable Manufacturer, airline or maintenance organization that (i) is experienced in maintaining aircraft and/or engines of the same type as the Aircraft and the Engines, (ii) possess a repair station certificate issued by the FAA under FAR Part 145 and/or by EASA under EASA Regulations Part 145, and by the Aviation Authority, (iii) is duly certified by the Aviation Authority and (iv) is not excluded by Lessor pursuant to Section 7.5.
Agreed Value	as set forth in Schedule 5.

1. *See* §3.03 of the text *supra*.

Aircraft	the aircraft described in Part 1 of Schedule 1 (which term includes, where the context admits, a separate reference to all Engines, Parts and Aircraft Documents).
Aircraft Documents	the documents, data and records identified in or pursuant to Part 2 of Schedule 1 and all additions, renewals, revisions and replacements from time to time made in accordance with this Agreement.
Airframe	the Aircraft, excluding the Engines and the Aircraft Documents.
Airframe Additional Rent	as defined in Section 5.4(a).
Airframe Additional Rent Rate	as set forth in Schedule 5.
Airframe Manufacturer	*[to be supplied]*
Airframe Reimbursable Expenses	as defined in Section 7.2(a)(i).
AMM	the Airframe Manufacturer's maintenance manual, as updated and modified from time to time.
Applicable Law	all applicable (i) laws, treaties and international agreements of any national government, (ii) laws of any state, province, territory, locality or other political subdivision of a national government, and (iii) rules, regulations, judgments, decrees, orders, injunctions, writs, directives, licences and permits of any Government Entity or arbitration authority.
Approved Maintenance Program	the Maintenance Program of Lessee approved by Lessor in writing on or before the Delivery Date, which shall at all times be based upon and in compliance with the Airframe Manufacturer's MPD and the Engine Manufacturer's MPD, as the same may be updated, amended and otherwise modified from time to time in accordance with this Agreement.
APU	(i) the auxiliary power unit listed in Part 1 of Schedule 1, (ii) any and all Parts, so long as such Parts are incorporated in, installed on or attached to such auxiliary power unit or so long as title to such Parts is vested in Lessor in accordance with the terms of Section 8.17 after removal from such auxiliary power unit, and (iii) insofar as the same belong to Lessor, all substitutions, replacements or renewals from time to time made in or to such auxiliary power unit or to any of the Parts referred to in clause (ii) above, as required or permitted under this Agreement.

APU Additional Rent	as defined in Section 5.4(a).
APU Additional Rent Rate	as set forth in Schedule 5.
APU Basic Shop Visit	any shop visit involving the disassembly, cleaning, inspection and repair of an APU which corrects the condition associated with the removal reason, accomplishes a minimum of a medium repair to the power section in accordance with the Manufacturer's workscope planning guide, and provides for a minimum interval of continued operation greater than or equal to the Manufacturer's mean time between shop visits.
APU Hour	each hour or part thereof (rounded up to one decimal place) that the APU is operated, whether for aircraft operations or testing.
APU Reimbursable Expenses	as defined in Section 7.2(e)(i).
ATC/Airport Authority	any air traffic control authority, including NavCanada and Eurocontrol, and any airport authority with jurisdiction over any aircraft operated by Lessee or any sublessee.
Aviation Authority	any and all Government Entities that, under the laws of the State of Registration, from time to time (i) have control or supervision of civil aviation; or (ii) have jurisdiction over the registration, airworthiness or operation of, or matters relating to, the Aircraft.
Basic Rent	all amounts payable pursuant to Section 5.3.
Basic Rent Amount	as set forth in Schedule 5.
Beneficiary	such party as may be identified in the Notice and Acknowledgment.
Business Day	a day (other than a Saturday or Sunday) on which business of the nature required by this Agreement is carried out in New York, New York and the city in which Lessee's office listed in Section 16.10(b) is located.

C-Check	a maintenance check on the Airframe under the Approved Maintenance Program designated as a "C" check (or the equivalent check if not so designated) and consisting of full and complete zonal, systems and structural check including the corresponding lower checks ("A" and "B" or equivalent) and any other maintenance and inspections tasks that are a part of such checks, all in accordance with the Approved Maintenance Program, or if the Approved Maintenance Program changes and no longer refers to a full and complete zonal, systems and structural block "C" check, then a check consisting of those items of maintenance characterized by the MPD and best industry practice as a "C" check (or its equivalent), but in any event not including repairs arising as the result of operational or maintenance mishandling or accidental damage.
Certificate of Acceptance	a certificate in the form attached as Exhibit A to be completed and executed by Lessor and Lessee at the time of Delivery.
Certificate of Delivery Condition	a certificate in the form attached as Exhibit B to be completed and executed by Lessor and Lessee at the time of Delivery.
Commitment Fee	as set forth in Schedule 5.
CPCP	Lessee's Corrosion Prevention and Control Program that is a part of the Approved Maintenance Program.
Cycle	one take-off and landing of the Airframe or, in the case of an Engine, of the airframe on which such Engine is installed.
Damage Notification Threshold	as set forth in Schedule 5.
Default	any Event of Default and any event which with the giving of notice, lapse of time, determination of materiality or fulfillment of other condition or any combination of the foregoing would constitute an Event of Default.
Delivery	the delivery of the Aircraft to Lessee in accordance with the terms of this Agreement.
Delivery Date	the date on which Delivery takes place, which shall be the Scheduled Delivery Date or such other date notified by Lessor to Lessee in accordance with the provisions of this Agreement.
Delivery Location	a location in [the continental United States][Western Europe] mutually agreeable to Lessor and Lessee.
Deregistration Power of Attorney	an irrevocable power of attorney by Lessee in substantially the form attached as Exhibit C.

Dollars and $	the lawful currency of the United States of America.
EASA	the European Aviation Safety Agency of the European Union established by Regulation (EC) No 1592/2002 of 15 July 2002, or any successor Government Entity succeeding to the functions thereof.
EASA Regulations	the requirements of Regulation (EC) No 1702/2003 and Regulation (EC) No 2042/2003, any successor thereto and all applicable certification specifications, acceptable means of compliance and guidance material issued by EASA pursuant thereto.
Engine	whether or not installed on the Aircraft: (a) each engine of the manufacture, model and serial number specified in Part 1 of Schedule 1, title to which shall belong to Lessor; or (b) any engine which replaces that engine, title to which passes to Lessor in accordance with Section 8.17(a); and in each case includes all modules and Parts from time to time belonging to, installed in or appurtenant to that engine.
Engine Additional Rent	as defined in Section 5.4(a).
Engine Additional Rent Rate	as set forth in Schedule 5.
Engine LLP Additional Rent	as defined in Section 5.4(a).
Engine LLP Additional Rent Rate	as set forth in Schedule 5.
Engine LLP Reimbursable Expenses	as defined in Section 7.2(c)(i).
Engine Loss	the occurrence, with respect to an Engine, of one of the events set forth in clauses (a) through (d) of the definition of "Total Loss" as if references to the "Airframe" were to such "Engine".
Engine Loss Date	the relevant date determined in accordance with the definition of "Total Loss Date" as if that definition applied to an Engine Loss.
Engine Manufacturer	[EngMfgr].

Engine Reimbursable Expenses	as defined in Section 7.2(b)(i).
Engine Shop Visit	[to be reviewed by technical for each lease].
Equipment Change	any modification, alteration, addition to or removal from the Aircraft during the Term.
Eurocontrol	the European Organization for the Safety of Air Navigation.
Event of Default	an event specified in Section 13.1.
Excusable Delay	with respect to delivery of the Aircraft, delay or non-performance due to or arising out of (i) acts of God or public enemy, civil war, insurrection or riot, fire, flood, explosion, earthquake, serious accident, epidemic, quarantine restriction or import restriction, (ii) any act of government, governmental priority, allocation, regulation or order affecting directly or indirectly, the Aircraft, any Manufacturer, Lessor or any materials or facilities, (iii) strike or labor dispute causing cessation, slowdown or interruption of work, (iv) inability after due and timely diligence to procure equipment, data or materials from manufacturers, suppliers, any existing owner, seller or lessee in a timely manner, (v) damage, destruction or loss, or adverse weather conditions preventing any services, inspections or flights of the Aircraft or (vi) any other cause to the extent that such cause is beyond the control of Lessor, whether above mentioned or not and whether or not similar to the foregoing.
Expiry Date	the Scheduled Expiry Date or, if earlier, the date on which: (a) the Aircraft has been redelivered in accordance with this Agreement and all obligations of Lessee have been satisfied; or (b) Lessor receives the Agreed Value following a Total Loss and any other amounts then due and owing in accordance with this Agreement.
FAA	the Federal Aviation Administration of the U.S. Department of Transportation, or any successor Government Entity succeeding to the functions thereof.
FAR	Federal Aviation Regulations issued by the FAA.
Final Inspection	the inspection of the Aircraft by Lessor and any other inspecting parties during any part of the inspections, checks and test flights required pursuant to Section 12 and Schedule 3 or otherwise performed in connection with the Return.

Final Maintenance Performer	an Agreed Maintenance Performer with the necessary experience and regulatory authority approvals for the Aircraft type in order to perform the required redelivery maintenance on the Aircraft needed to meet the requirements of Section 12 and Schedule 3.
Financial Indebtedness	any indebtedness in respect of: (a) moneys borrowed; (b) any liability under any debenture, bond, note, loan stock, acceptance credit, documentary credit or other security; (c) the acquisition cost of any asset to the extent payable before or after the time of acquisition or possession; or (d) the capitalized value (determined in accordance with accounting practices generally accepted in the United States of America) of obligations under finance leases; or (e) any guarantee, indemnity or similar assurance against financial loss of any Person in respect of the above.
Financing Documents	any loan agreement, credit agreement or similar agreement between Lessor and any Financing Party under which funds are advanced to Lessor or any Affiliate of Lessor and the obligations of Lessor or any Affiliate of Lessor to such Financing Parties relate to the Leased Property or the Operative Documents.
Financing Parties	collectively (i) Beneficiary, (ii) Security Trustee, (iii) any Person that has advanced funds to Lessor or an Affiliate of Lessor pursuant to a Financing Document, (iv) any Person that holds a Security Interest in the Leased Property or the Lessor's right, title and interest in any Operative Document to secure the Lessor's and/or any Affiliate's obligations under Financing Documents, (v) any agent, loan agent, trustee, security trustee, collateral trustee or similar Person acting pursuant to any Financing Document, and (vi) the successors and permitted assigns of such Persons.
Financing Security Document	any Financing Document whereby Lessor grants to a Financing Party a Security Interest in the Leased Property and/or in its right, title and interest in any Operative Document.

Flight Charges	all flight charges, route navigation charges, navigation service charges and all other fees, charges or Taxes payable for the use of or for services provided at any airport or otherwise payable to any airport, airport authority, navigation or flight authority or other similar entity or for any services provided in connection with the operation, landing or navigation of aircraft.
Flight Hour	each hour or part thereof (rounded up to one decimal place) elapsing from the moment the wheels of the Airframe leave the ground on take off until the moment the wheels of the Airframe next touch the ground or, in the case of an Engine, of the airframe on which such Engine is installed.
GAAP	generally accepted accounting principles as in effect from time to time in the State of Organization and, subject to changes in such principles from time to time, consistently applied in accordance with the past practices of a Person.
Government Entity	(a) any national, state or local government, political subdivision thereof or local jurisdiction therein; (b) any board, commission, department, division, instrumentality, court, agency or political subdivision thereof; and (c) any association, organization or institution of which any of the above is a member or to whose jurisdiction any thereof is subject or in whose activities any of the above is a participant.
Habitual Base	the State of Organization or, subject to the prior written consent of Lessor, any other state, province or country in which the Aircraft is for the time being habitually based.
Hull Insurance Deductible	as set forth in Schedule 5.
IATA	the International Air Transport Association.
Indemnitees	Lessor, Servicer, any Financing Party, the respective successors and assigns of such Persons and the shareholders, members, partners, Affiliates, directors, officers, employees, agents and servants of such Persons.
Insurances	as defined in Section 9.1.
Landing Gear	the landing gear assemblies (nose, left main and right main) of the Aircraft identified by the respective serial numbers in the Certificate of Acceptance, and any landing gear assembly substituted therefor in accordance with this Agreement and title to which has passed to Lessor in accordance with this Agreement.

Landing Gear Additional Rent	as defined in Section 5.4(a).
Landing Gear Additional Rent Rate	as set forth in Schedule 5.
Landing Gear Overhaul	an overhaul of the Landing Gear to full Manufacturer specification and operating condition (excluding any rotable components such as wheels, tires, brakes and consumable items).
Landing Gear Reimbursable Expenses	as defined in Section 7.2(d)(i).
Leased Property	the Aircraft and the Aircraft Documents.
Lessee Installed Part	any part installed on the Aircraft at Delivery title to which is held by Lessee, and any part installed on the Aircraft after Delivery not in replacement for a Part and not required under Applicable Law on the Aircraft title to which is either held by Lessee (which title may be subject to a Security Interest in favor of an unrelated third party) or held by an unrelated third party and such part is leased or conditionally sold to Lessee.
Lessor's Counsel	*[to be advised]*, counsel to Lessor in each of the State of Organization and the State of Registration.
Lessor Lien	(a) any Security Interest from time to time created by or arising through Lessor or any Financing Party in connection with the financing or refinancing of the Aircraft; (b) any other Security Interest in respect of the Aircraft that results from acts or omissions of, or claims against, Lessor or any Financing Party not related to the operation of the Aircraft or the transactions contemplated by or permitted under the Operative Documents; and (c) Security Interests in respect of the Aircraft for Non-Indemnified Taxes.
Letter of Credit	as defined in Section 5.15.
Letter of Credit Bank Minimum Rating	a senior, unsecured and unguaranteed long-term debt rating of "A + " from Standard & Poor's Ratings Group (a division of The McGraw-Hill Companies, Inc.) or "A1" from Moody's Investors Service, Inc.
Letter of Credit Validity Date	at any date of determination, the date which is three months after the Scheduled Expiry Date.
LLPs	life limited Parts.

Maintenance Program	an Aviation Authority approved maintenance program for the Aircraft encompassing scheduled maintenance, condition monitored maintenance and/or on-condition maintenance of Airframe, Engines and Parts, including servicing, testing, preventative maintenance, repairs, structural inspections, system checks, overhauls, approved modifications, service bulletins, engineering orders, ADs, corrosion control, inspections and treatments.
Major Checks	any C-Check, Engine Shop Visit, APU Basic Shop Visit and Landing Gear Overhaul.
Mandatory Equipment Change	an Equipment Change that is required by or performed to comply with an AD or a Manufacturer's service bulletin
Manufacturer	with respect to the Airframe, Engine or any Part of the Aircraft, the Airframe Manufacturer, Engine Manufacturer or manufacturer of such Part, respectively.
Minimum Liability Coverage	as set forth in Schedule 5.
MPD	for any Manufacturer, such Manufacturer's maintenance planning document or EMP-Engine MFG maintenance program/planning guide, as updated and modified from time to time.
Non-Incident/ Non-Accident Statement	a statement produced on Lessee's letterhead confirming that the Airframe and Engines have not been involved in any abnormal operational or maintenance events that could have resulted in significant damage (incidents) or that did result in significant damage (accidents), executed by Lessee's appropriately qualified quality assurance manager.
Non-Indemnified Taxes	(a) Taxes imposed as a direct result of activities of any Tax Indemnitee in the jurisdictions imposing the liability unrelated to such Tax Indemnitee's dealings with Lessee pursuant to the Operative Documents or to the transactions contemplated by the Operative Documents or the operation of the Aircraft by Lessee; (b) Taxes imposed on the income, profits or gains of any Tax Indemnitee by (i) any Federal Government Entity in the United States of America, (ii) any Government Entity in the jurisdictions where such Tax Indemnitee is incorporated, formed or organized or has its principal place of business, or (iii) any Government Entity in any other jurisdiction where such Tax Indemnitee is liable for such Taxes and such liability has or would have arisen in the absence of the transactions contemplated by the Operative Documents;

	(c) Taxes imposed with respect to any period commencing or event occurring before the date of this Agreement or after Return and unrelated to any Tax Indemnitee's dealings with Lessee pursuant to the Operative Documents or to the transactions contemplated by the Operative Documents; (d) Taxes imposed as a direct result of the sale or other disposition of the Aircraft, unless such sale or disposition occurs as a consequence of an Event of Default; (e) Taxes imposed by a taxing jurisdiction for a particular tax period unless imposed as a result of any of the following for that tax period: (i) the operation, maintenance, registration, location, presence or use of the Aircraft, the Airframe, any Engine or any Part thereof in such jurisdiction, (ii) the place of incorporation, commercial domicile or other presence in such jurisdiction of Lessee, any sublessee or any user of or Person in possession of the Aircraft, the Airframe, any Engine or any Part thereof in such jurisdiction, or (iii) any payments made under the Operative Documents and related documents being made from such jurisdiction; (f) Taxes to the extent caused by the gross negligence or willful misconduct of any Tax Indemnitee; and (g) Taxes to the extent caused by a failure by any Tax Indemnitee to furnish in a timely manner notice or information that it is required to furnish to Lessee by the terms of this Agreement.
Notice and Acknowledgment	a notice and acknowledgment between Lessor and Lessee in substantially the form attached as Exhibit D.
OEM	the original equipment manufacturer of a Part.
Operative Documents	this Agreement, the Certificate of Acceptance, the Certificate of Delivery Condition, the Deregistration Power of Attorney and the Notice and Acknowledgment.
Overdue Rate	at any time and from time to time, 7.0% plus the base commercial lending rate as announced by Citibank, N.A.

Part	whether or not installed on the Aircraft: (a) any appliance, part, component, module, navigation, avionic and communication equipment, computer, instrument, appurtenance, accessory, furnishing and equipment of whatever nature (including the APU and Landing Gear but excluding a complete Engine) furnished with, installed on or appurtenant to the Airframe and Engines on Delivery, which may from time to time be removed, incorporated or installed in or attached to the Airframe or any Engine; and (b) any other appliance, part, component, module, navigation, avionic and communication equipment, computer, instrument, appurtenance, accessory, furnishing or equipment of whatever nature (other than a complete Engine) title to which has, or should have, passed to Lessor pursuant to this Agreement,but excludes any such items title to which has, or should have, passed to Lessee pursuant to Section 8.17 and any Lessee Installed Part.
Permitted Lien	(a) any Security Interest for Taxes not assessed or, if assessed, not yet due and payable, or being contested in good faith by appropriate proceedings; (b) any Security Interest of a repairer, mechanic, carrier, hangar keeper, unpaid seller or other similar lien arising in the ordinary course of business or by operation of law in respect of obligations which are not overdue in accordance with Applicable Law (or, if applicable, generally accepted accounting principles and practices in the relevant jurisdiction) or are being contested in good faith by appropriate proceedings; and (c) any Lessor Lien;but only if, in the case of (a) and (b), (i) adequate reserves have been provided by Lessee for the payment of the Taxes or obligations in accordance with GAAP; and (ii) such proceedings, or the continued existence of the Security Interest, do not give rise to any reasonable likelihood of the sale, forfeiture or other loss of the Aircraft or any interest therein or of criminal liability on the part of Lessor or any Financing Party.
Person	any individual, corporation, partnership, limited liability company, limited liability partnership, joint venture, association, joint stock company, trust, unincorporated organization or Government Entity.

PMA Part	a non type-certificated Part whose design and/or manufacture has been accomplished by any entity other than the OEM and which has received parts manufacture approval from an Aviation Authority.
Redelivery Location	the facility of the Final Maintenance Performer, or such other location mutually acceptable to Lessor and Lessee.
Reimbursable Expenses	collectively, Airframe Reimbursable Expenses, APU Reimbursable Expenses, Engine Reimbursable Expenses, Engine LLP Reimbursable Expenses and Landing Gear Reimbursable Expenses.
Rent	collectively, Basic Rent, Additional Rent and Supplemental Rent.
Rent Date	the Delivery Date and the corresponding day of each calendar month during the Term or, for any calendar month that does not have a corresponding day, the last day of such calendar month.
Rental Period	each period ascertained in accordance with Section 5.2.
Return	the return of the Aircraft by Lessee to Lessor at the Redelivery Location in the condition and manner required by Section 12 and Schedule 3 and the other provisions of this Agreement, as evidenced by the execution by Lessor, and the delivery to Lessee, of a Return Certificate.
Return Certificate	the return certificate to be delivered by Lessor to Lessee pursuant to Section 12.3, substantially in the form attached as Exhibit E.
Scheduled Delivery Date	_______, 200_ or such other date mutually agreed by Lessor and Lessee.
Scheduled Expiry Date	the day corresponding to the Delivery Date in the ____ calendar month after the month in which the Delivery Date occurs or, if such calendar month does not have a corresponding day, the last day of such calendar month.
Security Interest	any security interest, mortgage, charge, pledge, lien, encumbrance, claim, assignment, hypothecation, right of set-off or other agreement or arrangement having the effect of creating a security interest.
Security Trustee	such party as may be identified in the Notice and Acknowledgment.
Servicer	[] or any other Person appointed by Lessor or Beneficiary to act as manager, administrative agent or remarketing agent for the Aircraft or any of the Operative Documents, as may be identified by Lessor to Lessee from time to time.
SRM	the Airframe Manufacturer's structural repair manual

State of Organization	*[to be supplied].*
State of Registration	*[to be supplied].*
Subsidiary	(a) in relation to any reference to accounts, any company wholly or partially owned by Lessee whose accounts are consolidated with the accounts of the Lessee in accordance with accounting principles generally accepted under accounting standards of the State of Organization; and (b) for any other purpose, an entity from time to time: (i) of which another has direct or indirect control or owns directly or indirectly more than 50% of the voting share capital; or (ii) which is a direct or indirect subsidiary of another under the laws of the jurisdiction of its incorporation.
Supplemental Rent	all amounts, liabilities and obligations (other than Basic Rent and Additional Rent) that Lessee assumes or agrees to pay under this Agreement to Lessor or any other Person, including payment of deposits, indemnities and the Agreed Value.
Tax Indemnitees	Lessor, Servicer, any Financing Party and the respective successors and assigns of Lessor, Servicer and each Financing Party (no such Person shall cease to be a Tax Indemnitee by reason of being a member of a group that files a consolidated tax return under the name of an affiliated Person).
Taxes	all present and future taxes, levies, imposts, duties or charges in the nature of taxes, whatever and wherever imposed, including customs duties, value added taxes or similar taxes and any franchise, transfer, sales, use, business, occupation, excise, personal property, stamp or other tax or duty imposed by any national or local taxing or fiscal authority or agency, together with any withholding, penalties, additions to tax, fines or interest thereon or with respect thereto.
Term	the period commencing on the Delivery Date and ending on the Expiry Date or any later date pursuant to Section 12.2.
Third Party Engine	any engine, title to which is either held by Lessee (which title may be subject to a Security Interest in favor of an unrelated third party) or held by an unrelated third party and such engine is leased or conditionally sold to Lessee.

Total Loss	with respect to the Airframe: (a) the actual, arranged or constructive total loss of the Airframe (including any damage to the Airframe which results in an insurance settlement on the basis of a total loss, or requisition for use or hire which results in an insurance settlement on the basis of a total loss); (b) the Airframe being destroyed, damaged beyond repair or permanently rendered unfit for normal use for any reason whatsoever; (c) the requisition of title, or other compulsory acquisition, capture, seizure, deprivation, confiscation or detention for any reason of the Airframe by the government of the State of Registration (whether *de jure* or *de facto*), but excluding requisition for use or hire not involving requisition of title; or (d) the hi-jacking, theft, condemnation, confiscation, seizure or requisition for use or hire of the Airframe which deprives any Person permitted by this Agreement to have possession and/or use of the Airframe for more than 60 consecutive days.
Total Loss Date	(a) in the case of an actual total loss, the actual date on which the loss occurs or, if such date is unknown, the day on which the Aircraft was last heard of; (b) in the case of any of the events described in subparagraph (a) of the definition of "Total Loss" (other than an actual total loss), the earlier of (i) 30 days after the date on which notice claiming such total loss is given to the relevant insurers, and (ii) the date on which such loss is admitted or compromised by the insurers; (c) in the case of any of the events described in subparagraph (b) of the definition of "Total Loss", the date on which such destruction, damage or rendering unfit occurs; (d) in the case of any of the events described in subparagraph (c) of the definition of "Total Loss", the date on which the relevant requisition of title or other compulsory acquisition, capture, seizure, deprivation, confiscation or detention occurs; and

	(e) in the case of any of the events described in sub-paragraph (d) of the definition of "Total Loss", the expiry of the period of 60 days referred to in such sub-paragraph (d);and, in each case, the Total Loss shall be deemed to have occurred at noon Greenwich Mean Time on such date.
Voluntary Equipment Change	an Equipment Change other than a Mandatory Equipment Change.

1.2 Interpretation

(a) In this Agreement, unless the contrary intention is stated, a reference to:
  (i) each of "Lessor", "Lessee", "Servicer", "Beneficiary", "Financing Party" or any other Person includes without prejudice to the provisions of this Agreement any successor in title to it and any permitted assignee;
  (ii) words importing the plural shall include the singular and vice versa;
  (iii) the term "including", when used in this Agreement, means "including without limitation" and "including but not limited to";
  (iv) any document shall include that document as amended, novated or supplemented from time to time unless expressly stated to the contrary; and
  (v) a law (1) includes any statute, decree, constitution, regulation, order, judgment or directive of any Government Entity; (2) includes any treaty, pact, compact or other agreement to which any Government Entity is a signatory or party; (3) includes any judicial or administrative interpretation or application thereof; and (4) is a reference to that provision as amended, substituted or re-enacted.
  (vi) A "Section", "Schedule" or "Exhibit" is a reference to a section of, a schedule to or an exhibit to this Agreement.
  (vii) The headings in this Agreement are to be ignored in construing this Agreement.

2. REPRESENTATIONS AND WARRANTIES[2]

2.1 Lessee's Representations and Warranties

Lessee represents and warrants to Lessor as follows:

(a) Status: Lessee is a ___________ duly organized, validly existing and in good standing under the laws of the State of Organization, has the corporate power

2. *See* §3.04 and Annex 7 of the text *supra*.

to own its assets and carry on its business as it is being conducted and is (or will at the relevant time be) the holder of all necessary air transportation licences required in connection therewith and with the use and operation of the Aircraft.

(b) Power and Authority: Lessee has the power to enter into and perform, and has taken all necessary corporate action to authorize the entry into, performance and delivery of, each of the Operative Documents and the transactions contemplated by the Operative Documents.

(c) Execution and Delivery: Lessee has duly executed and delivered this Agreement, and on or before Delivery shall have duly executed and delivered each of the Operative Documents to which Lessee is a party.

(d) Legal validity: Each of the Operative Documents to which Lessee is a party constitutes Lessee's legal, valid and binding agreement, enforceable against Lessee in accordance with its terms.

(e) Non-conflict: The entry into and performance by Lessee of, and the transactions contemplated by, the Operative Documents to which Lessee is a party do not and will not:

(i) conflict with any Applicable Laws binding on Lessee;

(ii) conflict with the constitutional documents of Lessee; or

(iii) conflict with or result in default under any document which is binding upon Lessee or any of its assets, or result in the creation of any Security Interest over any of its assets, other than Permitted Liens.

(f) Authorization: All authorizations, consents and registrations required by, and all notifications to be given by, Lessee in connection with the entry into, performance, validity and enforceability of, the Operative Documents and the transactions contemplated by the Operative Documents have been (or will on or before Delivery have been) obtained, effected or given (as appropriate) and are (or will on their being obtained or effected be) in full force and effect.

(g) No Immunity:

(i) Lessee is subject to civil and commercial law with respect to its obligations under the Operative Documents.

(ii) Neither Lessee nor any of its assets is entitled to any right of immunity and the entry into and performance of the Operative Documents by Lessee constitute private and commercial acts.

(h) Financial Statements: The audited consolidated financial statements of Lessee and its Subsidiaries most recently delivered to Lessor:

(i) have been prepared in accordance with GAAP; and

(ii) fairly present the consolidated financial condition of the Lessee and its Subsidiaries as at the date to which they were drawn up and the consolidated results of operations of the Lessee and its Subsidiaries for the periods covered by such statements.

(i) Restricted Countries: Lessee does not hold a contract or other obligation to, and does not, operate the Aircraft to or from any of the countries that are the subject of sanctions under U.N. Security Council directives.

(j) Pari Passu: The obligations of Lessee under the Operative Documents rank at least *pari passu* with all other present and future unsecured and unsubordinated obligations (including contingent obligations) of Lessee, with the exception of such obligations as are mandatorily preferred by law and not by virtue of any contract.

(k) Choice of Law: The choice by Lessee of the law of England and Wales to govern this Agreement as set out in Section 15.1 and the submission by the Lessee to the non-exclusive jurisdiction of the courts as set out in Section 15.2 are valid and binding.

(l) Allowances: Lessee has not claimed and will not claim any capital or depreciation allowances in respect of the Aircraft.

2.2 Lessee's Further Representations and Warranties

Lessee further represents and warrants to Lessor that:

(a) No Default:

(i) No Event of Default has occurred and is continuing or might reasonably be expected to result from the entry into or performance of any of the Operative Documents.

(ii) No event has occurred and is continuing that constitutes, or with the giving of notice, lapse of time, determination of materiality or fulfillment of any other applicable condition, or any combination of the foregoing, might constitute, a material default under any document that is binding on Lessee or any assets of Lessee.

(b) Registration:

(i) It is not necessary or advisable under the laws of the State of Organization, the State of Registration or the Habitual Base in order to ensure the validity, effectiveness and enforceability of the Operative Documents or to establish, perfect or protect the property rights of Lessor or any Financing Party in the Leased Property that any instrument relating to the Operative Documents, other than *[to be supplied by Lessee]*, be filed, registered or recorded or that any other action be taken or, if any such filings, registrations, recordings or other actions are necessary, the same have been effected or will have been effected on or before Delivery.

(ii) Under all Applicable Laws, including the laws of the State of Organization, the State of Registration and the Habitual Base, the property rights of Lessor and any Financing Parties notified to Lessee in the Leased Property have been fully established, perfected and protected and this Agreement will have priority in all respects over the claims of all creditors of Lessee, with the exception of such claims as are mandatorily preferred by law and not by virtue of any contract.

(c) Litigation: No litigation, arbitration or administrative proceedings are pending or, to Lessee's knowledge, threatened against Lessee that, if adversely determined, would have a material adverse effect upon its financial condition or business or its ability to perform its obligations under the Operative Documents.

(d) Taxes: Lessee has delivered all necessary returns and payments due to all tax authorities having jurisdiction over Lessee, including those in the State of Organization, the State of Registration and the Habitual Base, and Lessee is not required by law to deduct or withhold any Taxes from any payments under this Agreement. The execution, delivery or performance by Lessee or Lessor of the Operative Documents will not result in the Lessor (i) having any liability in respect of Taxes in the State of Organization, State of Registration or Habitual Base or (ii) having or being deemed to have a place of business in the State of Organization, State of Registration or Habitual Base.

(e) Material Adverse Change: No material adverse change in the financial condition of Lessee has occurred since the date of the financial statements most recently provided to Lessor on or before the Delivery Date.

(f) Information: The financial and other information furnished by Lessee in connection with the Operative Documents does not contain any untrue statement of material fact or omit to state any fact the omission of which makes the statements therein, in light of the circumstances under which they were made, materially misleading, and does not omit to disclose any material matter. All forecasts and opinions contained in the financial and other information furnished by Lessee in connection with the Operative Documents were honestly made on reasonable grounds after due and careful inquiry by Lessee.

(g) Air Traffic Control: Lessee is not in default in the payment of any sums due by Lessee to any ATC/Airport Authority in respect of any aircraft operated by Lessee.

(h) Insurances: On the Delivery Date, the Insurances will not be subject to any Security Interest except as may be created pursuant to the Operative Documents.

2.3 Repetition

The representations and warranties in Section 2.1 and Section 2.2 will survive the execution of this Agreement. The representations and warranties contained in Section 2.1 and Section 2.2 will be deemed to be repeated by Lessee on Delivery with reference to the facts and circumstances then existing. The representations and warranties contained in Section 2.1 will be deemed to be repeated by Lessee on each Rent Date as if made with reference to the facts and circumstances then existing.

2.4 Lessor's Representations and Warranties

Lessor represents and warrants to Lessee that:

(a) Status: Lessor is duly formed and validly existing under the laws of the place of its organization. Lessor has the power to own the Leased Property and carry on the business contemplated of Lessor under the Operative Documents.

(b) Power and Authority: Lessor has the power and authority to enter into and perform, and has taken all necessary action to authorize the entry into, performance and delivery of, the Operative Documents and the transactions contemplated by the Operative Documents.

(c) Enforceability: Each of the Operative Documents constitutes Lessor's legal, valid and binding agreement, enforceable against Lessor in accordance with its terms.

(d) Non-conflict: The entry into and performance by Lessor of, and the transactions contemplated by, the Operative Documents do not and will not:
   (i) conflict with any Applicable Laws binding on Lessor;
   (ii) conflict with the organizational documents of Lessor; or
   (iii) conflict with or result in a default under any document that is binding upon Lessor or any of its assets.

(e) Authorization: So far as concerns the obligations of Lessor, all authorizations, consents, registrations and notifications required in connection with the entry into, performance, validity and enforceability of, and the transactions contemplated by, the Operative Documents by Lessor have been (or will on or before Delivery have been) obtained or effected (as appropriate) and are (or will on their being obtained or effected be) in full force and effect.

(f) No Immunity:
   (i) Lessor is subject to civil and commercial law with respect to its obligations under the Operative Documents.
   (ii) Neither Lessor nor any of its assets is entitled to any right of immunity and the entry into and performance of the Operative Documents by Lessor constitute private and commercial acts.

(g) Right to Lease: On the Delivery Date, Lessor shall have the right to lease the Aircraft to Lessee under this Agreement.

2.5 Repetition

The representations and warranties in Section 2.4 will survive the execution of this Agreement. The representations and warranties contained in Section 2.4 will be deemed to be repeated by Lessor on Delivery as if made with reference to the facts and circumstances then existing.

3. CONDITIONS PRECEDENT[3]

3.1 Lessor's Documentary Conditions Precedent

Lessor's obligation to lease the Leased Property to Lessee under this Agreement is subject to the receipt of the following by Lessor from Lessee no less than three Business Days before Delivery in form and substance satisfactory to Lessor, provided, that it shall not be a condition precedent to the obligations of Lessor that any document be produced, or action taken, which is to be produced or taken by Lessor or any Person within its control:

(a) Constitutional Documents: a copy of the constitutional documents of Lessee[, together with an English translation thereof];

(b) Resolutions: a true copy of a resolution of the board of directors (or the equivalent) of Lessee approving the terms of, and the transactions contemplated by, the Operative Documents to which it is a party, resolving that it enter into the Operative Documents to which it is a party, and authorizing a specified individual or individuals to execute the Operative Documents to which it is a party and accept delivery of the Leased Property on its behalf;

(c) Operative Documents: a copy of each of the Operative Documents, duly executed and, if necessary, notarized by Lessee, including the chattel paper original counterpart of this Agreement;

(d) Opinions: (i) an opinion, in form and substance satisfactory to Lessor, in respect of Lessee's obligations under the Operative Documents issued by independent legal counsel to Lessee acceptable to Lessor, and (ii) an opinion from Lessor's Counsel as to such matters as Lessor may reasonably request;

(e) Approvals: evidence of the issuance of each approval, licence and consent which may be required in relation to, or in connection with, the performance by Lessee of its obligations under the Operative Documents;

(f) Filings and Registrations: evidence that the Aircraft has been validly registered under the laws of the State of Registration and that all filings, registrations, recordings and other actions have been taken or made that are necessary or advisable to ensure the validity, effectiveness and enforceability of the Operative Documents and to protect the property rights of Lessor in the Leased Property;

(g) Licences: copies of Lessee's air transport licence, air operator's certificate and all other licences, certificates and permits required by Lessee in relation to, or in connection with, the operation of the Aircraft;

(h) Certificate: a certificate of a duly authorized officer of Lessee:

   (i) setting out a specimen of each signature of an officer of Lessee referred to in Section 3.1(b); and

---

3. *See* §3.05 and Annex 8 of the text *supra*.

(ii) certifying that each copy of a document specified in Section 3.1(a) and (b) is correct, complete and in full force and effect;

(i) Insurances: certificates of insurance, certificates of reinsurance, insurance brokers' undertakings, reinsurance broker's undertakings and other evidence satisfactory to Lessor that Lessee is and will be in compliance with the provisions of this Agreement as to insurances on and after Delivery;

(j) ATC/Airport Authority: letters from Lessee addressed to any ATC/Airport Authority designated by Lessor pursuant to which Lessee authorizes such authority to issue to Lessor, upon Lessor's request from time to time, a statement of account of all sums due by Lessee to such authority in respect of all aircraft (including the Aircraft) operated by Lessee;

(k) Acceptance by Process Agent: a letter from the process agent appointed by Lessee pursuant to Section 15.4(a) accepting its appointment;

(l) Aviation Authority Letter: to the extent available, a letter from the appropriate Aviation Authority confirming that, upon the occurrence of an Event of Default under this Agreement and a request for deregistration by Lessor, the Aviation Authority will deregister the Aircraft and authorize the export of the Aircraft from the State of Registration; and

(m) General: such other documents as Lessor may reasonably request.

3.2 Lessor's Other Conditions Precedent

The obligation of Lessor to deliver and lease the Leased Property under this Agreement is also subject to the following additional conditions precedent:

(a) Representations and Warranties: the representations and warranties of Lessee under Sections 2.1 and 2.2 are correct and would be correct if repeated on Delivery; and

(b) Payments: all payments due to Lessor under this Agreement on or before Delivery, including the Basic Rent due on the Delivery Date and the Commitment Fee, shall have been received by Lessor.

3.3 Lessor's Waiver

The conditions specified in Sections 3.1 and 3.2 are for the sole benefit of Lessor and may be waived or deferred in whole or in part and with or without conditions by Lessor. If any of those conditions are not satisfied and Lessor (in its absolute discretion) nonetheless agrees to deliver the Leased Property to Lessee, then Lessee will ensure that those conditions are fulfilled within one month after the Delivery Date and Lessor may treat as an Event of Default the failure of Lessee to do so.

3.4 Lessee's Conditions Precedent

Lessee's obligation to accept the Leased Property on lease from Lessor under this Agreement is subject to the satisfaction by Lessor of the following conditions precedent:

(a) Representations and Warranties: the representations and warranties of Lessor under Section 2.4 are correct and would be correct if repeated on Delivery; and
(b) Delivery Condition: the Aircraft shall be in the condition set forth in Schedule 2.

3.5 Lessee's Waiver

The conditions specified in Section 3.4 are for the sole benefit of Lessee and may be waived or deferred in whole or in part and with or without conditions by Lessee. If any of those conditions are not satisfied on or before Delivery and Lessee (in its absolute discretion) nonetheless agrees to lease the Leased Property from Lessor, then Lessor will ensure that those conditions are fulfilled within one month after the Delivery Date.

3.6 Indemnity for Non-Occurrence of or Delay in Delivery

Lessee shall hold harmless and indemnify Lessor, without prejudice to any of Lessor's other rights under the Operative Documents, from and against all costs, expenses, liabilities, break funding costs and losses incurred by Lessor as a result of or arising out of or directly connected with a delay in or the non-occurrence of Delivery by reason of the failure of Lessee to satisfy all or any of the conditions set out in Sections 3.1 and/or 3.2 within the time set out therein for satisfaction of such conditions.

4. COMMENCEMENT[4]

4.1 Agreement to Lease

(a) Lessor will lease the Leased Property to Lessee and Lessee will take the Leased Property on lease at the Delivery Location on the Delivery Date in accordance with the Operative Documents for the duration of the Term.
(b) Lessor and Lessee intend that this Agreement constitute a "true lease" and a lease for all United States federal income tax purposes.

4. *See* §3.06 of the text *supra*.

4.2 Delivery

(a) Delivery Condition: Lessor shall deliver the Aircraft and the Aircraft Documents to Lessee at the Delivery Location in a condition complying with Schedule 2 except for any items mutually agreed between Lessor and Lessee which are set forth on Annex 2 to the Certificate of Delivery Condition.

(b) Correction of Discrepancies: The obligation of Lessee to lease the Leased Property from Lessor is subject to Lessor delivering the Leased Property to Lessee in compliance with the conditions set forth on Schedule 2. If Lessor corrects all material discrepancies from the conditions set forth on Schedule 2 before Delivery, or if Lessor and Lessee agree that Lessor will correct or pay for their correction as set forth on Annex 2 to the Certificate of Delivery Condition, then Lessee shall accept the Leased Property. If, on the Scheduled Delivery Date, the Aircraft is not, in all material respects, in the condition set forth in Schedule 2 and either Lessor does not correct all material discrepancies or Lessor and Lessee do not agree upon the correction of such material discrepancies within 360 days after the Scheduled Delivery Date, then Lessee may by notice to Lessor terminate this Agreement, in which event neither Lessor nor Lessee shall have any further obligations under this Agreement except as set forth in Section 7.4. If Lessee fails to give any such termination notice within 360 days following the Scheduled Delivery Date, Lessee shall be deemed to have accepted the Leased Property for all purposes of this Agreement.

4.3 Delayed Delivery

If, as a result of the occurrence of damage to the Aircraft not constituting a Total Loss or any Excusable Delay, Lessor delays in the delivery of, or fails to deliver, the Aircraft under this Agreement on the Scheduled Delivery Date, and so long as such failure does not result from the gross negligence or willful misconduct of Lessor, then in any such case:

(a) Lessor will not be responsible for any losses, including loss of profit, costs or expenses arising from or in connection with the delay or failure suffered or incurred by Lessee; and

(b) if the Aircraft is not in the condition provided in Section 4.2(b) within 360 days after the Scheduled Delivery Date, either Lessor or Lessee may terminate this Agreement upon giving five Business Days prior written notice to the other, in which event neither Lessor nor Lessee shall have any further obligations under this Agreement except as set forth in Section 7.4.

4.4 Acceptance and Risk

(a) The Leased Property will be delivered to, and will be accepted by, Lessee at the Delivery Location on the Delivery Date immediately following satisfaction of the conditions precedent specified in Sections 3.1, 3.2 and 3.4 (or their waiver or deferral by the party entitled to grant such waiver or deferral).

(b) Immediately following satisfaction of the conditions precedent specified in Sections 3.1, 3.2 and 3.4 (or their waiver or deferral by the party entitled to grant such waiver or deferral), Lessee and Lessor shall forthwith complete the annexes to the Certificate of Delivery Condition specifying, among other things, the maintenance status of the Airframe, Engines, APU and Landing Gear, and Lessor and Lessee shall sign and deliver to each other the Certificate of Acceptance and the Certificate of Delivery Condition. Delivery of the signed Certificate of Acceptance to Lessor shall constitute deemed delivery of the Aircraft to Lessee.

(c) On and from Delivery, the Leased Property will be in every respect at the sole risk of Lessee, which will bear all risk of loss, theft, damage or destruction to the Leased Property from any cause whatsoever.

(d) On or concurrent with Delivery, Lessee shall take all actions necessary to cause the Aircraft to be registered with the Aviation Authority and permit the operation of the Aircraft by Lessee in its normal passenger operations, including if required, causing this Agreement and the Certificate of Acceptance to be registered with the Aviation Authority.

5. PAYMENTS[5]

5.1 Commitment Fee

On the date that is three (3) Business Days prior to the Scheduled Delivery Date, Lessee shall pay the Commitment Fee to Lessor in immediately available funds. Lessee acknowledges that the Commitment Fee constitutes consideration to Lessor for leasing the Aircraft to Lessee and upon payment irrevocably and unconditionally becomes the unencumbered property of Lessor, free of any claims or rights thereto by Lessee.

5.2 Rental Periods

The first Rental Period will commence on the Delivery Date and end on the day preceding the numerically corresponding day one (1) month after the Delivery Date. Each subsequent Rental Period will commence on the day of each month during the Term which numerically corresponds with the Delivery Date, and will end on the day immediately preceding the first day of the next Rental Period, except that if a Rental Period would otherwise overrun the Expiry Date, it will end on the Expiry Date.

5. *See* §3.07 and §3.08 of the text *supra*.

5.3 Basic Rent

(a) Time of Payment: For each Rental Period during the Term, Lessee shall pay to Lessor or its order Basic Rent in advance on each Rent Date. Lessee shall initiate payment adequately in advance of the Rent Date to ensure that Lessor receives the payment of Basic Rent on the Rent Date.

(b) Amount: The Basic Rent payable in respect of each Rental Period will be the Basic Rent Amount, except that if the final Rental Period contains less than thirty (30) days, the amount of Basic Rent payable in respect of such final Rental Period will be a pro rata amount of the Basic Rent Amount obtained by dividing the Basic Rent Amount by thirty (30) and multiplying the result by the number of days elapsed from, and including, the last Rent Date to, and including, the Expiry Date.

5.4 Additional Rent

(a) Amount: Lessee will pay to Lessor Additional Rent in relation to each calendar month (or portion thereof) during the Term on the 10th day following the end of that calendar month (but not later than the Expiry Date for the last full calendar month and the portion of the calendar month in which the Expiry Date occurs) as follows:
   (i) in respect of the Airframe, Lessee shall pay the Airframe Additional Rent Rate for that calendar month ("Airframe Additional Rent");
   (ii) in respect of each Engine, Lessee shall pay the Engine Additional Rent Rate for that calendar month ("Engine Additional Rent");
   (iii) in respect of each Engine, Lessee shall pay the Engine LLP Additional Rent Rate for that calendar month ("Engine LLP Additional Rent");
   (iv) in respect of the Landing Gear, Lessee shall pay the Landing Gear Additional Rent Rate for that calendar month ("Landing Gear Additional Rent"); and
   (v) in respect of the APU, Lessee shall pay the APU Additional Rent Rate for that calendar month ("APU Additional Rent").

(b) Adjustment: The Additional Rent rates set forth in Section 5.4(a) shall be adjusted as follows:
   (i) the Airframe Additional Rent Rate, the Engine Additional Rent Rate, the Landing Gear Additional Rent Rate and the APU Additional Rent Rate are based on [month][year] Dollars and each such rate, as otherwise adjusted by this Section 5.4(b), shall be increased on the Delivery Date and on the first day of each calendar month in which an anniversary of the Delivery Date occurs at an annual rate of []%, and the adjusted amounts of such rates as of the Delivery Date shall be set forth on the Certificate of Acceptance;

(ii) the Engine LLP Additional Rent Rate shall be adjusted on the Delivery Date and on the first day of each calendar month in which an anniversary of the Delivery Date occurs based on changes in the respective Manufacturer's then current catalog list price, and the adjusted Engine LLP Additional Rent Rate as of the Delivery Date shall be set forth on the Certificate of Acceptance; and

(iii) the Engine Additional Rent Rate is based upon an assumed Flight Hour-to-Cycle ratio of [___]:1.0 or greater, and if any Engine's Flight Hour-to-Cycle ratio is less than [___]:1.0 in any 12-month period (or portion thereof) commencing on the first day of the month in which the Delivery Date or any anniversary of the Delivery Date occurs, Lessee shall pay to Lessor an amount equal to (i) the number of Cycles in such year in excess of a [___]:1.0 Flight Hours-to-Cycles ratio, multiplied by (ii) the Engine Additional Rent Rate in effect on the last day of such period.

5.5 <u>Charged Moneys</u>:

(a) Lessee acknowledges that the Additional Rent constitutes additional Rent payable for the use of the Aircraft and shall irrevocably and unconditionally become the unencumbered property of Lessor upon payment thereof by Lessee, free of any claims or rights thereto by Lessee.

(b) Notwithstanding the intent of Lessor and Lessee stated in Sections 5.1 and 5.5(a), if and to the extent that the Commitment Fee and/or the Additional Rent, or any part thereof, under any Applicable Law or otherwise, is determined to be security deposits or otherwise the property of Lessee or a debt owed to Lessee, or that Lessee shall have any interest in the Commitment Fee and/or the Additional Rent, then Lessee and Lessor agree that Sections 5.5(b)(i) and (ii) below shall apply to the Commitment Fee and/or the Additional Rent (as the case may be) (collectively, the "Charged Moneys"):

(i) To the fullest extent permitted by law and by way of continuing security, Lessee grants a Security Interest in the Charged Moneys and all rights of Lessee to payment thereof, the debt represented thereby and all interest thereon and/or any and all interest of Lessee therein to Lessor by way of first priority Security Interest as security for Lessee's obligations and liability under the Operative Documents (the "Secured Liabilities"). Except as expressly permitted under this Agreement, Lessee will not be entitled to payment of the Charged Moneys. Lessee will not assign, transfer or otherwise dispose of all or part of its rights or interest in the Charged Moneys and Lessee agrees that it will enter into any additional documents and instruments necessary or reasonably requested by Lessor to evidence, create or perfect Lessor's rights to the Charged Moneys.

(ii) If any Event of Default has occurred and is continuing, Lessor may immediately or at any time thereafter, without prior notice to Lessee,

(1) offset all or any part of Secured Liabilities against the liabilities of Lessor in respect of the Charged Moneys, or (2) apply or appropriate the Charged Moneys in or towards the payment or discharge of Secured Liabilities in such order as Lessor sees fit. Upon any offset or application of any portion of the Charged Moneys to the Secured Liabilities, Lessee shall immediately pay to Lessor an amount equal to the amount of the Charged Moneys so offset or applied.

5.6 Payments

(a) All payments of Rent by Lessee to Lessor under this Agreement will be made for value on the due date, for the full amount due, in Dollars and in same day funds, settled through the New York Clearing House System or such other funds as may for the time being be customary for the settlement in New York City of payments in Dollars by telegraphic transfer to the following account for Lessor:

[to be supplied]

or to such other account in North America or the European Union as Lessor may direct by at least five Business Days prior written notice.

(b) If any Rent or other payment would otherwise become due on a day which is not a Business Day, it shall be due on the immediately preceding Business Day.

(c) At the time of each Basic Rent, Additional Rent or other payment, Lessee will complete and fax or email to Lessor a wire transfer disbursement report stating (i) the amount of the payment being made by Lessee, (ii) the allocation of such payment to the Commitment Fee, Basic Rent, Additional Rent, interest at the Overdue Rate, indemnity payments and other charges, and (iii) if any payment includes Additional Rent, the allocation of such payment of Additional Rent to the applicable Additional Rent categories. Notwithstanding the allocation set forth in Lessee's report, during the continuance of an Event of Default, Lessor will have complete discretion to allocate all payments by Lessee as Lessor determines.

5.7 Gross-up

(a) All payments by Lessee under or in connection with the Operative Documents will be made without offset or counterclaim, free and clear of and without deduction or withholding for or on account of any Taxes (other than Taxes that Lessee is compelled by law to deduct or withhold).

(b) All Taxes (other than Non-Indemnified Taxes) in respect of payments under the Operative Documents shall be for the account of Lessee.

(c) If Lessee is compelled by law to make payment to an Indemnitee under or in connection with the Operative Documents subject to any Tax and such Indemnitee does not actually receive for its own benefit on the due date a net amount equal to the full amount provided for under the Operative Documents (other than Non-Indemnified Taxes that Lessee is compelled by law to deduct or withhold), Lessee will pay all necessary additional amounts to ensure receipt by such Indemnitee of the full amount (other than Non-Indemnified Taxes that Lessee is compelled by law to deduct or withhold) provided for under the Operative Documents.

5.8 Taxation

(a) Lessee will on demand pay and indemnify each Tax Indemnitee against all Taxes (other than Non-Indemnified Taxes) levied or imposed against or upon such Tax Indemnitee and relating to or attributable to Lessee, the Operative Documents or the Leased Property directly or indirectly in connection with the importation, exportation, registration, ownership, leasing, subleasing, purchase, delivery, possession, use, operation, repair, maintenance, overhaul, transportation, landing, storage, presence or redelivery of the Aircraft or any part thereof or any rent, receipts, insurance proceeds, income or other amounts arising therefrom.

(b) If any Tax Indemnitee shall, based upon its own reasonable interpretation of any relevant laws or regulations, realize any Tax savings (by way of refund, deduction, credit or otherwise) in respect of any amount with respect to which Lessee shall have made a payment (or increased payment) pursuant to Section 5.7, 5.9 or 5.11 or shall have indemnified such Tax Indemnitee pursuant to Section 5.8(a), or in respect of the occurrence or transaction which gave rise to such payment or indemnification, and such Tax savings shall not have been taken into account previously in calculating any indemnity payment made by Lessee, then such Tax Indemnitee shall, to the extent that it can do so without prejudice to the retention of the relevant savings and subject to Lessee's obligations to repay such amount to such Tax Indemnitee if the relevant savings are subsequently disallowed or canceled, pay to Lessee such amount as such Tax Indemnitee shall in its opinion have concluded to be the amount of such Tax savings (together with, in the case of a refund, any interest received thereon); provided, that such Tax Indemnitee shall not be obliged to make any payment to Lessee pursuant to this Section 5.8(b) to the extent that the amount of any Tax savings in respect of which such payment is to be made would exceed the aggregate amount of all prior payments made by Lessee to, on behalf of or as indemnification of such Tax Indemnitee under this Agreement for Taxes less the amount of all prior payments made pursuant to this Section 5.8(b) in respect of such Tax savings. Lessee acknowledges that nothing contained in this Section 5.8(b) shall interfere with the right of any Tax Indemnitee to arrange its tax affairs in whatsoever proper manner it thinks fit (or give Lessee any right to investigate, or impose any obligation on any Tax Indemnitee to disclose, the same) and, in particular, no Tax Indemnitee shall be under any obligation to claim any Tax savings in priority to any other savings available to it; provided, that subject to the foregoing Lessor shall use reasonable good faith diligence to realize Tax savings as described above.

5.9 Value Added Tax

(a) For purposes of this Section 5.9, "VAT" means value added tax and any goods and services, sales or turnover tax, imposition or levy of a similar nature, and "supply" includes anything on or in respect of which VAT is chargeable.
(b) Lessee shall pay each Tax Indemnitee or the relevant taxing authority, as the case may be, the amount of any VAT chargeable in respect of any supply for VAT purposes under the Operative Documents.
(c) Each amount stated as payable by Lessee under the Operative Documents is exclusive of VAT (if any), and if VAT is payable in respect of any amount payable by Lessee under the Operative Documents, Lessee shall pay all such VAT and shall indemnify each Tax Indemnitee against any claims for the same, and where appropriate Lessee shall increase the payments that would otherwise be required to be made under the Operative Documents so that such Tax Indemnitee is left in the same position as it would have been had no VAT been payable. Lessee shall provide evidence to Lessor, if available, in respect of payment of any VAT paid by Lessee with respect to the Operative Documents.

5.10 Information

If Lessee is required by any Applicable Law, or by any third party, to deliver any report or return in connection with any Taxes, then Lessee will duly complete the same and, in particular, will not state therein that any Person other than Lessee is responsible for the use and operation of the Aircraft and for the Taxes (other than Non-Indemnified Taxes) arising therefrom, and Lessee will, on request, supply a copy of the report or return to any Tax Indemnitee. If Lessee requires any information or cooperation from any Tax Indemnitee in order to satisfy its obligations as set forth above, such Tax Indemnitee shall promptly furnish such information or cooperation as Lessee may reasonably request in writing. If actual notice is given by any taxing authority to Lessor that a report or return is required to be filed with respect to any Taxes (other than Non-Indemnified Taxes), Lessor shall promptly notify Lessee of such required report or return.

5.11 Taxation of Indemnity Payments

(a) If and to the extent that any sums payable to any Tax Indemnitee by Lessee under the Operative Documents by way of indemnity are insufficient, by reason of any Taxes payable in respect of those sums, for such Tax Indemnitee to discharge the corresponding liability to the relevant third party (including any taxation authority), or to reimburse such Tax Indemnitee for the cost incurred by it to a third party (including any taxation authority), Lessee will pay to such Tax Indemnitee such sum as will, after the tax liability has been fully satisfied, leave such Tax Indemnitee with the same amount as it would have been entitled to receive in the absence of that liability, together with interest on the amount of the deficit at the Overdue Rate in respect of the period commencing on the date on which the payment of taxation is finally due until payment by Lessee (both before and after judgment).

(b) If and to the extent that any sums constituting (directly or indirectly) an indemnity to any Tax Indemnitee but paid by Lessee to any Person other than such Tax Indemnitee are treated as taxable in the hands of such Tax Indemnitee, then Lessee will pay to such Tax Indemnitee such sum as will, after the tax liability has been fully satisfied, indemnify such Tax Indemnitee to the same extent as it would have been indemnified in the absence of such liability, together with interest on the amount payable by Lessee under this Section 5.11(b) at the Overdue Rate in respect of the period commencing on the date on which the payment of taxation is finally due until payment by Lessee (both before and after judgment).

5.12 Default Interest

[aa)] If Lessee fails to pay any amount payable under the Operative Documents on the due date, Lessee will pay on demand from time to time to any Indemnitee interest (both before and after judgment) at the Overdue Rate on such amount from the due date to the day of payment in full by Lessee to such Indemnitee. All such interest shall be compounded monthly and calculated on the basis of the actual number of days elapsed assuming a year of 360 days.

[aa)] If, at any time during the Term, either (x) Lessee fails to make any two (2) consecutive payments of Basic Rent, Additional Rent or Commitment Fee installments (or any combination thereof) as and when required by this Agreement or (y) any single Basic Rent, Additional Rent or Commitment Fee installment payment remains due and unpaid for more than sixty (60) days, then the Basic Rent Amount payable by Lessee in accordance with Section 5.3 will automatically increase by five percent (5%) for the remainder of the Term, commencing with the Basic Rent payable immediately after the first to occur of (x) or (y) above. Nothing in this Section 5.12(b) will limit Lessor's right to receive interest at the Overdue Rate on such late payments or Lessor's rights and remedies pursuant to Sections 13.2 and 13.3 on account of such Events of Default.]

5.13 Contest

If a written claim is made against any Tax Indemnitee for or with respect to any Taxes (other than Non-Indemnified Taxes), such Tax Indemnitee shall promptly notify Lessee. If reasonably requested by Lessee in writing within 30 days after such notification, such Tax Indemnitee shall, upon receipt of indemnity satisfactory to such Tax Indemnitee and at the expense of Lessee (including all costs, expenses, losses, legal and accountants' fees and disbursements, penalties and interest), in good faith contest or to the extent permissible by law allow Lessee to contest in Lessee's or such Tax Indemnitee's name, other than the Financing Parties, the validity, applicability or amount of such Taxes by either (i) resisting payment thereof if practicable and permitted by Applicable Law, or (ii) if payment is made, using reasonable efforts to obtain a refund thereof in appropriate administrative and judicial proceedings, and in the contest of any such claim by any Tax Indemnitee, such Tax Indemnitee shall apprise Lessee of all material developments with respect to such contest, shall forward copies of all material submissions made in such contest and shall materially comply in good faith with any reasonable request concerning the conduct of any such contest; provided, that no Tax Indemnitee will be obliged to take any such action:

(a) that such Tax Indemnitee considers, in its reasonable discretion, may prejudice it; or
(b) that such Tax Indemnitee reasonably considers does not have a reasonable prospect of success; or
(c) for which Lessee has not made adequate provision to the reasonable satisfaction of such Tax Indemnitee in respect of the expense concerned; or
(d) that gives rise to any reasonable likelihood of the Aircraft or any interest of any Tax Indemnitee in the Aircraft being sold, forfeited or otherwise lost, or of criminal liability on the part of any Tax Indemnitee.

If any Tax Indemnitee, in accordance with the foregoing, determines to pay such Taxes and seek a refund, Lessee will either pay such Taxes on such Tax Indemnitee's behalf and pay such Tax Indemnitee any amount due with respect to such payment or will promptly reimburse such Tax Indemnitee for such Taxes. If any Tax Indemnitee shall obtain a refund of all or any part of such Taxes paid by Lessee, such Tax Indemnitee shall pay Lessee the amount of such refund; provided, that such amount shall not be payable before such time as Lessee shall have made all payments or indemnities to any Tax Indemnitee then due with respect to Taxes and so long as no Default has occurred and is continuing. If in addition to such refund any Tax Indemnitee shall receive an amount representing interest, attorneys fees or any other amount with respect to such refund, Lessee shall be paid that proportion of such interest, attorneys fees or any other amount which is fairly attributable to the Taxes paid by Lessee prior to the receipt of such refund. No Tax Indemnitee shall enter into a settlement or other compromise with respect to, or otherwise concede, any claim by a taxing authority on account of Taxes being contested by Lessee pursuant to this Section 5.13 without the written consent of Lessee, which consent shall not be unreasonably withheld, unless such Tax Indemnitee waives its right to be indemnified by Lessee with respect to such claim (but not with respect to any future claims).

5.14 Absolute

Lessee's obligations under this Agreement are absolute and unconditional irrespective of any contingency whatever including (but not limited to):

(a) any right of offset, counterclaim, recoupment, reduction, defense or other right which either party to this Agreement may have against the other;
(b) any unavailability of the Aircraft for any reason, including a requisition of the Aircraft or any prohibition or interruption of, interference with or other restriction against Lessee's use, operation or possession of the Aircraft;
(c) any lack or invalidity of title or any other defect in title, airworthiness, merchantability, fitness for any purpose, condition, design or operation of any kind or nature of the Aircraft for any particular use or trade, or for registration or documentation under the laws of any relevant jurisdiction, or any Total Loss in respect of or any damage to the Aircraft;
(d) any insolvency, bankruptcy, reorganization, arrangement, readjustment of debt, dissolution, liquidation or similar proceedings by or against Lessor or Lessee;
(e) any invalidity, unenforceability or lack of due authorization of, or other defect in, this Agreement; or
(f) any other cause which, but for this provision, would or might otherwise have the effect of terminating or in any way affecting any obligation of Lessee under this Agreement;

provided always, however, that this Section 5.14 shall be without prejudice to Lessee's right to claim damages and other relief from the courts in the event of any breach by Lessor of its obligations under this Agreement, or in the event that, as a result of any lack or invalidity of title to the Aircraft on the part of Lessor, Lessee is deprived of its possession of the Aircraft.

5.15 Substitution of Letter of Credit

(a) At any time on or before three (3) Business Days prior to the Delivery Date, so long as no Default is then continuing, Lessee shall have the option to substitute (which once exercised shall be irrevocable) for the Commitment Fee a letter of credit (the "Letter of Credit"), as security for all of the Secured

Liabilities, with a stated amount equal to the Commitment Fee. The Letter of Credit:

(i) shall be in the form set out in Exhibit F or such other form as Lessor may agree or require, acting reasonably;

(ii) shall be issued or confirmed by a first class international bank (or branch thereof) in New York or Los Angeles having at least the Letter of Credit Bank Minimum Rating; and

(iii) shall remain in full force and effect until the Letter of Credit Validity Date (or, if the Letter of Credit is at any time due to expire prior to the Letter of Credit Validity Date, then Lessee shall cause a valid renewal to be issued in a form satisfactory to Lessor not later than 30 days prior to such expiry date, each such renewal being for a period of not less than one year or, if less, until the Letter of Credit Validity Date).

(b) Upon valid substitution by Lessee of a Letter of Credit for the Commitment Fee in accordance with the provisions of this Section 5.15, Lessor shall apply that portion of the Commitment Fee which has not previously been applied or retained as provided for in any Operative Document, without interest, against the next payments of Basic Rent that may come due.

(c) In the event that at any time prior to the Letter of Credit Validity Date the bank issuing or confirming the Letter of Credit no longer has at least the Letter of Credit Bank Minimum Rating, Lessee shall within fourteen days of demand therefor by Lessor provide Lessor with a replacement "Letter of Credit" issued or confirmed by a first class international bank in New York or Los Angeles having at least the Letter of Credit Bank Minimum Rating and otherwise meeting the terms of this Agreement.

(d) If for any reason Lessor is paid under the Letter of Credit, then (a) Lessor may at any time as an agreed remedy, apply or retain all or any portion of the amounts so paid in full or partial payment for amounts constituting or corresponding to the Secured Liabilities and/or may retain all or any portion of the amounts so paid as security for the performance of the Secured Liabilities and any interest earned on the amounts so drawn shall be for Lessor's sole account, and (b) Lessee shall cause an additional "Letter of Credit" to be issued, or shall pay Lessor such amount in cash, so that the Lessor shall at all times have the benefit of cash and/or a Letter of Credit for the full Commitment Fee which would otherwise be required under Section 5.1.

(e) Unless the Letter of Credit is fully drawn, Lessor shall return the Letter of Credit to Lessee not later than 30 days after the date upon which the Aircraft is returned to Lessor in accordance with this Agreement and all of the Secured Liabilities which are then due and payable have been satisfied in full.

6. MANUFACTURER'S AND OTHER WARRANTIES[6]

6.1 Assignment

Notwithstanding this Agreement, Lessor will remain entitled to the benefit of each warranty, express or implied, and any unexpired customer and/or product support given or provided in respect of the Aircraft, any Engine or Part by any manufacturer, vendor, maintenance performer, subcontractor or supplier. Unless an Event of Default shall have occurred and be continuing, Lessor hereby authorizes Lessee during the Term to pursue any claim thereunder in relation to defects affecting the Aircraft, any Engine or Part, and Lessee agrees diligently to pursue any such claim that arises at its own cost. Lessee will notify Lessor promptly upon becoming aware of any such claim. Lessor will provide such assistance to Lessee in making a claim under any such warranties or customer and/or product support as Lessee may reasonably request, and, if requested by Lessee and at Lessee's expense, will pursue a claim in its own name where the relevant manufacturer, vendor, maintenance performer, subcontractor or supplier has refused to acknowledge Lessee's right to pursue that claim, but subject to Lessee first ensuring that Lessor is indemnified and secured to Lessor's reasonable satisfaction against all losses, damages, costs, expenses and liabilities (including fees and disbursements) that Lessor may incur in the taking of any such actions.

6.2 Proceeds

All proceeds of any such claim as is referred to in Section 6.1 and which exceed $100,000 will be paid directly to Lessor at the account set forth in Section 5.6(a), but if and to the extent that such claim relates:

(a) to defects affecting the Aircraft which Lessee has rectified; or
(b) to compensation for loss of use of the Aircraft, an Engine or any Part during the Term; or
(c) to costs incurred by Lessee in pursuing such claim (whether or not proceeds of such claim are payable to Lessee);

and provided no Default shall have occurred and be continuing, the proceeds will be promptly paid to Lessee by Lessor but, in the case of (a), only on receipt of evidence reasonably satisfactory to Lessor that Lessee has rectified the relevant defect.

6.3 Parts

Except to the extent Lessor otherwise agrees in a particular case, Lessee will procure that all engines, components, furnishings or equipment provided by the manufacturer, vendor, maintenance performer, subcontractor or supplier as a replacement for a

6. *See* §3.09 of the text *supra*.

defective Engine or Part pursuant to the terms of any warranty or customer and/or product support arrangement comply with Section 8.13(a), are installed on the Aircraft promptly and that title thereto vests in Lessor in accordance with Section 8.17(b). On installation those items will be deemed to be an Engine or Part, as applicable.

6.4 Agreement

To the extent any warranties or customer and/or product support relating to the Aircraft are made available under an agreement between any Manufacturer, vendor, maintenance performer, subcontractor or supplier and Lessee, this Section 6 is subject to that agreement. However, Lessee will:

(a) pay the proceeds of any claim thereunder to Lessor at the account set forth in Section 5.6(a) to be applied pursuant to Section 6.2 and, pending such payment, will hold the claim and the proceeds in trust for Lessor; and
(b) take all such steps as are necessary and requested by Lessor at the end of the Term to ensure the benefit of any of those warranties or customer and/or product support which have not expired are vested in Lessor.

6.5 Lessee Warranties

Lessee acknowledges that during the Term it might contract with Manufacturers, maintenance and overhaul agencies, subcontractors, suppliers and vendors (each an "MRO") to maintain, provide and service the Airframe, Engines and Parts. At Return, Lessee will irrevocably assign to Lessor all of Lessee's rights regarding the Aircraft under any warranty (express or implied), service policy, maintenance or product agreement provided by any MRO to the extent that such rights are assignable. Lessee will provide such assistance to Lessor in making a claim under any such warranties or customer and/or product support as Lessor may reasonably request. After Return, Lessee will promptly enforce on Lessor's behalf all such rights that are not assignable.

6.6 Final Maintenance Performer Warranties

To the extent that Lessee uses a Final Maintenance Performer for the Return, Lessee will cause its maintenance contracts with each Final Maintenance Performer to contain a provision, satisfactory in form and substance to Lessor, expressly stating that all warranties (express or implied) and product support is made for the benefit of Lessor and its assigns and may be relied upon and enforced directly by Lessor and its assigns without the involvement of Lessee.

7. LESSOR'S COVENANTS AND DISCLAIMERS[7]

7.1 Quiet Enjoyment

Provided no Event of Default shall have occurred and be continuing, none of Lessor, its successors and assigns, any Financing Party or any Person claiming by, through or on account of any of such parties will interfere with the quiet use, possession and enjoyment of the Aircraft by Lessee.

7.2 Lessor's Maintenance Contribution

(a) Airframe Reimbursable Expenses:

(i) Upon the performance by Lessee of a C-Check during the Term of this Agreement, the Lessee's Actual Costs incurred in completing all routine and non-routine C-Check tasks (or the equivalent thereof), but not including the cost of repairs caused by accident, premature or catastrophic failure, faulty maintenance or installation, incident, improper operations, abuse, neglect or misuse or the cost of modifications, interior reconfiguration, the accomplishment of ADs and any overhaul of time controlled components accomplished during the C-Check except such as are part of the tasks included at such C-Check interval, shall constitute "Airframe Reimbursable Expenses".

(ii) Upon the completion of a C-Check, Lessee shall present written evidence satisfactory to Lessor as to the completion of such C-Check, the workscope of such C-Check and the amount of the Airframe Reimbursable Expenses for approval by Lessor. Such evidence shall include a full hardcopy or digital copy of the entire maintenance event and a list of all routine and non-routine work cards with corresponding references to the MPD and an itemized labor and materials report. Upon receipt of such written evidence, and provided there then exists no Default or Event of Default, Lessor shall pay to Lessee (in the case where Lessee performed the work or upon proof that Lessee had paid the independent repair facility that performed such work) or to the independent repair facility performing such work if directed in writing by Lessee and upon receipt of written confirmation from such repair facility that it will apply such payments solely against the costs due for such C-Check, an amount equal to the lesser of (i) the Airframe Reimbursable Expenses or (ii) an amount equal to (1) all Airframe Additional Rent previously paid by Lessee under this Agreement as of the date of completion of the C-Check, minus (2) all previous payments by Lessor under this Section 7.2(a).

7. *See* §3.10 of the text *supra*.

(b) Engine Reimbursable Expenses:

(i) Upon the accomplishment of an Engine Shop Visit of an Engine during the Term, excluding any cost of such Engine Shop Visit to the extent incurred in respect of foreign object damage, ingestion, accident, premature or catastrophic failure, faulty maintenance or installation, incident, abuse, neglect or misuse, Lessee's Actual Costs incurred in completing such Engine Shop Visit, other than costs resulting from elective parts replacement (except to the extent ordinarily accomplished during such maintenance or overhaul) or covered by Engine Manufacturer's service bulletins or which is reimbursable by a claim under the Engine Manufacturer's warranties or by insurance (but including deductibles for purposes of this provision), shall constitute "Engine Reimbursable Expenses".

(ii) Upon accomplishment of any Engine Shop Visit for an Engine, Lessee, within six months of such accomplishment, shall present written evidence satisfactory to Lessor as to the completion of such Engine Shop Visit and the amount of Engine Reimbursable Expenses for approval by Lessor. Such evidence shall include a full hardcopy or digital copy of the entire maintenance event and a description of the reason for removal, a shop tear down report, a shop findings report, a full description of the workscope of the Engine Shop Visit and complete disk records for such Engine both prior to and after the Engine Shop Visit. Both the invoice supplied by the Engine repair facility and that submitted by Lessee to Lessor with respect to such Engine will state whether or not credits were provided due to life remaining on any Parts removed from such Engine and the amount of any such credits will be itemized. Upon receipt of such written evidence, and provided there then exists no Default or Event of Default, Lessor shall pay to Lessee (in the case where Lessee performed the work or upon proof that Lessee had paid the independent repair facility that performed such work) or to the independent repair facility performing such work if directed in writing by Lessee and upon receipt of written confirmation from such repair facility that it will apply such payments solely against the costs due for such Engine Shop Visit, an amount equal to the lesser of (i) the Engine Reimbursable Expenses with respect to such Engine or (ii) an amount equal to (1) all Engine Additional Rent previously paid by Lessee with respect to such Engine pursuant to this Agreement as of the date of completion of the Engine Shop Visit, minus (2) all previous payments by Lessor under this Section 7.2(b) with respect to such Engine (the "Net Available Engine Additional Rent"), subject to the further limitations that such amount payable by Lessor and attributable to:

(A) the high-pressure turbine of such Engine shall not exceed 43 % of the Net Available Engine Additional Rent;

(B) the low-pressure turbine of such Engine shall not exceed 19% of the Net Available Engine Additional Rent;

(C) the high-pressure compressor of such Engine shall not exceed 17% of the Net Available Engine Additional Rent;

(D) the low-pressure compressor of such Engine shall not exceed 13% of the Net Available Engine Additional Rent; and

(E) the fan and gear box of such Engine shall not exceed 8% of the Net Available Engine Additional Rent.

(iii) provided, however, that if the Engine Shop Visit includes a performance restoration in all modules of the Engine then the preceding module percentages shall not apply to the Net Available Engine Additional Rent.

(c) Engine LLP Reimbursable Expenses:

(i) During the performance of an Engine Shop Visit for an Engine during the Term, in the event Lessee is obligated to replace an Engine LLP (the "Replaced LLP") in accordance with the Approved Maintenance Program, excluding any replacements caused by foreign object damage, ingestion, accident, premature or catastrophic failure, faulty maintenance or installation, incident, abuse, neglect, misuse, elective parts replacement (except to the extent ordinarily accomplished during such maintenance) or covered by Manufacturer's service bulletins or which is reimbursable by a claim under the Manufacturer's warranties or by insurance (but including deductibles for purposes of this provision), the Lessee's actual cost to purchase a replacement Engine LLP (the "Replacement LLP") shall constitute "Engine LLP Reimbursable Expenses". For the avoidance of doubt, Engine LLP Reimbursable Expenses shall not include any late charges, mark-ups, interest, handling fees or similar charges associated with the purchase, import or shipping of such Replacement LLP, or any labor associated with the removal or replacement of such Replaced LLP or Replacement LLP.

(ii) Within six months following the accomplishment of any Engine Shop Visit for an Engine, Lessee shall deliver written evidence satisfactory to Lessor as to the amount of Engine LLP Reimbursable Expenses for each Replacement LLP in accordance with the preceding Section 7.2(c)(i). Upon receipt of such written evidence, and provided there then exists no Default or Event of Default, Lessor shall pay to Lessee (in the case where Lessee performed the work or upon proof that Lessee had paid the independent repair facility that performed such work) or to the independent repair facility performing such work if directed in writing by Lessee and upon receipt of written confirmation from such repair facility that it will apply such payments solely against the costs due for such Engine Shop Visit, an amount equal to the product of the following formula with respect to such Replacement LLP:

$$(A - B) \times (C \div D) \times E$$

where

(A) is the number of remaining Cycles on the Replacement LLP at installation;

(B) is the number of remaining Cycles on the Replaced LLP at removal;

(C) is the relevant Manufacturer's catalog price for the Replacement LLP at the time of installation;

(D) is the relevant Manufacturer's catalog price for the entire Engine LLP stack at the time of installation of the Replacement LLP; and

(E) is the weighted mean of the Engine LLP Additional Rent Rates (weighted by the number of months in which each successive adjusted figure for the Engine LLP Additional Rent Rate applies during the period in question) in effect since the previous Engine Shop Visit for such Engine (or since the Delivery Date, if later).

Notwithstanding the foregoing formula, however, Lessor shall not be required to pay to Lessee pursuant to this Section 7.2(c) more than either (A) the Engine LLP Reimbursable Expenses with respect to such Replacement Engine LLP, or (B) all Engine LLP Additional Rent previously paid by Lessee with respect to such Engine as of the date of completion of the Engine Shop Visit minus all previous payments by Lessor under this Section 7.2(c) with respect to such Engine.

(d) Landing Gear Reimbursable Expenses:

(i) Upon the performance by Lessee of a Landing Gear Overhaul during the Term in accordance with the Approved Maintenance Program, excluding a Landing Gear Overhaul caused by accident, faulty maintenance or installation, incident, abuse, neglect or misuse or covered by Manufacturer's service bulletins or which is reimbursable by a claim under the Manufacturer's warranties or by insurance (but including deductibles for purposes of this provision), Lessee's Actual Cost incurred in completing such Landing Gear Overhaul shall constitute "Landing Gear Reimbursable Expenses".

(ii) Upon accomplishment of a Landing Gear Overhaul, Lessee shall, within six months of such accomplishment, present written evidence satisfactory to Lessor as to the completion of such Landing Gear Overhaul, including a full hardcopy or digital copy of the entire maintenance event, and the amount of Landing Gear Reimbursable Expenses for approval by Lessor. Upon receipt of such written evidence, and provided there then exists no Default or Event of Default, Lessor shall pay to Lessee (in the case where Lessee performed the work or upon proof that Lessee had paid the independent repair facility that performed such work) or to the independent repair facility performing such work if directed in writing by Lessee and upon receipt of written confirmation from such repair facility that it will apply such payments solely against the costs due for such Landing Gear Overhaul, an amount equal to the lesser of (i) the Landing Gear Reimbursable Expenses or (ii) an amount equal to (1) all Landing Gear Additional Rent previously paid by Lessee pursuant to this Agreement as of the date of completion of the Landing Gear Overhaul, minus (2) all previous payments by Lessor under this Section 7.2(d).

(e) APU Reimbursable Expenses:

(i) Upon the accomplishment of any APU Basic Shop Visit of the APU during the Term in accordance with the Approved Maintenance Program, but excluding any APU Basic Shop Visit caused by foreign object damage, ingestion, accident, faulty maintenance or installation, incident, abuse, neglect, misuse, elective parts replacement (except to the extent ordinarily accomplished during such APU Basic Shop Visit), the cost of modifications, the accomplishment of Manufacturer's service bulletins or ADs, or costs which are reimbursable by claim under the Manufacturer's warranties or by insurance, Lessee's Actual Cost incurred in completing such APU Basic Shop Visit shall constitute "APU Reimbursable Expenses".

(ii) Upon accomplishment of any APU Basic Shop Visit of the APU, Lessee shall, within six months of such accomplishment, present written evidence satisfactory to Lessor as to the completion of such APU Basic Shop Visit, including a full hardcopy or digital copy of the entire maintenance event, and the amount of APU Reimbursable Expenses for approval by Lessor. Upon receipt of such written evidence, and provided there then exists no Default or Event of Default, Lessor shall pay to Lessee (in the case where Lessee performed the work or upon proof that Lessee had paid the independent repair facility that performed such work) or to the independent repair facility performing such work if directed in writing by Lessee and upon receipt of written confirmation from such repair facility that it will apply such payments solely against the costs due for such APU Basic Shop Visit, an amount equal to the lesser of (i) the APU Reimbursable Expenses or (ii) an amount equal to (1) all APU Additional Rent previously paid by Lessee for the APU pursuant to this Agreement as of the date of completion of the APU Basic Shop Visit, minus (2) all previous payments by Lessor under this Section 7.2(e).

(f) Additional Provisions:

(i) Notwithstanding anything to the contrary contained in this Section 7.2, any such maintenance and the extent and nature of such maintenance to be performed shall be conducted at an Agreed Maintenance Performer. Lessor shall be entitled to have representatives present during the performance of such maintenance to oversee and approve all aspects of such performance, including the workscope thereof. Lessor shall be notified by Lessee prior to the commencement of any maintenance work described in this Section 7.2, including as to the Agreed Maintenance

Performer and for Lessor's reasonable approval of the workscope. If required by the Agreed Maintenance Performer, Lessee shall give written authorization to the Agreed Maintenance Performer granting Lessor and its representatives full access to the maintenance event and all documents and correspondence generated during and as a result of such maintenance event.

(ii) Lessee acknowledges that Lessee is required to pay the full cost of and to perform (or cause to be performed) any check, shop visit, overhaul or other maintenance required by the Approved Maintenance Program, whether or not Lessor is required to make any payments pursuant to this Section 7.2, and any costs incurred by Lessee in performing any such check, shop visit, overhaul or other maintenance required by the Approved Maintenance Program shall be for Lessee's account solely.

(iii) As soon as practicable but, in any case, within 30 days after receipt of a claim for reimbursement of Reimbursable Expenses, Lessor shall (i) notify Lessee in writing of any portion of such claim to which it reasonably objects or for which it reasonably requires additional supporting documentation, and (ii) pay all portions of such claim to which it does not reasonably object or need additional documentation.

7.3 Registration and Filings

Lessor shall, at Lessee's cost:

(a) take all actions reasonably requested by Lessee to enable Lessee to perform its obligations under Section 8.10 regarding the registration of the Aircraft with the Aviation Authority, and not do or suffer to be done anything which might reasonably be expected to adversely affect that registration; and

(b) do all acts and things (including making any filing or registration with the Aviation Authority or any other Government Entity) as may be required following any change in the ownership or financing of the Aircraft.

7.4 Lessor's Obligations Following Termination

So long as no Default has occurred and is continuing, within five Business Days of:

(a) termination of this Agreement before Delivery pursuant to Section 4.2(b), 4.3(b) or 11.1; or

(b) redelivery of the Aircraft to Lessor in accordance with and in the condition required by this Agreement; or

(c) receipt by Lessor of the Agreed Value following a Total Loss and all other amounts due under Section 11.2;

or in any such case at such later time as Lessee has irrevocably paid to Lessor all amounts that are then outstanding under this Agreement, Lessor shall, unless Lessee shall have substituted for the Commitment Fee a Letter of Credit under Section 5.15, pay to Lessee an amount equal to that portion of the Commitment Fee that has not been applied or retained as provided for in any Operative Document without interest.

7.5 Agreed Maintenance Performers

Lessor may object to and may exclude any maintenance organization (other than Lessee) being included as an "Agreed Maintenance Performer" or "Final Maintenance Performer" for a valid business reason. If Lessor wishes to exclude a maintenance organization from being an Agreed Maintenance Performer or Final Maintenance Performer, Lessor shall deliver written notice to such effect to Lessee, which exclusion may be amended by Lessor from time to time. At the request of Lessee, Lessor shall consult in good faith with Lessee regarding any organizations excluded by Lessor pursuant to this Section.

7.6 Exclusion

UPON EXECUTION OF THE CERTIFICATE OF ACCEPTANCE, THE AIRCRAFT IS ACCEPTED BY LESSEE "AS IS, WHERE IS WITH ALL FAULTS" AND LESSEE AGREES AND ACKNOWLEDGES THAT, SAVE AS IS EXPRESSLY STATED IN THIS AGREEMENT, LESSOR WILL HAVE NO LIABILITY IN RELATION TO, AND LESSOR HAS NOT AND WILL NOT BE DEEMED TO HAVE MADE OR GIVEN, ANY WARRANTIES OR REPRESENTATIONS, EXPRESS OR IMPLIED, WITH RESPECT TO THE AIRCRAFT, INCLUDING:

(a) THE DESCRIPTION, AIRWORTHINESS, MERCHANTABILITY, FITNESS FOR ANY USE OR PURPOSE, VALUE, CONDITION, OR DESIGN, OF THE AIRCRAFT OR ANY PART; OR
(b) ANY OBLIGATION, LIABILITY, RIGHT, CLAIM OR REMEDY IN TORT, WHETHER OR NOT ARISING FROM LESSOR'S NEGLIGENCE, ACTUAL OR IMPUTED (BUT EXCLUDING ANY SUCH OBLIGATION, LIABILITY, RIGHT, CLAIM OR REMEDY IN TORT WHICH ARISES FROM LESSOR'S GROSS NEGLIGENCE OR WILFUL MISCONDUCT); OR
(c) ANY OBLIGATION, LIABILITY, RIGHT, CLAIM OR REMEDY FOR LOSS OF OR DAMAGE TO THE AIRCRAFT, FOR ANY LIABILITY OF LESSEE TO ANY THIRD PARTY, OR FOR ANY OTHER DIRECT, INDIRECT, INCIDENTAL OR CONSEQUENTIAL DAMAGES.

7.7 Lessee's Waiver

LESSEE HEREBY WAIVES, AS BETWEEN ITSELF AND LESSOR, ALL ITS RIGHTS IN RESPECT OF ANY WARRANTY OR REPRESENTATION, EXPRESS OR IMPLIED, ON THE PART OF LESSOR AND ALL CLAIMS AGAINST LESSOR HOWSOEVER AND WHENEVER ARISING AT ANY TIME IN RESPECT OF OR OUT OF THE CONDITION, OPERATION OR PERFORMANCE OF THE AIRCRAFT OR THIS AGREEMENT EXCEPT AS IS OTHERWISE EXPRESSLY STATED IN THIS AGREEMENT.

7.8 Lessee's Confirmation

LESSEE CONFIRMS THAT IT IS FULLY AWARE OF THE PROVISIONS OF SECTIONS 7.6 AND 7.7 AND ACKNOWLEDGES THAT BASIC RENT, ADDITIONAL RENT AND ALL OTHER AMOUNTS PAYABLE BY LESSEE UNDER THIS AGREEMENT HAVE BEEN CALCULATED NOTWITHSTANDING ITS PROVISIONS.

7.9 Conclusive Proof

DELIVERY BY LESSEE TO LESSOR OF THE CERTIFICATE OF ACCEPTANCE WILL BE CONCLUSIVE PROOF AS BETWEEN LESSOR AND LESSEE THAT LESSEE HAS EXAMINED AND INVESTIGATED THE AIRCRAFT, THAT THE AIRCRAFT AND THE AIRCRAFT DOCUMENTS ARE SATISFACTORY TO LESSEE AND THAT LESSEE HAS IRREVOCABLY AND UNCONDITIONALLY ACCEPTED THE AIRCRAFT FOR LEASE HEREUNDER WITHOUT ANY RESERVATIONS WHATSOEVER (EXCEPT FOR ANY DISCREPANCIES WHICH MAY BE NOTED IN THE CERTIFICATE OF DELIVERY CONDITION).

8. LESSEE'S COVENANTS[8]

8.1 Duration

The undertakings in Sections 8, 12 and Schedule 3 will:

(a) except as otherwise stated, be performed at the expense of Lessee; and
(b) remain in force until redelivery of the Aircraft to Lessor in accordance with this Agreement and thereafter to the extent of any accrued rights of Lessor in relation to those undertakings.

8. *See* §3.10 and Annex 9 of the text *supra*.

8.2 Information

Lessee shall:

(a) furnish to Lessor:

(i) within 60 days after the last day of the first three fiscal quarters of each fiscal year of Lessee, unaudited consolidated quarterly financial statements of Lessee prepared for such quarter, including a consolidated balance sheet of Lessee and its Subsidiaries as of the last day of such quarter and consolidated statements of income and retained earnings for such fiscal quarter and for the year to date and, on a comparative basis, figures for the corresponding periods of the immediately preceding fiscal year, all in reasonable detail, each such statement to be certified in a certificate of Lessee's chief financial officer or chief accounting officer as fairly presenting the financial position and the results of operations of the Lessee as at its date and for such quarter (subject to year-end audit adjustments) and as having been prepared in accordance with GAAP;

(ii) as soon as available but not in any event later than 90 days after the last day of each fiscal year of Lessee, audited consolidated financial statements of Lessee prepared for such year, including a consolidated balance sheet of Lessee and its Subsidiaries as of the last day of such year, consolidated statements of income and retained earnings of Lessee and its Subsidiaries for such fiscal year, a consolidating balance sheet of Lessee and its Subsidiaries as of the last day of such year and consolidating statements of income and retained earnings of Lessee and its Subsidiaries for such fiscal year and in all cases on a comparative basis figures for the immediately preceding fiscal year, all in reasonable detail, each prepared in accordance with GAAP and certified without qualification by one of the largest international firms of independent certified public accountants as fairly presenting the financial position and the results of operations of Lessee and its Subsidiaries at the end of and for such fiscal year and as having been prepared in accordance with GAAP;

(iii) in lieu of delivering to Lessor the financial statements referred to in Sections 8.2(a)(i) and (ii) above, Lessee may cause such financial statements to be publicly available on the internet within the time periods set forth in Sections 8.2(a)(i) and (ii) above at a location identified to Lessor in writing;

(iv) concurrently with the financial statements furnished pursuant to Sections 8.2(a)(i) and (ii) above, an officer's certificate signed by the chief financial officer or chief accounting officer of Lessee certifying to the best knowledge after due inquiry of such officer that no Default occurred during the period covered by such financial statements and no Default exists on the date of such officer's certificate or, if a Default occurred or exists, stating that fact and specifying the nature and period of existence of such Default and the actions Lessee took or proposes to take with respect to such Default;

(v) at the same time as it is issued to the creditors of Lessee, a copy of each notice or circular issued to Lessee's creditors as a group; and

(vi) on request from time to time such other information regarding Lessee and its business and affairs as Lessor may reasonably request, including copies of all statements of account of any Government Entity or other Person in respect of any Flight Charges;

(b) on request, inform Lessor as to the current location of the Airframe and Engines, the serial number and owner of any engine installed on the Airframe and the serial number, registration mark and owner of any airframe on which an Engine is installed;

(c) promptly furnish to Lessor all information that Lessor from time to time reasonably requests regarding the Aircraft, any Engine or any Part and its use, location and condition, including the hours available on the Aircraft and any Engine until the next scheduled check, inspection, overhaul or shop visit, as the case may be;

(d) on request, furnish to Lessor evidence reasonably satisfactory to Lessor that all Taxes and charges incurred by Lessee with respect to the Aircraft have been paid and discharged in full;

(e) provide to Lessor, within five days following the end of each calendar month during the Term, a monthly report on the Aircraft in the form set out in Exhibit E or such other form as Lessee may select providing substantially the same information;

(f) promptly notify Lessor of:

(i) any Total Loss, any Engine Loss, any theft of the Airframe or any Engine, any damage to the Aircraft if the potential cost of repair may reasonably be expected to exceed the Damage Notification Threshold or any modification to the Aircraft if the potential cost may reasonably be expected to exceed the Damage Notification Threshold;

(ii) any claim or other occurrence likely to give rise to a claim under the Insurances (but, in the case of hull claims only, in excess of the Damage Notification Threshold) and details of any negotiations with the insurance brokers over any such claim; and

(iii) any litigation, arbitration or administrative proceedings that are pending or, to Lessee's knowledge, threatened against Lessee which, if adversely determined, would have a material adverse effect upon its financial condition or business or its ability to perform its obligations under the Operative Documents; and

(iv) as soon as any officer of Lessee obtains knowledge thereof, any Default or Event of Default.

8.3 Operation of the Aircraft

Lessee shall:

(a) comply with all Applicable Law for the time being in force in any country or jurisdiction in which the Aircraft is being operated which is applicable to the Aircraft or the use and operation of the Aircraft;

(b) not use the Aircraft in any manner contrary to any recommendation of the Aviation Authority or any applicable Manufacturer, contrary to any rule or regulation of the Aviation Authority or for any purpose for which the Aircraft is not designed or reasonably suitable;

(c) ensure that the crew and engineers employed by it in connection with the operation and maintenance of the Aircraft have the qualifications and hold the licences required by the Aviation Authority and Applicable Law;

(d) use the Aircraft solely in commercial or other operations for which Lessee is duly authorized by the Aviation Authority and Applicable Law;

(e) not knowingly use the Aircraft (or use it when Lessee ought reasonably to have known that it was being so used) for the carriage of:

  (i) whole animals, living or dead, except in the cargo compartments according to IATA regulations, and except domestic pet animals carried in a suitable container to prevent the escape of any liquid and to ensure the welfare of the animal;

  (ii) acids, toxic chemicals, mercury, other corrosive materials, explosives, nuclear fuels, nuclear wastes or any nuclear assemblies or components, except as permitted for cargo aircraft under the "Restriction of Goods" schedule issued by IATA from time to time and provided that all the requirements for packaging or otherwise contained therein are fulfilled;

  (iii) any other goods, materials or items of cargo which could reasonably be expected to cause damage to the Aircraft and which would not be adequately covered by the Insurances; or

  (iv) any illegal item or substance;

(f) not utilize the Aircraft for purposes of training, qualifying or re-confirming the status of cockpit personnel except for the benefit of Lessee's cockpit personnel, and then only if the use of the Aircraft for such purpose is not disproportionate to the use for such purpose of other aircraft of the same type operated by Lessee;

(g) not (other than for bona fide safety reasons) cause or permit the Aircraft to proceed to, or remain at, any location which is for the time being the subject of a prohibition order (or any similar order or directive) by:

  (i) any Government Entity of the State of Registration or the Habitual Base; or

  (ii) any Government Entity of the country in which such location is situated; or

(iii) any Government Entity having jurisdiction over Lessor, any Financing Party or the Aircraft;

(h) obtain and maintain in full force all certificates, licences, permits and authorizations required for the use and operation of the Aircraft for the time being, and for the making of payments required by, and the compliance by Lessee with its other obligations under, this Agreement;

(i) not change the location of the Habitual Base of the Aircraft; and

(j) not operate the Aircraft to, from or in any country that is the subject of sanctions under United Nations Security Council directives that prohibit use of the Aircraft.

8.4 Taxes and Other Charges

As between Lessor and Lessee, Lessee shall be responsible for all fees, expenses, charges and other costs related to the use, operation and maintenance of the Leased Property, and shall promptly pay:

(a) all licence and registration fees, Taxes, Flight Charges and other amounts of any nature imposed by any Government Entity that are imposed on Lessee or for which Lessee is responsible under the Operative Documents with respect to the Aircraft, including the purchase, ownership, delivery, leasing, possession, use, operation, return, sale or other disposition of the Aircraft;

(b) all rent, fees, charges, Taxes imposed on Lessee and other amounts in respect of any premises where the Aircraft or any Part thereof is located from time to time during the Term; and

(c) all sums due by Lessee to any relevant ATC/Airport Authority in respect of all aircraft (including the Aircraft) operated by Lessee before such sums become overdue and in default,

except to the extent that such payment is being contested in good faith by appropriate proceedings in accordance with Section 5.13.

8.5 Subleasing

Lessee will not sublease or otherwise part with possession of the Aircraft, the Engines or any Part except that Lessee may part with possession:

(a) with respect to the Aircraft, the Engines or any Part, to the relevant manufacturers for testing or similar purposes, or to an Agreed Maintenance Performer or Final Maintenance Performer for service, repair, maintenance or overhaul work or for alterations, modifications or additions to the extent required or permitted by this Agreement;

(b) with respect to an Engine or Part, as expressly permitted by this Agreement;

(c) provided that no Default shall have occurred and be continuing, with respect to the Aircraft or an Engine, pursuant to an ACMI (aircraft, crew, maintenance and insurance) or "wet" lease or charter of the Aircraft in which operational control of the Aircraft remains with Lessee at all times (each a "Wet Lease"), provided (i) the Aircraft remains registered with the Aviation Authority, (ii) the Aircraft shall be maintained, insured and otherwise operated in accordance with the provisions of this Agreement, (iii) Lessee has given written notice to Lessor of such Wet Lease at least two (2) days prior to the date on which it is proposed that such Wet Lease begin, (iv) prior to the start of the Wet Lease, Lessee delivers to Lessor an original executed counterpart of the agreement documenting the Wet Lease and (v) prior to the start of such Wet Lease, the party contracting with Lessee for such service shall deliver to Lessor a written confirmation, in form and substance satisfactory to Lessor, that it will recognize the respective rights, title and interest of Lessor and any Financing Party in the Aircraft, that it will not seek to exercise any rights whatsoever in relation thereto and that it agrees that any right between it and Lessee is subject and subordinate to this Agreement; and

(d) with respect to the Aircraft, pursuant to a code-sharing arrangement so long as operational control of the Aircraft remains with Lessee at all times.

8.6 Inspection

(a) Lessor, any Financing Party and any Person designated by Lessor or any Financing Party may at any time visit, inspect and survey the Aircraft, any Engine or any Part and for such purpose may, subject to any applicable Aviation Authority regulation, travel on the flight deck as observer. Lessor, any Financing Party or any designee shall not be restricted during such inspection from opening any panels, bays or doors on the Aircraft or from inspecting any part of the Aircraft.

(b) Lessee shall have no responsibility for the costs and expenses of Lessor and any Financing Party in connection with any such visit, inspection or survey unless an Event of Default has occurred and is continuing or the visit, inspection or survey discloses that Lessee is in breach of its material obligations under this Agreement, in which case such costs and expenses shall be paid by Lessee on demand.

(c) Lessor shall:

  (i) have no duty to make, or liability arising out of, any such visit, inspection or survey; and

  (ii) so long as no Default has occurred and is continuing, not exercise such right other than on reasonable notice and so as not to disrupt unreasonably the maintenance or operation of the Aircraft.

8.7 Protection of Title

Lessee acknowledges that title to the Aircraft shall at all times be and remain solely and exclusively vested in Lessor and that the Operative Documents constitute for all purposes, including tax purposes, an agreement by Lessor to lease the Aircraft to Lessee and, accordingly, Lessee shall:

(a) not do or knowingly permit to be done or omit or knowingly permit to be omitted to be done any act or thing which might reasonably be expected to jeopardize the respective rights, title and interest of any Financing Party as mortgagee of the Aircraft and assignee of this Agreement or Lessor as owner of the Aircraft and lessor under this Agreement, or the validity, enforceability or priority of any Financing Security Document or which would be likely to expose Lessor or any Financing Party to any criminal or civil liability;
(b) on all occasions when the ownership of the Aircraft, any Engine or any Part is relevant, make clear to third parties that title is held by Lessor and is subject to any Financing Security Document;
(c) not at any time:
  (i) represent or hold out Lessor or any Financing Party as carrying goods or passengers on the Aircraft or as being in any way connected or associated with any operation or carriage (whether for hire or reward or gratuitously) which may be undertaken by Lessee; or
  (ii) pledge the credit of Lessor or any Financing Party;
(d) ensure that there is always affixed, and not removed or in any way obscured, a fireproof plate (having dimensions of not less than 6 in. x 4 in.) in a reasonably prominent position on the Aircraft stating:
  (i) "This Aircraft (msn [msn]) is owned by [Insert Name and Address of Lessor]"
(e) ensure that there is always affixed on each Engine, and not removed or in any way obscured, a fireproof plate in a prominent position near such Engine's data plate stating:

(e) "This Engine (esn [Insert esn]) is owned by [Insert Name of Lessor]"

(f) not create or permit to exist any Security Interest upon the Aircraft, any Engine or any Part, except Permitted Liens and will promptly take, or cause to be taken, such actions as may be necessary to discharge any such Security Interest (other than Permitted Liens) that may at any time arise, exist or be levied upon the Aircraft, any Engine or Part;
(g) not do or permit to be done anything which may reasonably be expected to expose the Aircraft, any Engine or any Part to penalty, forfeiture, impounding, detention, appropriation, damage or destruction and, without prejudice to the foregoing, if any such penalty, forfeiture, impounding, detention, appropriation, damage or destruction occurs, give Lessor notice and use its best efforts

to procure the immediate release of the Aircraft, such Engine or such Part, as the case may be;

(h) not abandon the Aircraft, any Engine or any Part;

(i) pay and discharge or cause to be paid and discharged when due and payable or make adequate provision by way of security or otherwise for all debts, damages, claims and liabilities which have given or might reasonably be expected to give rise to a Security Interest over or affecting the Aircraft, any Engine or any Part; and

(j) not attempt, or hold itself out as having any power, to sell, lease or otherwise dispose of the Aircraft, any Engine or any Part other than as expressly permitted by this Agreement.

8.8 General

Lessee will:

(a) not make any substantial change in the nature of the business in which it is engaged if such change, in the reasonable opinion of Lessor, might reasonably be expected to have a material adverse effect on Lessee's performance of its obligations under the Operative Documents;

(b) preserve its corporate existence, and will not merge or consolidate with any Person, or sell all or substantially all of its assets to any Person, unless the successor Person resulting from such merger or consolidation or purchasing all or substantially all of Lessee's assets (in each event, the "Successor"):

   (i) is a Person incorporated, formed or organized under the laws of the State of Organization, any state or province of the United States of America or the Dominion of Canada, a member of the European Union or another jurisdiction consented to in writing by Lessor;

   (ii) has a net worth immediately after such merger, consolidation or purchase of Lessee's assets that is not less than Lessee's net worth immediately prior to such transaction;

   (iii) is authorized under Applicable Law to perform Lessee's obligations under the Operative Documents to the same extent as Lessee;

   (iv) delivers to Lessor an agreement in form and substance reasonably satisfactory to Lessor containing an assumption by the Successor of Lessee's representations and warranties under this Agreement, together with the due and punctual performance of all of Lessee's obligations under the Operative Documents; and

   (v) delivers to Lessor an opinion of counsel reasonably satisfactory in form and substance to Lessor covering the Operative Documents and the agreement referred to in Section 8.8(b)(iv) above and substantially in the form of the legal opinion delivered pursuant to Section 3.1(d)(i).

8.9 Records

Lessee shall procure that accurate, complete and current records of all flights made by, and all maintenance, repairs, replacements, removals, modifications, alterations and additions carried out on or made to, the Aircraft (including, in relation to each Engine or Part subsequently installed, before its installation) are kept in English, and shall keep the records in such manner as the Aviation Authority, EASA and the FAA may from time to time require. In addition, all Airframe and Engine LLPs installed or replaced during the Term shall have documentation substantiating traceability "back-to-birth" to confirm current accumulated Flight Hours and Cycles. The records will form part of the Aircraft Documents.

8.10 Registration and Filings

Lessee shall at its cost:

(a) maintain the registration of the Aircraft with the Aviation Authority reflecting (so far as permitted by Applicable Law) the interests of the Lessor and not do or suffer to be done anything which might reasonably be expected to adversely affect that registration;

(b) do all acts and things (including making any filing or registration with the Aviation Authority or any other Government Entity) and execute and deliver all documents (including any amendment of this Agreement) as may be required by the Lessor:

   (i) following any change or proposed change in the ownership or financing of the Aircraft or in the manner of securing the Lessor's obligations to the Financing Parties;

   (ii) following any modification of the Aircraft, any Engine or any Part or the permanent replacement of any Engine or Part in accordance with this Agreement, so as to ensure that the respective rights of the Lessor and any Financing Party under this Agreement apply with the same effect as before; or

   (iii) to establish, maintain, preserve, perfect and protect the rights of Lessor under this Agreement and in and to the Aircraft; and

(c) without limitation to the generality of Section 8.10(b) above, if at any time in the State of Registration there shall be, or be brought into force, any legislative or other provisions giving effect to the Geneva Convention of 1948 or the Cape Town Convention on International Interests in Mobile Equipment and the Aircraft Equipment Protocol thereto (the "Cape Town Convention") or otherwise relating to the recognition of rights in aircraft, do and join with Lessor in doing all such acts as may be necessary to perfect recognition of Lessor's title and interest in, and the interests of any Financing Party in, the Aircraft in accordance with such legislative or other provisions. Lessee hereby irrevocably consents to Lessor's registering this Agreement under the Cape Town Convention.

8.11 Maintenance and Repair

Lessee shall:

(a) keep the Aircraft airworthy in all respects and in good repair and condition, and all maintenance will be carried out to the standards of major international air carriers;

(b) incorporate in the Approved Maintenance Program (i) a CPCP as recommended by the Airframe Manufacturer, (ii) any aging aircraft program as recommended by the Airframe Manufacturer, (iii) any SID program approved by the Airframe Manufacturer, and (iv) an anti-fungus and anti-biological growth and contamination prevention, control and treatment program for all fuel tanks in accordance with the Airframe Manufacturer's approved procedures;

(c) maintain the Aircraft in accordance with FAR Part 121 and all rules and regulations of the Aviation Authority as are applicable to passenger aircraft of the same type as the Aircraft, and maintain the Aircraft to as to comply at all times with the type certificate specification and data sheets for the Aircraft;

(d) maintain the Aircraft in accordance with the Approved Maintenance Program through Agreed Maintenance Performers and perform (at the respective intervals provided in the Approved Maintenance Program) all Major Checks, and (i) Lessor shall be notified by Lessee prior to the commencement of any Major Checks, including as to the Agreed Maintenance Performer and for Lessor's reasonable approval of the workscope, (ii) Lessor shall be entitled to have representatives present during the performance of all Major Checks to oversee and approve all aspects of such performance, including the workscope thereof and (iii) if required by the Agreed Maintenance Performer, Lessee shall give written authorization to the Agreed Maintenance Performer granting Lessor and its representatives full access to the Major Check and all documents and correspondence generated during and as a result of such maintenance event.

(e) advise Lessor in writing of all material changes to the Approved Maintenance Program, and shall not (i) change the intervals between Major Checks under the Approved Maintenance Program without the written consent of Lessor, or (ii) change the Approved Maintenance Program in any other material respect without the written consent of Lessor unless recommended by the applicable Manufacturer or mandated by the Aviation Authority;

(f) comply with all mandatory inspection and modification requirements, ADs and similar requirements applicable to the Aircraft, any Engine or Part having a compliance date on or before the Expiry Date and that are required by the Aviation Authority, EASA or the FAA;

(g) comply with all alert service bulletins issued by any manufacturer of the Aircraft, Engines or Parts, and comply (including scheduling compliance work and then performing such work on schedule) with all other service bulletins issued by any such manufacturer if and to the extent that Lessee brings or schedules to bring in compliance at least one-half of the applicable aircraft it operates (excluding for purposes of such calculation aircraft acquired from unrelated third parties that already comply with such other service bulletins);

(h) comply with all Applicable Laws and the regulations of the Aviation Authority and any other aviation authorities with jurisdiction over Lessee or the Aircraft, any Engine or Part that relate to the maintenance, condition, use or operation of the Aircraft or require any modification or alteration to the Aircraft, any Engine or Part;

(i) maintain in good standing a certificate of airworthiness for the Aircraft in the appropriate category for the nature of the operations of the Aircraft issued by the Aviation Authority except when the Aircraft is undergoing maintenance, modification or repair required or permitted by this Agreement, and from time to time Lessee shall provide to Lessor a copy on request;

(j) if required by the Aviation Authority, maintain a current certification as to maintenance issued by or on behalf of the Aviation Authority in respect of the Aircraft and shall from time to time provide to Lessor a copy on request;

(k) maintain the Engines with respect to overhaul build standards and disc replacements at a level which is consistent with the level applied by Lessee in relation to other engines of the same type as the Engines in its fleet;

(l) maintain the Engines and the APU in an "on condition" program as set forth in the respective Manufacturer's maintenance manual;

(m) not enter into any engine maintenance cost per flight hour, power-by-the-hour or similar agreement with the Engine manufacturer or any other engine maintenance facility or organization that includes any Engine without Lessor's prior written consent;

(n) subject to Section 11.3, procure promptly the replacement of any Engine or Part which has become time, cycle or calendar expired, lost, stolen, seized, confiscated, destroyed, damaged beyond repair, unserviceable or permanently rendered unfit for use, with an engine or part complying with the conditions set out in Section 8.13(a);

(o) accomplish all repairs, modifications and alterations in accordance with the SRM or, if the repair, modification or alteration is outside the scope of the SRM, as recommended in writing by the applicable manufacturer and approved by the Aviation Authority;

(p) provide Lessor with a written summary of all sampling programs involving or affecting the Aircraft;

(q) ensure that overhauls are accomplished following the respective Manufacturer's recommendations and using maintenance and quality control procedures approved by the Aviation Authority, and that each Agreed Maintenance Performer provides a complete record of all work performed during the course of such overhaul was accomplished in accordance with Aviation Authority, EASA and FAA requirements; and

(r) comply with the provisions of Section 11.4 in connection with any accident or incident involving the Aircraft.

8.12 <u>Removal of Engines and Parts</u>

Lessee will ensure that no Engine or Part installed on the Aircraft is at any time removed from the Aircraft other than:

(a) if replaced as expressly permitted by this Agreement; or

(b) if the removal is of an obsolete item and is in accordance with the Approved Maintenance Program; or

(c) pursuant to, and in accordance with, Section 8.15; or

  (i) during the course of maintaining, servicing, repairing, overhauling or testing that Engine or the Aircraft, as the case may be; or

  (ii) as part of a normal engine or part rotation program; or

  (iii) for the purpose of making such modifications to the Engine or the Aircraft, as the case may be, as are permitted under this Agreement,

(d) and then in each case only if it is reinstalled or replaced by an engine or part complying with Section 8.13(a) as soon as practicable and in any event no later than the Expiry Date.

8.13 <u>Installation of Engines and Parts</u>

(a) Lessee will ensure that, except as permitted by this Agreement, and (in the case of an engine) subject to Section 8.13(d), no engine or part is installed on the Aircraft unless:

  (i) in the case of an engine, it (1) is an engine of the same model as, or an improved or advanced version of the Engine it replaces (provided, in the case of an improved or advanced version, it can be installed and operated on the Airframe without modification of the Airframe or the engine, whether or not the other installed Engine is also such an improved or advanced version), (2) is in the same or better operating condition, has substantially similar hours available until the next scheduled checks, inspections, overhauls and shop visits and has the same or greater value and utility as the replaced Engine, (3) has attached to it a current "serviceable tag" issued by the Engine Manufacturer or an approved vendor indicating that the engine is new, serviceable or overhauled (and Lessee shall retain all such tags), and (4) shall be accompanied by documentation establishing traceability "back-to-birth" for all installed LLPs;

(ii) in the case of a part, it (1) is in as good operating condition, (2) has substantially similar hours available until the next scheduled checks, inspections, overhauls and shop visits, is of the same or a more advanced make and model, and is of the same interchangeable modification status as the replaced Part, (3) has attached to it a current "serviceable tag" issued by the manufacturer or approved vendor indicating that the part is new, serviceable or overhauled (and Lessee shall retain all such tags), and (4) is accompanied by documentation establishing traceability "back-to-birth";

(iii) in the case of a part that is replacing a Part in an Engine, Landing Gear or APU, the part is an OEM Part unless Lessee has obtained Lessor's prior written approval to use a non OEM Part, which approval, if given, will generally be given only for the installation of PMA Parts manufactured in accordance with FAR Part 21.303 (or its EASA equivalent) that are consumable parts such as brackets, gaskets and seals; the use of stationary or high energy rotating PMA Parts in the Engine or APU gas path will generally not be approved by Lessor; any proposed repair to an OEM Part or PMA Part in an Engine, Landing Gear or APU that has been approved by an FAA Designated Engineering Representative (DER) (or its EASA equivalent) must also be approved by Lessor prior to performance of the repair;

(iv) in the case of a part, it has become and remains the property of Lessor free from Security Interests and on installation on the Aircraft will, without further act, be subject to this Agreement, in which case title to the removed part shall automatically become vested in Lessee without further action or warranty on the part of Lessor except that such Part shall be free of Lessor Liens; and

(v) in each case, Lessee has full details as to its source and maintenance records.

(b) If no Default has occurred and is continuing, Lessee will be entitled to install any engine or part on the Aircraft by way of replacement notwithstanding Section 8.13(a), but (in the case of an engine) subject to Section 8.13(d), if:

(i) there is not available to Lessee at the time and in the place that engine or part is required to be installed on the Aircraft a replacement engine or part complying with the requirements of Section 8.13(a);

(ii) it would result in an unreasonable disruption of the operation of the Aircraft or the business of Lessee to ground the Aircraft until an engine or part complying with Section 8.13(a) becomes available for installation on the Aircraft; and

(iii) as soon as practicable after installation of the same on the Aircraft but, in any event, no later than the earlier of (1) 60 days after such installation and (2) the Expiry Date, Lessee removes any such engine or part and replaces it with the Engine or Part replaced by it or by an engine or part complying with Section 8.13(a).

(c) If no Default has occurred which is continuing, Lessee will be entitled to install Third Party Engines and Lessee Installed Parts on the Airframe by way of replacement notwithstanding Section 8.13(a)(i) and (ii), respectively, so long as:
  (i) the terms of any lease, conditional sale agreement or security agreement, as the case may be, covering such Third Party Engine or Lessee Installed Part will not have the effect of prejudicing the title and interest of Lessor in and to the Aircraft (including its Engines and Parts);
  (ii) the secured party, lessor or conditional vendor, as the case may be, of such Third Party Engine or Lessee Installed Part has confirmed and acknowledged in writing (which confirmation and acknowledgment may be contained in the lease, conditional sale agreement or security agreement covering such Third Party Engine or Lessee Installed Part, as applicable) to Lessor that it will recognize the respective rights, title and interest of Lessor in and to the Aircraft (including its Engines and Parts) and that it will not seek to exercise any rights whatever in relation thereto, and Lessee so agrees to the extent that title is held by it; and
  (iii) before the Expiry Date (1) Lessee removes any such Third Party Engine and replaces it with the Engine replaced by it, and (2) Lessee removes any such Lessee Installed Part and replaces it with the Part replaced by it or by another part, in either case complying with Section 8.13(a).

(d) Lessor agrees, for the benefit of any mortgagee, conditional vendor or holder of any other Security Interest in any Third Party Engine installed on the Airframe that Lessor shall not claim any title to or interest in any such Third Party Engine as the result of such Third Party Engine being installed on the Airframe; provided, that the agreement by Lessor set forth in this Section 8.13(d) is subject to Lessor's rights to take possession of the Aircraft under Section 13.2(c)(i) and/or to require Lessee to redeliver the Aircraft under Section 13.2(c)(ii) with such Third Party Engine installed. Lessee shall have full authority at all relevant times to comply with the provisions of this Section 8.13(d) in respect of any engine installed by it on the Aircraft pursuant to Section 8.13(a) or 8.13(c).

8.14 <u>Non-Installed Engines and Parts</u>

(a) Lessee shall ensure that any Engine or Part that is not installed on the Airframe (or any other airframe as permitted by this Agreement) is, except as expressly permitted by this Agreement, properly and safely stored and kept free from Security Interests (other than Permitted Liens), with insurance thereon complying with the requirements of this Agreement.

(b) Lessee shall notify Lessor whenever an Engine is removed from the Aircraft and, from time to time, upon request procure that any Person to whom possession of an Engine is given acknowledges in writing to Lessor, in form and substance satisfactory to Lessor, that such Person will respect the interests of Lessor in such Engine and will not seek to exercise any rights whatsoever in relation to such Engine.

(c) Notwithstanding Section 8.14(a), Lessee shall be permitted, if no Default has occurred and is continuing, to install any Engine on an airframe and any Part on an airframe or engine:
   (i) owned and operated by Lessee free from Security Interests, other than Permitted Liens;
   (ii) leased or hired to Lessee pursuant to a lease or conditional sale agreement on a long-term basis and on terms whereby Lessee has full operational control of that aircraft or engine; or
   (iii) acquired or financed by Lessee and operated by Lessee on terms that ownership of that aircraft or engine, as the case may be, pursuant to a lease, conditional sale agreement or Security Interest is vested in or held by any other Person;

(d) provided, that in the case of (ii) and (iii):
   (i) the terms of any such lease, conditional sale agreement or Security Interest will not have the effect of prejudicing the title and interest of Lessor in and to that Engine or Part or the interest of any Financing Party in respect thereof under any Financing Security Document;
   (ii) the lessor under such lease, the seller under such conditional sale agreement or the secured party of such Security Interest, as the case may be, has confirmed and acknowledged in writing (which confirmation and acknowledgment may be contained in the lease, conditional sale agreement or document creating the Security Interest covering that Engine or Part) to Lessor, in form and substance satisfactory to Lessor, that it will recognize the respective rights, title and interest of Lessor to and in that Engine or Part and that it will not seek to exercise any rights whatever in relation thereto; and
   (iii) Lessee shall have delivered to Lessor evidence reasonably satisfactory to Lessor of the matters set forth in clauses (1) and (2) above, which may be by written confirmation, in form and substance reasonably satisfactory to Lessor, from the applicable lessor, seller or secured party, or by Lessee providing a copy (certified as being true, correct and complete by Lessee) of the applicable provisions of the applicable lease, conditional sale agreement or security agreement.

8.15 Pooling of Engines and Parts

Lessee will not enter into nor permit any pooling agreement or arrangement in respect of an Engine or Part without the prior written consent of Lessor except, so long as no Default has occurred which is continuing, for pooling agreements or arrangements satisfying the following conditions:

(a) Lessee has entered into the pooling agreement or arrangement in the ordinary course of its airline business;
(b) the other parties to the pooling agreement or arrangement are reputable, solvent commercial air carriers or the manufacturers or suppliers of the Engine or Part (or other reputable, solvent organizations whose business includes the administration of and participation in such pooling agreements or arrangements);
(c) the Engine or Part is leased, let on hire or otherwise made available by Lessee on terms conferring no more than a contractual right *in personam* against Lessee and not a right *in rem* against such Engine or Part;
(d) in the case of an Engine, the pooling agreement or arrangement does not contemplate the transfer of title to such Engine; and
(e) the pooling agreement or arrangement either provides that Lessor (or any Financing Party designated by Lessor) will be sole loss payee in respect of any loss or damage to the Engine or Part, or provides for Lessor to acquire title to a substitute engine or part satisfying the conditions set out in Section 11.3(a) if the Engine or Part is destroyed.

8.16 <u>Equipment Changes</u>

(a) Lessee will not make any Voluntary Equipment Change expected to cost over $250,000 or that deviates from the Aircraft's original type design or configuration without the prior written consent of Lessor, which consent shall not be unreasonably withheld.
(b) Lessor may review Lessee's proposed designs, plans, engineering drawings and diagrams, and flight and maintenance manual revisions for any proposed Equipment Change. If requested by Lessor, Lessee will furnish Lessor (at Lessee's expense) with such documents in final form and any other documents required by Applicable Law as a result of an Equipment Change. All Equipment Changes made to the Aircraft will be properly documented in the Aircraft Documents and be fully approved by the Aviation Authority.
(c) Lessee shall not make any Voluntary Equipment Change that has the effect of diminishing or impairing the value, utility, condition or airworthiness of the Aircraft.
(d) All permanent or structural Equipment Changes, all Mandatory Equipment Changes and all Voluntary Equipment Changes will, upon installation, become a part of the Aircraft and the property of Lessor. At Lessor's request, all Voluntary Equipment Changes will be removed from the Aircraft before return of the Aircraft to Lessor and the Aircraft will be restored to its condition prior to that Equipment Change, and upon such removal and restoration will revert to become the property of Lessee; provided, that Lessee may not remove a Voluntary Equipment Change without Lessor's consent during the continuation of a Default.

8.17 Title to Engines and Parts

(a) Any Engine at any time removed from the Aircraft will remain the property of Lessor until a replacement has been made in accordance with this Agreement and title to that replacement has passed, according to Applicable Laws, to Lessor subject to this Agreement free of all Security Interests, whereupon title to the removed Engine will, provided no Default has occurred and is continuing, pass to Lessee free of Lessor Liens. At any time when requested by Lessor, Lessee will provide evidence to Lessor's reasonable satisfaction (including the provision, if required, to Lessor of one of more legal opinions) that title has so passed to Lessor.

(b) Title to all Parts installed on the Aircraft, whether by way of replacement, as the result of an Equipment Change or otherwise (except Lessee Installed Parts or those installed pursuant to Section 8.15) will on installation, without further act, vest in Lessor subject to this Agreement free and clear of all Security Interests. Lessee will at its own expense take all such steps and execute, and procure the execution of, all such instruments that are necessary to ensure that title so passes to Lessor according to all Applicable Laws. At any time when requested by Lessor, Lessee will provide evidence to Lessor's reasonable satisfaction (including the provision, if required, to Lessor of one of more legal opinions) that title has so passed to Lessor.

(c) Except as referred to in Section 8.17(b), any Part at any time removed from the Aircraft will remain the property of Lessor until a replacement has been made in accordance with this Agreement and until title to that replacement has passed, according to Section 8.17(b) and Applicable Laws, to Lessor subject to this Agreement free of all Security Interests, whereupon title to the removed Part will, provided no Default has occurred and is continuing, pass to Lessee free of Lessor Liens.

(d) If any Lessee Installed Part title to which is held by Lessee is not removed prior to the return of the Aircraft to Lessor, then upon return of the Aircraft to Lessor, title to all such Lessee Installed Parts will, without further act, vest in Lessor free and clear of all Security Interests. Lessee will at its own expense take all such steps and execute, and procure the execution of, all such instruments that are necessary to ensure that title so passes to Lessor.

8.18 Third Parties

Lessee shall procure that no Person having possession of the Aircraft during the Term will act in any manner inconsistent with Lessee's obligations under this Agreement, and that all such Persons shall comply with those obligations as if references to "Lessee" included a separate reference to those Persons. Lessee shall authorize the release by such Persons to Lessor of all details pertaining to the maintenance and Lessee shall, upon Lessor's request, provide Lessor with letters to all such Persons allowing the disclosure to Lessor of all matters relating to the Aircraft.

8.19 Non-Discrimination

(a) Lessee shall not discriminate against the Aircraft in its use, maintenance or operation of the Aircraft compared to similar aircraft owned or operated by Lessee, and Lessee shall service, repair, maintain and overhaul the Aircraft so as to keep the Aircraft maintained in the same manner and with the same care as used by Lessee with similar aircraft owned or operated by Lessee.

(b) Subject to a sublease permitted pursuant to Section 8.5, Lessee shall continue to use the Aircraft in its regular commercial passenger operations until delivery to the Redelivery Location immediately prior to the Final Inspection.

(c) Lessee further agrees that normal progressive maintenance will continue to be performed on the Aircraft throughout the Term, and no unusual maintenance procedures or cessation of maintenance shall occur during the one year period prior to the Expiry Date.

9. INSURANCE[9]

9.1 Insurances

Lessee will maintain in full force and effect during the Term insurances in respect of the Aircraft in form and substance reasonably satisfactory to Lessor (the "Insurances") through such brokers and with such insurers and having such deductibles and being subject to such exclusions as are usual and customary in the worldwide aviation insurance marketplace for major international air carriers operating similar equipment who are similarly situated with Lessee. The Insurances will be effected either:

(a) on a direct basis with insurers of recognized standing who normally participate in aviation insurances in the leading international insurance markets and led by reputable underwriters approved by Lessor, or

(b) with a single insurer or group of insurers approved by Lessor who does not retain the risk, but effects substantial reinsurance in the leading international insurance markets and through reinsurance brokers of recognized standing and acceptable to Lessor for a percentage acceptable to Lessor of all risks insured.

9.2 Requirements

Lessor's current requirements as to Insurances are as specified in this Section 9 and in Schedule 4. Except for the amount of the Agreed Value, the Minimum Liability Coverage and the deductible under Lessee's hull and war risk insurance policies, Lessor may from time to time stipulate such other requirements for the Insurances as Lessor reasonably considers necessary to ensure that the scope and level of cover is

9. *See* §3.12 of the text *supra*.

maintained in accordance with the then prevailing industry practice in relation to aircraft of the same type as the Aircraft and in relation to operators of similar standing to Lessee. In the event that it proposes any such stipulation, Lessor shall notify Lessee accordingly and Lessor and/or its brokers will then consult in good faith with Lessee and Lessee's brokers (as for the time being approved by Lessor) with regard to such proposed stipulation. Following the consultation, if Lessor is satisfied that the stipulation should be made, Lessee shall then comply with the stipulated requirements.

9.3 Insurance Covenants

Lessee shall:

(a) ensure that all legal requirements as to insurance of the Aircraft, any Engine or any Part that may from time to time be imposed by the laws of the State of Registration or any jurisdiction to, from or over which the Aircraft may be flown, in so far as they affect or concern the operation of the Aircraft, are complied with and, in particular, those requirements compliance with which is necessary to ensure that:
   (i) the Aircraft does not become subject to detention or forfeiture;
   (ii) the Insurances remain valid and in full force and effect; and
   (iii) the interests of the Indemnitees in the Insurances and the Aircraft or any Part are not thereby prejudiced;

(b) not use, cause or permit the Aircraft, any Engine or any Part to be used for any purpose or in any manner not covered by the Insurances or outside any geographical limit imposed by the Insurances;

(c) comply with the terms and conditions of each policy of the Insurances and not do, consent or agree to any act or omission that:
   (i) invalidates or may reasonably be expected to invalidate the Insurances;
   (ii) renders or may reasonably be expected to render void or voidable the whole or any part of any of the Insurances; or
   (iii) brings any particular liability within the scope of an exclusion or exception to the Insurances;

(d) not take out without the prior written approval of Lessor any insurance in respect of the Aircraft other than those of the type required under this Agreement unless relating solely to hull total loss, business interruption, engine break-down, profit commission and deductible risk;

(e) provide to Lessor copies of those documents evidencing the Insurances which Lessor may reasonably request;

(f) on request, provide to Lessor evidence that the Insurance premiums have been paid;

(g) not make any modification or alteration to the Insurances material and adverse to the interests of any of the Indemnitees;

(h) be responsible for any deductible under the Insurances; and

(i) provide any other insurance related information, or assistance, in respect of the Insurances as Lessor may reasonably request.

9.4 Renewal of Insurances

Lessee shall commence renewal procedures at least 30 days prior to the expiration of any of the Insurances and provide to Lessor:

(a) if requested by Lessor, a written status report of renewal negotiations 14 days prior to each expiration date;
(b) telefaxed confirmation of completion of renewal prior to each expiration date; and
(c) a certificate of insurance and broker's letter of undertaking substantially in the form delivered to Lessor on the Delivery Date, detailing the coverage and confirming the insurers' agreement to the specified insurance requirements of this Agreement within seven days after each renewal date.

9.5 Failure to Insure

If Lessee fails to maintain the Insurances in compliance with this Agreement:

(a) Lessee shall immediately ground the Aircraft and shall keep it grounded until such time as the Insurances shall again be in full force and effect.
(b) Lessee shall immediately notify Lessor of the non-compliance of the Insurances with the requirements of this Agreement, and Lessee shall provide Lessor with full details of all steps that Lessee is taking or proposes to take in order to remedy such non-compliance.
(c) Each of the Indemnitees will be entitled but not obligated (without prejudice to any other rights of Lessor under this Agreement):
    (i) to pay the premiums due or to effect and maintain insurances satisfactory to it or otherwise remedy Lessee's failure in such manner (including to effect and maintain an "owner's interest" policy) as it considers appropriate, and any sums so expended by it will become immediately due and payable by Lessee to Lessor on demand (such demand being made as soon as reasonably practicable following the incurring of such expenditure), together with interest thereon at the Overdue Rate from the date of expenditure by it up to the date of reimbursement by Lessee (before and after any judgment); and
    (ii) at any time while such failure is continuing to require the Aircraft to remain at any airport or to proceed to and remain at any airport designated by it until the failure is remedied to its reasonable satisfaction.

9.6 Continuing Insurance for Indemnity

(a) Lessee shall effect and maintain insurance after the Expiry Date with respect to its liability under the indemnities in Section 10 for two years, providing for each Indemnitee to be named as an additional insured pursuant to the provisions of the airline finance/lease contract Endorsement AVN 99.

(b) Lessee's obligation under this Section 9.6 shall not be affected by Lessee ceasing to be lessee of the Aircraft or any of the Indemnitees ceasing to have any interest in respect of the Aircraft, and upon a Transfer pursuant to Section 14.2, Lessee shall continue to name the Indemnitees as additional insureds under the Insurance policies covered by Section 1(d) of Schedule 4 for two years after the Transfer date.

9.7 Application of Insurance Proceeds

As between Lessor and Lessee, and except to the extent otherwise required pursuant to the provisions of the airline finance/lease contract Endorsements AVN 67C and AVN 67C (Hull War) adopted by the Lloyd's Aviation Underwriter's Association (or any successor endorsements), if applicable:

(a) All insurance payments, up to the Agreed Value, received as the result of a Total Loss occurring during the Term will be paid to Lessor (unless or until Lessor notifies Lessee that said payments should be made to a specified Financing Party).

(b) All insurance proceeds in respect of any damage or loss to the Aircraft, any Engine or any Part occurring during the Term not constituting a Total Loss and involving insurance proceeds in excess of the Damage Notification Threshold will be paid to Lessor (unless or until Lessor notifies Lessee that said payments should be made to a specified Financing Party) and applied in payment (or to reimburse Lessee) for repairs or replacement property upon Lessor being reasonably satisfied that the repairs or replacement have been effected in accordance with this Agreement. Insurance proceeds in amounts less than the Damage Notification Threshold may be paid by the insurer directly to Lessee. Any balance remaining shall be paid to or may be retained by Lessee.

(c) All insurance proceeds in respect of third party liability will be paid to the relevant third party.

(d) Notwithstanding Sections 9.7(a) and (b), if at the time of the payment of any such insurance proceeds a Default has occurred and is continuing, all such proceeds will be paid to or retained by Lessor (unless or until Lessor notifies Lessee that said payments should be made to a Financing Party) to be applied toward payment of any amounts that may be or become payable by Lessee in such order as Lessor sees fit or as Lessor may elect. In the event that Lessee remedies any such Default to the reasonable satisfaction of Lessor, then

Lessor shall procure that all such insurance proceeds then held by Lessor or any Financing Party, as the case may be, in excess of the amounts (if any) applied by Lessor or any Financing Party, as the case may be, in accordance with this Section 9.7(d) shall be paid promptly to Lessee.

9.8 Aggregate Limits

If any of the Insurances is subject to an annual aggregate yearly or other periodic limit, and, by reason of any claims made thereunder during the course of a year or other period in respect of any property subject to such policy, the aggregate amount of coverage available thereunder in respect of the balance of such year or other period shall have been reduced:

(a) Lessee shall forthwith notify Lessor of the amount of any such claim; and
(b) Lessee shall not operate the Aircraft during the balance of such year or other period either (i) without the prior written consent of Lessor or (ii) until Lessee has increased forthwith upon request of Lessor the aggregate limit under the relevant policy for such year or other period to such amount as Lessor may reasonably require.

9.9 Form LSW555D Exclusions

In this Section 9.9, the term "**Uninsured Risks**" shall mean the matters set out in the exclusions to form LSW555D (or any successor provision approved by Lessor) for chemical or biological weapons, so called "dirty bombs" and electromagnetic pulse weapons. Lessee undertakes that if cover in respect of the Uninsured Risks is, or becomes, available in the London insurance markets or elsewhere at commercially reasonable rates (having reference to the extent to which such cover is commonly taken by first class international airlines) it shall, if requested by Lessor, obtain and maintain, or cause to be obtained and maintained, insurance cover for the Uninsured Risks to the fullest extent available in the leading international insurance markets.

10. INDEMNITY[10]

10.1 General

(a) Lessee shall defend, indemnify and hold harmless each of the Indemnitees for, from and against any and all claims, proceedings, losses, liabilities, suits, judgments, costs, expenses, penalties or fines (each a "Claim") regardless of when the same is made or incurred, whether during or after the Term (but not before):

10. *See* §3.11 of the text *supra*.

(i) that may at any time be suffered or incurred directly or indirectly as a result of or connected with possession, repossession, delivery, performance, management, registration, deregistration, control, maintenance, condition, service, repair, overhaul, leasing, subleasing, use, operation or return of the Aircraft, any Engine or Part (either in the air or on the ground) whether or not the Claim may be attributable to any defect in the Aircraft, any Engine or any Part or to its design, testing, use or otherwise, and regardless of when the same arises or whether it arises out of or is attributable to any act or omission, negligent or otherwise, of any Indemnitee;

(ii) that arise out of any act or omission that invalidates or that renders voidable any of the Insurances; or

(iii) that may at any time be suffered or incurred as a consequence of any design, article or material in the Aircraft, any Engine or any Part or its operation or use constituting an infringement of patent, copyright, trademark, design or other proprietary right or a breach of any obligation of confidentiality owed to any Person.

(b) Notwithstanding the provisions of Section 10.1(a), Lessee shall not have to indemnify an Indemnitee for any Claim to the extent that:

(i) it arises directly as a result of the willful misconduct or gross negligence of that Indemnitee;

(ii) it arises directly as a result of a breach by Lessor of its express obligations under this Agreement or as a result of a representation or warranty given by Lessor in this Agreement not being true and correct at the date when, or when deemed to have been, given or made;

(iii) it constitutes a Non-Indemnified Tax or Lessor Lien;

(iv) it represents a Tax or loss of tax benefits (Lessee's liabilities for which, including exclusions, are set out in Sections 5.7, 5.8, 5.9 and 5.11);

(v) it constitutes a cost or expense that is required to be borne by Lessor in accordance with another provision of this Agreement;

(vi) it results from any disposition not caused by Lessee of all or any part of Lessor's rights, title or interest in or to the Aircraft or under this Agreement, unless such disposition occurs as a consequence of an Event of Default;

(vii) it is attributable to an event occurring after the Term unless the Claim results from or arises out of an act or omission by Lessee, or any circumstance existing, during the Term; or

(viii) it is brought after the Term and relates to a claimed patent infringement by the applicable Manufacturer.

10.2 Mitigation

(a) Lessor agrees that it shall notify Lessee in writing as soon as reasonably practicable after it becomes aware of any circumstances that would, or would reasonably be expected to, become the subject of a claim for indemnification pursuant to Section 10.1. Lessor (and any other Indemnitee seeking indemnification, as the case may be) and Lessee shall then consult with one another in good faith in order to determine what action (if any) may reasonably be taken to avoid or mitigate such Claim. Lessee shall have the right to take all reasonable action (on behalf and, if necessary, in the name of Lessor or such other Indemnitee) in order to resist, defend or settle (provided such settlement is accompanied by payment) any claims by third parties giving rise to such Claim, provided always that Lessee shall not be entitled to take any such action unless adequate provision, reasonably satisfactory to Lessor and such other Indemnitee, shall have been made in respect of the third party claim and the costs thereof. Lessee or, if the Claim is covered by Lessee's Insurances, Lessee's insurers shall be entitled to select any counsel to represent it or them, Lessor and such other Indemnitee in connection with any such action, subject in the case of Lessee to the approval of Lessor and such other Indemnitee (such approval not to be unreasonably withheld) and any action taken by Lessee shall be on a full indemnity basis in respect of Lessor and such other Indemnitee.

(b) Any sums paid by Lessee to Lessor or any Indemnitee in respect of any Claim pursuant to Section 10.1 shall be paid subject to the condition that, in the event that Lessor or such Indemnitee is subsequently reimbursed in respect of that Claim by any other Person, Lessor or such Indemnitee shall, provided no Default shall have occurred and be continuing, promptly pay to Lessee an amount equal to the sum paid to it by Lessee, including any interest on such amount to the extent attributable thereto and received by Lessor or such Indemnitee, less any Tax payable by Lessor or such Indemnitee in respect of such reimbursement.

10.3 Duration

The indemnities contained in this Agreement will survive and continue in full force after the Expiry Date.

11. EVENTS OF LOSS[11]

11.1 Total Loss Before Delivery

If a Total Loss occurs before Delivery, this Agreement will immediately terminate and neither party will have any further obligation or liability under this Agreement except as expressly stated herein.

11. *See* §3.11 and §3.12 of the text *supra*.

11.2 Total Loss After Delivery

(a) If a Total Loss occurs after Delivery, Lessee will pay the Agreed Value to Lessor (or any Financing Party designated by Lessor) on the earlier of:
   (i) the date of receipt of the insurance proceeds payable as a result of the Total Loss, or
   (ii) the 30th day after the Total Loss Date (the "Settlement Date"),

(b) in either case unless the Aircraft is restored to Lessor or Lessee within that period (or, in the case of a Total Loss coming within paragraph (c) of the definition of Total Loss and involving the loss of Lessor's title to the Aircraft, if both the Aircraft and Lessor's title thereto are restored to Lessor or, in the case of the Aircraft, to Lessee).

(c) The receipt by Lessor or any Financing Party (on behalf of Lessor) of the insurance proceeds in respect of the Total Loss on or prior to the Settlement Date shall discharge Lessee from its obligation to pay the Agreed Value to Lessor pursuant to this Section 11.2, provided such proceeds are not less than the Agreed Value. In the event that the insurance proceeds are paid initially to Lessee and not to Lessor or any Financing Party designated by Lessor, they may be retained by Lessee if Lessee shall have paid the Agreed Value to Lessor or any Financing Party (on behalf of Lessor); otherwise Lessee shall pay the Agreed Value to Lessor or any Financing Party (on behalf of Lessor) not later than the next Business Day following receipt by Lessee of such proceeds. In the event that Lessee pays the Agreed Value to Lessor or any Financing Party (on behalf of Lessor) in accordance with this Section 11.2, Lessor shall promptly assign to Lessee its rights under the Insurances to receive the insurance proceeds in respect of the Total Loss to the extent that such proceeds shall not have been paid to Lessee.

(d) Subject to the rights of any insurers or other third parties, upon irrevocable payment in full to Lessor or any Financing Party (on behalf of Lessor) of the Agreed Value and all other amounts that are payable to Lessor under the Operative Documents, Lessor shall without recourse or warranty (except as to the absence of Lessor Liens), and without further act, be deemed to have transferred to Lessee all of Lessor's rights to any Engines or Parts not installed when the Total Loss occurred, all on an "as-is where is" basis, and shall, at Lessee's expense, execute and deliver such bills of sale and other documents and instruments as Lessee may reasonably request to evidence (on the public record or otherwise) the transfer and the vesting of Lessor's rights in such Engines and Parts in Lessee, free and clear of all rights of Lessor and any Lessor Liens.

11.3 Engine Loss

(a) Upon the occurrence of an Engine Loss in circumstances in which there has not also occurred a Total Loss (including, for the avoidance of doubt, at a time when the Engine is not installed on the Airframe), Lessee shall give Lessor written notice promptly upon becoming aware of the same and shall, within 60 days after the Engine Loss Date, convey or cause to be conveyed to Lessor, as replacement for such Engine, title to a replacement engine that is in the same or better operating condition, and has the same or greater value and utility, as the lost Engine (assuming the lost Engine was, immediately before the Engine Loss, in the condition required by this Agreement) and that complies with the conditions set out in Section 8.13(a).

(b) Lessee will at its own expense take all such steps and execute, and procure the execution of, a full warranty bill of sale covering such replacement engine, a supplement to this Agreement adding such replacement engine to the Leased Property and all such other agreements and instruments that are necessary to ensure that title to such Engine passes to Lessor and is subject to the Security Interest created by any Financing Security Document and such replacement engine becomes an "Engine", all according to Applicable Laws. At any time when requested by Lessor, Lessee will provide evidence to Lessor's reasonable satisfaction (including the provision, if required, to Lessor of one of more legal opinions) that title has so passed to Lessor and is subject to the Security Interest created by any Financing Security Document.

(c) Upon compliance with the foregoing title transfer provisions, the leasing of the replaced Engine that suffered the Engine Loss shall cease and title to such replaced Engine shall (subject to any salvage rights of insurers) vest in Lessee free of Lessor Liens. If Lessor or any Financing Party subsequently receives any insurance proceeds relating to such Engine Loss, Lessor shall promptly remit such proceeds, or cause such proceeds to be remitted, to Lessee.

(d) No Engine Loss with respect to any Engine that is replaced in accordance with the provisions of this Section 11.3 shall result in any increase or decrease in Basic Rent, Additional Rent or the Agreed Value.

11.4 <u>Damage or Incident Not Constituting a Total Loss</u>

Following the occurrence of any damage to the Aircraft, any Engine or any Part that does not constitute a Total Loss or an Engine Loss and where either (i) the potential cost of repair may reasonably be expected to exceed the Damage Notification Threshold or (ii) Lessor notifies Lessee in writing that Lessor reasonably believes the damage will permanently affect the value of the Aircraft, Lessee shall take the following actions:

(a) Lessee shall consult with, and comply with, all reasonable instructions of Lessor with respect to the accomplishment of repairs;

(b) Lessee shall obtain Lessor's consent prior to agreeing any repair workscope or seeking Manufacturer approval in connection with any such repairs; and

(c) Lessee shall obtain a written certification satisfactory to Lessor from all relevant Manufacturers as to the accomplishment of repairs.

11.5 Requisition

During any requisition for use or hire of the Aircraft, any Engine or Part that does not constitute a Total Loss:

(a) the Basic Rent, Additional Rent and Supplemental Rent payable under this Agreement will not be suspended or abated either in whole or in part, and Lessee will not be released from any of its other obligations under this Agreement (other than operational obligations with which Lessee is unable to comply solely by virtue of the requisition);
(b) so long as no Default has occurred and is continuing, Lessee will be entitled to any compensation payable by the requisitioning authority in respect of the Term;
(c) Lessee will, as soon as practicable after the end of any such requisition (with the Term being extended if and to the extent that the period of requisition continues beyond the Scheduled Expiry Date), cause the Aircraft to be put into the condition required by this Agreement; and
(d) Lessor will be entitled to all compensation payable by the requisitioning authority in respect of any change in the structure, state or condition of the Aircraft arising during the period of requisition, and Lessor will apply such compensation in reimbursing Lessee for the cost of complying with its obligations under this Agreement in respect of any such change; provided, that, if any Default has occurred and is continuing, Lessor may apply the compensation in or towards settlement of any amounts owing by Lessee under this Agreement.

12. RETURN OF AIRCRAFT[12]

12.1 Redelivery

On the Expiry Date or termination of the leasing of the Aircraft under this Agreement, Lessee shall, unless a Total Loss has occurred, at its expense, return and redeliver the Aircraft and Aircraft Documents to Lessor at the Redelivery Location in a condition complying with Schedule 3, free and clear of all Security Interests and Permitted Liens (other than Lessor Liens).

12.2 Non-Compliance

To the extent that, at the time of Final Inspection, the condition of the Aircraft or the Aircraft Documents does not comply with this Agreement, Lessee shall, at the option of Lessor:

12. *See* §3.13 of the text *supra*.

(a) immediately rectify the non-compliance and, to the extent the non-compliance extends beyond the Expiry Date, the Term will be automatically extended until the earlier to occur of the date on which the non-compliance has been rectified and the date (if any) on which Lessor notifies Lessee to redeliver the Leased Property in accordance with Section 12.2(b); or

(b) redeliver the Aircraft and the Aircraft Documents to Lessor and indemnify Lessor, and provide security reasonably acceptable to Lessor for that indemnity, against the cost of putting the Aircraft and the Aircraft Documents into the condition required by this Agreement.

During any extension of the Term pursuant to Section 12.2(a), this Agreement will remain in full force and effect, including the obligation to pay lease rental (which Lessee shall pay on a *per diem* basis weekly in advance in an amount equal to half of the Basic Rent Amount per week); provided, however, that Lessee shall not operate, or permit others to operate, the Aircraft after the Expiry Date except for acceptance flights pursuant to Schedule 3 and a ferry flight to the Redelivery Location or, in accordance with Section 12.5, from the Redelivery Location.

12.3 Acknowledgment

Following redelivery of the Aircraft by Lessee to Lessor at the Redelivery Location in compliance with the requirements of this Agreement and Lessee's satisfaction of its other obligations under the Operative Documents, Lessor will deliver to Lessee the Return Certificate.

12.4 Storage

(a) If Lessor so requests, and subject to the availability of the requisite space, Lessee shall park and store the Aircraft at a secure storage area, which may be at the Redelivery Location or at any other suitable facility of Lessee selected by Lessee, wherever located (the "Storage Location"), on behalf of Lessor for a period not exceeding 30 days from the Expiry Date. During that period the Aircraft shall be at Lessee's risk (save as to any loss or damage caused by Lessor's willful misconduct or gross negligence), and Lessee shall maintain the Aircraft under the Lessee's EASA Continuing Airworthiness Maintenance Organization (CAMO) including but not limited to, oversight of continuing maintenance requirements in compliance with the Approved Maintenance Program, monitoring of the Aircraft maintenance and records keeping under the Lessee's quality control procedures, organize appropriate continuing maintenance and AD compliance actions and maintain appropriate technical records keeping practices, all such actions to be in compliance with EASA Part M subpart G requirements. The Lessee will invoice the Lessee's incremental Actual Costs associated with EASA Part M subpart G requirements. Lessee shall insure the Aircraft in accordance with a "ground risk only" policy usual and customary in the worldwide aviation insurance marketplace. All storage, maintenance and insurance costs shall be borne by Lessee.

(b) If Lessor so requests, and subject to the availability of the requisite space, Lessee shall continue to park and store the Aircraft at the Storage Location on behalf of Lessor for a further period not exceeding 60 days. During that further period the Aircraft shall be at Lessor's risk (save as to any loss or damage caused by Lessee's willful misconduct or gross negligence), but Lessee shall continue to maintain, store and insure the Aircraft in accordance with this Section 12.4. All reasonable storage, maintenance and insurance costs incurred by Lessee (excluding any profit element accruing to Lessee) during such further period shall be reimbursed by Lessor promptly upon presentation of supporting invoices and receipts.

12.5 Ferry Flight

After acknowledgment of redelivery of the Aircraft pursuant to Section 12.3 or storage of the Aircraft pursuant to Section 12.4, Lessee will ferry the Leased Property to a location designated by Lessor in the continental United States of America or the European Union.

13. DEFAULT[13]

13.1 Events

Each of the following events will constitute an Event of Default and a repudiation of this Agreement by Lessee:

(a) Non-payment: Lessee (i) fails to pay the Agreed Value and all other amounts required under Section 11.2 on the Settlement Date, (ii) fails to make any payment of Basic Rent or Additional Rent within two Business Days after the date on which such payment is due, or (iii) fails to pay any other amount payable by it under this Agreement within five Business Days after written notice from Lessor that such amounts are due; or

(b) Material Covenants: Lessee (i) fails to rectify the non-compliance of the Leased Property with the conditions of Section 12 and Schedule 3 or redeliver the Leased Property to Lessor in accordance with Section 12.2, (ii) fails to maintain in full force and effect any insurance required to be maintained under Section 9, or (iii) transfers possession of the Airframe or any Engine to another Person other than as permitted by this Agreement; or

(c) Breach: Lessee fails to comply with any other provision of this Agreement and, if such failure is, in the reasonable opinion of Lessor, capable of remedy, the failure continues for 14 days after notice from Lessor to Lessee, provided,

13. *See* §3.14, §3.15 and Annex 10 of the text *supra*.

that if such failure cannot reasonably be remedied within such 14 day period and Lessee is diligently undertaking all necessary remedial action, the 14 day period shall be extended for a further 14 days; or

(d) Representation: any representation or warranty made (or deemed to be repeated) by Lessee in the Operative Documents or in any document or certificate furnished to Lessor pursuant to or in connection with the Operative Documents is or proves to have been incorrect in any material respect when made or deemed to be repeated and Lessee's ability to comply with its obligations under the Operative Documents, and/or Lessor's rights, title and interest to and in the Aircraft and/or under the Operative Documents, are thereby materially and adversely affected; or

(e) Cross Default:
   (i) any Financial Indebtedness of Lessee or any of its Affiliates that exceeds $[] is not paid when due and any applicable grace period shall have expired;
   (ii) the security for any Financial Indebtedness of Lessee or any of its Affiliates is enforced;
   (iii) any lease, conditional sale, installment sale or forward purchase agreement of Lessee or any of its Affiliates in respect of an aircraft is terminated as a consequence of an event of default or termination event (however described); or
   (iv) an event of default (however described) occurs under any lease, conditional sale, installment sale or forward purchase agreement between Lessor or any of its Affiliates and Lessee or any of its Affiliates;

(f) provided always, in any such case, it shall not constitute an Event of Default under this Agreement:
   (i) if the relevant Financial Indebtedness constitutes non-recourse borrowing or financing; or
   (ii) if the non-payment, acceleration, termination or event in question is being contested by Lessee in good faith and on reasonable grounds and any declaration of default, termination of agreement or enforcement of security has been stayed by a court of competent jurisdiction; or

(g) Approvals: any consent, authorization, licence, certificate or approval of or registration with or declaration to any Government Entity in connection with this Agreement, including:
   (i) any authorization required by Lessee of, or in connection with, the execution, delivery, validity, enforceability or admissibility in evidence of the Operative Documents or the performance by Lessee of its obligations under the Operative Documents; or
   (ii) any airline licence, air transport licence, franchise, concession, permit, certificate, right or privilege required by Lessee for the conduct of its business,

(h) is modified, withheld, revoked, suspended, canceled, withdrawn, terminated or not renewed, or otherwise ceases to be in full force and is not reissued, reinstated or renewed within 30 days, provided however that any such modification, withholding, revocation, suspension, cancellation, withdrawal, termination or non-renewal shall only constitute an Event of Default if it has a material adverse effect on Lessee's ability to perform its obligations under the Operative Documents or on Lessor's rights, title and interest to and in the Aircraft or under the Operative Documents; or

(i) Insolvency:

(i) Lessee or any of its Affiliates is, or is deemed for the purposes of any relevant law to be, unable to pay its debts as they fall due or to be insolvent; or

(ii) Lessee or any of its Affiliates suspends making payments on all or any class of its debts or announces an intention to do so, or a moratorium is declared in respect of any of its indebtedness; or

(j) Bankruptcy and Similar Proceedings

(i) Lessee shall consent to the appointment of a receiver, trustee or liquidator for itself or for a substantial part of its property; or

(ii) Lessee shall admit in writing its inability to pay its debts generally as they become due, or Lessee shall make a general assignment for the benefit of creditors; or

(iii) Lessee shall file a voluntary petition in bankruptcy or a voluntary petition or answer seeking reorganization in a proceeding under any laws dealing with bankruptcy, insolvency, moratorium or creditors' rights generally (any or all of which are hereinafter referred to as "Bankruptcy Laws"), or an answer admitting the material allegations of a petition filed against Lessee in any such proceeding, or Lessee shall by voluntary petition or answer consent to or fail to oppose the seeking of relief under the provisions of any Bankruptcy Laws; or

(iv) any order, judgment or decree is entered by a court of competent jurisdiction appointing a receiver, trustee or liquidator of Lessee or a substantial part of its property, or ordering a substantial part of Lessee's property to be sequestered, is instituted or done with the consent of Lessee or, if instituted by another Person, the order, judgment or decree is not dismissed, remedied or relinquished within 30 days; or

(v) a petition against Lessee in a proceeding under any Bankruptcy Laws shall be filed and shall not be withdrawn or dismissed within 30 days thereafter, or if, under the provisions of any Bankruptcy Laws that may apply to Lessee, any court of competent jurisdiction shall assume jurisdiction, custody or control of Lessee or of any substantial part of its property; or

(vi) any step (including petition, proposal or convening a meeting) is taken with a view to a composition, assignment or arrangement with any creditors of, or the reorganization, rehabilitation, administration, liquidation, or dissolution of, Lessee or any of its Affiliates or any other insolvency proceedings involving Lessee or any of its Affiliates; or

(k) Other Jurisdiction: there occurs in relation to Lessee or any of its Affiliates any event anywhere which, in the reasonable opinion of Lessor, corresponds with any of those mentioned in Section 13.1(h); or

(l) Unlawful: it becomes unlawful for Lessee to perform any of its material obligations under the Operative Documents, or any of the Operative Documents becomes wholly or partly invalid or unenforceable, provided that any such partial invalidity or unenforceability shall only constitute an Event of Default if it has a material adverse effect on Lessee's ability to perform its obligations under the Operative Documents or Lessor's rights, title and interest in and to the Aircraft or under the Operative Documents; or

(m) Suspension of Business: Lessee or any of its Affiliates suspends or ceases to carry on all or a substantial part of its business; or

(n) Disposal: Lessee or any of its Affiliates disposes or threatens to dispose of all or a material part of its assets, whether by one or a series of transactions, related or not, other than pursuant to a merger or consolidation as referred to in, and subject to, Section 8.8(b) or for the purpose of any other reorganization or amalgamation the terms of which have received the previous consent in writing of Lessor; or

(o) Rights: the existence, validity, enforceability or priority of the rights of Lessor as owner and lessor in respect of the Aircraft or the rights of any Financing Party as mortgagee of the Aircraft or assignee of this Agreement are challenged by Lessee or any other Person claiming by or through Lessee; or

(p) Change of Ownership: any single Person or group of Persons acquire control, directly or indirectly, of Lessee without the previous consent in writing of Lessor (which consent shall not be withheld unless Lessor is of the reasonable opinion that such acquisition of control will have a materially adverse effect on Lessee's ability to perform its obligations under the Operative Documents or Lessor's rights, title and interest in and to the Aircraft or under the Operative Documents), not including (i) individuals or other Persons that are currently in control of Lessee, (ii) spouses of any such individuals, (iii) any lineal ancestor or descendant of any such individual, (iv) any spouse of any individual covered by clause (iii), or (v) a partnership or trust set up for the benefit of individuals identified in clauses (i) through (iv); or

(q) Delivery: Lessee fails to accept delivery of the Aircraft when validly tendered pursuant to this Agreement by Lessor (provided that Lessor shall have satisfied the conditions precedent set out in Section 3.4); or

(r) Adverse Change: any event or series of events occurs which, in the reasonable opinion of Lessor, could be expected to have a material adverse effect on the financial condition or operations of Lessee and its Affiliates or on the ability of Lessee to comply with its obligations under the Operative Documents or to have a prejudicial effect on Lessor's or any Financing Party's rights, title and/or interest in, to or under the Aircraft and/or the Operative Documents; or

(s) Nationalization: all or a material part of the undertakings, rights, assets or revenues of, or shares or other ownership interests in, Lessee are seized, nationalized, expropriated or compulsorily acquired by or under the authority of any Government Entity.

13.2 Rights

If an Event of Default occurs, and for as long as it shall continue, Lessor may at its option (and without prejudice to any of its other rights under this Agreement or that may arise by operation of Applicable Law), at any time thereafter:

(a) accept such repudiation by Lessee of its obligations under this Agreement and by notice to Lessee with immediate effect terminate the leasing of the Aircraft (but without prejudice to the continuing obligations of Lessee under this Agreement), whereupon all rights of Lessee under this Agreement shall cease; and/or

(b) proceed by appropriate court action or actions to enforce performance of this Agreement or to recover damages for the breach of this Agreement; and/or

(c) either:

  (i) take possession of the Aircraft, for which purpose Lessor may enter any premises belonging to, occupied by or under the control of Lessee (for which purpose Lessee hereby grants to Lessor an irrevocable licence to the extent permitted by Applicable Law) where the Aircraft may be located, or cause the Aircraft to be redelivered to Lessor at the Redelivery Location (or such other location as Lessor may require), and Lessor is hereby irrevocably authorized and empowered, to the extent permitted by Applicable Law, to direct pilots of Lessee or other pilots to fly the Aircraft to that airport and will have all the powers and authorizations necessary for taking such action; or

  (ii) by serving notice, require Lessee to redeliver the Aircraft to Lessor at the Redelivery Location (or such other location as Lessor may require) in the condition required by Section 12 and Schedule 3.

(d) If an Event of Default occurs, Lessor may sell, lease or otherwise deal with the Leased Property in such manner as Lessor in its absolute discretion considers appropriate.

(e) If an Event of Default occurs, Lessee shall at the request of Lessor take all steps necessary to deregister the Aircraft from the aircraft registry of the State of Registration and export the Aircraft from the country where the Aircraft is for the time being registered or situated and any other steps necessary to enable the Aircraft to be redelivered to Lessor in accordance with this Agreement. Lessee hereby irrevocably and by way of security for its obligations under the Operative Documents authorizes and empowers Lessor as its attorney-in-fact and agent (such agency being coupled with an interest), in Lessor's own name or in the name of Lessee, to execute and deliver any documentation and to do any act or thing required in connection with the foregoing.

13.3 Default Payments

If an Event of Default occurs, Lessee will indemnify and pay to Lessor on demand against any loss (including loss of profit), damage, expense, cost or liability that Lessor may sustain or incur directly or indirectly as a result, including:

(a) all unpaid Basic Rent, Additional Rent and Supplemental Rent then due and unpaid;

(b) any loss of profit (calculated on an after-tax basis) suffered by Lessor because of Lessor's inability to place the Aircraft on lease with another lessee on terms as favorable to Lessor as this Agreement or because whatever use, if any, to which Lessor is able to put the Aircraft upon its return to Lessor, or the funds arising upon a sale or other disposal of the Aircraft, is not as profitable (calculated on an after-tax basis) to Lessor as this Agreement would have been but for such Event of Default;

(c) in the event that the Aircraft is sold prior to Lessor entering into a replacement lease, the amount (if any) by which (i) the aggregate of (1) the net sale proceeds (calculated by deducting the costs of sale together with the cost of preparing the Aircraft for sale and the repayment of any outstanding indebtedness in relation to the financing of the Aircraft) plus (2) the present value of the anticipated after-tax net income to be derived from such net sale proceeds up to the Scheduled Expiry Date, discounted on a monthly basis using 3.0%*per annum* as the discount rate, are less than (ii) the aggregate of (1) the anticipated net sale proceeds (computed on the same basis as the net sale proceeds referred to in (i)(1) above), assuming that the Aircraft would have been sold as soon as reasonably practicable following the Scheduled Expiry Date plus (2) the present value of the income that would have been derived from the future Basic Rent payable until the Scheduled Expiry Date, discounted on a monthly basis using 3.0%*per annum* as the discount rate;

(d) any amount of principal, interest, fees or other sums whatsoever paid or payable on account of funds borrowed in order to carry any amount unpaid by Lessee;

(e) any loss, premium, penalty or expense that may be incurred in repaying funds raised to finance the Aircraft or in unwinding any swap, forward interest rate agreement or other financial instrument relating in whole or in part to Lessor's financing of the Aircraft; and

(f) any loss, cost, expense or liability sustained or incurred by Lessor owing to Lessee's failure to redeliver the Aircraft on the date, at the place and in the condition required by this Agreement.

13.4 Waiver of Certain Article 2A Rights

To the fullest extent permitted by Applicable Law, each of Lessor and Lessee hereby agrees that no rights or remedies referred to in Article 2A of the Uniform Commercial Code shall be conferred upon either Lessor or Lessee unless otherwise expressly granted in this Agreement.

14. ASSIGNMENT, TRANSFER AND FINANCING[14]

14.1 No Assignment by Lessee

Lessee shall not assign any of its right, title, interests, duties, obligations or liabilities in, to or under the Operative Documents, or create or permit to exist any Security Interest (other than Permitted Liens) over any of its rights under the Operative Documents, and any such purported assignment or grant of a Security Interest shall be void *ab initio* and of no force or effect. Without limiting the foregoing, if any assignment prohibited under the foregoing sentence shall be valid by operation of any non-waivable provision of Applicable Law, Lessee shall nevertheless remain fully liable for the payment and performance of all of Lessee's obligations to be paid and performed hereunder as fully and to the same extent as if such assignment had not been effected, without prejudice to the obligations of such assignee.

14.2 Lessor Assignment

Lessor may sell, assign or transfer all or any of its rights under the Operative Documents and in the Leased Property (a "Transfer") and Lessor will, other than in the case of an assignment for security purposes, have no further obligation under the Operative Documents following a Transfer but, notwithstanding any Transfer, will remain entitled to the benefit of each indemnity under this Agreement.

(a) In connection with any Transfer, the following conditions shall apply:
  (i) Lessor shall give Lessee written notice of such Transfer at least 10 Business Days before the date of such Transfer, specifying the name and address of the proposed purchaser, assignee or transferee (the "Transferee");
  (ii) the Transferee will either (1) be an Affiliate of Lessor or (2) be a Person reasonably experienced in aircraft leasing (or the Transferee's rights and powers under this Agreement shall be exercised or serviced on its behalf pursuant to an appropriate management or servicing agreement by a Person having such experience);

14. *See* §3.16 of the text *supra*.

(iii) the Transferee will have full corporate power and authority to enter into and perform the transactions contemplated by this Agreement on the part of "Lessor";

(iv) such Transfer shall not result in a change of State of Registration (unless otherwise agreed with Lessee);

(v) on the Transfer date Lessor and the Transferee shall enter into an agreement or agreements in which the Transferee confirms that it shall be deemed a party to this Agreement and agrees to be bound by all the terms of, and to undertake all of the obligations of, Lessor contained in this Agreement arising on or after the time of the Transfer; and

(vi) such Transfer shall not violate any Applicable Law.

(b) Upon any Transfer, the Transferee shall be deemed Lessor for all purposes of this Agreement, each reference in this Agreement to "Lessor" shall thereafter be deemed for all purposes to refer to the Transferee, and the transferor shall be relieved of all obligations of "Lessor" under this Agreement arising after the time of such Transfer except to the extent attributable to acts or events occurring prior to the time of such Transfer.

(c) Upon compliance by Lessor and a Transferee with the terms and conditions of Section 14.2(a), Lessee shall at the time of Transfer, at the specific written request of Lessor and with Lessor paying all of Lessee's reasonable out-of-pocket costs and expenses:

(i) execute and deliver to Lessor and to such Transferee an agreement, in form and substance satisfactory to Lessor, Lessee and such Transferee, dated the date of such Transfer, consenting to such Transfer, agreeing to pay all or such portion of the Basic Rent, Additional Rent and other payments under this Agreement to such Transferee or its designee as such Transferee shall direct, and agreeing that such Transferee shall be entitled to rely on all representations and warranties made by Lessee in the Operative Documents or in any certificate or document furnished by Lessee in connection with the Operative Documents as though such Transferee was the original "Lessor";

(ii) execute and deliver to Lessor or such Transferee, as appropriate, precautionary Uniform Commercial Code financing statements or amendments reflecting the interests of such Transferee in the Aircraft and the Operative Documents;

(iii) deliver to Lessor and to such Transferee a certificate, signed by a duly authorized officer of Lessee, dated the date of such Transfer, to the effect that (1) no Event of Default has occurred and is continuing or, if one is then continuing, describing such Event of Default, and (2) the representations and warranties set forth in Section 2.1 are true and correct as of such date;

(iv) cause to be delivered to Lessor and such Transferee certificates of insurance and broker's letters of undertaking substantially in the form delivered to Lessor on the Delivery Date, detailing the coverage and confirming the insurers' agreement to the specified insurance requirements of this Agreement and listing Lessor and Transferee as additional insureds and the Transferee as sole loss payee (subject to other direction by any Financing Party);

(v) deliver to Lessor and to such Transferee an opinion of Lessee's counsel (which may be Lessee's General Counsel), addressed to Lessor and such Transferee to the effect that the agreement referred to in Section 14.2(c)(i) has been duly authorized and executed by Lessee and constitutes the legal, valid and binding obligation of Lessee, enforceable against Lessee in accordance with its terms (subject to customary exceptions), and to the effect that such Transferee may rely on the opinion delivered by such counsel or its predecessor counsel in connection with the Operative Documents on the Delivery Date with the same force and effect as if such Transferee was an original addressee of such opinion when given;

(vi) deliver to Lessor and such Transferee information on the location of the Airframe and Engines at all times requested by Lessor in order to permit the Transfer to take place at a time and on a date so as to eliminate or minimize any Taxes applicable to the Transfer; and

(vii) such other documents as Lessor or such Transferee may reasonably request.

14.3 Financing Parties; Grants of Security Interests

(a) On or before the Delivery Date, and from time to time thereafter, Lessor shall advise Lessee in writing of any Financing Parties, and of any Financing Documents relevant to such Financing Parties status as Additional Insureds and of any Financing Security Documents providing to any Financing Parties a Security Interest in the Leased Property or Lessor's right, title and interest in any Operative Documents. On the Delivery Date, pursuant to Section 3.1(c), Lessee shall execute and deliver to Lessor the Notice and Acknowledgment.

(b) Lessor shall be entitled at any time after Delivery to grant a Security Interest in the Leased Property or its right, title and interest in any Operative Document in replacement of or with a priority senior, equal or subordinate to any previous grant of a Security Interest. In the case of any such grant after Delivery, Lessee shall promptly, at the specific written request of Lessor and with Lessor paying all of Lessee's reasonable out-of-pocket costs and expenses:

(i) execute and deliver to Lessor a notice and acknowledgment referring to the new Financing Security Document and otherwise substantially in the form of the Notice and Acknowledgment;

(ii) deliver to Lessor and any new Financing Parties identified by Lessor a certificate, signed by a duly authorized officer of Lessee, dated the date of the grant of the additional Security Interest by Lessor, to the effect that

(1) no Event of Default has occurred and is continuing or, if one is then continuing, describing such Event of Default, and (2) the representations and warranties set forth in Section 2.1 are true and correct as of such date;

(iii) cause to be delivered to Lessor certificates of insurance and broker's letters of undertaking substantially in the form delivered to Lessor on the Delivery Date, detailing the coverage and confirming the insurers' agreement to the specified insurance requirements of this Agreement, adding the additional Financing Parties identified by Lessor as additional insureds and, if requested by Lessor, as loss payees; and

(iv) such other documents as Lessor may reasonably request.

14.4 Sale and Leaseback by Lessor

In addition to the Transfers and grants of Security Interests permitted by Sections 14.2 and 14.3, Lessor shall be entitled to transfer its right, title and interests in and to the Leased Property to any Person and lease the Aircraft from such Person (a "Head Lessor"), and in such event Lessor shall retain its rights and obligations as "Lessor" under this Agreement. In the event of such a sale and lease-back by Lessor, (a) the Head Lessor shall meet the requirements for a "Transferee" as defined in Section 14.2(a)(ii) above, (b) Lessor shall be entitled to assign its rights in this Agreement to such Head Lessor as security for its obligations under the head lease, (c) the Head Lessor shall be entitled to grant to one or more purchase money lenders, or to an indenture trustee on behalf of such lenders, a Security Interest covering the Leased Property and the Operative Documents, (d) Lessee shall execute and deliver to Lessor, such Head Lessor and such secured parties, as appropriate, the documents specified in Sections 14.2(c) and 14.3(b) above, and Lessee shall cooperate with Lessor to make such other changes to the Operative Documents, such as including such Head Lessor and such secured parties as additional insureds and "Indemnitees", as Lessor may reasonably request.

14.5 Further Acknowledgments

Lessee further acknowledges that any Transferee shall in turn have the rights of, and be subject to the conditions to, transfer and grants of Security Interests set forth above in this Section 14.

14.6 Certain Protections for Lessee's Benefit

The rights of Lessee under this Agreement shall be superior to the rights of any Financing Party or Head Lessor, and Lessor shall require each Financing Party holding a Security Interest in this Agreement and each Head Lessor to agree in writing with Lessee that such Financing Party's and Head Lessor's rights in and to the Leased

Property and/or this Agreement shall be subject to the terms of this Agreement, including to Lessee's rights to the quiet use, possession and enjoyment provisions contained in this Agreement. Lessor's obligations to perform the terms and conditions of this Agreement shall remain in full force and effect notwithstanding the creation of any Financing Security Document or head lease. No Transfer shall cause or result in any increase in or additional payment obligations (including with respect to Taxes) of Lessee under this Agreement based on the laws in effect at the time of such Transfer. Lessor shall not enter into any Financing Security Document or head lease that violates the terms of this Section 14.6.

15. GOVERNING LAW AND JURISDICTION[15]

15.1 Governing Law

THIS AGREEMENT SHALL, IN ALL RESPECTS, INCLUDING ALL MATTERS OF CONSTRUCTION, VALIDITY AND PERFORMANCE, BE GOVERNED BY AND CONSTRUED IN ACCORDANCE WITH THE LAWS OF ENGLAND AND WALES THE LAWS OF ENGLAND AND WALES SHALL ALSO GOVERN ANY NON-CONTRACTUAL OBLIGATIONS ARISING OUT OF OR IN CONNECTION WITH THIS AGREEMENT AND EACH OTHER OPERATIVE DOCUMENT, UNLESS OTHERWISE EXPRESSLY PROVIDED THEREIN.

15.2 Consent to Jurisdiction

Each of Lessor and Lessee hereby agrees that the English courts are to have non-exclusive jurisdiction to settle any disputes which may arise out of or in connection with this Agreement or any other Operative Document, and by execution and delivery of this Agreement each of Lessor and Lessee hereby irrevocably submits to and accepts with regard to any such action or proceeding, for itself and in respect of its assets, generally and unconditionally, the jurisdiction of the aforesaid courts. Each of Lessor and Lessee waives objection to the English courts on grounds of inconvenient forum or otherwise as regards proceedings arising out of or in connection with this Agreement and any other Operative Document and agrees that a judgment or order of an English court in any such proceedings is conclusive and binding on it and may be enforced against it in the courts of any other jurisdiction. Nothing herein shall limit the right of either Lessor or Lessee from bringing any legal action or proceeding or obtaining execution of judgment against the other in any other appropriate jurisdiction or concurrently in more than one jurisdiction. Each of Lessor and Lessee further agrees that, subject to applicable law, a final judgment in any action or proceeding arising out of or relating to this Agreement or any other Operative Document shall be conclusive

15. *See* §3.17 and §3.18 of the text *supra*.

and may be enforced in any other jurisdiction outside England by suit on the judgment, a certified or exemplified copy of which shall be conclusive evidence of the fact and the amount of the indebtedness or liability therein described, or in any other manner provided by law.

15.3 Waiver of Jury Trial

LESSEE AND LESSOR HEREBY WAIVE TRIAL BY JURY IN ANY JUDICIAL PROCEEDING TO WHICH THEY ARE PARTIES INVOLVING, DIRECTLY OR INDIRECTLY, ANY MATTER ARISING OUT OF OR RELATING TO THIS AGREEMENT.

15.4 Service of Process

(a) Lessor hereby irrevocably designates, appoints and empowers [] of [] as its authorized agent to receive on its behalf and on behalf of its property service of copies of the summons and complaint and any other process which may be served in any action or proceeding arising out of or in connection with to this Agreement and/or any Operative Document. Such service may be made by mailing or delivering a copy of such process in care of the appropriate process agent described in this Section 15.4 and Lessor hereby irrevocably authorizes and directs its designated process agent to accept such service on its behalf. Lessor further agrees that failure by a process agent appointed in accordance with the foregoing terms to notify Lessor of the process shall not invalidate the proceeding concerned. Notwithstanding the foregoing, nothing herein shall affect the rights of either party to serve process in any other manner permitted by law.

(b) Lessee hereby irrevocably designates, appoints and empowers [] of [] as its authorized agent to receive on its behalf and on behalf of its property service of copies of the summons and complaint and any other process which may be served in any action or proceeding arising out of or in connection with to this Agreement and/or any Operative Document. Such service may be made by mailing or delivering a copy of such process in care of the appropriate process agent described in this Section 15.4 and Lessee hereby irrevocably authorizes and directs its designated process agent to accept such service on its behalf. Lessee further agrees that failure by a process agent appointed in accordance with the foregoing terms to notify Lessee of the process shall not invalidate the proceeding concerned. Notwithstanding the foregoing, nothing herein shall affect the rights of either party to serve process in any other manner permitted by law.

16. MISCELLANEOUS[16]

16.1 Waivers, Remedies Cumulative

The rights of Lessor or Lessee under this Agreement may be exercised as often as necessary, are cumulative and not exclusive of that party's rights under any law and may be waived only in writing and specifically. Delay in exercising or non-exercise of any such right is not a waiver of that right.

16.2 Delegation

Lessor may delegate to any Person or Persons all or any of the trusts, powers or discretions vested in it by this Agreement and any such delegation may be made upon such terms and conditions and subject to such regulations (including power to sub-delegate) as Lessor in its absolute discretion thinks fit.

16.3 Appropriation

If any sum paid or recovered in respect of the liabilities of Lessee under this Agreement is less than the amount then due, Lessor may apply that sum to amounts due under this Agreement in such proportions and order and generally in such manner as Lessor may determine.

16.4 Currency Indemnity

(a) If Lessor receives an amount in respect of the Lessee's liability under this Agreement or if such liability is converted into a claim, proof, judgment or order in a currency other than the currency (the "contractual currency") in which the amount is expressed to be payable under this Agreement:
   (i) Lessee will indemnify Lessor, as an independent obligation, against any loss arising out of or as a result of such conversion;
   (ii) if the amount received by Lessor, when converted into the contractual currency (at the market rate at which Lessor is able on the relevant date to purchase the contractual currency in New York City with that other currency) is less than the amount owed in the contractual currency, Lessee will, forthwith on demand, pay to Lessor an amount in the contractual currency equal to the deficit; and
   (iii) Lessee will pay to Lessor on demand any exchange costs and Taxes payable in connection with the conversion.

16. *See* §3.19 of the text *supra*.

(b) Lessee waives, to the extent permitted by Applicable Law, any right it may have in any jurisdiction to pay any amount under this Agreement in a currency other than that in which it is expressed to be payable.

16.5 Payment by Lessor

Lessor will not be obliged to pay any amounts to Lessee under this Agreement so long as any sums which are then due from Lessee under this Agreement remain unpaid and any such amounts which would otherwise be due will fall due only if and when Lessee has paid all such sums.

16.6 Severability

If a provision of this Agreement is or becomes illegal, invalid or unenforceable in any jurisdiction, that will not affect:

(a) the legality, validity or enforceability in that jurisdiction of any other provision of this Agreement; or
(b) the legality, validity or enforceability in any other jurisdiction of that or any other provision of this Agreement.

16.7 Remedy

If Lessee fails to comply with any provision of this Agreement, Lessor may, without being in any way obliged to do so or responsible for so doing and without prejudice to the ability of Lessor to treat the non-compliance as a Default, effect compliance on behalf of Lessee, whereupon Lessee shall become liable to pay immediately any sums expended by Lessor together with all costs and expenses (including reasonable legal costs) necessarily incurred in connection therewith.

16.8 Expenses

(a) Lessor and Lessee shall each bear their respective expenses (including legal, professional and out-of-pocket expenses) incurred or payable in connection with the negotiation, preparation and execution of the Operative Documents, except that Lessee shall be responsible for (i) all registration and filing fees in connection with the registration of the Aircraft in the State of Registration, (ii) all fees in connection with the filing and translation of any Operative Document or related document, and (iii) the legal fees and out-of-pocket expenses of Lessor's Counsel.

(b) Lessee shall pay to Lessor on demand all expenses (including legal, professional and out-of-pocket expenses) incurred or payable by Lessor in connection with the granting of any waiver or consent under this Agreement.

(c) Lessee will pay to Lessor on demand all expenses (including legal, survey and other costs) payable or incurred by Lessor in contemplation of, or otherwise in connection with, the enforcement of or preservation of any of Lessor's rights under the Operative Documents, or in respect of the repossession of the Aircraft.

(d) Lessor will pay to Lessee on demand all expenses (including legal costs) payable or incurred by Lessee in contemplation of, or otherwise in connection with, the enforcement of or preservation of any of Lessee's rights under this Agreement.

16.9 Time of Essence

The time stipulated in this Agreement for all payments payable by Lessee to Lessor and for the performance of Lessee's other obligations under this Agreement that are due on a specified or determinable date will be of the essence of this Agreement (subject always to any applicable grace period).

16.10 Notices

(a) All notices and other communications given under or in connection with this Agreement shall be in writing (including telefax and e-mail) and in English, and shall be deemed to be received as follows:

  (i) If the notice or other communication is sent by telefax, it shall be deemed to be received at the time of receipt by the sender of a transmission report indicating that all pages of the telefax transmission were properly transmitted (unless the recipient notifies the sender promptly, or if received after 17:00 local time, by no later than 10:00 local time the following Business Day, that the transmission was incomplete or illegible, in which case the telefax shall be deemed to have been received at the time of receipt by the sender of a further clear transmission report on retransmitting the telefax), provided the relevant telefax transmission (or retransmission, as the case may be) was transmitted to the receiver between 09:00 and 17:00 local time. If it was transmitted later, then it shall be deemed to have been received at 09:00 local time on the succeeding Business Day.

  (ii) In any other case, the notice or other communication shall be deemed to be received when delivered to the address or e-mail address (if any) specified in Section 16.10(b).

(b) All such notices, requests, demands and other communications shall be sent:

(i)	to Lessor at:	[Name of Lessor] [Lessor's Address] U.S.A. Attention: Telephone: Telefax: E-mail:
(ii)	to Lessee at:	[Name of Lessee] [Lessee's Address] Attention: Telephone: Telefax: E-mail:

or to such other address, e-mail address or telefax number as shall have been notified by one party to the other in the manner set out in this Section 16.10.

16.11 Sole and Entire Agreement

This Agreement is the sole and entire agreement between Lessor and Lessee in relation to the leasing of the Aircraft, and supersedes all previous agreements in relation to that leasing. The terms and conditions of this Agreement can only be varied by an instrument in writing executed by both parties or by their duly authorized representatives.

16.12 Indemnities

All rights expressed to be granted to each Indemnitee under this Agreement (other than any Financing Party) are given to Lessor as agent for and on behalf of that Indemnitee.

16.13 Counterparts

This Agreement may be executed in one or more counterparts, each of which shall constitute an original and, when taken together, all of which shall constitute one and the same Agreement.

16.14 English Language

All documents delivered to the Lessor pursuant to this Agreement will be in English or, if not in English, will be accompanied by a certified English translation. If there is any inconsistency between the English version of this Agreement and any version in any other language, the English version will prevail.

16.15 Further Assurances

Lessee shall promptly and duly execute and deliver to Lessor such further documents and assurances and take such further action as Lessor may from time to time reasonably request in order to carry out more effectively the intent and purpose of the Operative Documents and to establish and protect Lessor's title to the Leased Property, the interests of any subsequent transferee and Lessor's rights and remedies created or intended to be created under the Operative Documents.

16.16 Confidentiality

Neither Lessor nor Lessee shall, without the other's prior written consent, communicate or disclose the terms of the Operative Documents or any information or documents furnished pursuant to the Operative Documents (except to the extent that the same are within the public domain) to any third party (other than any Financing Party, any prospective Transferee, any material investor in Lessee or creditor in Lessee, Head Lessors, the respective external legal advisers, auditors, insurance brokers or underwriters of Lessor, Lessee and such parties, and the Airframe Manufacturer and Engine Manufacturer); provided, that disclosure will be permitted, to the extent required:

(a) pursuant to an order of any court of competent jurisdiction; or
(b) pursuant to any procedure for discovery of documents in any proceedings before any such court; or
(c) pursuant to any law or regulation having the force of law; or
(d) pursuant to a lawful requirement of any authority with whose requirements the disclosing party is legally obliged to comply; or
(e) in order to perfect any assignment of any assignable warranties.

[signature page follows]

IN WITNESS WHEREOF Lessor and Lessee have executed this Lease Agreement [msn] on the date shown at the beginning of this Agreement.

[NAME OF LESSOR]
By:______________________________
Name:
Title:
[NAME OF LESSEE]
By:______________________________
Name:
Title:

SCHEDULE 1 – DESCRIPTION OF LEASED PROPERTY

Part 1 Aircraft Specification

Identification:

Aircraft Model:	[mfgr] Model [model]
Registration Mark:	______
Serial Number:	[msn]
Date of Manufacture:	___________

Weight Data:

Maximum Gross Taxi Weight:	_______ lbs.
Maximum Gross Takeoff Weight:	_______ lbs.
Maximum Landing Weight:	_______ lbs.
Maximum Zero Fuel Weight:	_______ lbs.
Operating Empty Weight:	_______ lbs.
Fuel Capacity:	_______ U.S. gallons

Airframe and Interior Equipment:

Galleys	Locations:	___ forward; ___ aft
Lavatories	Locations:	___ forward; ___ aft
Air Stairs	Locations:	___ forward
Passenger Seats	Types:	

Engines:

Manufacturer:	[EngMfgr]	
Position	No.1	No.2
Model:	[EngModel]	[EngModel]
Serial Numbers:	[esn1]	[esn2]

APU:

Manufacturer:	[...........]
Model:	[...........]
Serial Number:	[...........]

Landing Gear:

Position:	Nose	Left Main	Right Main
Manufacturer:	[...........]	[...........]	[...........]
Part Number:	[...........]	[...........]	[...........]
Serial Number:	[...........]	[...........]	[...........]

Major Avionics Equipment:

Description	Manufacturer	Part No.	Qty.

SCHEDULE 1 – DESCRIPTION OF LEASED PROPERTY

Part 2 Aircraft Documents

1. Manuals: The following manuals shall be delivered with the Aircraft. Each manual shall be current and include all temporary revisions. Each manual shall be in the English language.
   (a) FAA-Approved Airplane Flight Manual.
   (b) Weight and Balance Control and Cargo Loading Manual and Supplements (load and trim sheet) to include last weight and balance paperwork and delivery equipment list.
   (c) Operations Manual and Quick Reference Handbook.
   (d) Structural Repair Manual
   (e) Aircraft Maintenance Manuals
   (f) Aircraft/Engine/APU Illustrated Parts Catalog (IPC) (Lessee Customized)
   (g) Wiring Diagram Manual
2. Airworthiness Directives Documentation: The following data will be provided as well as all records associated with A.D. compliance:

(a) a single, complete and current status list of each AD to the Airframe, each Engine and each Part (at redelivery, the list shall be typed, certified and signed by authorized quality assurance representative of Lessee);

(b) legible copies of the completion documentation that accomplish each AD, and if the AD involves repetitive inspection, documentation from the last accomplishment is sufficient (if the original completion documents are not available, at a minimum a copy of the job card of engineering order that accomplished the AD shall be provided, plus a certification letter (at redelivery, signed by Lessee's airworthiness department) stating that the AD in question was accomplished at a certain Flight Hour, Cycle and date and referencing all pertinent support documentation (i.e., engineering order, alternate means of compliance, etc.); however, any AD that was complied with by an alternate means of compliance must have all original documentation and necessary air authority approvals); and

(c) exemptions or deviations, if any, granted by any aviation authority on AD compliance, including copy of exemption request.

3. Engineering Documentation:

(a) A single, current list in English language of the following shall be provided:

(i) Service Bulletin status.

(ii) Major repairs list, if applicable.

(iii) Supplement Type Certificate list, if any.

(b) Data package covering all non-manufacturer or non-aviation authority approved repairs or alterations, including any submittals to aviation authorities for an approval, if applicable.

4. Additional Documentation:

(a) Quarterly Published Reliability Reports for last 3 months (one year, if available)

(b) Location map of emergency equipment with description

(c) Interior configuration drawings

(d) Passenger/Cargo Equipment List (seats, galleys, lavatories)

(e) Complete paperwork for last "D" Check overhaul.

(f) Compass card calibration documentation

(g) All life records for the assemblies and rotable parts installed during the last overhaul for each nose, left hand and right hand main landing gears

5. Individual Aircraft and Engine Records:

(a) Letter of Declaration for each major aircraft/engine accident or major incident which shall include supporting documentation, if any

(b) Engine trend monitoring data for each Engine.

(c) Aircraft Technical Log for the last six (6) months of operation (at redelivery)

(d) Serviceable/overhaul tags for all life limited parts and hard time components listed in the rotable components list (for Term only).

(e) Listing of Aircraft, Engine and APU components status by P/N-S/N-Description Position TBO-TSO-TSN, total time, next due time, including interpretation keys, (Rotable Component List)
(f) Engine and APU logbooks
(g) Aircraft and Engine time status at redelivery with serial number, total time, total cycles and times of the last letter check inspection
(h) All (i) Engine and APU records for the last heavy maintenance shop visit, (ii) back to birth history for each Engine life limited part, and (iii) last power plant test cell run documents for Engines and APU
(i) Aircraft Readiness Log (from aircraft manufacturer)
(j) Copies of all applicable Master Changes (M.C.) performed on the Aircraft, if any
(k) aviation authority approvals and operator certification reports for major modifications alterations and repairs that are not covered by manufacturer's service bulletins.
(l) Fire blocking status for all seats, interior fabrics/material, including burn test documentation and certification.
(m) Current CPCP Status Report
(n) Current list outlining all waiver items/components not approved by FAR Part 121.

SCHEDULE 2 – OPERATING CONDITION AT DELIVERY

On the Delivery Date the Aircraft will be in the condition set out below:

1. General Condition

The Aircraft will:

(a) be clean by major international airline standards;
(b) be airworthy, conform to type design and be in a condition for safe operation with all equipment, components and systems operating in accordance with their intended use and within limits established by the manufacturer and approved by the FAA, and all pilot discrepancies and deferred maintenance items cleared on a terminating action basis;
(c) have a valid export certificate of airworthiness with respect to the Aircraft issued by the ________ Aviation Authority;
(d) have zero Flight Hours (except for test and acceptance flights) since undergoing a block "C" Check in accordance with the MPD before the Scheduled Delivery Date;
(e) have had accomplished all outstanding ADs and mandatory orders affecting that model of Aircraft issued by the FAA or EASA that are due before the Delivery Date on a terminating action basis;
(f) have no special or unique manufacturer inspection or check requirements specific to the Aircraft that exist unless there is no terminating action available from any source;

(g) be free of any system-related leaks;
(h) have all fluid reservoirs (including fuel, oil, oxygen, hydraulic and water) full, and the waste tank serviced in accordance with the Manufacturer's instructions;
(i) have all signs and decals clean, secure and legible; and
(j) be painted white in accordance with standard industry practices and the paint manufacturer's instructions and avoiding any overspray on other surfaces.

2. Parts
   (a) Each life limited or hard time controlled Part, excluding Engine Parts, shall have not less than 3,600 Flight Hours, 3,600 Cycles or 18 months (whichever is the most limiting factor) remaining to the next scheduled removal in accordance with the MPD intervals or OEM recommendations in the event that the MPD does not provide intervals.
   (b) Each calendar limited Part (including hard time controlled Parts with calendar limits but excluding Engine Parts) will have at least 18 months remaining to its next scheduled removal or overhaul in accordance with the Airframe Manufacturer's MPD recommendations or OEM recommendations in the event that the Airframe Manufacturer's MPD does not provide intervals.
   (c) Each "on-condition" and "condition monitored" Part will be serviceable in accordance with the MPD.
3. Engines
   (a) Each Engine shall have at least 2,500 Cycles remaining until the next scheduled CER or LLP replacement under the existing maintenance program.
   (b) No Engine shall be "on engineering watch", on a reduced interval inspection or otherwise have any defect that reduces the Flight Hours or Cycles (whichever is more limiting) of remaining life pursuant to Engine Manufacturer's or airworthiness requirements until overhaul to less than 2,500.
   (c) Each Engine shall be in a condition that can operate at maximum rated take-off power at sea level with an E.G.T. margin of 15 degrees Celsius.
   (d) Lessor shall perform a maximum power assurance run and condition, acceleration and bleed valve scheduling checks on each Engine in accordance with the AMM. Lessor will record and evaluate each Engine's performance, with Lessee's representatives entitled to be present. Each Engine shall pass such tests without operational limitations throughout the operating envelope in accordance with the AMM.
   (e) Lessor shall perform a video borescope inspection of all accessible gas path sections of each Engine (accessible whether by borescope port or other means), including the low pressure and high pressure compressors and the turbine area of such Engine, and Lessee's representatives will be entitled to observe such borescope inspection. All items beyond the

Engine Manufacturer's maintenance manual serviceable limits will be rectified at Lessor's sole cost and expense.

4. Fuselage, Windows and Doors
   (a) The fuselage will not contain any dents, corrosion or abrasions that exceed the SRM limitations and shall be free of scab patches and loose, pulled or missing rivets.
   (b) The windows will not contain any delamination, blemishes or crazing that exceed the prescribed parameters under the AMM and will be properly sealed.
   (c) The doors will be free moving, correctly rigged and fitted with serviceable seals.
5. Wings and Empennage
   (a) The leading edges will not contain any damage that exceeds the SRM limitations.
   (b) All unpainted cowlings and fairings will be polished.
   (c) All wings will be free of fuel leaks.
6. Interior
   (a) The interior will be fully serviceable.
   (b) All emergency equipment having a calendar life will have a minimum of one year or 100% of its total approved life remaining, whichever is less.
   (c) All curtains, carpets, seat covers and seat cushions will be clean and free from stains and worn out (threadbare) areas and will conform to EASA/FAR fire resistance regulations as applicable to an EASA/FAR Part 121 operator.
7. Cockpit
   (a) All fairing panels shall be free of stains and cracks, clean, secure and repainted as necessary.
   (b) All floor coverings will be clean and effectively sealed.
   (c) All seat covers will be in good condition, clean and free of stains and will conform to EASA/FAR fire resistance regulations as applicable to an EASA/FAR Part 121 operator.
   (d) All seats will be serviceable, in good condition and repainted as necessary.
8. Cargo Compartments
   (a) All panels will be in good condition and effectively sealed.
   (b) All nets will be in good condition.
   (c) The cargo compartments will comply with EASA/FAR fire resistance and containment regulations as applicable to an EASA/FAR Part 121 operator.
9. Landing Gear
   (a) The installed main and nose landing gear components and their associated actuators and parts will be cleared of all inspections for not less than 12 months, 3,000 Flight Hours or 3,000 Cycles of operation (whichever is more limiting).

(b) The tires and brakes will have 50% of the wear, as specified by the manufacturer as serviceable limits, remaining until next removal.
(c) The landing gear and wheel wells will be clean, free of leaks and repaired as necessary.

10. APU
(a) The APU shall be serviceable in accordance with the MPD.
(b) The APU shall have not more than 1,500 Flight Hours of operation since its last hot section inspection.
(c) Lessor shall perform a video borescope inspection and an electrical and pneumatic load analysis of the APU, and Lessee's representatives will be entitled to observe such borescope inspection. All items beyond the Manufacturer's recommended serviceable limits will be rectified at Lessor's sole cost and expense.

11. Aircraft Documents
The Aircraft will be accompanied by the Aircraft Documents listed on Part 2 of Schedule 1. Lessor will also provide to Lessee all historical and current maintenance manuals, aircraft and engine technical records and data, and other aircraft documentation in the possession of Lessor. Upon the request of Lessee, Lessor shall use reasonable efforts to obtain any required maintenance and technical records or documents not in its custody. All Aircraft Documents provided to Lessee at Delivery shall be listed and included as an attachment to the Certificate of Delivery Condition.

12. Acceptance Flight
Before the Delivery Date, Lessor shall cause an acceptance flight of the Aircraft to be performed of up to three hours at Lessor's cost (with up to two representatives of Lessee on-board as observers), and such further acceptance flights as may be necessary in the event that the first or subsequent flights do not confirm that the Aircraft complies with the delivery conditions set forth in this Schedule 2.

13. Delivery Inspection
Before the Delivery Date, Lessor shall make the Leased Property available for Lessee to conduct a ground inspection of the Aircraft and an inspection of the Aircraft Documents to its satisfaction

SCHEDULE 3 – OPERATING CONDITION AT REDELIVERY

On the Expiry Date the Aircraft, subject to fair wear and tear generally, will be in the condition set out below:

1. General Condition
The Aircraft will:
(a) be clean by major international airline standards;
(b) have installed the full complement of engines and other equipment, parts and accessories and loose equipment installed at Delivery and

required under the Approved Maintenance Program and usually installed in the other aircraft of the same model operated by Lessee (together with any additions and improvements thereto, or replacements thereof, effected pursuant to and in accordance with this Agreement) and be in a condition suitable for immediate operation in commercial service;

(c) be airworthy, conform to type design and be in a condition for safe operation with all equipment, components and systems operating in accordance with their intended use and within limits established by the manufacturer and approved by the Aviation Authority, and all pilot discrepancies and deferred maintenance items cleared on a terminating action basis;

(d) have a standard transport category Certificate of Airworthiness issued by the Aviation Authority in accordance with the Aviation Law and the FAR's or, if requested by Lessor, a valid export certificate of airworthiness with respect to the Aircraft issued by the Aviation Authority for a country designated by Lessor, and unconditionally meet all Aviation Authority requirements for immediate operations and be in a condition which makes it eligible for the issuance of an FAA Certificate of Airworthiness;

(e) comply with the manufacturer's original specification to the extent that it so complied on the Delivery Date and subject to any alterations made pursuant to and in accordance with this Agreement after such date;

(f) have undergone, at Return immediately prior to redelivery of the Aircraft, the next sequential block "C" check or equivalent block-type maintenance on the Airframe performed by the Final Maintenance Performer in accordance with the then current Airframe Manufacturer's MPD, including all corresponding and lower level checks, and Lessee shall perform all other inspections and maintenance tasks (including corrosion prevention and control and aging aircraft inspections, if any and as applicable), all structural/systems/zonal inspections and out-of-sequence inspections due at that time, and all routine and non-routine tasks, all with full fault rectification, sufficient to clear the Aircraft for operation until its next scheduled C-Check per the then current Airframe Manufacturer's MPD and in any event not less than 6,000 Flight Hours, 4,000 Cycles and 24 months. If the Approved Maintenance Program permits such "C" check, inspections, checks and other tasks to be performed in phases, Lessee shall ensure that the Final Maintenance Performer performs all phases of such maintenance check, inspections and other tasks immediately prior to the Return in order to align fully such maintenance of the Aircraft with the then latest revision of the Airframe Manufacturer's "block type" MPD schedule to the same extent as if the Approved Maintenance Program did not permit such maintenance check, inspections and other tasks to be performed in phases;

(g) have had accomplished all outstanding ADs and mandatory orders affecting that model of Aircraft issued by the Aviation Authority, EASA or the FAA that are due during the Term or by the next block C-Check or within the next 6,000 Flight Hours, 4,500 Cycles or 18 months therafter on a terminating action basis; ADs and mandatory orders that do not have a terminating action will be accomplished at the highest level of inspection or modification permitted;

(h) no special or unique manufacturer inspection or check requirements specific to the Aircraft will exist unless there is no terminating action available from any source;

(i) have installed all applicable vendor's and manufacturer's service bulletin kits received free of charge by Lessee that are appropriate for the Aircraft and, to the extent not installed, those kits retained by Lessee will be furnished free of charge to Lessor;

(j) be free of any system-related leaks;

(k) all fluid reservoirs (including fuel, oil, oxygen, hydraulic and water) will be full, and the waste tank serviced in accordance with the manufacturer's instructions;

(l) all fuel tanks and hydraulic systems will have recently undergone an anti-fungus/biological growth contamination laboratory evaluation, and any excessive levels of contamination corrected;

(m) have had the Aircraft interior fumigated prior to Return;

(n) have all Lessee specific corporate branding and Lessee unique external and interior markings, decals and signs removed and blended, and Lessee shall have restored such areas to the original condition that existed prior to the application of such markings;

(o) have all signs and decals clean, secure and legible; and

(p) in conjunction with the redelivery check, be stripped of Lessee's livery, with all exterior markings removed and replaced, and either painted white or painted in the livery of the next operator, as identified by Lessor, in either case in accordance with standard industry practices and the paint Manufacturer's instructions and avoiding any overspray on other surfaces; the Aircraft will be painted at an appropriate time in the Return process so that the paint will have a uniform and continuous finish, without damage caused by the removal of panels, and after painting the Aircraft will be weighed and any flight surfaces will be removed and balanced as required by the Manufacturer's MPD.

2. Parts

(a) Each life limited or hard time controlled Part, excluding Engine Parts, shall have not less than 6,000 Flight Hours, 4,500 Cycles or 18 months (whichever is the most limiting factor) remaining to the next scheduled removal in accordance with the MPD intervals or OEM recommendations in the event that the MPD does not provide intervals.

(b) Each calendar limited Part (including hard time controlled Parts with calendar limits but excluding Engine Parts) will have at least 13 months remaining to its next scheduled removal or overhaul in accordance with the Airframe Manufacturer's current MPD recommendations or OEM recommendations in the event that the Airframe Manufacturer's MPD does not provide intervals.

(c) Each "on-condition" and "condition monitored" Part will be serviceable and have been maintained in accordance with the Manufacturer's recommendations and the MPD.

3. <u>Engines</u>

(a) Each Engine shall, at Return, to the extent not previously provided to Lessor, be accompanied by all documentation Lessor may require to evidence that title thereto is properly vested in Lessor in accordance with Section 8.17.

(b) Each Engine shall have no more than 4,000 Flight Hours since its last Engine Shop Visit and no less than 4,000 Flight Cycles remaining until the next anticipated Engine Shop Visit (based on the Engine Manufacturer's MTBR for this type engine operating at the agreed upon hour to cycle ratio). No Engine shall be "on engineering watch," on a reduced interval inspection or otherwise have any defect that reduces the Flight Hours or Cycles (whichever is more limiting) of remaining life pursuant to Engine Manufacturer's or airworthiness requirements until overhaul to less than 4,000.

(c) Each Engine shall be in a condition that can operate at maximum rated take-off power at sea level with an E.G.T. margin of 30°C at an I.A.T. of 32°C.

(d) Each Engine LLP shall have not less than [] Cycles of life remaining.

(e) Within the first week of induction into the final maintenance check (or within one week of installation of an Engine if it is installed during the redelivery check), in accordance with the AMM, Lessee shall perform a maximum power assurance run test and condition, acceleration and vibration study on each Engine. Lessee will record and evaluate each Engine's performance, with Lessor and its representatives entitled to be present. Each Engine shall pass such tests without operational limitations throughout the operating envelope in accordance with the published AMM.

(f) Following the last flight prior to the Return and ground performance tests, Lessee shall perform a video borescope inspection of all accessible gas path sections of each Engine (accessible whether by borescope port or other means), including the low pressure and high pressure compressors and the turbine area of such Engine. All items beyond the Airframe Manufacturer's published maintenance manual serviceable limits will be rectified at Lessee's sole cost and expense.

4. Fuselage, Windows and Doors
   (a) The fuselage will not contain any dents, corrosion or abrasions.
   (b) The windshields and windows will not contain any delamination, blemishes or crazing.
   (c) The doors will be free moving, correctly rigged and fitted with serviceable seals.
5. Wings and Empennage
   (a) The leading edges will not contain any damage that exceeds the SRM limitations.
   (b) All unpainted cowlings and fairings will be polished.
   (c) All wings will be free of fuel leaks.
6. Interior
   (a) The interior will be fully serviceable.
   (b) All emergency equipment having a calendar life will have a minimum of 18 months or 100% of its total approved life remaining, whichever is less.
   (c) All curtains, carpets, seat covers and seat cushions will be clean and free from stains and worn out (threadbare) areas and will conform to EASA/FAR fire resistance regulations as applicable to an EASA/FAR Part 121 operator.
7. Cockpit
   (a) All fairing panels shall be free of stains and cracks, clean, secure and repainted as requested by Lessor.
   (b) All floor coverings will be clean and effectively sealed.
   (c) All seat covers will be in good condition, clean and free of stains and will conform to EASA/FAR fire resistance regulations as applicable to an EASA/FAR Part 121 operator.
   (d) All seats will be fully inspected per the seat CMM, be in good condition and repainted as requested by Lessor.
8. Cargo Compartments
   (a) All panels will be in good condition without repairs and effectively sealed.
   (b) All nets will be in good condition without any repairs.
   (c) The cargo compartments will comply with EASA/FAR fire resistance and containment regulations as applicable to an EASA/FAR Part 121 operator.
9. Landing Gear
   (a) The installed main and nose landing gear components and their associated actuators and parts will be in serviceable condition with no less than 3,000 Cycles or 12 months (whichever is the most limiting factor) remaining until the next scheduled Landing Gear Overhaul under the Approved Maintenance Program.
   (b) The tires and brakes will have 50% of the wear, as specified by the manufacturer as serviceable limits, remaining until next removal.
   (c) The landing gear and wheel wells will be clean, free of leaks and repaired as necessary.

10. APU
   (a) The APU shall be serviceable in accordance with the Approved Maintenance Program parameters.
   (b) The APU shall have not more than 500 Flight Hours of operation since its last APU Basic Shop Visit.
   (c) Within the first week of induction into the final maintenance check (or within one week of installation of an APU if it is installed during the redelivery check), Lessee shall perform a video borescope inspection and an electrical and pneumatic load analysis of the APU, and all items beyond the Manufacturer's recommended limits will be rectified at Lessee's sole cost and expense.
11. Corrosion
   (a) The Aircraft will be in compliance with the CPCP.
   (b) Fuel tanks will be free from contamination and corrosion and the fuel tank treatment program that is part of the Approved Maintenance Program will be current.
   (c) Lessee shall perform (or have performed by an Agreed Maintenance Performer), at Return immediately prior to redelivery of the Aircraft, an internal and external corrosion inspection in accordance with the CPCP, and correct any discrepancies in accordance with the recommendations of the Airframe Manufacturer and the SRM. In addition, all inspected areas will be properly treated with corrosion inhibitor as recommended by Airframe Manufacturer.
12. Structural Inspections
   If Lessee performed any structural inspections or tasks on a sampling basis but did not perform such inspections on the Aircraft, such work shall also be performed on the Aircraft.
13. Trend Monitoring
   If any historical and technical records, condition trend monitoring data, power assurance runs or borescope inspection indicate an abnormal acceleration or shift in the rate of performance deterioration or oil consumption in any Engine or the APU, Lessee shall correct such conditions causing the accelerated rate of deterioration or oil consumption.
14. Additional Work
   (a) Lessee shall also perform or cause to be performed, to the extent it is able, any other work reasonably required by Lessor (and not otherwise required under this Agreement) so long as such work does not prevent Lessee from returning the Aircraft on the Expiry Date, and Lessor shall reimburse Lessee for the Actual Cost of such work.
   (b) At the request of Lessor, Lessee shall perform "bridging" maintenance procedures for the purpose of standardizing the Aircraft to the maintenance program of any subsequent operator of the Aircraft; provided, that Lessor shall pay to Lessee the Actual Cost of all "bridging" procedures that are in excess of or not in lieu of the final checks and maintenance

work to be performed pursuant to this Schedule 3 and that are in excess of "bridging" maintenance work required to align the Leased Property to the Airframe Manufacturer's MPD.

15. Final Inspection

During the 30 days prior to Return, Lessee will make the Aircraft and Aircraft Documents available at one single location to representatives of Lessor for inspection ("Final Inspection") in order to verify that the condition of the Leased Property complies with this Agreement. The Final Inspection will be long enough to permit the representatives of Lessor to inspect, at their own cost, the Aircraft Documents, the Aircraft and any uninstalled Parts and Engines. The representatives of Lessor shall attend and conduct the Final Inspection diligently and, without limiting their right to conduct the full Final Inspection permitted by this Agreement, will cooperate with Lessee in order to complete the Final Inspection as soon as reasonably practical. In addition, Lessor's representatives shall be entitled to review the workscope for, and be present at, all redelivery checks, maintenance work and meetings in connection with the Return, including, for the avoidance of doubt, all production meetings between Lessee and the Final Maintenance Performer. During the redelivery checks, Lessor's representatives shall not be restricted from opening any accessible panel or bay door.

16. Acceptance Flight

Prior to Return, Lessor shall also be entitled, as part of the Final Inspection, to require Lessee to perform an acceptance flight of up to three hours at Lessee's cost (with up to four representatives of Lessor on-board as observers) and such further acceptance flights as may be necessary in the event that the first or subsequent flights do not confirm to Lessor that the Aircraft complies with the redelivery requirements of this Agreement.

17. Aircraft Documents

Lessee shall redeliver to Lessor on the Expiry Date all Aircraft Documents delivered with the Aircraft on the Delivery Date in the form and condition in which such Aircraft Documents were delivered by Lessor to Lessee, and all other Aircraft Documents acquired or prepared by Lessee during the Term, including time logs showing Flight Hours and Cycles for the Airframe, Engines, Landing Gear and APU on any given date, documents, manuals (revised up to and including the most current revisions issued by the applicable Manufacturer), data, overhaul records, time controlled part and hard time part traceability to last overhaul and/or repair/test (as applicable) and total Flight Hours/Cycles/calendar time since new or since last overhaul or repair (as applicable), LLP traceability to original source of origin (back to birth) and last overhaul and "zero time since new" for time controlled and hard time parts that have been replaced by Lessee, log books, and serviceable parts tags (such as FAA Form 8130-3 or EASA Form One) for all Parts that have been replaced by Lessee, component teardown/inspection and shop findings reports or alternative compliance as described in Section 8.13 for time controlled parts that have been replaced by Lessee, Aviation Authority forms (as applicable), modification records, inspection reports (including non-destructive test documentation such as x-ray and eddy current documentation), Non-Incident/Non-Accident Statements for the Airframe and Engines and all other documentation such as reliability reports and the like pertaining to the Aircraft, Engines and Parts. If Lessee's maintenance program did not track tasks using the MPD numbering system, Lessee will produce a cross reference that will enable Lessor to track each Lessee maintenance program task to the MPD. Lessee will provide a list of all maintenance program tasks last accomplished and "next due" status. All discrepancies found in the Aircraft Documents shall be corrected, and any missing Aircraft Documents shall be reconstructed by Lessee at Lessee's sole cost and expense prior to the return of the Aircraft. All Aircraft Documents shall be in the English language.

18. Assignment of Warranties

At Return, Lessee shall assign or novate to Lessor any remaining Airframe, Engine, Part or other warranties with respect to the Aircraft pursuant to a written agreement in form and substance satisfactory to Lessor, including warranties pursuant to Section 6.5 and the warranties from the Final Maintenance Performer pursuant to Section 6.6, and Lessee shall arrange for all necessary consents to such assignment or novation.

19. Non-Incident/Non-Accident Statement

At Return, Lessee shall provide Lessor with Non-Incident/Non-Accident Statements for the Airframe and Engines in a form satisfactory to Lessor.

20. Maintenance Program

(a) During the 60-day period preceding the Scheduled Expiry Date and upon Lessor's request, Lessee will provide Lessor or its agent access to the Approved Maintenance Program and the Aircraft Documents in order to facilitate the Aircraft's integration into any subsequent operator's fleet. Lessor agrees that it will not disclose the contents of the Approved Maintenance Program to any Person except to the extent necessary to monitor Lessee's compliance with this Agreement and to bridge the maintenance program for the Aircraft from the Approved Maintenance Program to another program after the Expiry Date.

(b) Concurrent with providing the Aircraft Documents for Lessor's review, Lessee shall provide to Lessor a written summary of all sampling programs involving or affecting the Aircraft.

21. Other

[].

22. Export and Deregistration

Upon Return and upon request by Lessor, Lessee shall (i) provide to Lessor all documents necessary to export the Aircraft from the State of Registration (including a valid and subsisting export licence for the Aircraft), and (ii) provide any documents requested by Lessor in connection with, and otherwise cooperate with, the deregistration of the Aircraft by the Aviation

Authority, including causing the Aviation Authority to issue an Export Certificate of Airworthiness to a country specified by Lessor.

SCHEDULE 4 – INSURANCE REQUIREMENTS

1. The Insurances required to be maintained are as follows:
   (a) HULL "ALL RISKS" of loss or damage while flying and on the ground with respect to the Aircraft for the Agreed Value and with a deductible not exceeding the Hull Insurance Deductible.
   (b) HULL WAR AND ALLIED PERILS, covering those war risks excluded from the Hull "All Risks" Policy to the extent such coverage is available from the leading international insurance markets, including confiscation and requisition by the State of Registration, for the Agreed Value (with form LSW555D exclusions being acceptable except to the extent applying while the Aircraft is under power and except to the extent that coverage in respect of such exclusions is commercially available in the insurance market);
   (c) "ALL RISKS" PROPERTY INSURANCE (INCLUDING WAR AND ALLIED RISK except when on the ground or in transit other than by air or sea) on all Engines and Parts when not installed on the Aircraft (to the extent not covered under the Aircraft hull insurances described in paragraphs (a) and (b) above), including Engine test and running risks, in an amount equal to replacement value in the case of the Engines; and
   (d) AIRCRAFT THIRD PARTY, BODILY INJURY/PROPERTY DAMAGE, PASSENGER, BAGGAGE, CARGO AND MAIL AND AIRLINE GENERAL THIRD PARTY (INCLUDING PRODUCTS) LEGAL LIABILITY for a combined single limit (Bodily Injury/Property Damage) of an amount not less than the Minimum Liability Coverage for the time being in respect of any one occurrence (but, in respect of products liability, this limit may be an aggregate limit for any and all losses occurring during the currency of the policy, and in respect of liability arising out of certain offences, the limit (within the said combined single limit) may be $25,000,000 in respect of any one offence and in the aggregate, and cargo and mail legal liability may be subject to a limit of $1,000,000 any one occurrence); War and Allied Risks are also to be covered under the Policy to the extent available in the leading international insurance markets. The Minimum Liability Coverage may be adjusted upwards from time to time to such an amount as Lessor may be advised by its insurance brokers constitutes the standard Minimum Liability Coverage applicable to aircraft of the make, model and series as the Aircraft operating internationally by an airline similarly situated as Lessee. If Lessee disputes any such adjustment, the matter shall be referred to a reputable independent insurance broker appointed by Lessor, whose decision, acting as expert, shall be conclusive and binding on Lessee.

2. All required hull and spares insurance specified in Sections 1(a), 1(b) and 1(c) above, so far as it relates to the Aircraft, will:
   (a) provide that any loss will be settled with Lessee (who undertakes to consult with Lessor in regard thereto), and any claim that becomes payable on the basis of a Total Loss shall be paid in Dollars to Lessor (unless or until the Lessor notifies Lessee that said payments should be made to a Financing Party) as sole loss payee up to the Agreed Value, and loss proceeds in excess of the Agreed Value shall be payable to Lessee, with any other claim being payable as may be necessary for the repair of the damage to which it relates;
   (b) if separate Hull "All Risks" and "War Risks" insurances are arranged, include a 50/50 provision in the terms of Lloyd's endorsement AVS103 or its equivalent; and
   (c) confirm that the Insurers are not entitled to replace the Aircraft in the event of a Total Loss.
3. All required liability insurances specified in Section 1(d) above will:
   (a) include the Indemnitees as additional insureds for their respective rights and interests; but the coverage provided will not include claims arising out of their legal liability as manufacturer, repairer or servicing agent of the Aircraft or any Engine or Part;
   (b) include a severability of interest clause;
   (c) contain a provision confirming that the policy is primary without right of contribution and that the liability of the insurers will not be affected by any other insurance of which any Indemnitee or Lessee have the benefit; and
   (d) accept and insure the indemnity provisions of this Agreement to the extent of the risks covered by the relevant policy or policies.
4. All Insurances specified in Sections 1(a) through (d) above will:
   (a) be in accordance with normal industry practice of Persons operating similar aircraft in similar circumstances;
   (b) provide coverage on a worldwide basis subject to those territorial exclusions which are usual and customary for carriers similarly situated with Lessee in the case of War Risks and Allied Perils coverage which are advised to and approved by Lessor, such approval not to be unreasonably withheld;
   (c) acknowledge that the insurers are aware that the Aircraft is owned by Lessor and is subject to this Agreement;
   (d) provide that, in relation to the interests of each of the additional insureds, the Insurances will not be invalidated by any act or omission of the Insured which results in a breach of any terms, conditions or warranty of the policies;
   (e) provide that the Insurers will waive any rights of recourse and/or subrogation against each additional insured to the same extent that

Lessee has waived or has no rights of recovery against such additional insured in the Lease;

(f) provide that the additional insureds will have no obligation or responsibility for the payment of any premiums (but reserve the right to pay the same should any of them elect to do so) and that the Insurers will waive any right of offset or counterclaim against the respective additional insureds other than for outstanding premiums in respect of the Aircraft, any Engine or Part;

(g) provide that, except in the case of any provision for cancellation or automatic termination specified in the policies or endorsements thereof, the Insurance can only be canceled or materially altered in a manner adverse to the additional insureds by giving at least 30 days' written notice to Lessor and each Financing Party, except in the case of war risks (or radioactive contamination), for which seven days' written notice (or such lesser period as is or may be customarily available in respect thereof) will be given; and

(h) include a services of suit clause.

5. Where any provision of this Schedule 4 conflicts with the provisions of the airline finance/lease contract Endorsements AVN 67C, AVN 67C (Hull War), and AVN 99 (Tail Cover Continuing Liability) adopted by the Lloyd's Aviation Underwriter's Association (or any successor endorsements), Lessor agrees that the provisions of AVN 67C, AVN 67C (Hull War) and AVN 99 (Tail Cover Continuing Liability), respectively, or any successor endorsements will apply to the exclusion of the provisions of this Schedule 4. For purposes of each of AVN 67C, AVN 67C (Hull War), and AVN 99 (Tail Cover Continuing Liability), the "Designated Contract Party" will be Lessor.

6. All Reinsurances will:

   (a) be on the same terms as the Insurances and will include the provisions of this Schedule;

   (b) provide that, notwithstanding any bankruptcy, insolvency, liquidation, dissolution or similar proceedings of or affecting the reinsured, the reinsurers' liability will be to make such payment as would have fallen due under the relevant policy of reinsurance if the reinsured had (immediately before such bankruptcy, insolvency, liquidation, dissolution or similar proceedings) discharged its obligations in full under the original insurance policies in respect of which the then relevant policy of reinsurance has been effected; and

   (c) contain a "cut-through" clause in the following form (or such other form as is reasonably satisfactory to Lessor):

> "The Reinsurers and the Reinsured hereby agree that in the event of any valid claim arising hereunder, the Reinsurers shall in lieu of payment to the Reinsured, its successors in interest and assigns pay to the party(ies) identified as Contract Part(ies) under the original insurance effected by the Insured that portion of any loss due for which the

Reinsurers would otherwise be liable to pay the Reinsured (subject to proof of loss), it being understood and agreed that any such payment by the Reinsurers shall fully discharge and release the Reinsurers from any and all further liability in connection therewith.

To provide for payment to be made notwithstanding (a) any bankruptcy, insolvency, liquidation or dissolution of the Reinsured, and/or (b) that the Reinsured has made no payment under the original insurances.

The Reinsurers reserve the right to set off against any claim payable under the Reinsurance policy in accordance with this Clause any outstanding premiums (applicable to the Equipment involved in the Loss) covered by the original insurance. Such set off shall first be applied to any financial interest of the Insured in the Equipment involved.

If Reinsurers exercise their right to set off any outstanding premium, upon subsequent receipt by Reinsurers of such outstanding premium, Reinsurers hereby agree to refund the set off premium to the Contract Part(ies).

Any payment due under this Clause shall not contravene any law, statute or decree of the Government of Lessee's jurisdiction."

7. For insurance coverage that includes the AVN67C endorsement (or the substantive equivalent), the Contract Parties (their addressees) and the Contracts that should be identified in the insurance/reinsurance certificates are set forth in the Notice and Acknowledgment.

SCHEDULE 5 – SCHEDULE OF PRINCIPAL ECONOMIC TERMS

Agreed Value	$___,000,000.
Airframe Additional Rent Rate	$___.00 per Flight Hour or Cycle flown by the Airframe, whichever is greater, as adjusted from time to time pursuant to Section 5.4(b).
APU Additional Rent Rate	$__.00 per APU Hour, as adjusted from time to time pursuant to Section 5.4(b).
Basic Rent Amount	$_______ per Rental Period.
Commitment Fee	$_______.
Damage Notification Threshold	$_______.
Engine Additional Rent Rate	$___.00 per Flight Hour or Cycle operated by such Engine, whichever is greater, as adjusted from time to time pursuant to Section 5.4(b).
Engine LLP Additional Rent Rate	$___.00 per Cycle operated by such Engine, as adjusted from time to time pursuant to Section 5.4(b).
Hull Insurance Deductible	$___,000.

Landing Gear Additional Rent Rate	$__.00 per Flight Hour flown by the Airframe, as adjusted from time to time pursuant to Section 5.4(b).
Minimum Liability Coverage	$__________ each occurrence.

EXHIBIT A – CERTIFICATE OF ACCEPTANCE

Certificate of Acceptance

This Certificate of Acceptance is delivered on the date set forth in paragraph 1 below by [NAME OF LESSEE] ("Lessee") to [NAME OF LESSOR] ("Lessor") pursuant to Lease Agreement [msn], dated [date of Lease], between Lessor and Lessee (the "Agreement"). Capitalized terms used but not defined in this Certificate of Acceptance shall have the meaning given to such terms in the Agreement.

1. Details of Acceptance. Lessee hereby confirms to Lessor that Lessee has at __:__ _.m. G.M.T. on this _____ day of _________ 200_, at ____________________, accepted the following, in accordance with the provisions of the Agreement.
   (a) one [mfgr] Model [model] airframe, bearing manufacturer's serial number [msn] and ________ registration mark _____;
   (b) two [EngMfgr] Model [EngModel] engines, bearing manufacturer's serial numbers [esn1] and [esn2];
   (c) all Parts installed on, attached to or appurtenant to the Airframe and Engines; and
   (d) the Aircraft Documents specified in Part 2 of Schedule 1 to the Agreement.
2. Lessee's Confirmation. Lessee confirms to Lessor that as at the time indicated above, being the time of Delivery:
   (a) Lessee's representations and warranties contained in Sections 2.1 and 2.2 of the Agreement are hereby repeated;
   (b) the Aircraft is insured as required by the Agreement; and
   (c) Lessee confirms that there have been affixed to the Aircraft and the Engines the fireproof notices required by the Agreement.
3. Lessor's Confirmation. Lessor confirms to Lessee that, as at the time indicated above, being the time of Delivery, Lessor's representations and warranties contained in Section 2.4 of the Agreement are hereby repeated.
4. Lease Information. Lessor and Lessee agree and confirm the following as of the date of this Certificate of Acceptance:
   (a) the date of this Certificate of Acceptance is the "Delivery Date" for purposes of the Lease Agreement; and
   (b) the Additional Rent rates as of the Delivery Date are as follows:

(i) Airframe Additional Rent Rate: $_____ per calendar month;
(ii) Engine Additional Rent Rate: $_____ per Flight Hour or Cycle;
(iii) Engine LLP Additional Rent Rate: $_____ per Cycle;
(iv) Landing Gear Additional Rent Rate: $_____ per Flight Hour or Cycle; and
(v) APU Additional Rent Rate: $_____ per APU Hour.

* * *

IN WITNESS WHEREOF Lessor and Lessee have executed this Certificate of Acceptance on the date set forth in Section 1 of this Certificate.
SIGNED on behalf of
[NAME OF LESSEE]
By:______________________________
Name:
Title:
SIGNED on behalf of
[NAME OF LESSOR]
By:______________________________
Name:
Title:

EXHIBIT B – CERTIFICATE OF DELIVERY CONDITION

Certificate of Delivery Condition

This Certificate of Delivery Condition is delivered on ____________, 200_ by [NAME OF LESSEE] (the "Lessee") to [NAME OF LESSOR] ("Lessor") pursuant to Lease Agreement [msn], dated [date of Lease], between Lessor and Lessee (the "Agreement"). Capitalized terms used but not defined in this Certificate of Delivery Condition shall have the meaning given to such terms in the Agreement.

1. Aircraft Acceptance. Lessee hereby confirms to Lessor that, pursuant to the Agreement, Lessee has accepted the [mfgr] Model [model] airframe bearing manufacturer's serial number [msn] and ________ registration mark ______, together with the two [EngMfgr] Model [EngModel] aircraft engines bearing manufacturer's serial numbers [esn1] and [esn2], all Parts installed on, attached to or appurtenant to the Airframe and Engines, as set forth on Annexes 4 and 6, and the Aircraft Documents, as set forth on Annex 5, and Lessor and Lessee agree that such Airframe, Engines and Parts are in the condition set forth as listed on the attached Annexes 1 and 3.
2. Confirmation of Delivery Condition. Lessee confirms to Lessor that at the time of acceptance of the Leased Property, the Leased Property complied in all respects with the condition required at Delivery under Schedule 2 of the Agreement, except for the items (if any) listed on the attached Annex 2 (the

"Discrepancies"). Lessor and Lessee agree that the Discrepancies (if any) shall be corrected as set forth on the attached Annex 2.

IN WITNESS WHEREOF Lessor and Lessee have executed this Certificate of Delivery Condition on the date set forth at the beginning of this Certificate.

SIGNED on behalf of [NAME OF LESSEE]	SIGNED on behalf of [NAME OF LESSOR]
By:____________________________ Name: Title:	By:____________________________ Name: Title:

ANNEX 1

STATUS OF AIRCRAFT

AIRFRAME:	**Date**	**Hours**	**Cycles**
Current:			
Last "C" Check:			
Last "D" Check:			

ENGINES: **Position/ Serial Number**	**Current:**		**Last Shop Visit:**		
	Hours	**Cycles**	**Date**	**Hours**	**Cycles**
1.					
2.					

APU:	**Current:**		**Last Overhaul:**		
Serial Number	**Hours**	**Cycles**	**Date**	**Hours**	**Cycles**

LANDING GEAR:		Current:	Last Overhaul:			
Position	**Serial Number**	**Hours**	**Cycles**	**Date**	**Hours**	**Cycles**
Nose:						
Right Main:						
Left Main:						

Fuel on board at Delivery: ________ (circle one) pounds / kilograms (________ gallons)

ANNEX 2

DISCREPANCIES

Description of Discrepancy	Agreed Corrective Action
1.	1.
2.	2.

ANNEX 3

ENGINE LLPs

Part Description	Cycles for Engine[esn1]	Cycles for Engine[esn2]

ANNEX 4
LOOSE EQUIPMENT AND ACCESSORIES
[TO BE INSERTED BY TECHNICAL REPRESENTATIVE]

ANNEX 5

AIRCRAFT DOCUMENTS AND TECHNICAL RECORDS
[TO BE INSERTED BY TECHNICAL REPRESENTATIVE]

ANNEX 6

AIRCRAFT STATUS – AVIONICS INVENTORY
[TO BE INSERTED BY TECHNICAL REPRESENTATIVE]

EXHIBIT C – FORM OF DEREGISTRATION POWER OF ATTORNEY

Irrevocable Power of Attorney

By this Irrevocable Power of Attorney, [NAME OF LESSEE], a company incorporated under the laws of ________ and having its registered office at *[to be supplied by Lessee]* (together with its successors and assigns, the "Lessee"), hereby irrevocably nominates and appoints [Name of Lessor] having its principal place of business at [Address of Lessor], acting alone and without the authorization of any other person, to be the Lessee's true and lawful attorney-in-fact (the "Lessor") so that the Lessor may take any of the following actions in the name of and for Lessee with respect to the [mfgr] Model [model] airframe bearing manufacturer's serial no. [msn] and ________ registration mark ______, including the engines and any and all parts installed on or appurtenant to such airframe (collectively, the "Aircraft"), leased by the Lessor to the Lessee pursuant to Lease Agreement [msn], dated [date of Lease], between the Lessor and the Lessee (the "Lease"):

1. In the exercise of the rights of the Lessor under the Lease to recover the Aircraft from Lessee after termination of the Lease due to an Event of Default under the Lease or for termination of the Lease for any other reason, the Lessor may take all action, and may execute in the Lessee's name and for and on behalf of the Lessee any and all documents, applications and instruments, that may at any time be required in order to (a) cause the Aircraft to be repossessed by the Lessor, (b) cause the Aircraft to be deregistered from the register of aircraft maintained by the ________ civil aviation authority (the "Aviation Authority"), (c) obtain any document (whether in the nature of an export license, certificate of airworthiness for export or otherwise) that is required for the purpose of canceling the registration of the Aircraft with the Aviation Authority and/or securing the export of the Aircraft from ________, and (d) export the Aircraft after the expiration of the Lease.
2. Pursuant to the Lease, Lessee is maintaining all risk hull and war risk insurance and reinsurance covering the Aircraft, and the Lessor has been named loss payee on such insurance and reinsurance policies in the event of a total loss or constructive total loss of the Aircraft, in the event of damage to the Aircraft in excess of $100,000 or in the event of damage to the Aircraft while an "Event of Default" under the Lease has occurred and is continuing. The Lessor may take all action, and may execute in the Lessee's name and for and on behalf of the Lessee any and all documents, applications and instruments, including executing on behalf of the Lessee an appropriate form of

discharge and release, that may at any time be required in order for the Lessor to collect such insurance proceeds or to adjust or settle any claim under such insurance policies.

3. In the exercise of the rights listed in paragraphs 1 and 2, the Lessor may take all such other actions and sign all such other documents as the Lessor considers necessary or appropriate in its absolute discretion. In connection with such documents, or in connection with any registrations or filings to which such documents are subject, the Lessor may represent the Lessee before and submit any such document, application or instrument to any applicable authorities, government department and agencies (including without limitation, the Aviation Authority) of ________ as shall be necessary to achieve the aforementioned purposes.
4. The Lessee hereby undertakes from time to time and at all times to indemnify the Lessor against all costs, claims, expenses and liabilities lawfully and reasonably incurred by such Lessor in connection with this Irrevocable Power of Lessor and, upon request, to ratify and confirm whatever the Lessor shall lawfully and reasonably do or cause to be done by virtue of this Irrevocable Power of Attorney.
5. The Lessee hereby grants to the Lessor the full power and authority to substitute and appoint in its place one or more attorney or attorneys to exercise for it as attorney or attorneys of the Lessee any or all the powers and authorities conferred on the Lessor by this Irrevocable Power of Attorney, and to revoke any such appointment from time to time and to substitute or appoint any other or others in the place of such attorney or attorneys, all as the Lessor shall from time to time deem appropriate.

Any person, agency or company relying upon this Irrevocable Power of Attorney need not and will not make any determination or require any court judgment as to whether an "Event of Default" has occurred under the Lease or whether the Lease has been terminated. Lessee hereby waives any claims against (i) any person acting on the instructions given by Lessor or its designee pursuant to this Irrevocable Power of Attorney and (ii) any person designated by Lessor or an officer of Lessor to give instructions pursuant to this Irrevocable Power of Attorney. Lessee also agrees to indemnify and hold harmless any person, agency or company that may act in reliance upon this Irrevocable Power of Attorney and pursuant to instructions given by Lessor or its designee.

This Power of Attorney is given as security by the Lessee for the performance of its obligations under the Lease. This Power of Attorney is irrevocable and coupled with an interest. Lessee hereby represents, warrants and covenants that this Irrevocable Power of Attorney is irrevocably granted to the Lessor, and constitutes the legal, valid and irrevocably binding obligation of the Lessee, enforceable against the Lessee in accordance with its terms.

This Power of Attorney shall be governed by the laws of ________.

IN WITNESS WHEREOF, [NAME OF LESSEE] has executed and delivered this Irrevocable Power of Attorney this ____ day of _________ 200_.
[NAME OF LESSEE]
By:________________________________
Name:
Title:

EXHIBIT D – NOTICE AND ACKNOWLEDGMENT

[to be supplied]

EXHIBIT E – MONTHLY UTILIZATION AND STATUS REPORT

MONTH ENDING___________, 20__
[NAME OF LESSOR]
[Address]
ATTN:
FAX:
E-mail:

A/C TYPE		**A/C SERIAL # I**	**REGIS. #**
	CALENDAR	**HOURS (1)**	**CYCLES**
A/C TOTAL HOURS & CYCLES SINCE NEW AS OF LAST REPORT	----		
A/C TOTAL HOURS & CYCLES SINCE NEW (CURRENT REPORT)	----		
AIRCRAFT HOURS & CYCLES FLOWN DURING MONTH	----		
DATE/HOURS/CYCLES @ ACCOMP OF LAST C CHECK OR EQUIV.			
INTERVALS FOR C CHECK OR EQUIVALENT			
DATE/HOURS/CYCLES @ ACCOMP OF LAST D CHECK OR EQUIV.			
INTERVALS FOR D CHECK OR EQUIVALENT			

ENGINE TYPE		**ENG SERIAL # I**	**THRUST RATING (Lbs)**
ORIGINAL POSITION			
CURRENT LOCATION (A/C & Position, In Shop, Spare, etc) See Note (2)			
	HOURS (1)	**CYCLES**	
ENG TOTAL HOURS & CYCLES SINCE NEW AS OF LAST REPORT			
ENG TOTAL HOURS & CYCLES SINCE NEW (CURRENT REPORT)			
TOTAL HOURS & CYCLES FLOWN DURING MONTH			
ENGINE LIMITER(S) (DESCRIPTION – ie C1 Disk, T1 Disk, etc.)			
ENGINE LIMITER HOURS/CYCLES REMAINING			
ENGINE HOURS & CYCLES SINCE LAST SHOP VISIT			

ENGINE TYPE		**ENG SERIAL # I**	**THRUST RATING (Lbs)**
ORIGINAL POSITION			
CURRENT LOCATION (A/C & Position, In Shop, Spare, etc) See Note (2)			
	HOURS (1)	**CYCLES**	
ENG TOTAL HOURS & CYCLES SINCE NEW AS OF LAST REPORT			
ENG TOTAL HOURS & CYCLES SINCE NEW (CURRENT REPORT)			

ENGINE TYPE	ENG SERIAL # I	THRUST RATING (Lbs)
TOTAL HOURS & CYCLES FLOWN DURING MONTH		
ENGINE LIMITER(S) (DESCRIPTION - ie C1 Disk, T1 Disk, etc.)		
ENGINE LIMITER HOURS/CYCLES REMAINING		
ENGINE HOURS & CYCLES SINCE LAST SHOP VISIT		

LANDING GEAR	CALENDAR	HOURS	*CYCLES*
NOSE GEAR SERIAL #	TOTAL HOURS & CYCLES	----	
TSO (Hrs/Cyc/Months as App)			
TIME SINCE INSTLLN (Hrs/Cyc/Months as App)			
____________			
OVERHAUL INTERVAL (Hrs/Cyc/Months as App)			
LH MAIN GEAR SERIAL #	TOTAL HOURS & CYCLES	----	
TSO (Hrs/Cyc/Months as App)			
TIME SINCE INSTLLN (Hrs/Cyc/Months as App)			
____________			
OVERHAUL INTERVAL (Hrs/Cyc/Months as App)			
RH MAIN GEAR SERIAL #	TOTAL HOURS & CYCLES	----	
TSO (Hrs/Cyc/Months as App)			
TIME SINCE INSTLLN (Hrs/Cyc/Months as App)			
____________			
OVERHAUL INTERVAL (Hrs/Cyc/Months as App)			

APU MFR		**APU MODEL**	**APU S/N**
CURRENT LOCATION (On A/C #, In Shop, etc)			
	HOURS	***CYCLES***	
TOTAL HOURS & *CYCLES* SINCE NEW (If available)			
HOURS & CYCLES FLOWN DURING MONTH			
HOURS & *CYCLES* SINCE LAST SHOP VISIT			

Notes:

(1) List Hours in Hours + Minutes format for this portion of the report where applicable.
(2) Record Engine data for only the engines owned by the Lessor whether or not installed on this aircraft. If collateral engine goes into the shop, provide TT, TC and date of removal. Also provide engine disk sheets & last workscope whenever an engine comes out of a shop visit.
(3) Please advise any routine checks, Airworthiness Directives and Service Bulletins performed during the month, as well as details of any repairs accomplished which were beyond SRM limits.
(4) Also advise any Airframe Maintenance Checks, Engine scheduled shop visits or landing gear or APU overhauls or replacements scheduled to be performed within the next 12 months.

EXHIBIT F – FORM OF LETTER OF CREDIT

[LETTERHEAD OF CONFIRMING BANK]
IRREVOCABLE LETTER OF CREDIT
Current Date:___________, 20__
Irrevocable Letter of Credit No. ___________
Re:Lease Agreement [msn], dated [date of Lease],
between [Name of Lessor] and [Name of Lessee]
relating to [model] bearing msn [msn]
Expiration Date: ___________, 20__
[Name of Lessor]
[Address of Lessor]
Ladies and Gentlemen:
We hereby issue in your favor, at the request of and for the account of [Name of Lessee] ("Lessee"), this Irrevocable Letter of Credit No. ______ in the amount of *[insert*

amount] United States Dollars (US$ __________) (the "Stated Amount") available upon presentation in accordance with this Letter of Credit of (i) a Sight Draft drawn on us dated on or before the date of such presentation and in the form attached as Annex 1 and (ii) a Drawing Certificate dated the date of such draft in the form attached as Annex 2 and signed by an individual being or purporting to be your authorized representative. Such presentation must be made on a Banking Day to our offices at *[insert address of Drawing Location]*, Facsimile Number: [__________], confirming Telephone Number: [_____________] on or before the Expiration Date set forth above or, if such date is not a Banking Day, then on or before the following Banking Day. "Banking Day" means a day other than a Saturday, a Sunday or a day on which banks are required or authorized to be closed in *[City/State of Drawing Location]*. Any such presentation may be made by means of electronic facsimile transmission and we shall be entitled to rely thereon as if such draft and certificate were presented in person, provided such draft and certificate are in conformity with the requirements for the same as set forth herein, but for the requirement of an original signature. In addition, any draft and certificate hereunder may be presented by U.S. Mail, express courier (e.g., Federal Express or DHL) or in person at the address set forth above.

A Sight Draft presented hereunder may be in an amount of up to the Stated Amount. More than one Sight Draft may be presented hereunder, provided the aggregate amount of such drafts shall not exceed the Stated Amount.

We hereby agree that, to the extent that within five (5) calendar days of any drawing by you hereunder, such drawing is reimbursed in full to us by, or on behalf of, Lessee, including any banking charges, such drawing shall not be considered as a drawing hereunder for the purposes of, and only for such purposes of, calculating the aggregate maximum amount of all drawings made hereunder.

We hereby agree that each draft presented hereunder in compliance with the terms hereof will be duly honored by the amount of such draft in immediately available funds in United States dollars to the account specified on the sight draft:

(a) not later than 3:00 p.m., *[City of Drawing Location]* time, on the day such draft is presented to us as aforesaid, if such presentation is made to us at or before 12:00 noon, *[City of Drawing Location]* time, or

(b) not later than 3:00 p.m., *[City of Drawing Location]* time, on the Business Day following the day such draft is presented to us as aforesaid, if such presentation is made to us after 12:00 noon, *[City of Drawing Location]* time.

Upon the earlier of (a) the Expiration Date set forth above or (b) irrevocable payment of the entire Stated Amount (in one or more drawings), this Letter of Credit shall automatically terminate.

This Letter of Credit shall be deemed automatically extended without amendment for a period of one year from the Expiration Date and from each anniversary of the Expiration Date unless, 30 days prior to such date, we shall notify you in writing by certified mail, courier or hand delivery that we elect not to consider this Letter of Credit renewed for any such additional period. In the event that we notify you that we elect not to renew this Letter of Credit, a drawing can be made by you by presenting a sight draft and a certificate in the forms attached hereto.

Except as otherwise provided herein, this Letter of Credit shall be governed by and construed in accordance with the Uniform Customs and Practice for Documentary Credits (2007 Revision), ICC Publication No. 600 (the "UCP"). Notwithstanding Article 36 of the UCP, if this Letter of Credit expires during an interruption of business as described in said Article 36, we agree to effect payment if a drawing is made against this Letter of Credit within 30 days after the resumption of business.

Upon request, but no more than once in any 30 day period, we will confirm to you in writing that this Letter of Credit is in full force and effect and is enforceable against us in accordance with its terms.

This Letter of Credit sets forth in full the terms of our undertaking and shall not in any way be modified, amended or amplified by reference to any documents, instruments or agreements referred to herein, or in which this Letter of Credit is referred to or to which this Letter of Credit relates, and any such reference shall not be deemed to incorporate herein by reference any such documents, instruments and agreements.

This Letter of Credit may be transferred by you to any person.

Communications with respect to this Letter of Credit shall be in writing, addressed to *[Name of Issuing Bank]* at *[address of Issuing Bank]*. Attention: [___________], specifically referring to the number of this Letter of Credit, and if directed to you, shall be addressed to you at *[insert address of beneficiary]*, Attention: ____________________.

All banking charges in connection with this Letter of Credit and any drawings made hereunder shall be for the account of Lessee. All payments made to you pursuant to this Letter of Credit shall be made free and clear of, and without deduction for, any present or future fees, taxes, restrictions or conditions of any nature, and without set off of counterclaim for any reasons whatsoever.

We hereby confirm and engage with drawers, endorsers and bonafide holders of Sight Drafts drawn and in compliance with the terms of this Letter of Credit that the same shall be duly honored upon presentation and delivery of documents as specified at this office, if negotiated on/or before the expiration date of this letter of Credit.

[NAME OF ISSUING BANK]

____

[Name]

[Title]

Annex 1 to Irrevocable Letter of Credit No. ______

SIGHT DRAFT

Irrevocable Letter of Credit No. _______Date of Draft: ________________

To the Order of [Name of Lessor]

Pay ______________________________________ ($____________) US DOLLARS

At SIGHT by wire transfer of such amount to the account of *[Name of Lessor]* at:

[Lessor's Bank]

ABA Number:[________]

Account Number:[________]

DRAWN UNDER IRREVOCABLE LETTER OF CREDIT NO. ________________.
TO: *[Name of Issuing Bank]*
[Address of Issuing Bank]
[NAME OF LESSOR]
By:____
Name:
Title:
[Endorse on back]
Annex 2 to Irrevocable Letter of Credit No. ______
DRAWING CERTIFICATE
Irrevocable Letter of Credit No. ___________
The undersigned, a duly authorized representative of [Name of Lessor] ("Beneficiary"), hereby certifies to *[NAME OF ISSUING BANK]* (the "Bank") with reference to Irrevocable Letter of Credit No. _________ (the "Letter of Credit"), issued by the Bank in favor of Beneficiary, as follows:

1. Beneficiary is presenting a sight draft herewith to draw funds under the Letter of Credit in the amount of US $[_____________].
2. Demand for payment under the Letter of Credit is being made prior to the expiration thereof.
3. Either
   (a) an Event of Default has occurred and is continuing under and as defined in Lease Agreement [msn], dated [date of Lease], between Beneficiary and [Name of Lessee] ("Lessee");
   (b) the Letter of Credit expires within 30 days of the date hereof and Lessee has not as of the date hereof provided Beneficiary with evidence of a renewal or extension of the Letter of Credit or with a substitute Letter of Credit, in each case, in form and substance satisfactory to Beneficiary; or
   (c) the bank issuing or confirming the Letter of Credit no longer has at least the Letter of Credit Bank Minimum Rating as defined in the Lease, and Lessee did not, within fourteen days of demand therefor by Lessor, provide Lessor with a replacement letter of credit meeting the requirements of the Lease.

IN WITNESS WHEREOF, Beneficiary has caused this Drawing Certificate and the accompanying Sight Draft to be executed as of the ____ day of _________, 20__.
[NAME OF LESSOR]
By:______________________________
Name:
Title:
EXHIBIT G – FORM OF RETURN CERTIFICATE
Return Certificate
This Return Certificate ("Return Certificate") is delivered on the date set forth in paragraph 1 below by [Name of Lessor] ("Lessor") to [Name of Lessee] ("Lessee")

pursuant to Lease Agreement [msn], dated [date of Lease], between Lessor and Lessee (the "Lease Agreement"). Capitalized terms used but not defined in this Return Certificate shall have the meanings given to such terms in the Lease Agreement.
Lessor hereby confirms to Lessee that Lessor has at __:__ G.M.T. on this _____ day of _________ 20__, at ____________________, accepted the following:

(c) one [mfgr] Model [model] airframe, bearing manufacturer's serial number [msn] and ________ registration mark _____;
(d) two [EngMfgr] Model [EngModel] engines, bearing manufacturer's serial numbers [esn1] and [esn2];
(e) all Parts installed on, attached to or appurtenant to the Airframe and Engines; and
(f) the Aircraft Documents specified in Part 2 of Schedule 1 to the Lease Agreement and all other Aircraft Documents acquired or prepared by Lessee during the Term.

and thereupon the leasing of such property under the Lease Agreement was terminated.
Lessor and Lessee hereby confirm that on the date and time hereof (i) the Aircraft was duly accepted by Lessor subject to correction of the discrepancies noted in Attachment 2 hereto and (ii) Lessee confirms its obligations under the Lease Agreement accruing prior to the date hereof, and those required to be performed after the date hereof, shall remain in full force and effect until all such obligations have been satisfactorily completed.
IN WITNESS WHEREOF, the parties hereto have caused this Return Certificate for MSN [msn] to be executed in their respective corporate names by their duly authorized representatives as of the day and year first above written.

[NAME OF LESSEE]	[NAME OF LESSOR]
(Lessee)	(Lessor)
By: ______________________	By: ______________________
Name:	Name:
Title:	Title:

ATTACHMENT 1

STATUS OF AIRCRAFT

AIRFRAME:	Date	Hours	Cycles
Current:			
Last "C" Check:			

AIRFRAME:	**Date**	**Hours**	**Cycles**
Last "D" Check:			

ENGINES: **Position/ Serial Number**	**Current:**		**Last Shop Visit:**		
	Hours	**Cycles**	**Date**	**Hours**	**Cycles**
1.					
2.					

APU:	**Current:**	**Last Overhaul:**			
Serial Number	**Hours**	**Cycles**	**Date**	**Hours**	**Cycles**

LANDING GEAR:		**Current:**	**Last Overhaul:**			
Position	**Serial Number**	**Hours**	**Cycles**	**Date**	**Hours**	**Cycles**
Nose:						
Right Main:						
Left Main:						

Fuel on board at Delivery: ________ (circle one) pounds / kilograms (________ gallons)

ATTACHMENT 2

DISCREPANCIES

Description of Discrepancy	**Agreed Corrective Action**
1.	**1.**
2.	**2.**

ATTACHMENT 3

LESSOR REQUESTED MAINTENANCE

Bibliography

Abeyratne R.I.R., *Aviation in Crisis*, Ashgate, 2004.

Abeyratne R.I.R., *Aviation Trends in the New Millenium*, Ashgate, 2001.

Abeyratne R.I.R., *Negligent Entrustment of Leased Aircraft and Crew: Some Legal Issues*, Annals of Air and Space Law, Volume XXXV, Part I, 2010.

Abeyratne R.I.R., *Registration of Aircraft: Legal and Regulatory Issues*, Annals of Air and Space Law, Volume XXXIV, 2009.

Abeyratne R.I.R., *The Unlawful Interference Compensation Convention of 2009 and Principles of State Responsibility*, Annals of Air and Space Law, Volume XXXV, Part I, 2010.

Aviation Working Group, *AWG Position on Eurocontrol and Air Navigation Route Charges*, August 2004.

Aviation Working Group, *Position Paper Objecting to Liens to Securing Airline Obligations under Rules Implementing the EU ETS*, February 2011.

Balfour J. (ed.), *Air Transport in 34 Jurisdictions Worldwide 2009*, Getting the Deal Through, 2009.

Bartlik M., *The Extension of the European Union's Emissions Trading Scheme to Aviation Activities*, Annals of Air and Space Law, Volume XXXIV, 2009.

Basch K. and Iezzi I., *Summary of Repossession Procedure in Brazil*, a paper presented to the American Bar Association Air and Space Law Forum annual meeting in Seattle, Washington on 11 October 2010.

Bisset M., *Taxes and Charges under the Chicago Convention, in From Lowlands to High Skies: A Multilevel Jurisdictional Approach Towards Air Law*, Nijhoff, 2013, 67–76.

Bisset M. and Sharman R., *Aviation Insurance: Issues in Law and Practice from the Lessor/Lender Perspective*, Clyde & Co., 2014.

Blumenkron J., *Implications of Transparency in the International Civil Aviation Organization's Universal Safety Oversight and Audit Programme*, Annals of Air and Space Law, Volume XXXIV, 2009.

Bunker D.H., *Aircraft Financing and Drugs*, Annals of Air and Space Law, Volume XVI, 1991.

Bunker D.H., *Aircraft Financing in the Future*, Annals of Air and Space Law, Volume XXVII, 2002.

Bunker D.H., *Aircraft Wet Leasing: The Perils and the Benefits*, Annals of Air and Space Law, Volume XXV, 2000.

Bunker D.H., *Canadian Aviation Finance Legislation*, McGill University, 1989.

Bunker D.H., *International Aircraft Financing*, 2nd Edition, IATA, Volumes 1 and 2, 2015.

Bunker D.H., *Securing Aircraft Financing*, Annals of air and Space Law, Volume XXIX, 2004.

Bunker D.H., *The Law of Aerospace Finance in Canada*, McGill University, 1988.

Bunker D.H., *The Legal Aspects of Aerospace Finance in Canada*, DCL Thesis, McGill University, 1987.

Butler G.F. and Keller M.R. (executive editors), *Handbook of Airline Finance*, 1st Edition, Aviation Week: McGraw-Hill, 1999.

Bushell S. (ed.), *Dispute Resolution in 50 Jurisdictions Worldwide 2008*, Getting the Deal Through, 2008.

Byrnes T.P. and Kass G.R., *Aircraft Lessor Liability*, Joint Presentation to 26th Annual Conference of the International Society of Transport Aircraft Trading, Scottsdale, Arizona, held on 17 March 2009.

Chassot L., *Les sources de la responsabilité du transporteur aérien international: entre conflict et complementarité*, Schulthess, Geneva, 2012.

Chrystal P., *The Aviation Insurance and Reinsurance Markets-Defying the Odds*, in Butler G.F. and Keller M.R., executive editors, *Handbook of Airline Finance*, 1st Edition, Aviation Week: McGraw-Hill, 1999.

Clark B., *The Law of Secured Transactions under the Uniform Commercial Code*, Volume 1, Thomson Financial, 2000.

Clark L. and Wool J., *International Aviation Finance Laws Revisited: A Report on the Development of the Proposed Unidroit Convention on International Interests in Mobile Equipment as Applied to Aircraft*, Annals of Air and Space Law, Volume XXIII, 1998.

Clark R.W. and Richardson T.M., *Is Lessor More?*, 75 Journal of Air Law & Commerce 69, 2010.

Clark T. (ed.), *Leasing Finance*, Euromoney, 1985.

Condon & Forsyth, *Attempts by Plaintiffs to Defeat Forum Non Conveniens Motions by Alleging Aircraft Owner or Lessor Liability*, Newsletter, Winter 2008.

Condon and Forsyth, *49 U.S.C. Section 44112(B): Limits on the Liability of Aircraft Owners and Lessor*, Newsletter, Spring 2008.

Crans B., *Aircraft Finance Below Sea Level*, Airfinance Journal, July, 2008 Supplement.

Crans B., *The Implications of the EU Accession to the Cape Town Convention*, Air and Space Lawyer, Volume 35, Issue 1, 2010.

Crans B. and Nath R., Aircraft *Repossession and Enforcement: Practical Aspects*, Wolters Kluwer, 2009.

Dameris T.T., Weiner D.J. and Crane A.R., *The United States Is No Longer the Courthouse for the World*, The Air and Space Lawyer,Volume 22, Number 1, 2008.

Dempsey P.S., *Public International Air Law*, McGill University, 2008.

Dempsey P.S. and Gesell L.E., *Air Commerce and the Law*, Coast Aire, 2004.

Dempsey P.S. and Milde M., *International Air Carrier Liability: The Montreal Convention of 1999*, McGill University, 2005.

Djojonegoro A., *The Unidroit Proposal for a Uniform Air Law: A New Aircraft Mortgage Convention?*, Annals of Air and Space Law, Volume XXII, Part II, 1997.

Escalada F.V., *L'article 83 bis de la Convention de Chicago. Importance de sa ratification*, Annals of Air and Space Law, Volume XV, 1990.

European Civil Aviation Conference, *Recommendation on Leasing of Aircraft*, Recommendation ECAC/21-1, 2–3 July 1997.

Fitzgerald G.F., *The Lease, Charter and Interchange of Aircraft in International Relations: Amendments to the Chicago and Rome Conventions*, Annals of Air and Space Law, Volume II, 1977.

Fitzgerald P.P., *In Defense of the Nationality of Aircraft*, Annals of Air and Space Law, Volume XXXVI, 2011.

French D., *Legal Considerations for Aircraft Engine Financiers*, Airfinance Journal, July, 2008 Supplement.

Furmston M.P., *Cheshire & Fifoot's Law of Contract*, 10th Edition, Butterworths, 1981.

Gaddis II P.G., *Registering Lease Aircraft in the US*, Airfinance Journal, May 1988, 48–49.

Gerber D.N., *Aircraft Finance Issues: The Blue Sky Ruling; The New ASU and the 'Home Country Rule'; and Recent Developments at the FAA Registry*, a paper presented at the American Bar Association Air and Space Law Forum 2010 Annual Meeting in Seattle, Washington on 26 October 2010.

Gesell L.E. and Dempsey P.S., *Aviation and the Law*, 4th Edition, Coast Aire Publications, 2005.

Giemulla E. and Schmid R. (eds), *Montreal Convention*, Kluwer Law International, 2006.

Gillick J.E., *The Impact of Citizenship Considerations on Aviation Financing*, in Butler G.F. and Keller M.R. (executive editors), *Handbook of Airline Finance*, 1st Edition, Aviation Week: McGraw-Hill, 1999, 41 et seq.

Goode CBE QC Sir Roy, *Commercial Law*, 2nd Edition, Penguin Books, 1995.

Goode CBE QC Sir Roy, *Convention on International Interests in Mobile Equipment and Protocol Thereto on Matters Specific to Aircraft Equipment: Official Commentary*, UNIDROIT, 2002, 4th Edition, 2019.

Goode CBE QC Sir Roy, *The International Interest as an Autonomous Property Interest*, European Review of Private Law, Volume 1, 2004.

Gullifer L. and Mokal R., *UK Restructuring Plan and Scheme of Arrangement Proceedings: Expert Opinion on Status under the Cape Town Convention*, 23 November 2020, revised 29 April 2021, at http://awg.aero/wp-content/uploads/2021/04/

CTC-status-of-RPs-and-Schemes-Expert-Report-Revised-29-Apr-2021.pdf on 9 September 2021.

Hall A., *New Regulations on Aviation Emissions Trading*, International Law Office, 13 April 2011.

Hamilton J.S., *Practical Aviation Law*. 4th Edition. Blackwell, 2005.

Hanley D.P., *Contractual and Property Rights in Leased Aircraft Engines*, in Singamsetty S.S.P. (editor in chief), *Air and Space Law: Contemporary Issues and Future Challenges*, Air and Space Books, 2011.

Hanley, D.P., *COVID-19 and International Aircraft Financing Law*, Air & Space Law, Volume 45, Special Issue, 2020, 155–172.

Hanley D.P., *Eurocontrol, EASA and the EU*, Low-Cost Airline World, UBM Aviation Publications, Issue 7, Second Quarter, 2010, 32–36.

Hanley D.P., *Eurocontrol, EASA and the EU*, Aircraft Finance Guide, UBM Aviation Publications, 2011 Edition, 104–107.

Hanley D.P., *Potential Risks and Liabilities for Owners and Lessors under Aircraft Operating Leases*, LL.M. (Adv.) Air and Space Law Thesis, Faculty of Law, Leiden University, August 2009.

Hanley D.P., *The Relationship Between the Geneva and Cape Town Conventions*, Cape Town Convention Journal, Volume 4, Issue 1, 2015, 103–113.

Havel B. and Sanchez G., *The Principles and Practice of International Aviation Law*, Cambridge University Press, 2014.

Ho A., *Does the Montreal Convention 199 Provide an Exclusive Remedy in the International Carriage of Good and Passengers*, Annals of Air and Space Law, Volume XXXIV, 2009.

Honnebier B.P., *Clarifying the Alleged Issues Concerning the Financing of Aircraft Engines: Some Comments to the Alleged Pitfalls Arising under Dutch, German and International Law as Proposed*, Zeitschrift für Luft- und Weltraumrecht, Volume 3, 2007.

Huang J., *Aviation Safety and ICAO*, PhD Thesis, Leiden University, 2008.

IBA Article, *Have Operating Lease Agreements Evolved with the Industry?*, 26 February 2020, at www.iba.aero/insight/have-operating-lease-agreements-evolved-with-the-industry-february-2020/ on 9 September 2021.

International Air Transport Association, *Master Short-Term Engine Lease Agreement*, IATA Document No. 5016-00, 2002.

International Civil Aviation Organization, *Annex 6 to the Convention on International Civil Aviation: Operation of Aircraft*, 8th Edition, 2001.

International Civil Aviation Organization, *Annex 8 to the Convention on International Civil Aviation: Airworthiness of Aircraft*, 10th Edition, 2005.

International Civil Aviation Organization, *Guidance on the Implementation of Article 83 bis of the Convention on International Civil Aviation*, 2002.

International Civil Aviation Organization, *International Conference on Air Law, Montreal, 10–28 May 1999, Minutes*, 1999.

International Civil Aviation Organization, *International Conference on Air Law, Montreal, 20 April to 2 May 2009, Draft Convention on Compensation for Damage to*

Third Parties, Resulting from Acts of Unlawful Interference Involving Aircraft, presented by Germany, ICAO DCCD Doc. No. 7, 13/03/09.

International Civil Aviation Organization, *Report of the Rapporteur: Draft Convention on Compensation for Damage Caused by Aircraft to Third Parties*, Legal Committee - 33rd Session, Montreal, 21 April–2 May 2008, in Annals of Air and Space Law, Volume XXXIV.

International Civil Aviation Organization, *Report of the Rapporteur: Draft Convention on Compensation for Damage Caused by Aircraft to Third Parties, In Case of Unlawful Interference*, Legal Committee - 33rd Session, Montreal, 21 April–2 May 2008, in Annals of Air and Space Law, Volume XXXIV.

International Civil Aviation Organization, *Study on Aircraft Leasing*, Air Transport Committee, 156th Session of the Council, ICAO, 1999.

Kennelly J.J., *Litigation and Trial of Air Crash Cases*, Callaghan and Co., 1958.

Krupski J., *Conflict of Laws in Aircraft Securitization*, Annals of Air and Space Law, Volume XXIV, 1999.

Lawrence W.H. and Minan J.H., *The Law of Personal Property Leasing*, Thomson West, 2003.

Lee J.W., *The Regime of Compensable Damage in the Modernized Rome Conventions: A Comparison Between Article 3 of the General Risks Convention of 2009 and Article 17 of the Montreal Convention of 1999*, Annals of Air and Space Law, Volume XXXV, Part I, 2010.

Legal Advisory Panel of the Aviation Working Group, *Advanced Contract and Opinion Practices Under the Cape Town Convention*, Cape Town Paper Series, Volume 2, UNIDROIT, 2008.

Legal Advisory Panel of the Aviation Working Group, *Practitioner's Handbook to the Cape Town Convention and Aircraft Protocol*, Cape Town Paper Series, Volume 3, UNIDROIT, 2010.

Leloudas G. and Haeck L., *Legal Aspects of Aviation Risk Management*, Annals of Air and Space Law, Volume XXVII, 2002.

Lessard M.N., et al., *Worldwide Aircraft Repossession Index*, 3rd Edition, Pillsbury, 2018.

Lobkowicz P. and Detrich B., *Operating Leasing: Who Wins Economically?*, Airfinance Journal: A Guide to Operating Lease, June, 1997.

Loukakos N. and Cabanes A., *Lex Aero: Guide du droit aérien*. 2e Edition. Librairie de l'Université d'Aix-en-provence, 1999.

McBain G., *Aircraft Finance: Registration, Security and Enforcement*, General Editor, Sweet & Maxwell, 2000.

McBain G., *Aircraft Liens & Detention Rights*, General Editor, Sweet & Maxwell, 2007.

MacCarthy R.J., *The Problem of Unpaid Eurocontrol Charges*, in Butler G.F. and Keller M.R., executive editors, *Handbook of Airline Finance*, 1st Edition, Aviation Week:McGraw-Hill, 1999.

Macintosh A., *Overcoming the Barriers to International Aviation Greenhouse Gas Emissions Abatement*, Air and Space Law, Volume XXXIII, Issue 5. Wolters Kluwer, November 2008, 403–429.

Margo R.D., *Aviation Insurance*, Butterworths Law; 3rd Revised edition, 1999.

Margo R.D., *Aviation Insurance in the United Kingdom: Law and Practice*, DCL Thesis, McGill University, 1979.

Margo R.D. and Houghton A.T., *The Role of Insurance in Aviation Finance Transactions* in Butler G.F. and Keller M.R., executive editors, *Handbook of Airline Finance*, 1st Edition, Aviation Week:McGraw-Hill, 1999.

Mauritz A.J., *Liability of the Operators and Owners of Aircraft for Damage Inflicted to Persons and Property on the Surface*. PhD Thesis, Leiden University, 2003.

Mendes de Leon P.M.J., *Introduction to Air Law*, 10th Edition, Kluwer Law, 2017.

Mendelsohn A.I., *Foreign Plaintiffs, Forum Non Conveniens and the 1999 Montreal Convention*, paper presented to the IATA Legal Symposium held in February 2011 at Vancouver, British Columbia, Canada.

Mercer A., *The Montreal Convention 1999: The Challenges of a New, Modern Liability Regime for International Civil Aviation – An Airline Perspective on Certain Features,* Civil Aviation Summit, 29–30 March 2005.

Miller G., *Liability in International Air Transport*, Kluwer, 1977.

Mönter R., *Another Mexico: Today's Challenges of Leasing Aircraft into Mexico*. Air and Space Law, Volume XXXIII, Issue 6. Wolters Kluwer, November 2008, 430–443.

Morrell P.S., *Airline Finance*, 3rd Edition, Ashgate, 2007.

Muriel A. and Yanboukhtin A., *Confiscation of Leased Aircraft by Customs*, International Law Office, Aviation – Russia, 20 May 2009.

Myburgh P., *Title to Sue under the Warsaw Convention: Construing a Dinosaur Text in the Digital Age,* New Zealand Business Law Quarterly, Volume 6, 2000, 305–313.

Neenan P., *The Effectiveness of the Exclusivity Provision in Foreign Serious Accidents: Does the Montreal Convention Channel Liability Against the Carrier?*, LLM (Adv) Thesis, Leiden University, 2011.

Nolan J.R. and Nolan-Haley J.M., *Black's Law Dictionary*, 6th Edition, West Publishing Co., 1990.

Official Journal of the European Union, L 134/4, 25 May 2007.

Olson U., *Interpretation of the Montreal 99 Convention in a Forum Non Conveniens Case*, http://www.mcgill.ca/files/iasl/Session_7_olson.pdf on 14 April 2011.

Organisation for Economic Co-operation and Development, *Sector Understanding on Export Credits for Civil Aircraft – Final Text*, 20 December 2010.

Peña S.F., *Defining Insurance Coverage Adequacy under the Montreal Convention of 1999*, Annals of Air and Space Law, Volume XXXIV, 2009.

Piera A., *Greenhouse Gas Emissions from International Aviation: Legal and Policy Challenges*, Eleven International Publishing, 2015.

Piera A. and Gill M., *Will the New ICAO-Beijing Instruments Build a Chinese Wall for International Aviation Security?*, Vanderbilt Journal of Transnational Law, Volume 47, Issue 1, January 2014, at 145–237.

Pimpongsuk P., *International Aircraft Leasing: Impact on International Air Law Treaties,* LLM Thesis, McGill University, Montréal, 1997.

Reuleaux M. and Tonnaer H., *Financing Aircraft Engines: Pitfalls and Solutions*, Zeitschrift für Luft- und Weltraumrecht, Volume 56, 2007.

Rollo V.F., *Aviation Law: An Introduction*. 5th Edition, Maryland Historical Press, 2000.

Rosales R., *Recordation of Rights in Aircraft and International Recognition: A Comparison Between the American and Canadian Situations*, Annals of Air and Space Law, Volume XVI, 1991.

Sand P., *The International Unification of Air Law,* Law and Contemporary Problems, Volume 30, Issue 2, 1965, 400–424, at 405.

Segal S., *Repossessions and Remarketing after the Repo Man*, Airfinance Journal, December 2008/January 2009.

Shawcross and Beaumont, *Air Law*, 4th Edition, Butterworth, 1991.

Speciale R.C., *Fundamentals of Aviation Law*, McGraw Hill, 2006.

Steppler U., *Air Travel Tax and Aircraft Lease Agreements*. International Law Office: Aviation - Germany, 1 December 2010.

Sterns G.C., *Lessor Liability; or Absence Thereof: Federal Immunity or Not for Lessors of Commercial Aircraft*, paper presented at McGill Institute of Air & Space Law Conference on International Aviation Liability & Insurance, Montreal, Canada, 6–7 May 2011.

The Aon Aviation Guide: The Banker's & Lessor's Guide to Insurance Aspects of Aircraft Financing, Aon Group Limited, Aviation, 2nd Edition, 2000.

The Cape Town Convention after Three Years: participatory seminar on advanced contract, registration and transaction practices held at Freshfields, London on 18 March 2009.

Thomson K., *Waving Goodbye to Your Rights*, Banking Update, Linklaters, 14 June 2009.

Tompkins Jr G.N., *The Continuing Development of Montreal Convention 1999 Jurisprudence*, Air and Space Law, Volume 35, Issue 6, 2010.

UNIDROIT, *Seminar Report: The European Community and the Cape Town Convention*, Rome, 26 November 2009.

Van Antwerpen N., *Cross-Border Provision of Air Navigation Services with Specific Reference to Europe: Safeguarding Transparent Lines of Responsibility and Liability*. PhD Thesis, Leiden University, 2007.

Vasigh B., Fleming K. and Humphreys B., *Foundations of Airline Finance: Methodology and Practice*, Routledge, 2015.

Verhaegen B.M., *The Entry into Force of Article 83 bis: Legal Perspectives in Terms of Safety Oversight*, Annals of Air and Space Law, Volume XXII, Part II, 1997.

Verna M.P., *Convenience Has Nothing to Do with FNC Motions*, The Air and Space Lawyer, Volume 22, Issue 1, 2008.

Weigand T.A., *Exclusivity, and Passenger Disturbances under the Warsaw Convention*, Weigand Published, 30 March 2001.

Whalen T.J., *The New Warsaw Convention: The Montreal Convention*, Annals of Air & Space Law, Volumber XXV, Issue 1, 2000.

Wickersham D.K., *When Should Courts Pierce the Veil Protecting Aircraft Financiers*, University of California, Los Angeles, May 2007, at http://works.bepress.com/david_wickersham/1 on 16 May 2011.

Wielinski P., et al., *Contractual Risk Transfer: Strategies for Contract Indemnity and Insurance Provisions*, International Risk Management Institute, Inc., 2000.

Wilson F.S., *Mastering Engine Leasing: The Master Short-Term Engine Lease Agreement Will Serve as Models for Future Standardization in the Aviation Industry*, Airfinance Journal, September 2007.

Wool J., *Lessor, Financier, and Manufacturer Perspectives on the New Third-Party Liability Conventions*, The Air & Space Lawyer, Volume 22, Issue 4, 2010.

Wool J. and Littlejohns A., *Cape Town Treaty in the European Context: The Case for Alternative A, Article XI of the Aircraft Protocol*, Airfinance Annual 2007/2008.

Wunnicke B., Wunnicke D.B. and Turner P.S., *Standby and Commercial Letters of Credit*, Wolters Kluwer, 3rd Edition, 2009.

Yodice J.S., *Aviation Lawyer's Manual: Representing the Pilot in FAA Enforcement Actions*, Maryland Historical Press, 1986.

Table of Cases

AAR Aircraft & Engine Group v. Aerowings, Court of Appeal, Den Bosch, The Netherlands, 15 August 2002, 98
ACG Acquisition XX LLV v. Olympic Airways [2010] EWHC 923 (Comm), [2012] EWHC 1070 (Comm), 48, 50
AerCap Ireland Ltd & Ors v. Hainan Airlines Holding Co Ltd [2020] EWHC 2025 (Comm), 145
Aercap Partners 1 Limited v. Avia Asset Management AB, 2010 EWHC 2431 (Comm), 23*AirAsia X Berhad v. BOC Aviation Limited* (WA-24NCC-467-10/2020), 23
Airbus S.A.S. v. Generali Italia S.P.A. & Ors [2019] EWCA Civ 805, 167
Air Canada v. UK (1995) 20 EHRR 150, 76
Air France v. Saks, 470 U.S. 392, 405, 105 S.Ct. 1338, 1345, 84 L.Ed.2d 289 (1985), 110
Air Mauritius v. Caribjet Inc., Royal Courts of Justice, 18 September 2007, 69
Air Transworld Limited v. Bombardier Inc [2012] EWHC 243 (Comm), 54
Arctic Aviation Assets Designate Activity Company & ors v. Companies Act, 2014 (Approved) [2021] IEHC 268, 145, 149
Austrian Airlines Oesterreichische Luftverkehrs AG v. UT Finance Corporation, 04 Civ 3854 (LAK) (2008), 47, 171
BAE Systems Management Service (Two) Limited & Another v. Trident Aviation Leasing Services (Jersey) Limited and AS Enimex, [2010] EWCA Civ 107, 63, 146
Blue Sky One Limited and others v. Blue Sky Airways LLC and others [2009] EWHC 3314 (Comm), [2010] EWHC 631 (Comm), 52, 96, 136
Bosphorus Airways v. Ireland, Grand Chamber Judgment of the European Court of Human Rights, 362 30.6.2005, 67, 79
Calgary Airport Authority v. AerCap Group Services Inc., 2009 ABCA 306, 77
Calgary Airport Authority and Others v. Zoom Airlines Incorporated, Court of Queen's Bench of Alberta, Judicial District of Calgary, Case No. 0801–10295, 5 September 2008, 77
Canada 3000 Inc.; Re: Inter-Canadian (1991) Inc. (Trustee of), 2006 SCC 24 (CanLII), 77
Celestial Aviation Trading 71 Limited v. Paramount Airways Private Ltd. [2009] EWHC 3142 (Comm), [2010] EWHC 185 (Comm), 2, 16, 54, 148, 171

CGTSN Limited and Global Knafaim Leasing Limited v. The Civil Aviation Authority and BAA Limited, Case No: CO/12012/2008, 75
Chan v. Korean Air Lines, Ltd., 490 U.S. 122, 134 (1989), 109
Cityjet Limited v. Irish Aviation Authority, 2005 [IEHC] 206, 138
Credit Suisse AG v. Arabian Aircraft & Equipment Leasing Co Ec and others [2013] EWCA Civ 1169, 160
Eid v. Alaska Airways, Inc., 621 F.3d 858 (9th Cir. 2010), 118
El Al Israel Airlines Ltd v. Tseng, 525 U.S. 155 (1999), 105, 107
Ellis v. AAR Parts Trading, Inc., 828 N.E. 2d 726, 730 (Ill. App. Ct. 2005), 106, 123
Esheva v. Siberia Airlines, 499 F. Supp. 2d, 498 (S.D.N.Y 2007), 122, 170
Euroatlantic Airways – Transportes Aéreos, S.A. v. Portugal [2015] ECHR 1077, 170
First Security Bank National Association (acting as owner trustee for the benefit of Leopard Leasing No 2 Ltd) v. Compagnie Nationale Air Gabon, Royal Courts of Justice, 10 May 1999, 40–41
Fishman Fishman v. Delta Airlines Inc, Nos 1818, 2038, Dockets 96–9345, 96–9457 (1998), 109
Fothergill v. Monarch Airlines Ltd [1981] AC 251; [1980] 2 All ER 696; [1980] 3 WLR 209; [1980] 2 Lloyd's Rep 295, (33 ICLQ 797), 110
Gambra v. International Lease Finance Corp., 377 F. Supp. 2d 810 (C. D. Cal. 2005), 169
Global Knafaim Leasing Ltd and another v. Civil Aviation Authority and others [2010] EWHC 1348 (Admin), 76
Grecoair v. John Tilling and Others [2004] EWHC 2851 (Comm), 133
Hassanati v. International Lease Finance Corporation, No. BC452279 (Cal. Super. Ct. 10 January 2011), 112
In re Air Crash Disaster Over Makassar Strait, Sulawesi, No. 09-cv-3805, MDL 2037, 2011 WL 91037 (N.D. Ill. 11 January 2011), 106
In re Air Crash Over the Mid-Atlantic on June 1, 2009, MDL Docket No. 10–2144-CRB (N.D. Cal. 4 October 2010), 111
In re Air Crash over the Taiwan Strait on May 25, 2002, 331 F. Supp. 2d 1176, 1187 (C. D. Cal 2004), 106
In re Charge Card Services Ltd. [1987] Ch. 150 (High Court), [1996] Ch. 245 (Court of Appeal), 56
In re Metrobility Optical Systems, Inc, 268 B.R. 326 (D.N.H) 2001, 61
Iris Helicopter Leasing Limited v. Elitaliana SRL and Point Holding SpA [2010] EWHC 2516, 161
JSD Corporation PTE Ltd v. Al Waha Capital PJSC and Second Waha Lease Limited [2009] EWHC 583 (Ch), 22
Kellogg v. Blue Quail Energy, Inc. (In re Compton Corp.), 831 F.2d 586 (5th Cir. 1987), 61
KLM Royal Dutch Airlines v. Morris [2001] Part 8 Case 2 [CAEW], 110
Kuwait Airways Corporation v. Iraqi Airways Company [2004] EWHC 2603 (Comm), 135
Kuwait Airways v. Republic of Iraq, 2010 SCC 40, 174

Layug v. AAR Parts Trading, Inc., No. 00 L 9599, 2003 WL 25744436 (Ill. Cir. Ct., Cook Cty. 16 May 2003), 123
Lithoprint (Scotland) Ltd. v. Summit Leasing Ltd. & Ors. [1998] ScotCS 36 (23 October 1998), 16, 172
Mardorf Peach & Co., Ltd. v. Attica Sea Carriers Corpn of Liberia, The Laconia [1977] AC 850 [1977] 1 All E R 545, 139
Me Raymond Dupont acting as appointed liquidator of SAS Noor Airways v. Aviation Capital Group Acquisition XX LLC, Case 119083, Commercial Court of Saint Nazaire, 2011, 149
Medellin v. Texas, 552 U.S. 491, 506 (2008), 109
Mitsui & Co., Ltd. and Tombo Aviation Inc v. Viacao Aerea Sao Paulo S.A. – VASP, Court File No. 99-CV-170574, Superior Court of Justice, Ontario, 1999, 150
Ministry of Defence v. Ashman (1993) 25 HLR 513, 135
Morris and others v. Rayners Enterprises Incorporated and Another [1997] UKHL 44, 56
Nordic Aviation Capital Designated Activity Company v. The Companies Act 2014 to 2018 (Approved) [2020] IEHC 445, 144
Novus Aviation Limited v. Alubaf Arab International Bank BSC [2016] EWHC 1575 (Comm), 21
Novus Aviation Limited v. Onur Air Tasimacilik AS [2009] EWCA Civ 122, 168
Oxford Aviation Services Limited v. Godolphin Management Company Limited [2004] EWHC 232 (QB), 134, 175
Pindell Limited and BBAM Aircraft Holdings 98 (Labuan) Limited v. AirAsia Berhad [2010] EWHC 2516, 136
Protea Leasing Limited v. Royal Air Cambodge Company Limited [2002] EWHC 2731 (Comm), 159, 164
Re MAB Leasing Limited [2021] EWHC 152 (Ch), 144
Retzler v. Pratt & Whitney Co., 309 Ill. App. 3d 906 (1st Dist. 1999), 123
Ross Leasing Ltd & Ors v. Nile Air [2021] EWHC 2201 (Comm), 145
Sabena Technics SA v. Singapore Airlines Limited [2003] EWHC 1318 (Comm), 36
Salam Air SAOC v. Latam Airlines Group SA [2020] EWHC 2414 (Comm), 161
Shiloh Spinners Ltd. v. Harding [1973] AC 691, 16
Sidhu v. British Airways, 1 Aviation and Space Law reports 217–219 (1994), 105
Societe Outremer Finance Limited, Counseil d'Etat, 2 juillet 2003, No. 254536, 75
Sunrock Aircraft Corporation Limited v. Scandinavian Airline Systems Denmark-Norway-Sweden [2007] EWHC Civ 882, 58, 135, 137
Tandrin Aviation Holdings Ltd v. Aero Toy Store LLC [2010] EWHC 40, 23
Tele2 International Card Company SA v. Post Office Ltd. [2009] All ER (D) 144 (Jan), 172
The Cristina [1938] A.C. 485, 173
The Emilie Millon [1905] 2 K.B. 817, 78
The Nippon Credit Bank Limited v. Air New Zealand Limited [1997] UKPC. 60, 164
The Queen on the application of Air Transport Association of America, Inc. and Others v. The Secretary of State for Energy and Climate Change, English High Court

(Administrative Court), Claim Co/15376/2009, referred to the Court of Justice of the European Union on 22 July 2010, Case C-366/10, 2010/C 260/12, 80

Tigris International N.C. v. China Southern Airways Company Limited [2014] EWCA Civ 1649, 172

Trident Turboprop (Dublin) Ltd v. First Flight Couriers Ltd. [2009] 1 All ER (Comm), 54

Trinity Products, Inc v. Burgess Steel, LLC, 486 F 3d 325, 329 (8th Cir 2007), 55

Union Eagle Ltd. v. Golden Achievement Ltd. [1997] AC 514, 171

UPS Supply Chain Solutions (f/k/a Menlo Worldwide Forwarding, Inc.) v. Qantas Airways Limited at al., U.S. Court of Appeals, 9th Circuit, No. 08-55281, 2 October 2010, 109

U.S. Bank National Association v. Southwest Airlines Co., 2009 WL 2163594 (S.D.N.Y. 20 July 2009), 92

Various Airfinance Leasing Companies & Ors v. Saudi Arabian Airlines Corporation [2021] EWHC 2330 (Comm), 52

VB Leaseco Pty Ltd (administrators appointed) v. Wells Fargo Trust Company, National Association (trustee) [2020] FCAFC 168, 149

Volvo Aero Leasing v. AVIA Air, Summary Proceedings, Court of First Instance of Aruba, 25 June 2003, No. 121, 98

Vreeland v. Ferrer, et al., Supreme Court of Florida, No. SC10–694, 8 July 2011, 123

Wilmington Trust Company, Orix Aviation Systems Limited v. Rolls Royce PLC, IAE International Aero Engines PLC [2010] CSOH 157, 73

Wilmington Trust SP Services (Dublin) Ltd & Ors v. Spicejet Ltd [2021] EWHC 1117 (Comm), 161

Table of International Conventions and Other Agreements

Additional Protocol No. 4 to Amend the Convention for the Unification of Certain Rules Relating to International Carriage by Air Signed at Warsaw on 12 October 1929 as Amended by the Protocol Done at The Hague on 28 September 1955, Signed at Montreal on 25 September 1975, 105, 108

Convention for the Protection of Human Rights and Fundamental Freedoms, signed at Rome on 4 November 1950 (European Convention on Human Rights), 75, 76, 79, 83, 170

Convention for the Suppression of Unlawful Acts against the Safety of Civil Aviation, signed at Montreal on 23 September 1971 (Montreal Convention 1971) 119–120

Convention for the Suppression of Unlawful Seizure of Aircraft, signed at The Hague on 16 December 1970 (Hague Convention), 118–119

Convention for the Unification of Certain Rules for International Carriage by Air, signed at Montreal on 28 May 1999 (Montreal Convention 1999), 6, 11, 104, 105, 107–116, 124, 125, 127–129, 179, 186, 187

Convention for the Unification of Certain Rules for International Carriage by Air, signed at Warsaw on 12 October 1929 (Warsaw Convention),11, 104–112, 114–116, 124, 125, 128, 129, 179

Convention for the Unification of Certain Rules Relating to the Precautionary Arrest of Aircraft, signed at Rome on 29 May 1933 (Rome Convention 1933), 148–151, 162

Convention on Compensation for Damage caused by Aircraft to Third Parties, signed at Montreal on 2 May 2009 (General Risks Convention), 103, 104, 112

Convention on Compensation for Damage to Third Parties, Resulting from Acts of Unlawful Interference Involving Aircraft, signed at Montreal on 2 May 2009 (Unlawful Interference Compensation Convention), 102–104, 111–114, 116, 183, 187

Convention on Damage caused by Foreign Aircraft to Third Parties on the Surface, done at Rome on 7 October 1952 (Rome Convention 1952), 101–103, 128, 129Convention on International Civil Aviation, signed at Chicago on 7 December 1944

(Chicago Convention) together with Annexes thereto, 6, 9–11, 17, 38, 40–42, 44, 68, 81, 83–91, 95, 100–102, 117, 124, 129, 153–158, 162, 179–182, 186, 188, 203

Convention on International Interests in Mobile Equipment signed at Cape Town on 16 November 2001 (Cape Town Convention), 6, 10, 11, 13, 17, 20, 22, 24, 25, 31, 65–67, 76, 96–100, 112, 139–147, 149, 151, 152, 157, 158, 162, 165, 166, 168, 170, 177, 179, 182–183, 185, 189, 190, 204, 215, 216, 275, 276

Convention on Offences and Certain Other Criminal Acts Committed on Board Aircraft, signed at Tokyo on 14 September 1963 (Tokyo Convention), 117–119, 188

Convention on the International Recognition of Rights in Aircraft, signed at Geneva on 19 June 1948 (Geneva Convention), 76, 94–100, 151–152, 179, 204, 275

Convention on the Recognition and Enforcement of Foreign Arbitral Awards, signed at New York on 10 June 1958 (New York Convention), 169, 204

Convention on the Suppression of Unlawful Acts Relating to International Civil Aviation, done at Beijing on 10 September 2010 (Beijing Convention), 119, 120

Convention relating to the Regulation of Air Navigation signed at Paris on 13 October 1919 (Paris Convention), 11, 40, 85

Eurocontrol International Convention relating to Cooperation for the Safety of Air Navigation signed in Brussels on 13 December 1960 (Eurocontrol Convention), 73, 75, 76, 100

European Convention on State Immunity, signed at Basle on 16 May 1972, 173

International Air Services Transit Agreement, signed at Chicago on 7 December 1944 (Transit Agreement), 86, 181

International Air Transport Agreement, signed at Chicago on 7 December 1944 (Transport Agreement), 38, 86, 87

Kyoto Protocol to the United Nations Framework Convention on Climate Change, done at Kyoto on 11 December 1997, 80

Open Skies Agreement (European Union and United States), done at Brussels on 25 April 2007 and at Washington on 30 April 2007, in duplicate, 80

Protocol to Amend the Convention for the Unification of Certain Rules Relating to International Carriage by Air, signed at Guatemala City on 8 March 1971 (Guatemala City Protocol), 105, 108

Protocol to Amend the Convention for the Unification of Certain Rules Relating to International Carriage by Air, signed at The Hague on 28 October 1955 (Hague Protocol), 128

Protocol consolidating the Eurocontrol International Convention relating to Cooperation for the Safety of Air Navigation signed at Brussels on 27 June 1997 (Protocol to the Eurocontrol Convention), 76

Protocol Supplementary to the Convention for the Suppression of Unlawful Seizure of Aircraft, signed at Beijing on 10 September 2010 (Protocol to the Hague Convention), 118

Protocol to the European Convention on Human Rights, done at Paris on 20 March 1952, 75

Protocol to the Convention on International Interests in Mobile Equipment on Matters specific to Aircraft Equipment, signed at Cape Town on 16 November 2001

(Aircraft Protocol), 24, 65, 67, 96, 97, 99, 141–145, 147, 149, 151, 152, 157, 158, 204, 215, 216
Unidroit Convention on International Financial Leasing, signed at Ottawa on 28 May 1988, 15, 127, 141, 146
Vienna Convention on the Law of Treaties, done at Vienna on 23 May 1969 (Vienna Convention), 108, 116

Table of Legislation and Regulations

Aviation Act 1946, 104

Australia

Damage by Aircraft Act 1999, 102

Babylon

Code of Hammurabi, 1

Canada

Airport Transfer (Miscellaneous Matters) Act, S. C. 1992, 77

Denmark

Aviation Act 1927, 104

England, United Kingdom

Air Navigation Order 2005, 154
Civil Aviation Act 1982, 102
Civil Aviation (Insurance) Regulations 2005, 129
Civil Aviation (Navigation Services Charges) Regulations 2000, 74
Companies Act 2006, 56, 144
Customs and Excise Management Act 1979, 70
Judicature Act 1873, 65, 163
Law of Real Property Act 1925, 65, 163
Misrepresentation Act 1967, 36
Sale of Goods Act 1893, 35
Tort (Interference with Goods) Act 1977, 136
Unfair Contract Terms Act (UCTA) 1977, 54, 55

European Union

Commission Regulation (EC) No. 474/2006, 124

Commission Regulation (EC) No. 859/2008, 38, 40, 44
Commission Regulation (EC) No. 1071/2010, 124
Commission Regulation (EC) No. 1702/2003, 138, 228
Council Directive 2008/101/EC, 78
Council Directive 2003/87/EC, 78
Council Directive 85/374, 51, 115, 116, 187
Council Regulation (EC) No. 216/2008, 69
Council Regulation (EC) No. 593/2008 (Rome I), 166, 216
Council Regulation (EC) No. 785/2004, 43, 129, 130
Council Regulation (EC) No. 864/2007 (Rome II), 166
Council Regulation (EC) No. 1008/2008, 42, 44, 85, 133, 149, 155
Council Regulation (EU) No. 421/2014, 78

Germany

Air Travel Tax Act (*Luftverkehrsgesetz*), 82–84
Civil Code (*Buergerliches Gesetzbuch*), 72
Fiscal Code (*Abgabenordnung*), 82

Greece

Civil Aviation Code, 104

Ireland

Irish Aviation Authority (Airworthiness of Aircraft Order) (S.I. No. 324 of 1996), 157
Irish Aviation Authority (Nationality and Registration of Aircraft) Order, 2005 (S.I. 634 of 2005), 89, 156
Irish Aviation Authority (Operations) Order (S.I. 19 of 1999), 157

Netherlands

Act of Air Navigation (*Wet luchtvaart*), 75
Civil Code (*Burgerlijk Wetboek*), 75

New Zealand

Civil Aviation Act 1990, 102

Nigeria

Civil Aviation Act, 2006, 130

Norway

Aviation Act 1993, 104
United States of America
Bankruptcy Code, 61, 141–142
Code of Federal Regulations, 69, 124
Federal Aviation Act, 88, 114, 122–124
Federal Aviation Regulations, 88

Foreign Sovereign Immunities Act, 174
Transportation Code, 88
Uniform Commercial Code, 16, 48, 55, 301, 302
US Code, 68

Index

A

Assignment, 28, 162–165, 301–305, 325
Aviation Working Group (AWG), 5, 75, 79, 102, 104, 144, 186, 189

C

Cape Town Convention, 142–145, 151, 182–183
Chicago Convention, 84–91, 181–182
Chicago Convention, Article 83 *bis*, 17, 42, 44, 86, 87, 89, 117, 153–158, 162, 181–182, 188, 217–222,
Conditions precedent, 26, 35–46, 178, 209–210, 244–246, 248, 298
Covenants, lessee's, 68–100, 267–284
Covenants, lessor's, 66–67, 260–267
Credit, letter of, 60–62

D

Default, events of, 28, 31, 34, 45, 139–145, 162, 177, 179, 213–214
Definitions, 25, 32–33, 224–239
Delivery, 25–27, 46–52, 134–139, 178–179
Deposit, security, 55–57
Deregistration, 88, 134, 150, 152–153, 157–159, 168, 181, 182, 204, 209, 215, 227, 245, 289, 325–326, 334–336
Dispute resolution, 28, 55, 145, 167–170, 179

E

Emissions, 78–83, 179, 183–185, 191
Engines, aircraft, 2, 71–73, 96, 98, 99, 151, 277, 325, 331
Entrustment, negligent, 120–126
Eurocontrol, 44, 73–78, 183–185
Execution, 7, 20, 28, 49, 153, 172, 175, 179, 189, 240, 242, 243, 266, 283, 292, 296, 305, 308

G

Geneva Convention, 76, 94–100, 151–152, 179, 275
Global Aircraft Trading Scheme, 163
Guarantee, 60–62, 137–138

H

Hague Convention, 118–119

IDERA, 157–159, 162, 182–184, 209

I
Immunity, sovereign, 173–175
Indemnities, 27, 101–127, 159–160

Insurance, 40–41, 125–134, 140
Intent, letter of, 9, 18, 20–23, 67
Interest, international, 22, 24, 65, 67, 76, 96–99, 162, 275
International Air Transport Association (IATA), 5, 185, 186
International Civil Aviation Organization (ICAO), 14, 38, 68, 78, 81, 84, 86, 102, 117, 125, 129, 155–157, 182, 219

J

Jurisdictional rankings, 189–190

L

Law, governing, 9, 21, 28, 36, 39, 52, 63, 93, 94, 139, 140, 145, 146, 165–167–169, 179, 185, 305–306
Lease
  definition of, 13–15
  finance, 3, 14–17, 27, 53, 88, 91, 123, 141, 146, 230, 287, 328
  operating, 13–18, 31–175
  standardization of, 185–186
  sublease, 9, 18, 19, 31, 41, 91, 136, 152, 154, 188, 211, 271, 284
Liability, product, 51, 115–116, 166
Liens, 70–84, 183–185

M

Miscellaneous, 28, 171–175, 179, 307–311
Montreal Convention 1971, 119–120
Montreal Convention 1999, 6, 11, 104, 105, 107–116, 124, 125, 127–129, 179, 186, 187

N

New York Convention, 169, 204

O

Opinion, legal, 23–25, 35, 38, 39, 88, 93, 98, 144, 167, 175, 205

P

Paris Convention, 11, 40, 85
Parties, 31, 101–120, 169–170
Parts, aircraft, 92
Payments, 37–38, 52–63, 67, 140
Power of attorney, deregistration, 153, 158, 209, 234–236

Q

Questionnaire, jurisdictional, 18, 23–24, 40, 167, 169, 170, 175, 203–204
Quiet enjoyment, 19, 39, 41, 66–67, 100, 152, 164, 180, 260

R

Recitals, 11, 25, 32, 155, 178, 223
Redelivery, 134–139
Registration, aircraft, 2, 20, 85, 89, 102, 203, 204, 211
Remedies, 145–162
Rent, 52–55, 59
Repossession, 146–149
Representations and warranties, 24, 25, 31, 34–36, 173, 178, 207–208, 239–243, 245, 246, 274, 302, 304
Reserves, maintenance, 21, 26, 31, 33, 39, 52, 53, 57–61, 63, 66, 67, 83, 140, 160, 164, 180
Restructuring, 144–145, 160–161
Rome Convention (1933), 148–151, 162
Rome Convention (1952), 101–103, 128, 129

T

Taxes, 63–64, 81–84
Term, lease, 11, 14, 16, 18, 21, 25, 27–29, 34, 39, 41, 52, 53, 65–67, 77, 91, 93, 127, 131, 140, 152, 161, 165, 179–180, 182
Tokyo Convention, 117–119, 188

W

Warranties, manufacturer's, 27, 64–66, 178, 261–264
Warsaw Convention, 11, 104–112, 114–116, 124, 125, 128, 129, 179

AEROSPACE LAW AND POLICY SERIES

1. Erwin von den Steinen, *National Interest and International Aviation*, 2006 (ISBN 90-411-2455-1).
2. Ludwig Weber, *International Civil Aviation Organisation: An Introduction*, 2007 (ISBN 978-90-411-2622-1).
3. Niels van Antwerpen, *Cross-Border Provision of Air Navigation Services with Specific Reference to Europe: Safeguarding Transparent Lines of Responsibility and Liability*, 2008 (ISBN 978-90-411-2688-7).
4. Brian F. Havel, *Beyond Open Skies: A New Regime for International Aviation*, 2009 (ISBN 978-90-411-2389-3).
5. Jiefang Huang, *Aviation Safety through the Rule of Law: ICAO's Mechanisms and Practices*, 2009 (ISBN 978-90-411-3115-7).
6. Marian Hoeks, *Multimodal Transport Law: The Law Applicable to the Multimodal Contract for the Carriage of Goods*, 2010 (ISBN 978-90-411-3246-8).
7. George N. Tompkins, Jr., *Liability Rules Applicable to International Air Transportation as Developed by the Courts in the United States: From Warsaw 1929 to Montreal 1999*, 2010 (ISBN 978-90-411-2646-7).
8. Daniel Calleja Crespo and Pablo Mendes de Leon (eds), *Achieving the Single European Sky: Goals and Challenges*, 2011 (ISBN 978-90-411-3730-2).
9. Donal Patrick Hanley, *Aircraft Operating Leasing: A Legal and Practical Analysis in the Context of Public and Private International Air Law, Third Edition*, 2022 (ISBN 978-94-035-4030-6).
10. Mikołaj Ratajczyk, *Regional Aviation Safety Organisations: Enhancing Air Transport Safety through Regional Cooperation*, 2015 (ISBN 978-90-411-5861-1).
11. Benjamyn I. Scott (ed.), *The Law of Unmanned Aircraft Systems: An Introduction to the Current and Future Regulation under National, Regional and International Law*, 2016 (ISBN 978-90-411-6126-0).
12. Stamatis Varsamos, *Airport Competition Regulation in Europe*, 2016 (ISBN 978-90-411-6831-3).
13. Katarzyna Malinowska, *Space Insurance: International Legal Aspects*, 2017 (ISBN 978-90-411-6784-2).
14. John Milligan, *European Union Competition Law in the Airline Industry*, 2017 (ISBN 978-90-411-6618-0).

15. Dejian Kong, *Civil Liability for Damage Caused by Global Navigation Satellite System*, 2019 (ISBN 978-94-035-1171-9).
16. Pablo Mendes de Leon and Niall Buissing (eds), *Behind and Beyond the Chicago Convention: The Evolution of Aerial Sovereignty*, 2019 (ISBN 978-94-035-1131-3).
17. Neta Palkovitz, *Regulating a Revolution: Small Satellites and the Law of Outer Space*, 2019 (ISBN 978-94-035-1762-9).
18. Federico Bergamasco, Roberto Cassar, Rada Popova & Benjamyn I. Scott, *Cybersecurity: Key Legal Considerations for the Aviation and Space Sectors*, 2020 (ISBN 978-94-035-0110-9).
19. Luis Fernando Fiallos Pazmiño, *The International Civil Operations of Unmanned Aircraft Systems under Air Law*, 2021 (ISBN 978-94-035-2854-0).
20. Merinda E. Stewart, *Freedom of Overflight: A Study of Coastal State Jurisdiction in International Airspace*, 2021 (ISBN 978-94-035-3804-4).